FIGHTING FOR TIME

FIGHTING FOR TIME

Rhodesia's Military and Zimbabwe's Independence

CHARLES D. MELSON

CASEMATE
academic
Philadelphia & Oxford

Published in the United States of America and Great Britain in 2021 by
CASEMATE PUBLISHERS
1950 Lawrence Road, Havertown, PA 19083, US
and
The Old Music Hall, 106–108 Cowley Road, Oxford OX4 1JE, UK

Hardback Edition: ISBN 978-1-95271-506-8
Digital Edition: ISBN 978-1-95271-507-5

A CIP record for this book is available from the British Library

Printed and bound in the United States of America by Integrated Books International

Typeset by Versatile PreMedia Services (P) Ltd.

For a complete list of Casemate titles, please contact:

CASEMATE PUBLISHERS (US)
Telephone (610) 853-9131
Fax (610) 853-9146
Email: casemate@casematepublishers.com
www.casematepublishers.com

CASEMATE PUBLISHERS (UK)
Telephone (01865) 241249
Email: casemate-uk@casematepublishers.co.uk
www.casematepublishers.co.uk

Front cover image courtesy of The Rhodesian African Rifles Regimental Association.

Contents

An image depicting aspects of the conflict used for contemporary recruiting posters as well as to project the image of the first line of defense. (RAA)

Foreword

Major Charles David "Chuck" Melson, USMC (Ret), is a military historian of distinction with that rare quality of practical experience, not just through military service but that of combat, in his case in Vietnam. He brings therefore not just a fresh eye to his examination of the counterinsurgency effort in Rhodesia but a practiced one.

His is a rare analytical study of the Rhodesian campaign. Almost all the writing on this subject is anecdotal narrative, inevitable as servicemen recall their experiences. Most of the unit histories are anthologies of experiences, useful in themselves.

Given the destruction of paper in March 1980 when the temporary governor of Rhodesia, Lord Soames, announced that Robert Mugabe had won what is still a disputed election, history has to be written from fragments. There is no continual military archival material, no full collection of situation reports, on which to base certainty. The newspaper archives are not a great assistance because the embattled Rhodesian government kept the press at arm's length. There was no embedding of journalists.

Given these difficulties, Chuck Melson provides a welcome and necessary forensic examination of a small force, starved for funds, forced to find ingenious solutions, but whose efforts were brought to naught, as in most counter-campaigns, because they depended upon a political outcome.

J. R. T. Wood, BA (Hons) (Rhodes) PhD (Edin) FRHistS

Preface

Senior wartime participants believed the study of the Rhodesia conflict was useful from their perspective. Police Commissioner S. F. S. Bristow noted at the war's start: "Too often in the present times we are inclined to regard history as dry and lacking in any form of appeal, yet the reading and learning of history is one of the best ways in which we can learn of, and benefit from, the mistakes of the past."[1] Lieutenant-General G. P. Walls, Commander, Combined Operations, echoed this at the war's end: "Assailed on every side by new violence day by day, the past tends to become vague and then forgotten. For this reason, this significant incident in the history of Africa has been recorded in a concrete manner. Those who become involved ... will keep alive that which the few defended even though the cause was lost."[2] Recent experience with the University of New South Wales and the Australian Defence Force Academy indicates that this research is still of current value and importance.[3] For Rhodesians of all persuasions this was not just an academic exercise, but life itself recalled by the Chindit Prayer on Remembrance Days: "Somewhere, somehow, I know not where, You will proudly stand and say: I was there." The Kohima Epitaph is still recited for those who did live to tell the tale: "For your tomorrow, We gave our today."[4]

From the 1960s through 1970s, there were a series of conflicts in Africa involving Rhodesia, South Africa, and Portugal in confrontation with the Frontline States. An international element was present with the Cold War and witnessed United States interest at the diplomatic, economic, and social level. In the post-Vietnam period, participation occurred with individual American soldiers, educators, politicians, and executives. By 1971, I developed a professional interest in conflicts in southern Africa in general and in Rhodesia (now Zimbabwe) in particular. As a military action officer and historian, my efforts were conducted at Headquarters, U.S. Marine Corps and the Marine Corps Education Command and University to include lectures, seminars, case studies, and a variety of research projects.[5] I followed the conflict through the 1980s and while preparing for post-graduate education in the 1990s. At the time, Professor J. R. T. Wood at the University of Durban-Westville and Professor D. F. S. Fourie of the University of South Africa (Pretoria) were my advisors. Career opportunities prevented completion of this goal but I collected the documentary material used for this narrative that now resides at the Pritzker Military Museum and Library of

Chicago, Illinois. I shared this with other authors, publishers, and institutions to ensure that lessons learned from the conflict remain available. This included original army, air force, and police records held by the Rhodesian Army Association (RAA), the British Empire and Commonwealth Museum (BECM), the National Archives of Zimbabwe (NAZ), and from the unselfish contributions of those who served during the conflict. Grateful acknowledgement is given to the journalists and academics that played a part in the undertaking with their own persistent research. In spite of their contributions, all opinions or errors remain mine alone. Place names used are those from the contemporary literature, and may not conform to post-colonial usage. A mix of imperial and metric units of measurement exists, again reflecting available records, coupled with the fact that Rhodesia converted from the imperial to metric system in 1970, midway through the conflict.

The title derives from the political and military interaction that made the goal of winning on the battlefield impossible without external intervention. All that could be gained was gained, an instant in time for a settlement. Published to date are journalism, academic work, unit histories, and personal accounts that lack balance or insights beyond the level of individual experience. In part, this is because senior Rhodesian leaders did not leave memoirs or analysis, with a prevailing belief that the Rhodesian diplomatic and political situation was too unique to learn from. To answer the reservations of whether there are lessons to learn from the study of this low-intensity conflict, the narrative divides into several parts and chapters. The first part consists of chapters 1 and 2 for background to describe the physical, historical, and public safety considerations that provided the starting point for a more detailed examination of the military response to the evolving revolutionary threat. The development of existing and then continuing measures provides the basis for general- and special-purpose units. The central part includes chapters 3 and 4 addressing the critical use of airpower as a force multiplier supporting civil, police, and army efforts, ranging from internal security and border control to internal and external combat operations. Chapter 5 examines the requirement for innovative units and full-time joint commands structures. This includes the use of helicopter-borne internal reaction forces described in detail with Chapter 6. As the conflict escalated, cross-border attacks and unconventional responses were conducted, as documented in chapters 7 and 8. The final section has the conclusions derived from the thesis. Original contributions are found at the level of tactics, techniques, and procedures, and the major finding of the transition of the Rhodesian armed services from a general-purpose force to a special-purpose force conducting intelligence-driven operations.

Appreciation and thanks go to Casemate's publisher Ruth Sheppard, managing editor Isobel Fulton, editorial administrator Felicity Goldsack, production designer Declan Ingram, and copy editor Chris Cocks, for their efforts and support throughout. The study is for an audience with little background in the story of modern

African conflicts or with previous regional history. My research approach was that of a trained staff officer dealing with administration, intelligence, operations, logistics, and communications concerns. Personal military experience provided practical appreciation of these differing needs. I have been present or participated in cordon and search, population and resource control, field interrogation, and burning of proscribed structures. War is always harsh, but the conditions of irregular warfare generate cruelties hard to match elsewhere. Both during and after the war these methods were condemned. Nevertheless, the "tactics, techniques, and procedures" portrayed are morally neutral and their utility depends upon the goals achieved (do the ends justify the means?). As a result, the focus of this examination is on methods used, as only by knowing the facts about the "how" is it possible to understand the opinions about the "why." Underlying the topic is the relation of necessity, law, and morality in insurgency campaigns and whether these are valid concerns in the ultimate conduct of war, for military forces on the ground and air, and for the desired goal of each.

Rhodesian

TERRORISM STOPS HERE

Introduction

Problem and Hypothesis

Strife between Europeans and Africans in Rhodesia existed as far back as the 1890s with the first *Chimurenga*[1] from which state security institutions developed that kept order well into the modern period. The Rhodesian conflict was part of a regional struggle for political control between African nationalists and European settlers. Both the Rhodesian forces and Zimbabwean guerrillas fought different wars and the tactics used were based upon conflicting strategic necessities. The settlers did so through expansion and employment of forces to search out and destroy the guerrillas; the nationalists through evasion and mobilization of the population to disrupt the national economy and power base. Each mounted active campaigns to shape and control the news media and public opinion through conflicting use of events.

On 11 November 1965, the British possession of Southern Rhodesia unilaterally declared independence from Britain to maintain rule under an existing constitution that ensured colonial dominance of an African majority by a European minority. Rhodesian Prime Minister Ian Douglas Smith declared to his supporters that "I don't believe in black majority rule ever in Rhodesia—not in a thousand years." Rhodesia's declaration of self-government presented African nationalist opponents with seemingly no other recourse for majority rule except through rebellion. Robert G. Mugabe, the succeeding prime minister of Zimbabwe at independence in 1980, acknowledged that the illegal declaration of self-rule "was based on a military threat, there was nothing we could do in those circumstances unless we armed ourselves." Thus began the violence that pursued to final resolution, polarized both sides, and drove out any hope of moderation or compromise.

From 1965, for some 15 years, Rhodesian security forces fought a successful conflict with limited resources in political isolation. This was based upon previous British Empire and Commonwealth experience, within the evolving dynamics of the struggle for power. Functioning within the context of developing policy, strategy, and operations geared to retaining European control of the government, the security forces achieved tactical victory in the face of escalating odds. By 1975, a comprehensive approach to insurgency was available in the form of a "doctrinal campaign plan" based upon the three interrelated elements of support to the civil power, anti-terrorist operations, and psychological action. However, it was still a piecemeal and delayed effort that by 1977 failed to address the critical strategic conditions of population imbalance and international isolation. Stalemate resulted instead of victory when security forces could not win militarily what was lost politically.

Are there lessons the American defense establishment can learn from the study of this low-intensity conflict and the way it was fought? These need to be examined in terms of small wars and conflict in Africa, and whether the principles assumed, learned, and applied hold true elsewhere or conform to the opinions of others. This was from traditional experience before 1945 and modern experience after that date.

How the Rhodesian security forces responded to the threat of the second *Chimurenga* is the subject of this narrative. The method compares and contrasts doctrine with practice to delineate the use of force: what worked, what did not, and why. By focusing on one determinant, the use of force as crucial to the events, analyzed were key elements to success or failure in conflict. The intent is to provide the basis for thought or action for others in similar circumstances, because an understanding of the utility of force is required if other approaches to conflict resolution are to succeed.

The argument follows the military thread through a complex Gordian knot of social, political, economic, and diplomatic issues, some of which are well documented and some of which are not. The study uses historic methods and sources, rather than social science techniques, to examine phenomena. Primary sources generated by events and published secondary sources that analyzed them were located and evaluated. Use was made of interviews and comments from participants looking back on their actions with the perspective of time. The result is an operational "nuts and bolts" narrative rather than "new" military history, popular at one time with American academia. The Rhodesian War has been dealt with at the University of South Africa (UNISA) as strategic studies, but it is now in the realm of history. I was impressed with what was considered by UNISA scholars of the conflict—Paul Moorcraft, J. K. Cilliers, Paresh Pandya—and Professor Dion F. S. Fourie, Department of Political Science for Strategic Studies, who established the writing framework. This is a departure from my personal experience, and it offers a different view than the participants', but it still provides background broad enough to appeal to other disciplines.[2]

The study of this war is an introduction to the type of fighting that America faces in a new era of "small wars." As the majority of local or regional wars of the last half of the 20th century were revolutions or counter-revolutions, this study of a specific conflict will serve a useful purpose for those who lack comparable experience. Civilian policymakers and special interest groups can learn from the indeterminable struggle. For military readers, the tactical insights pay dividends not found in doctrinal or school solutions, with insight provided into a region of continued significance that Americans have had little access to. This is timely considering the renewed interest in Africa, low-intensity conflict, peace operations, conflict resolution, and the legacy of complex prolonged wars. The account offers perspectives into social disruption of traditional societies, with related issues of refugees, tribal infighting, child soldiers, landmines, terrorism, and guerrilla warfare. Efforts made by government forces to counter the nationalists and their insurgency have been considered here. Conducted outside of international law and public scrutiny, these actions represented a "purist's dream" of counterinsurgency operations according to Australian Defence Force Academy Professor Michael Evans. There is a cautionary tale with this of carrying a struggle beyond its conclusion. Subsequent inquiry can consider whether the principles assumed, learned, and applied conformed to the conclusions of others in analogous situations. There is still work left for others to complete.

Just what is documented from a study of this war and the way it was fought? I found that though the campaign elements examined were interrelated in theory; in practice they were often times diluted by conflicting institutions and resources that resulted in "too little too late." Others have argued along similar lines: Professor J. R. T. Wood, at the University of Durban-Westville, felt that Rhodesians did not display a high level of strategic leadership because the talent of the small European community (4 percent of the total population) was spread thin across the needs of society—military leaders reflecting the available ability in just one area of Clausewitz's trinity of the "people, army, and state." Elsewhere, Professor Paul L. Moorcraft with the University of South Africa at Pretoria argued that paradoxically the Rhodesian military leadership became preoccupied with political solutions while the political leadership looked for military resolution to the conflict. While fighting a losing struggle, Wood further notes that for a brief period, military action changed the strategic situation to put victory in sight, but this moment passed unrealized. Military students Charles M. Lohman and Robert I. MacPherson, at the Marine Corps Command and Staff College, concluded that this dichotomy in authority, resources, and goals resulted in what they termed "tactical victory and strategic defeat."[3]

One aspect of the conflict was that it was a "four-star" corporal's war depending heavily on junior leaders on the ground. Scholars Peter M. McLaughlin at the University of Rhodesia and Eugene P. J. Pomeroy of Portland State University examined the historical factors that concentrated the Rhodesian military's focus on the small-unit level. However, why study at the tactical and technical level? It is difficult to research or generalize and is of little real interest to scholars. Even current military professionals dismiss this level and often view insurgencies as internal wars best fought by forces prepared for conventional tasks in major conflicts (classical warfare). One reason is that it is the realm of Clausewitz's friction that Jomini (and others) have tried to organize or ignore. As experience at this level is the most perishable, it is a necessity to be prepared for, or policy miscalculations might occur if not fully understood (Afghanistan and Iraq being examples).[4]

In the story of southern Africa, Zimbabwe still occupies a position of political and economic significance. The same terrain, weather, personalities, and forces are present today. For this reason alone, the period is of interest to those who implement American foreign or military policy. The absence of visibility in America of the 1965–80 fighting reflected preoccupation with the war in Vietnam and a lack of public concern for southern Africa (for example, there was no discussion in Max Boot's 2013 *Invisible Armies: An Epic History of Guerrilla Warfare from Ancient Times to the Present*). Despite this, the war in Rhodesia was significant for at least one American president, several administrations, and a number of special interest groups. Some viewed it as a conflict between the Free World and Communism over a source of critical raw materials; others viewed it in moral terms over perceived social injustices.

Insurgency and counterinsurgency have continued to be a concern that has not ended by changes to the world order. The American approach to low-intensity conflict was formed by the experience of the Vietnam, Afghanistan, and Iraq wars. Other countries also dealt with insurgencies in the Cold War era, noticeably the British Commonwealth and former colonies and dependencies—such as Rhodesia. Professor Colin McInnes, at the University of Wales and a former lecturer with the Department of War Studies at Sandhurst, surveyed the warfare strategies of the British Army since 1945 and identified a distinctive style of its approach to this type of warfare:

> From the hills of Korea to the desert of Kuwait, and from the jungles of Malaya to the streets of Northern Ireland, the army has retained a remarkable consistency of approach. Further, despite the changes in Britain's world position since 1945, the place and role of the army in defense policy has remained relatively unchanged. Together, the military's approach to war and its pivotal role in the formulating defense policy constitutes the British Army's "way in warfare."[5]

This is a theme found in Thomas Mokaitis, Bruce Hoffman, and Raffi Gregorian. This broad context of "approach" and "policy" is needed for wars of less than national significance. In this context, did the conflict in Rhodesia really mark the "end of empire" for Great Britain? As a final colonial war, Rhodesia provided a classic study of communist-style revolutionary war and British-style counterrevolutionary war—an example of a low-intensity conflict that was labor intensive and low technology oriented.

Findings and Reconsideration

What is the role of history in this, specifically with what is called "operational" history? Defined by function, it is to provide in narrative form an account of military operations (who, what, when, where, and, as far as possible, why). This is so commanders, staff officers, and students have the essential facts of previous events for use in current or future military actions. It should be noted that it also organizes and provides a historical record that allows contemporary and future "operators" to draw their own conclusions, lessons, and argues as Marine General Philip D.

Shutler observed, that the writers of your doctrine should not be the writers of your history—this can lead to bad doctrine and history.[6]

The study of the Rhodesian bush war has been a reoccurring theme among a small number of U.S. Marines (and others) as far back as 1973 at Quantico, Virginia, and has continued to date as seen in this study including the negligible number who actually served in the conflict.[7] For example, Jon A. Custis picked Fire Force as an interesting "Foreign Military" development to link to present Marine Corps operations as a possible solution to a perceived problem. Custis found excellent references: Richard Wood's superb "Fire Force: Helicopter Warfare in Rhodesia" published on both the internet and in Al J. Venter's *The Chopper Boys: Helicopter Warfare in Africa*, and reviewed in the *Marine Corps Gazette* in May 1995, and, moreover, as expanded with Wood's *Counter-Strike from the Sky*.[8]

A question was whether the circumstances faced by the Rhodesian security forces were really that similar to those faced by currently deployed Marine Air-Ground Task Force commanders as deeper analysis here has indicated? For the Rhodesians, the enemy consisted of six to 12 men on foot in relatively open terrain who generally tried to avoid direct confrontation with security forces and would try to evade contact when spotted. Larger forces dug-in to fight required more conventional combined arms efforts, even if smaller Rhodesian units consistently took on numerically larger opponents. This was as much a reflection of motivation, training, and superior use of available technology—for example, the payloads of helicopters and transports—were of necessity and not choice.

A formal effort was called for that should systematically consider the Rhodesian approach to insurgency based as much upon people as machinery—solutions Marines foster. In the decades that have passed since the conflict's conclusion, memories have become fewer and documentation scarcer; perhaps the *Marine Corps Gazette* or *University Journal* could help encourage the study of a subject that most American service personnel would identify with and benefit from.

Accepted was that the definition of low-intensity conflict included the problems of terrorism, insurgency, and counterinsurgency, and peacetime contingency or peacekeeping operations. Assumptions were essential to this: some hypotheses concluded that American and British counterinsurgency experience resulted in "models" or "styles" of dealing with insurgencies with distinctive approaches. It was further assumed in the broadest sense that it was possible to transfer elements of one model to the other as a matter of choice or doctrine.

To conclude, my task is to relate the subject of low-intensity conflict, the British Commonwealth experience over the last decades, and to propose what occurred is of use to the United States for further study and consideration in the Post-Cold War world. As seen by this study, methods differed from the American model and are worth considering as an alternative.[9] At first the Rhodesian example seemed appropriate, but more with form rather than content. The conflict was more in common with other regional conflicts: Angola, Mozambique, South West Africa, and South Africa. The lesson learned was for political transition rather than military capitulation.

There has not been a universal approach to the problem of internal war by either the insurgent or the counterinsurgent, other than to gain or to retain power with or without outside influence and intervention. The problems themselves are not the same despite similar elements. Relative positions of force, the strong versus the weak, define how responses can be used and what their impact would be, but the means to fight does not equate to the ability to fight. Experience rather than theory has shown neither offers victory in the inevitable sense that it is a product of existing conditions and trends—tactical and strategic victory may not determine the winners, just as losses on the battlefield will not guarantee the losers. To quote the combatants, "*A luta continua!*" ... "The struggle continues!"

CHAPTER I

Colonial Heritage

These events took place in southern Africa in the 1960s and 1970s. Because this narrative is part of a longer story, some context is needed. With a focus on the security forces, the diplomatic, political, economic, and social story has been left to others. Space allows only passing mention of the civil basis for the counterinsurgency efforts, in spite of the major lesson of the conflict that military measures alone could not ensure success. A review of the larger picture was based upon relative perspective of the following considerations: the legitimacy of the original occupation of Matabeleland and Mashonaland and the subsequent acquisition of land; the ultimate responsibility of the United Kingdom for the African peoples of these territories; and the relative positions of 19th-century colonialism versus 20th-century self-determination and Cold War views about the strategic resources and location in regards to regional and global conflicts.

Rhodesia was a self-governing British colony established in 1890 by Cecil Rhodes in the heyday of the British Empire. This colonial past limited its Commonwealth future with the retreat from Empire after the world wars. Rhodesia became one of the last colonies to be granted independence due to efforts to retain "responsible" government in European hands. This began with federalization in 1953 and continued until breaking with Great Britain over the constitutional basis for independence after 1961. A unilateral declaration of independence (UDI) was declared from Great Britain on 11 November 1965. The actors were the colonial government in revolt from Great Britain over the issue of independence under minority rule. This was opposed by Zimbabwean nationalists in the name of majority rule operating domestically and from nearby countries. With Rhodesia in diplomatic and economic isolation, armed attempts by nationalists to force either a negotiated settlement by the British or to effect a revolutionary victory through increased violence put government forces at a strategic disadvantage that got worse over time. Without a viable political solution, Rhodesian military actions only delayed the inevitable despite tactical victory.

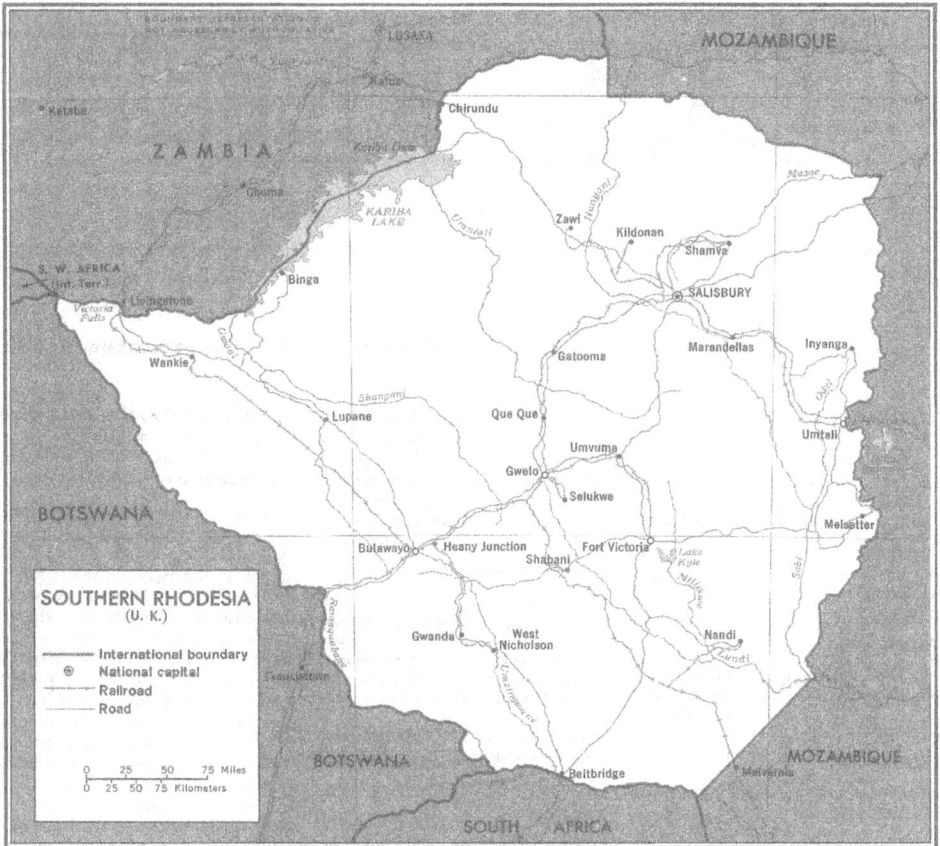

Southern Rhodesia (Department of State, public domain)

Land and People

At the start of the conflict, the then Southern Rhodesia occupied some 150,333 square miles of landlocked territory in southern Africa. This was slightly larger than the American state of Montana. It was bounded on the north by Zambia (445 miles of border along the Zambezi River), in the northeast and east by Mozambique (725 miles of border along the Zambezi valley in the north and the Umtali mountain range in the east), in the south by the Republic of South Africa (135 miles of border along the Limpopo River), and to the west by Botswana (490 miles of border, along the Shashe River in the southern part). There was also a point of contact with South West Africa's Caprivi Strip between Botswana and Zambia.

Most of Rhodesia is 3,000 to 5,000 feet above sea level (the highest feature being the 8,514-foot Mount Inyangani). Across the country from the northeast to southwest there is a central plateau about 400 miles long and 50 miles wide known as the High Veld. This central ridge forms the main watershed and rivers flow in roughly parallel courses down both sides to the Indian Ocean. Either side of this plateau is described as the Middle Veld, with the basins of the Zambezi, Limpopo, and Sabi rivers comprising the Low Veld.

The weather is temperate (comparable to California), described as "one of the finest climates in the world" in government literature. In general, temperatures decrease and rainfall increases with altitude ranging from cool and wet in the Eastern Highlands to hot and dry in the river valleys. The High Veld is "pleasant and healthy," with adequate rainfall for agriculture and European settlement. The lower areas of the Middle Veld are hot and dry and mostly settled by Africans. The Low Veld is unsuitable for settlement, as it is very hot and inhospitable with malaria and sleeping sickness in the depressions. Rainfall—averaging 25 to 30 inches a year with maximum up to 48 inches—in the Eastern Highlands allows the growth of tropical evergreen trees, while the High Veld precipitation permits savannah tree growth and temperate grasses. Semi-arid conditions in the western and southern regions support tufts of stunted coarse grass and acacia thornbush where only along the permanent rivers are there thicket forests of evergreens. The underlying granite, schist, and igneous rocks of the High Veld produce loamy or sandy soils, while the Low Veld sandstone is generally lacking in mineral or agricultural value. While market agriculture is vital to the economy, a majority of the tribal areas are engaged in subsistence farming.

Land allocation and conventions reflect commercial concerns for productivity. As a result, it became a source of the conflict. There were designated European urban (with one million Africans and a ratio of 3.7 Africans to 1 European) and rural areas (24 Africans to 1 European); African tribal and purchase lands (with a population of some three million and a ratio of 1,450 Africans to 1 European), and wildlife or national parks (a population density of 1/20th of the designated African areas and a ratio of 45 Africans to 1 European). By 1969, overall population figures were 5,099,344 with 72 percent living in rural areas (mainly Black) and 28 percent in the urban areas (mainly White). About 94 of every 100 were Black, 4 of every 100 were White, and the remainder Asian or Colored (mixed race). The Mashona and the Matabele are the largest African tribal groups. The Mashona language is Chishona (colloquially Shona) and the Matabele speak Sindebele (colloquially Nedebele); English is the primary European language.

Europeans provided the commercial and professional classes, with Africans providing labor for farming, mining, and manufacturing. The Rhodesian economy was based upon agriculture, producing tobacco, corn, sorghum, wheat, sugar, cotton, and cattle; industry produced transportation equipment, ferrochrome, textiles, and processed food; natural resources provided hydroelectric power, chrome, coal, nickel, gold, and iron ore. Que Que (iron), Wankie (coal), and Kariba (power) are important industrial locations. Trade was disrupted by United Nations sanctions but continued through systematic international evasion.[1]

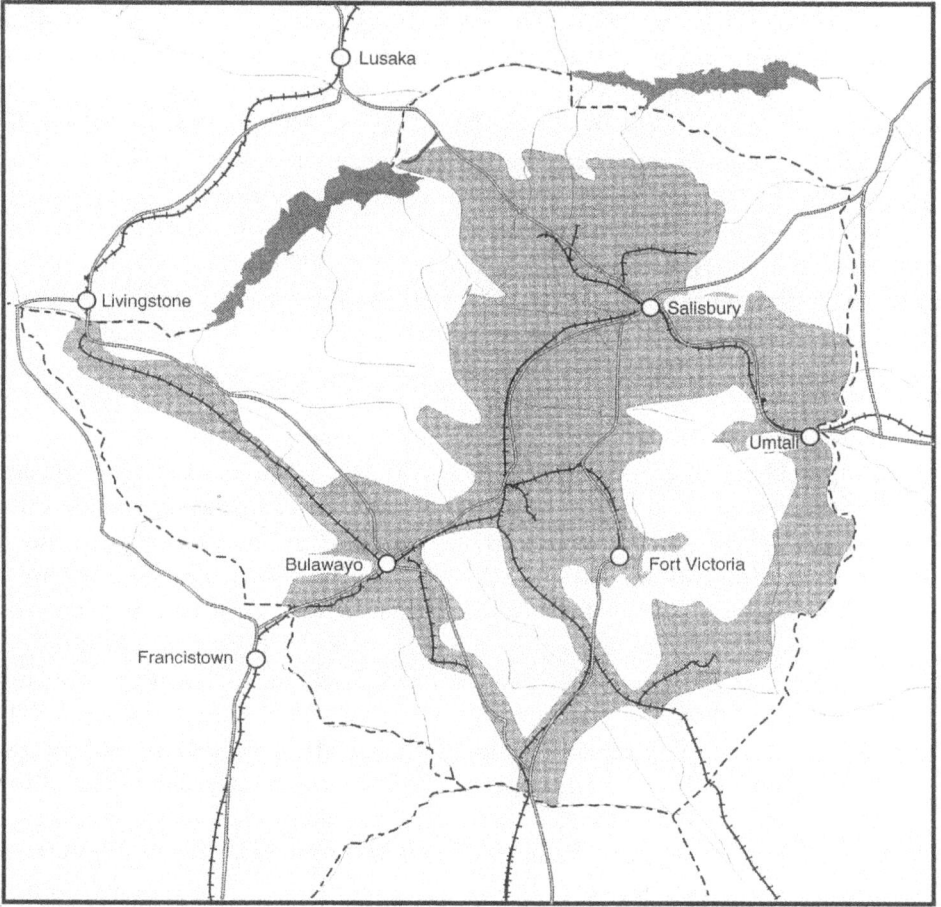

Legend

- - - - = railway lines
~~~~~ = roads
.... = rivers

████ = Vital Asset Ground

Vital Asset Ground (VAG), c. 1979

Military concerns for geography and demographics included the cover provided during the rainy season (October through April) for guerrilla movement and attacks along the watershed (the Rhodesian Intelligence Corp regarded guerrillas as "riparian" creatures in this attachment to watercourses). When rains were heavy, vehicle movement was restricted to improved roads. A cold season (May through September) occurs until about mid-July with temperatures as low as 37°F (3°C), after which they rise to 100°F (38°C) until the rainy season begins again. While lines of communications radiated from Salisbury and Bulawayo, the border locations were underdeveloped, which favored the guerrillas with large areas and large African populations with little day-to-day government control. As most of the border regions were either national park or designated for tribal use, any guerrilla incursion would have to pass through unoccupied territory or African populations before reaching European areas.[2]

Rhodesian society consisted mainly of two separate groups: one of predominately urban Europeans and the other of primarily rural Africans with little in common except the colonial structure. This was a gap the minority government was never able to bridge or take advantage of when in the end both the moderate and radical nationalists called for majority rule. The result was a society divided against itself, and to some extent a civil war evolved between those portions of the African society that supported the minority government and the progress it meant for them and those that were in opposition to what it stood for. In retrospect, the differing social and economic circumstances of the minority and majority populations created attitudes that were never going to be compromised without the submission of one to the other, and over time, both sides knew this. The question was one of who could hold out the longest under changing conditions. These were all policy considerations that provided the strategic or moral background to this topic. But these are not the subject of this study, rather, the police and military security measures taken to ensure the continued existence of an established government in response to nationalist confrontation within state boundaries and in adjacent territories. For this we need to understand the nature of the several challenges and the effectiveness of the various responses.

In 1890, Cecil Rhodes's Pioneer Column marched into this part of central Africa, bringing armed settlers to as yet undeveloped land. Conflict began when Europeans first occupied the territory in search of mineral and agricultural wealth using local Africans for labor. The resulting state, called Southern Rhodesia, was first administered by the commercial British South Africa Company until 1923, when it became a self-governing crown colony instead of joining the neighboring Union of South Africa. A three-way struggle evolved between Great Britain, the White settlers and Black nationalists that intensified with the breakup of the British Empire after World War II.

There were tortuous efforts to unify the three territories of Northern Rhodesia, Southern Rhodesia, and Nyasaland. The architects of this last British imperial experiment in Africa had conflicting motives. Britain wished to ease its colonial burdens and perhaps to provide a liberal counter to South African chauvinism. Rhodesian and Nyasaland Europeans sought freedom from British control and to secure self-government on their own terms. The result was the colonies of Northern Rhodesia, Southern Rhodesian, and Nyasaland formed the Federation of Rhodesia and Nyasaland in 1953. The brief but significant life of the Federation brought euphoria when her government assumed power, and achievements—the greatest being the mammoth Kariba hydroelectric scheme. Revealed were abrasions between the three territorial governments and their leading personalities as the Federal cabinets of prime ministers Godfrey Huggins (Lord Malvern) and Sir Roy Welensky attempted to circumvent British and territorial policies which might tear the Federal fabric. All sides ignored African opinion in this constitutional conflict.

Hampered by the Federal constitution's limitations and growing African nationalist unrest, led in the main by Hastings Banda, Kenneth Kaunda, and Joshua Nkomo, the various government administrations failed in their task. Always hostile to the Federation, African nationalism flowered in the 1956 post-Suez climate. The conflicting demands for African independence and European retrenchment turned to internal disorder by the early 1960s. The Federation did not endure and could not control its fate because Whitehall retained ultimate constitutional power. The inevitable result was British Prime Minister Harold Macmillan's concession to Nyasaland and Northern Rhodesia of the right to secede. Sensing the "wind of change," Britain chose to disengage from Africa and seek its destiny with Europe. In 1963, the Federation of Rhodesia and Nyasaland dissolved, creating independent Zambia and Malawi.[3]

Rhodesia to Zimbabwe

However, because of failure to reach agreement over the constitutional issue, Southern Rhodesia remained a self-governing possession of Great Britain. The Rhodesians were slow to abandon established practices and the Foreign Office was determined to advance rapidly to independence all its colonies on the basis of universal adult suffrage. In 1963, the British government listed five principles about which it needed to be satisfied before agreeing to Rhodesian independence: guaranteed majority rule, no retrogressive amendment to the constitution, improved political status of the African population, progress towards ending racial discrimination, and the basis for independence to be acceptable to the people of Rhodesia as a whole. The British further added the stipulation in 1966, that regardless of race, there must be no oppression of majority by minority or minority by majority.

In the bitter aftermath of the breakup of Federation, this decision drove Southern Rhodesia towards a UDI. On 11 November 1965, the Rhodesian government declared sovereignty and wrote a new constitution. Britain declared the Rhodesian government illegal and in December imposed sanctions, which were adopted as mandatory by the United Nations (UN) Security Council later the following year.

Rhodesian Government Senior Leadership, c. 1965–80[4]

President
Hon C. Dupont, 1965–75
Hon J. Wrathall, 1975–8
Hon H. B. Everard, 1978–9 (acting)
Hon J. Z. Gumede, 1979

Prime Minister
Hon I. D. Smith, 1965–79
Hon A. T. Muzorewa, 1979

Minister of Internal Affairs
Hon W. J. Harper, 1965–8
Hon L. B. Smith, 1968–74
Hon B. H. Mussett, 1974–7
Hon G. R. Haymen with Hon Kayisa Ndiweni, 1978
Hon W. D. Walker with Hon Monwadisa Malumisa, 1978–9
Hon H. Zimuto, 1979

Minister of Law and Order
Hon D. W. Lardner-Burke, 1965–75
Hon H. G. Squires, 1975–8
Hon J. C. Andersen with Hon B. R. M. Hove, Hon F. J. Zindoga, 1978–9
Hon F. J. Zindoga, 1979

Commissoner, Police
F. E. Barfoot, 1965–8
J. Spink, 1968–70
S. F. S. Bristow, 1970–4
P. D. W. R. Sherren, 1974–8
P. K. Allum, 1978–80

Director General, Central Intelligence Organization
K. Flower, 1965–80

Minister, Defense
Hon C. Dupont, 1965
Hon Lord J. A. Graham, 1965–8
Hon J. H. Howman, 1968–74
Hon P. K. F. V. van der Byl, 1974–6
Hon R. E. D. Cowper, 1976–7
Hon M. H. H. Partridge, 1977
Hon R. T. R. Hawkins with Hon John Kadzwiti, 1977–8
Hon H. G. Squires with Hon N. G. Mukono, 1978–9
Hon A. T. Muzorewa, 1979

Minister, Combined Operations
Hon R. T. R. Hawkins with Hon John Kadzwiti, 1977–8
Hon H. G. Squires with Hon N. G. Mukono, 1978–9
Hon A. T. Muzorewa, 1979

Commander, Combined Operations
Lt-Gen G. P. Walls, 1977–80

Commander, Army
Maj-Gen R. R. J. Putterill, 1965–8
Lt-Gen K. R. Coster, 1968–72
Lt-Gen G. P. Walls, 1972–7
Lt-Gen J. S. V. Hickman, 1977–9
Lt-Gen A. L. C. MacLean, 1979–80

Commander, Air Force
AVM H. Hawkins, 1965–9
AM A. O. G. Wilson, 1969–73
AM M. J. McLaren, 1973–7
AM F. W. Mussell, 1977–80

Commander, Guard Force
Maj-Gen G. A. D. Rawlins, 1976–9
Brig W. A. Godwin, 1979–80

Terror attacks by nationalists from neighboring Zambia began at this time. Negotiations for a settlement failed in 1966 aboard HMS *Tiger* and again in 1968 aboard HMS *Fearless*. Rhodesia declared itself a republic in 1970 while still seeking to reconcile with Great Britain on favorable terms. Although an agreement was reached in 1971, the Pearce Commission reported that it was unacceptable to the people as a whole. In 1972, guerrilla war began in earnest with Operation *Hurricane* on Rhodesia's northern border fought against nationalists operating from Mozambique.

Throughout this period there was a conflict that saw no major battles, liberated territory, or decisive actions. The situation broadened sharply with the Portuguese withdrawal from Mozambique in 1974. In 1975, the Victoria Falls Conference broke down before it had really begun. This year also saw the Geneva Conference with new Anglo-American proposals, but again this failed. Another initiative was launched in 1977 which included the Frontline States, and these talks continued in Malta and South Africa.

A rising level of guerrilla activity was met by settler mobilization and resistance. During the fighting both sides were able to sustain morale, raise manpower, and develop the means to fund the fighting under increasingly demanding conditions, which after nearly two decades of civil war, ended in a military stalemate and a negotiated transition of power from White to Black Zimbabweans. In 1978, with acceptance of the principle of majority rule and adult suffrage, Prime Minister Smith began talks with nationalist leaders inside Rhodesia (excluding the Patriotic Front) that culminated in the Salisbury Agreement. Elections took place in April 1979 and a new (unrecognized) administration led by Bishop Abel Muzorewa took office on 1 June. At Lusaka in August, the Commonwealth heads of government approved a British plan to convene a constitutional conference on Rhodesia as part of the usual process of bringing a dependency to independence. The Lancaster House Conference began on 10 September, resulting in the return to colonial status on the arrival of the governor, Lord Soames, on 12 December. This was followed by the signing of the ceasefire agreement on 21 December 1979.

By then, the Europeans retained one party, the Rhodesian Front (RF) led by Ian Smith, although some of the seats in the House of Assembly were sought by independents. The RF held all the European seats in the last Parliament. There were nine other factions, the most important of which were Bishop Abel Muzorewa's United African National Council (UANC), Joshua Nkomo's Zimbabwe African People's Union (ZAPU, later Patriotic Front-PF), and Robert Mugabe's Zimbabwe African National Union (later ZANU-PF). The loyalty of six other parties was divided between these three. Ethnic loyalties naturally affected the election results although in their elections speeches, all parties made a great play on the breaking down of tribal barriers. However, Nkomo got his support from Matabeleland and Mugabe from Mashonaland, with a very "gray" area in the center of the country where crucial seats were fought over. These were the parties to the subsequent election of an independent state.

Previous Experience and Doctrine

The modern African nationalist movements began when Europeans and Africans were unable to find acceptable means of integrating their interests within the existing form of government, economy, and society. This exposed long-term grievances caused by the original occupation of the country in the 1890s and subsequent *Chimurenga* rebellions which established traditions of resistance for both sides. Both security force and nationalist approaches to resistance and repression had their roots in the breakup of the Federation. A number of processes were set in motion that took on a life of their own. At first this was in the urban areas, and only later did rural disturbance become a reality in the countryside. The Rhodesian response to the nationalist threat was not made in a vacuum and reflected assumptions and experience with a constantly shifting threat. This overview reflects the security force view of the threat and the terms of reference they considered when devising countermeasures. It provides a background for the specific situations addressed by the narrative.

Terms and Concepts Used by the Rhodesian Security Forces

- Civil disobedience—A campaign, with political motives, designed to disobey laws in order to exert pressure on the authorities.[5]
- Infiltration—The entry into the country of any person for subversive purposes.[6]
- Insurgent—An indigenous or foreign national not recognized as a belligerent by international law, aiming to overthrow a government by force. In revolutionary war the terms guerrilla, revolutionary, terrorist, dissident, and rioter are used on occasions to indicate differences in the opposition. When it is not necessary to indicate specific differences, however, insurgent is used to cover all the roles implied by the foregoing terms. It is also taken to include such additional terms as saboteur, enemy, insurrectionist or rebel when applicable.[7]
- Insurgency—A form of rebellion in which a dissident faction instigates the commission of acts of civil disobedience, sabotage, and terrorism, and wages irregular warfare in order to overthrow the government. In its ultimate stages it could escalate to a conflict on conventional lines. Although insurgency often starts internally, it has seldom been known to succeed without outside assistance, support, and encouragement.[8]
- Intimidator—A person who by inspiring fear tries to impose his will on others.[9]
- Passive resistance—An act or acts of a nonviolent nature carried out willfully to defy the authorities.[10]
- Revolutionary warfare—The process which includes the use of political, economic and military measures that militant dissidents employ to weaken and overthrow the existing government.[11]

- Saboteur—A supporter of a dissident faction who damages property, equipment or plant for political purposes.[12]
- Terrorist—A supporter of a dissident faction (in fact, an insurgent), who is trained for or resorts to organized violence for political ends.[13]
- Terrorist hide—A place where terrorists may temporarily conceal themselves; terrorist camp—a place within the country, temporarily occupied by terrorists from which operations are conducted and training may take place; terrorist holding center—an establishment outside the country where provision is made for the accommodation, indoctrination and training of terrorists.[14]

General George P. (Peter) Walls served throughout the conflict, along with others, and dealt with its evolution from the tactical to the policy level.[15] In a mid-war interview with South African journalist Al J. Venter, he commented at length on the Rhodesian approach to counterinsurgency and these remarks feature throughout this study as representative security force thinking.[16]

Walls qualified his views:

We don't acknowledge that this is a guerrilla war. We say this is terrorism. Of this I am quite convinced [if] you look at the background to it, the motives of the people, their methods of operating and so on. You might as well say that in America, in the days of the mafia or in prohibition days that the forces of law and order couldn't succeed. They did succeed—and we're going to succeed because we are merely supporting law and order. I believe we have a tremendous fund of good will in this country amongst the masses that one might call uncommitted. I'm not talking politics now because I don't get involved in politics. But you've got a whole lot of people who are slightly perhaps "in the middle," if I can use that phrase, and I believe they want desperately to support law and order. This is borne out and shown in so many different ways, but they're jolly well afraid to. I think this is something one has to bear in mind with these masses of people. I believe we've got the good will there, we've got the means of doing it, and the people are getting sick and tired of these terrorists who can't even decide amongst themselves who their leaders are, and what they are trying to achieve.[17]

In regards to metropolitan threats, "I would take you to task about calling it urban guerrilla warfare. I would prefer you to refer to urban terrorism. But all I can say is that as far back as I've been in the army, we have trained and been prepared for urban disturbances, urban terrorism, and we are prepared for it now."[18]

According to Walls:

Exactly what form it might take or how we would counter it, I don't think you could expect me to comment on. Again, we are ready for any eventuality. The terrorists who are rather like parasites living off these people. They come [the terrorists] and demand food and information and shelter; they ask for intelligence about security forces movements, and when they don't get it, they resort to brutal intimidation, torture. In the meantime, they make their demands and take them the hard way. Every now and then they murder somebody to make it clear that they are going to demand help, and the very fact that they have to resort to intimidation and murder shows they are not getting help easily in the area where they have to carry out this practice.[19]

Even so:

> You get some terrorists who are absolute punks, but others when cornered will put up a reasonable fight. It varies, I would say, from man to man. Whereas you occasionally come across the odd hard-core chap, who knows that he's had it if he is captured, or in sheer fright, or in many cases because he's drugged [with marijuana] he will put up a good fight.[20]

He added:

> We reckon there is no part of Rhodesia which is dominated by terrorists—we dominate all of it, although we have terrorists in certain areas … We operate as much by night as by day. We reckon that 24 hours of the day we've got to be in control of the situation, so there is no difference between day and night as far as our operations are concerned. … I think if one uses common sense, one can see the sort of thing we are liable to do, a) to contact the terrorist, b) to cut them off from the local population, and c) to give confidence to the local population that we are there.[21]

Concluding:

> I wouldn't like to be drawn or in any way quoted on numbers and distances, because I believe [that] in counterinsurgency far too much emphasis is placed on these. I hear journalists at press conferences on television and so on ask, 'how many in this area?' I think this is probably because this is a child's guide to how the terrorist war is going. But it doesn't work that way [in terms of how] insurgency and terrorism operate. And again, I wouldn't want to be drawn on distances. I don't think you can talk about penetration up to this distance or that distance. But taking your point that there are vast areas of Rhodesia to be looked after to counter terrorism, I would say it is a question of priorities. We have certain resources and finances available to us, and we have to use it [sic] to best advantage. What is quite definite is that we are getting the support of the government in our military and civil administrative efforts as far as possible, and they are quite determined to give us what we need, so I'm not worried on this score.[22]

Paul Moorcraft and Peter McLaughlin, journalistic and academic witnesses, felt that "There was no discernable philosophical basis to the Rhodesian counterinsurgency war, and Rhodesian officers would have been surprised at the suggestion that there should be one."[23] It could be argued that they were only looking at open literature, as a continuing debate about the nature of the war and how to fight it occurred within the confines of the armed services.[24] That there never was a viable strategy had more to do with the situation and policy constraints than from any lack of intellect or leadership. Rajesh Ragagopalan observed that:

> The lack of a formal, explicitly stated doctrine does not mean that no doctrine exists. Military doctrine is a military organization's view of future war and its conduct. Defined thus, all organized military forces operate with at least an implicit military doctrine. Understanding military doctrines in such cases requires detecting and bringing to the surface the elements that make up the doctrine. These elements can be detected in what military officers say and write about war, by examining official and unofficial unit histories, as well as relevant contemporaneous accounts. Examining army operations is yet another method of getting at the elements of the

doctrine. However, this is a rather risky method because military operations might differ from doctrine, which might lead to the 'detection' of non-existent elements of doctrine.[25]

Doctrine was a way of overcoming the unknown of the future to allow for organization, equipment, and training military forces. One benefit of a common doctrine is that it allowed for centralized ideas and decentralized action. The Rhodesia Army's Operations Branch published a version of doctrine as used in Malaya and Kenya in a similar format. This was with the 1967 *Military Support to the Civil Power*, known as the *MCP*. It was amplified by counterinsurgency aide-mémoires for ease in instruction and application. While incorporating aspects from other services, it was more a collection of army techniques than joint doctrine.[26] The Operations Coordinating Committee (OCC) brought these techniques together in a more comprehensive form for the Rhodesian security forces in 1975 in the four-part *Counter-Insurgency Operations Manual*, the so-called *COIN* manual. This consisted of general discussion, anti-terrorist operations in rural areas, psychological actions, and operations in support of the civil authorities. This applied as a "guide" for the conduct of military operations and "for training purposes."[27]

Covered were principles and techniques for the unit and sub-unit level, with specific "battle drills" being left to the on-the-spot commander. As stated, "users should constantly regard its contents with a healthy contempt, aiming for meaningful improvement" based on experience.[28] Again, the *COIN* manual counseled that commanders "must be allowed the necessary freedom of action to fit any particular requirement within the framework covered by this publication."[29] Printed material was in a restricted form with limited availability in the form of outlines and summaries. It is important to note that while documents were used as a source of doctrine in this study, application was based upon training and unwritten or even nonverbal execution. At the troop level participants might not even realize it was doctrine they were following.

Walls recalled:

> Well, we started a very long time ago, shortly after the start of the Federation, in fact, with training camps concentrating on anti-terrorist operations. A few people had been to Malaya, plus the odd officer like Major [R. R. J.] Putterill, as he was [later major-general and army commander]—who had been up to Kenya to study the Mau Mau campaign—and others who had some knowledge or experience of anti-terrorist campaigns, pooled their knowledge and experience which we passed on to the ... territorial forces and reserve. So way back in the mid-fifties, we started preparing for counter-insurgency in Rhodesia.[30]

About experience in Malaya:

> I think the main difference is that the Malayan campaign was fought by the British in one of their overseas territories, if I may use that phrase. I don't know exactly what its constitutional status was at the time. They had a High Commissioner there, and this was virtually run from Britain through their high commissioner; and their normal military command system. So you had soldiers from the British forces, plus various Commonwealth forces—Rhodesian, Australian,

New Zealand—plus forces raised in Malaya such as the Malayan Police, the Malay Regiment, and then during the time we were there the Federation Regiment, fighting communist terrorists.

He added, "Originally they were called bandits, but they were people trying to break down law and order in one of Britain's overseas territories. In Rhodesia, this is our homeland. This is Rhodesians fighting for Rhodesia."[31] He continued:

> Again it is very difficult to compare. … They've got better weapons than the Malayan [communist terrorists] had. I wouldn't want to be forced to compare them really. … From the terrorist point of view, the best terrorists in Malaya were the Chinese. There was the odd Indian and the odd Malay, but by and large, the toughest chaps we were up against were the Chinese with pure communist background and driving force. And of course the terrorists we're up against have been trained and armed and driven along by communists.[32]

He explained, "We haven't slavishly followed the Malayan way of doing things. In fact, some of our critics in the past have accused us of slavishly following them. We have tried to study methods from all over the world."[33] Then expanding, "I took part in some things that were perhaps new techniques, and I think generally soldiers of all ranks and levels are taught to contribute new ideas and so on. But we came back with the principles of counter-insurgency in our minds, and we tried to adapt these principles from the jungle type of country to Rhodesian bush warfare."[34]

About Kenya:

> I don't believe that you can compare terrorists in different parts of the world. You get well-trained terrorists and badly trained terrorists. You get the part timers, the militia, the supporters, the cadres … It is very different to make a comparison. The training methods are perhaps similar, but have been developed along normal communist lines, and perhaps the terrorists' weaponry is better than the Mau Mau had in Kenya. But again, it's not as good as ours. As their weapons and ammunition have improved, so have ours. So we still have better weapons than the terrorists.[35]

Continuing on Kenya:

> There are lessons to be learned from the Kenyan campaign but again it's a different situation. There are certain similarities, but other things are rather different. You are dealing with the same sort of people, who think and operate the same way. You are dealing with the communist tactics of living off the local population where possible, intimidating them, and avoiding contact wherever possible with security forces, although in places they will make a bit of gesture to try and impress the locals. But generally speaking they try to avoid any kind of contact, so there are those similarities. But again, this is Rhodesia, and Rhodesians of all races—and I do emphasize all races—are looking after their homeland. This is where our kraals are, where our towns are, where our farms are, and so on. Whereas this wasn't the case with *all* of the people involved in Kenya, it was the case with some. Their government policy came from London. Our government policy comes from Rhodesia.[36]

He went on to outline that:

> We have studied methods from all over the world. Every now and then, just in case I am getting into a rut, I call for certain books and so on to be brought forward again. On my desk

right now I've got "Quelling Insurgency" [sic] which is a British forces manual on this sort of thing. My previous chief of staff, General [G. A. D.] Rawlings ... produced a précis of Sir Robert Thompson's book, which I like to look through every now and then just to remind myself of principles. But it's a case of refreshing your memory of basic principles, and then deciding whether your methods are out of date or whether you can try something new, change it or what have you.[37]

Rhodesian doctrine stated counterinsurgency warfare "probably places a greater burden of responsibility on the individual than does any other form of conflict. It connotes small groups and light scales. Catch words are: thorough training, self-discipline, skill-at-arms, initiative, guile, endurance and above all, the will to win."[38] Individual training emphasized following the rules until the rules no longer worked. This promoted a focus in technique common to most high-risk occupations, "attention to detail and mental alertness." It was a thread reflected in most narratives. An article of faith was that "Rhodesia's security forces are potentially among the best in the world. This potential will only be realized by hard training and sound professional knowledge."[39]

Just as insurgency, insurgent, and terrorist were defined, so were the Rhodesian responses.

Terms and Concepts Used by the Rhodesian Security Forces

- Anti-terrorist operations (ATOPS), rural versus urban—Any military operations against terrorists.[40] Anti-terrorist operations are fought on a wide front: the security forces, various government departments and the civilian population all have a role to play. In implementing the anti-terrorist actions, members of the security forces must appreciate the vital need for cooperation and the understanding of each other's characteristics and capabilities.[41]
- Counter-insurgency (COIN)—All measures, both civil and military, undertaken by the government, independently or with the assistance of friendly nations to prevent or defeat insurgency.[42] Efforts by the armed forces were defined to include the following:
- Military support to the civil power (MSCP), urban versus rural— Any military operation in support of civil authorities, which involves primarily the maintenance of law and order and essential services, in the face of civil disturbance and disobedience.[43] Also referred to as operations in support of civil authorities (OSCA) or military assistance to the civil power.
- Psychological actions (PSYAC), European versus African—An action conducted over a predetermined time and consisting of the application

of various coordinated measures, directed at the population, own armed forces, or at the enemy in accordance with determined doctrine and techniques. They are conducted by military forces, civil authorities or by both in conjunction with each other, to achieve an objective of psychological action.[44]

This analysis considers interrelated and concurrent employment concepts; they are presented as they developed in time and space, which is how they were considered in the text. Methods of employment evolved with resulting command and control structures, beginning with the national Operations Coordinating Committee (OCC) in October 1964, the various provincial joint operations centers (JOCs) and sub-joint operations centers (sub-JOCs) from 1966, up to the 1977 formation of Combined Operations (ComOps) and a National Joint Operations Center (NatJOC). Each system answered to the prime minister, whether Smith or later Muzorewa, for police, joint, or military operations. [45] The term "operation" had a variety of meanings, or at least could be used vaguely. In general, the Rhodesian military actions could be considered geographically as internal and external.

"Internals" included: a. Internal Security Operations: from 1963, the civil and police effort conducted as aid to the civil power with due regard for the early application of these measures in the breakup of the Federation; b. Border Control Operations: from 1964, the Zambezi valley incursions as temporary joint operations. The primarily military border control effort in the Zambezi valley up to the start of operations in the northeast and with the collapse of Portuguese East Africa; and c. Area Control Operations: from December 1972, response to guerrilla incursions marked the beginning of a series of internal counterinsurgency operations that did not cease until the war's end. The military area control efforts were standing joint operations in the northeast and expanded throughout the country.

"Externals" were employments conducted beyond the borders of the country. Included were actions by intelligence and security officers and agents, by members of the army special forces, and ultimately by general-purpose army and air forces. These were customarily joint operations involving more than one of the Rhodesian security forces, but unilateral actions did occur under certain circumstances. The air force provided support in most cases and carried out some notable independent tasks of its own. Employment of the first two tiers of forces was centralized at the highest level while those at the third tier were decentralized at lower echelons of command.[46]

Terrorism Stops Here: A Thin White Line

Fundamental to this study are the armed forces that conducted the bush war using both established methods and unique local innovations. An understanding of the organizational structure of these forces and how they evolved is needed to comprehend their employment during the conflict. This gives form to the substance of the analysis.[56] Accounts of the growth of the Rhodesian security forces vary. Emotional and structural aspects were often mixed together, as might be expected, ranging from "regimental" narratives to polemics by outsiders. Only recently, scholars have seriously studied the security forces as social institutions. This began with writings by the late Professor Lewis H. Gann and his collaborators that described the armed forces as reflecting the needs of a settler state.[48] Peter McLaughlin conducted further research into the evolution of the Southern Rhodesian military system in 20th century's first three decades, pivoting on the experience of World War I.[49] Eugene Pomeroy has examined the origins and development of the defense forces of Northern and Southern Rhodesia through 1945, as the basis for the institutions that were in place at UDI, and to explain the emphasis on aviation, special forces, armor, and artillery.[50]

From the time of the Pioneer Column until the state of emergency against terrorist incursions, Rhodesians were proud of their military record. The foundation of Rhodesia's armed forces was the British South Africa Company police, which first accompanied and safeguarded the Pioneer Column on its journey north from South Africa. Garrisons were established at Macloutsie, Fort Tuli, Fort Victoria, and Fort Charter. Early settlers fought against bitter odds in the Matabele and Mashona rebellions and their columns rode in the Anglo-Boer War of 1899–1902 to the relief of Mafeking. The colony contributed to Empire and Commonwealth needs during two world wars and postwar conflicts, including with the *askari* of the Rhodesia Native Regiment (RNR) and Rhodesian African Rifles (RAR).

The Rhodesian Army incorporated sizable African components and included women. The basis for organization was individual regiments and corps, controlled by a headquarters staff structure through regional brigade or area commands. National and territorial service was embodied into most elements of the security forces as the conflict went on. It was active in providing support of Empire and Commonwealth commitments. In 1950, the Staff Corps organized a unit deployed to Malaya from April 1951 to March 1953 as C Squadron, 22 Special Air Service. In 1952, the Rhodesian African Rifles (RAR) served in the Suez Canal zone, followed by a tour in Malaya from April 1956 to February 1958.[51] In July 1962, the SAS squadron deployed with 22SAS to Aden.[52] The army's Regular Force served at the apex of an ever-expanding manpower pool that included part-time Territorial Force (TF) units and a Reserve Holding Unit (RHU) of individuals to keep it fully engaged.

This military tradition should be considered a characteristic element of the European settler society. This was reflected in the conduct of operations and was a part of any discussion because of the distinct outlook it created. It was a monopoly on the forms of power that were an essential element of social control that far exceeded the actual level of coercion involved. The British South Africa Police (BSAP) was considered Rhodesia's first line of defense, backed up by the small regular Rhodesia Staff Corps (RhSC), and expanded by the conscripted and part-time Royal Rhodesia Regiment (RRR, later RR). If endangered, more and more of the European population were called upon to serve to avoid, as it was termed, "arming the natives." But in reality most regular soldiers, policemen, and protection forces were Black. [53]

A defining period for the security forces was the formation of the Federation in 1953. The consolidation of the militaries of Southern Rhodesia, Northern Rhodesia, and Nyasaland into the Federal Defense Force resulted in an expansion of existing manpower and material and incorporation into the Central Africa Command in January 1954. The Rhodesian Air Force became a separate service and the police were removed from the military side of national defense and a national intelligence agency came into being. "The three territories of the Federation of Rhodesia and Nyasaland have always made a major contribution to the common cause," was the conclusion reached by Federation leadership.[54] Both police and military forces participated in a number of the Cold War actions of the British Empire and Commonwealth, a fact recalled during Rhodesia's upsurge in nationalist protest and at the time of independence.[55] The Kenyan and Congo emergencies saw all services employed, at a time when British policies towards African colonies were in a state of flux. African participation expanded, but in a clearly subservient role, using the image of the "horse and rider," with no doubt who the rider was. This witnessed the formation of new all-White units in response to a perceived threat of rising African nationalism: the Rhodesian Light Infantry (RLI), the light armor Selous Scout Regiment (not the same as the later special force unit), and the Rhodesian Special Air Service (SAS). The modern Rhodesian security forces were a byproduct of the Federation's dissolution. At the end of 1963, the Federal Army had a strength of some 5,323 regulars and 8,528 reservists of all arms of service.[56] The 1,158-man air force supported some six squadrons of fighter, bomber, transport, and utility aircraft.[57] It was noted that on 1 January, 1964, "all the units in Southern Rhodesia reverted to their own names, incorporating the name of the territory, and a great deal of reorganization was necessary."[58]

Present at independence in 1965 (UDI) was a rudimentary armed force of all arms with continued experience in action. The available security forces were diverse (even at odds) by age, race, sex, obligation, training, and resources. At that time, the formal roles of the security forces were: a. military assistance to the civil power in the event of national disasters; b. military aid to the civil power in the following circumstances: internal security operations, to restore law and order in urban and rural contexts and counterinsurgency operations; c. border control operations to prevent insurgency or illegal transborder commutation; d. external commitments, operations in hot pursuit; and finally e. classical warfare, international armed conflict. The stated purposes then were first, to defend Rhodesian territory from external attack; second, to maintain internal security; third, in the event of war, to contribute to the maximum to the British Commonwealth cause. It was the need to maintain internal security that translated into the counterinsurgency effort that came to the fore during this period.[59]

Internal Security as Law and Order

The British South Africa Police of Rhodesia provided a classic example of a counterinsurgency dilemma in recent times, albeit in a colonial environment. Originally a force serving a dual role of Southern Rhodesia's police and standing military, the BSAP evolved to a position analogous to the Royal Canadian Mounted Police and other lesser constabularies with a reputation of "always getting their man." A national police force, the BSAP was neither British nor South African. It was a competent law enforcement institution, which claimed to solve some 85 percent of crimes within seven days.[60] This was by firm but seemingly fair methods, including physical punishment for African culprits. It normally recruited outside the colony, mainly from the United Kingdom. Its recruits were then able to stay on in Rhodesia and contribute to the civil society, which explains in part the social prestige the police had.[61] By tradition and institution, the force was the senior service over the more junior Rhodesian army and air force (even its uniforms and mess were of a better quality, reminiscent of a Victorian cavalry regiment).[62]

The police gave extensive support to British government needs in Bechuanaland (1950, 1951, 1952), Nyasaland (1953, 1959), and Northern Rhodesia (1956) with detachments varying from 54 to 253 men. By 1953, a complete separation from military duties occurred with the BSAP maintaining control of rural and urban African areas through provincial and district stations, and patrols, along with the courts and prison system. A Special Branch (SB) provided a countrywide intelligence-gathering system that was without competition until the formation of an externally focused Central Intelligence Organization (CIO) in 1963—headed by a former career policeman. In addition to full-time members, the regular police force organized an extensive reserve, providing an opportunity to serve to those not otherwise employed in the security effort, including women and Africans. According to Inspector Richard Hamley, the Police Act (1964) established a Police Reserve consisting of the Police General and Special Reserves. The General Reserve broke down in turn to the A and Field Reserves. The A reservists served with regular members at police stations a minimum of 16 hours a month and during contingencies. Field reservists attended a minimum of annual training periods and when called up for service. The Field Reserve included specialized categories: ex-regulars, Reconnaissance Car, Signals, and Air Wing sections. The Special Reserve encompassed Residential and Key-point Special Reservists who performed patrolling duties in neighborhoods or places of employment. This allowed the general distribution of small arms and personal equipment for protection purposes to the European population with aspects of militia service. Police forces would be deployed in areas where the army was not present because of a lack of threat or priority. [63]

Of initial concern here were the police and policing approach based on established support to the civil power precedence in both the United Kingdom and Commonwealth. The position of the police in the security force hierarchy hindered the army and air force from establishing a separate command and staff structure that could have matured its own view of dealing with insurgency. As a result, previous experience by local and expatriate members was relied on, again from Commonwealth models in the postwar era. The police maintained an institutional hold on the intelligence field, both internally and externally. This worked as long as the insurgency was in its initial phases, but the differences between analysis and target acquisition only became wider with time. The police wanted to solve crimes for convictions, the army and air force wanted to anticipate enemy actions for their own responses. This institutional friction would be reflected in the evolution of the command structure that did develop, but always seemed to be behind what was called for and ultimately reflected political control exerted by Prime Minister Smith.

Interestingly, insurgencies often originate from social and economic causes that are more open to civil than military solutions. The irony is that this is seldom recognized by law enforcement at the time, and past a certain point the police are ineffective in what becomes a military problem. In democracies, particularly those from British traditions, the desire to maintain the rule of law exhibits an effort to treat insurgents as criminals or at most terrorists committing criminal acts (and they can be the same). Early attempts are at detection, gathering evidence, and bringing perpetrators to trial. As security regulations became more draconian, this allowed the suspension of normal police processes within a perceived legal framework. The responsibility of first the police and then the military from accountability for their own actions ceases with "indemnity and compensation" regulations. Gradually, in a losing situation, martial law takes over, moving farther from the intended purpose of maintaining the rule of law.

When African nationalists began a campaign of subversion and intimidation, the police were firmly in control and kept the army and air force in a supporting role (despite military experience with counterinsurgency in Egypt, Somalia, Malaya, and Kenya). The BSAP expanded, particularly with part-time reserves mobilized for security and riot duties. In 1965, the police numbered some 5,700 regulars compared to 2,320 in the army and 1,200 in the air force. Police reserves added a further 27,350 to the total of which 11,500 were African. Police ascendance was challenged by 1966 when it began to lose its edge in controlling terrorist infiltration, particularly in remote areas and with escalating firefights. The BSAP responded by fielding the paramilitary part-time Police Anti-Terrorist Unit (PATU), Urban Emergency Unit (UEU), and the full-time armed Police Support Unit (PSU). Military manpower needs impacted hardest on the police and expanded security efforts saw more and more of the older and less fit put into the police reserve.

Throughout, the intelligence effort was with the Special Branch and even military intelligence depended upon it for information processing and prisoner handling. This was first with expanded ground coverage and then with a "pseudo" concept that had its origins in the need to make up internal losses from terrorist intimidation. The internal pseudo concept was taken over by an army hybrid unit and army-led cross-border efforts needed more specific targeting than the police could provide. Civil and military cross-purposes continued to cause friction—even after all intelligence collecting was brought under the umbrella of the Central Intelligence Organization. In the end, the army and air force asserted control only after much bureaucratic resistance. Disagreement between civil and military use of force was the fissure that deserves some consideration, highlighting the essential moral rather than physical aspects of law enforcement and highlighting that "solving crime" does not defeat insurgent challenges that have moved to armed phases and that military solutions in themselves cannot restore legitimacy to a challenged regime unless based on law rather than necessity.

The police were the ones who ensured political and social conformity for both European and African communities. Recognition that maintenance of law and order could be seen as oppressive did not occur to them, with the exception of some post-independence memoirs. Not discussed was the structure of the force that kept the senior leadership in European hands, as any European member was automatically superior to any African regardless of length of service. In presenting their story, the members of this police force saw themselves as upholders of law and order "to serve and protect" citizens rather than as combatants to close with and destroy the enemy. An insight is provided into an aspect of state security in modern times, particularly in the specific case of the conflicts in southern Africa in the colonial period.[64] The police force always had mixed feelings about the UDI that marked the final effort to maintain European rule in this Africa colony, if not pleased with Zimbabwe independence in 1980. The legality that British Empire and Commonwealth membership gave to suppressing the majority population was harder to live with when carried out in seclusion. Holding on in isolated outposts, deprived of majority civil support, found the police longing for a return to legitimacy rather than victory. In 1980, the BSAP became the Zimbabwe Republic Police (ZRP) and passed into history.[65]

Emergency Powers to Martial Law

Emergency powers and regulations were used in Rhodesia. Legislation was based on English common and colonial law, some South African Roman Dutch law, and the colony's own experience and existing legal system (pass laws, land apportionment, and other native-affairs stipulations). In practice, in the rural areas district commissioners and police through tribal authorities directly governed a majority of the African population. These measures were intended to function in a "state of emergency" between constitutional "law of the land" and "martial law" by degree in defense of the realm from subversion and revolution. After the initial act, regulations were drafted by the various governmental agencies and were put into effect during a declared emergency, with renewal required every six to 12 months. Allowed were the enactment and implementation of additional measures without debate or review, administered through the prime minister, the ministers, and provincial governors.[66] Chief considerations were negating requirements for due process in arrest and confinement along with the rules of evidence. Areas addressed included the use of special courts, censorship, collective fines and punishments, death penalties for terrorist acts, confiscations, requisitions, use of public transportation, suspension of labor strikes, access to key points and protected buildings, military support to the civil power (including arrest, search, and seizure), and military trials of servicemen for civil offenses.[67]

Similar emergency regulations were used in Malaya and Kenya during their crises. These addressed admission of confessions made at any time, detention, deportation, restriction, controlled areas protected by deadly force (protected places, danger areas, perimeter fences), curfews, arrest and detention, search and seizure, requisitions, destruction of property, control of roads/rail/waterways, clearance orders, forced labor, disconnection of communications equipment, and control of foodstuffs and other supplies. It is of interest here how the focus on law and order would lead to martial law, internal security, population and resource control and an array of protective or self-defense forces that ultimately provided the solid base from which the other security forces operated. Some of these were under the police control while others were considered as Internal Affairs (IntAf) and administered accordingly. [68]

CHAPTER 2

From Border Control to Cross-border Operations

General-purpose and Special Forces

Although funded, organized, trained, and equipped for national defense, between 1966 and 1972, the Rhodesian security forces had only a fraction of its full strength deployed at any one time for active service. At maximum mobilization, this reached some 20,000 but was supportable only for brief periods of national emergency, such as elections.[1] The basis for unit deployments evolved and changed over time as the threat altered. This was from internal security, to border control, to area control (reactive to proactive), with extensive external operations. A later further development was the assignment of priorities to which areas would be actively protected (the so-called Lindner strategy).[2]

At the conflict's start, the police occupied a number of stations throughout the country but at any one time only a percentage was on duty conducting law enforcement rather than security or paramilitary operations. The Police Support Unit could reinforce threatened areas, normally where the army and air force were not present. Rural Police Anti-Terrorist Unit and Urban Police Emergency Unit were placed on rotating duty assignments. The use of the South African Police in the border areas between 1966 and 1976 provided a full-time force that part-time units were ill-prepared to replace with anything other than police reservists and other protection services. As the need for security expanded, this included armed members of Internal Affairs and the Guard Force.

The army started with the rotating deployment of a company from the RAR, a commando from the RLI, and an RR company to the border and operational areas, using them on Fire Force or eventually for external roles. These had to be augmented by the SAS, who did border control and Fire Force deployments of their own, often at odds with their stated mission and strength. As national service increased, independent companies were stationed at key locations, augmented by armor and artillery units at the most critical locations (all being draftees led by regular officers and noncommissioned officers). The RAR expanded battalions to the limits of available resources, but the all-White RLI and SAS did not, despite

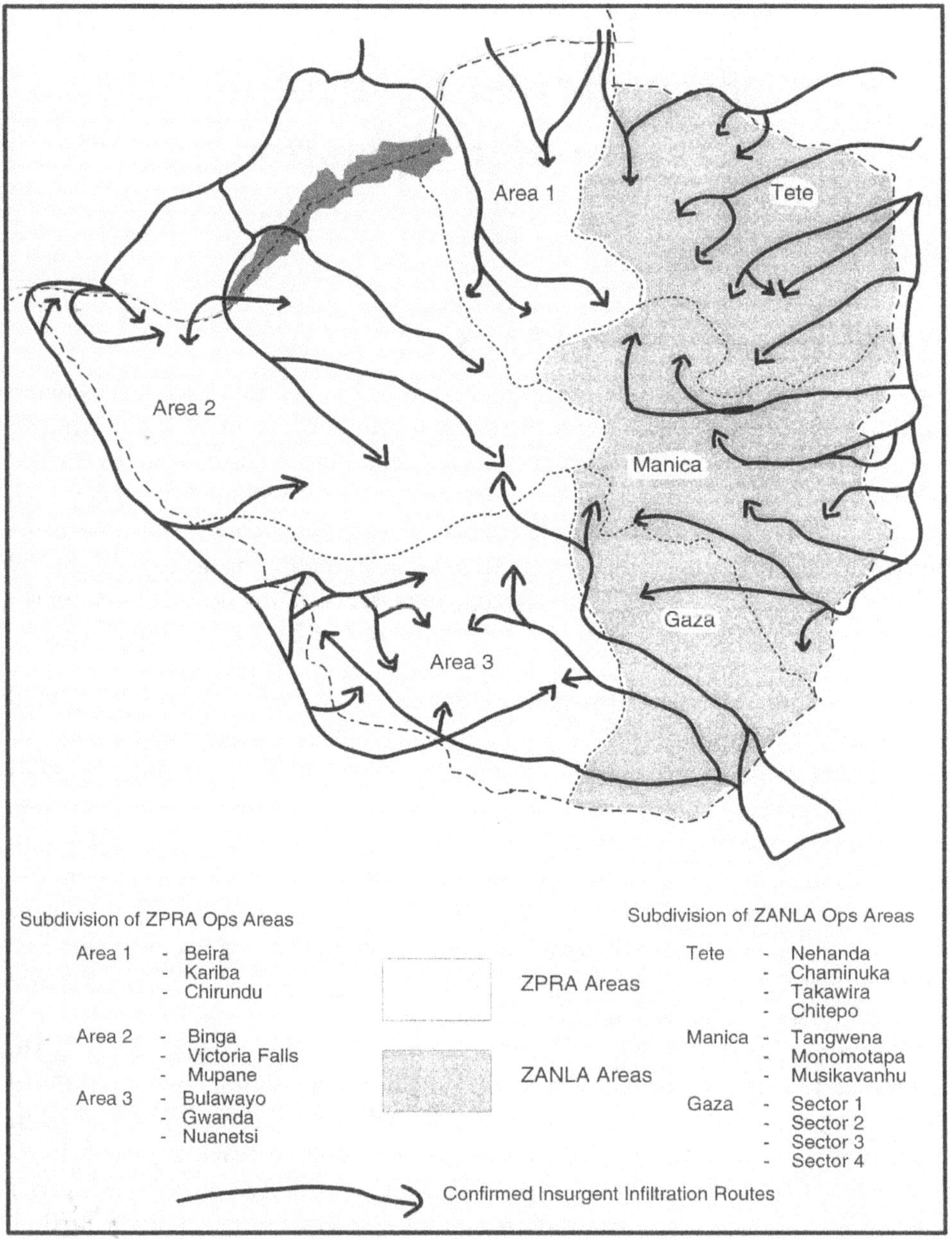
Area 1
Tete
Area 2
Manica
Gaza
Area 3
Subdivision of ZPRA Ops Areas
Area 1 - Beira
- Kariba
- Chirundu
Area 2 - Binga
- Victoria Falls
- Mupane
Area 3 - Bulawayo
- Gwanda
- Nuanetsi
ZPRA Areas
ZANLA Areas
Subdivision of ZANLA Ops Areas
Tete - Nehanda
- Chaminuka
- Takawira
- Chitepo
Manica - Tangwena
- Monomotapa
- Musikavanhu
Gaza - Sector 1
- Sector 2
- Sector 3
- Sector 4
Confirmed Insurgent Infiltration Routes

Major guerrilla infiltration routes and areas, from Zambia in 1966 and from Mozambique in 1971 accepting national servicemen into their ranks. There was also the limit on available European leadership and labor that would impact the economy as well.

The air force had full-time duties that depended upon a rotation into the border and operational areas for six-week stints at forward airfields (FAFs)—making the helicopter and counterinsurgency squadrons the most deployed forces. South African aircraft and crews between 1966 and 1976 augmented them. The continued expansion of requirements was met with a relatively limited number of aircraft and crews, at times there being fewer pilots than aircraft.

The security forces could be considered to comprise special, general-purpose, and protection forces. Throughout the course of the conflict it was seen that special forces set a standard for others to follow. The transition from "general-purpose" to "special" operations spans the spectrum of command and control, intelligence, and anti-terrorist operations reflecting the diverse nature of Rhodesian forces and operations during the bush war. How these came to be employed by general-purpose ground and air forces will be expanded upon in the narrative. A point of interest was whether they were an adjunct to conventional operations, a "classical" warfare assumption not always the case in internal war, or whether at some point special operations became the main effort supported by conventional forces. The emphasis was on unit employment, rather than any individual skills and qualifications, and begins with an overview of what Rhodesians defined as "special forces:" the Special Air Service (SAS)[3] and the later Selous Scouts.[4] Related were the creation of the Tracker Combat Unit (TCU) and Bush Warfare School as part of the evolution of tactics and techniques begun by these special units.[5] Special operations forces of the Rhodesia Army had competing and complementary capabilities: the SAS was small, highly trained, racially exclusive, and reliable; the Selous Scouts was larger, adaptable, of mixed races, and not as responsive to control.

Army structure at UDI in 1965 included:

- The Royal Rhodesia Regiment
- The Rhodesian African Rifles
- The Rhodesian Light Infantry
- C Squadron (Rhodesian), Special Air Service
- 1 Field Regiment, Rhodesian Artillery
- Rhodesian Corps of Engineers
- Rhodesian Army Service Corps
- Rhodesian Corps of Signals
- Rhodesian Army Medical Corps
- Rhodesian Corps of Military Police
- Rhodesian Army Pay Corps
- Rhodesian Army Educational Corps
- Rhodesian Corps of Chaplains

Army structure after UDI to meet the needs of the conflict:

- Rhodesian Defense Unit, 1972
- Rhodesian Armored Car Regiment, 1972
- Rhodesian Intelligence Corps, 1973
- Selous Scouts, 1973
- Protection Companies, 1974
- Rhodesian Women's Service, 1975
- Grey's Scouts, 1975
- Rhodesian Corps of Artillery, 1976
- 1 Psychological Operations Unit, 1977
- Rhodesian Defense Regiment, 1978
- 1 (Rhodesian) Special Air Service Regiment, 1978

Neither the Rhodesian *Military Support to the Civil Power (MCP)* nor *Counter-Insurgency Operations (COIN)* doctrinal manuals dealt with special forces or operations, perhaps because they were considered infantry employment in a more refined form. Lieutenant-Colonel Ron F. Reid-Daly felt doctrine was "designed for normal infantry soldiers not special forces." [6] A matter-of-fact explanation was that these were: "High-risk covert or clandestine operations that are conducted by specially trained and equipped troops, normally supported by elements of the army, air force or navy. ... These operations are normally conducted beyond the borders ... to promote national objectives, without the risk of military escalation." This South African view was more durable than equivalent American or British definitions. To be kept in mind was that special operations could be carried out by either civil or military agencies.[7]

A review of Rhodesian special operations provided a useful framework for this analysis. While special forces followed a common mission profile (planning, preparation, approach, actions at the objective, and withdrawal), what took place at the objective was the defining factor. Special operations could be described in effect-based terms: to detect, to destroy/disrupt/delay, and to deceive or destabilize a targeted opponent. A further factor for scrutiny was whether the task was "close," "deep," or "distant" from the base of operations. These actions also had to be calculated out to the second or third order of effect.[8] Reconnaissance tasks (detection) were observation and information-gathering about the enemy, including the capture of prisoners or wiretapping communications. By their nature these were covert ("gray") actions. Combat tasks (destroy/disrupt/delay) were camp attacks, demolition raids, and ambushes, including mining. These were overt ("white") actions when carried out. Unconventional warfare and "pseudo" tasks were clandestine ("black") methods that used the enemy's own resources to cause deception or destabilization. All were considered "top secret" at the time.[9]

Assorted military and civil actions were codenamed, including those planned as well as those executed and it was reasonable to presume some actions also went unnamed. Air force files do not indicate whether air attacks were independent or jointly undertaken in conjunction with others. Refinement or at least caution should be used with operation listings. Portuguese and South African combined efforts appeared as well.[10] Operations included internals, border control or counterinsurgency deployments within Rhodesia. Externals were tasks conducted beyond the borders of the country. Early external operations were run for OCC by the CIO and by the military in Portuguese East Africa (Mozambique). Intelligence and security officers and agents, members of the army special forces, and ultimately general-purpose army and air forces, undertook them. Of direct interest here were incursions conducted into the Frontline States of Zambia, Botswana, Mozambique and Tanzania that provided support, basing, and access to Rhodesia for the nationalists.[11]

The origins of Rhodesian special forces were based as much on personalities as institutions. The colonial period saw irregulars used alongside conventional units, with both citizen-mounted columns and scouting efforts. The Anglo-Boer and world wars saw Rhodesians fighting in Africa and elsewhere in unconventional circumstances. A substantial tradition existed with Great Britain including airborne and seaborne commandos, long-range raiders, and a variety of "private armies" ranging from individuals to groups, most notably World War II service with the British Long Range Desert Group, Special Air Service, and the Chindit Long Range Penetration Groups.[12]

In the modern period, Rhodesians served in special warfare roles in Malaya, Kenya, and Yemen and were viewed as prime candidates for such tasks. Chindit and SAS commander, Brigadier J. Michael "Mad Mike" Calvert[13] reportedly told receptive Rhodesian audiences in 1950:

> We have a new war in the Malayan Emergency, and we need more men to help fight it. Not just any kind of soldier will do for this job. We need men who can work independently of their command headquarters, men with flair for the unorthodox, men who can stay out in those jungles for weeks and months. Men we can rely on to help beat those terrorists.[14]

Special Air Service: Who Dares Wins

The Southern Rhodesia Far East Volunteers under Major George P. Walls served in Malaya from April 1951.[15] They were assigned to Calvert's Malayan Scouts as C Squadron (A Squadron was formed in theater and B Squadron came from the territorial 21 Special Air Service in Great Britain). The Malayan Scouts were redesignated as 22 Special Air Service (22SAS) in 1952, eventually including New Zealand D and Parachute Regiment P squadrons. Walls recalled, "that many of the successes of the Rhodesian War had their beginnings in Malaya. We learned what it was like to be ambushed; what the principles were in establishing our own ambushes; what gives you away; and learned the technique of tracking."[16] Rhodesians learned evolving counterinsurgency doctrine, one lesson being the need for patience with some 1,800 man hours of patrolling needed for every terrorist contact made, if not eliminated.[17] They were also exposed to Sir Harold R. Briggs's "hearts and minds" strategy. Upon returning to Rhodesia in March 1953, the unit disbanded and most members went their separate ways. Ron Reid-Daly was one, who said he had only volunteered for duty because football clubmates had. He served in Malaya as a noncommissioned officer and, with others, later performed with distinction in the bush war.[18]

An SAS squadron was reformed in 1961 affiliated with the British 22SAS Regiment as part of a Commonwealth defense contribution. Number 1 Training Unit was established to provide European regulars for the SAS as well as the newly formed Rhodesian Light Infantry and Selous Scout armored car squadron. A small group of officers and noncommissioned officers under Major Curt E. Welch went to the United Kingdom to participate in SAS selection and continuation training.[19] They returned to Bulawayo to conduct a similar course for volunteers from the Federal Army. By the end of 1961, the first qualified members moved to Ndola Barracks in Northern Rhodesia.[20] It became operational on 1 August 1962, known as C Squadron (Rhodesian) Special Air Service. It built up to 200 men in six troops.[21] A close relationship developed with the Royal Rhodesian Air Force who provided parachute training and transport aircraft.[22]

The SAS assisted during the Congo emergency and certainly with the death of UN Secretary-General Dag Hammarskjöld in an air crash at Ndola, Northern Rhodesia, on 17 September 1961. Operation *Mackerel* saw SAS teams deployed by parachute in September 1962 to Melsetter, Inyanga, and Domboshawa in response to rural unrest and arson, as a "strong deterrent."[23] In July 1962, C Squadron went with 22SAS to Aden during the ongoing confrontation there. On returning to Southern Rhodesia, another rash of rural arson caused SAS personnel to be dropped by parachute to hinder these disturbances.[24]

At the breakup of the Federation, reduced to 31 men, the SAS moved to Southern Rhodesia, stationed at Cranborne Barracks under SAS Malayan veteran Major E. W. Dudley Coventry.[25] Without adequate resources, the essential concept for special operations and skills survived with emphasis on ground, air, and amphibious mobility similar to its parent regiment. Retained were the sand beret, blue stable belt, operator wings, and winged dagger badge of its predecessors and the creed, "Who Dares Wins." Needed were a real enemy and mission.[26]

The Rhodesian SAS organized with headquarters and three to four mobile troops based around Land Rover "Sabre" vehicles.[27] The four-man patrol was the prime SAS building block with a leader, communicator, machine-gunner, and medic (or demolitions man, linguist). Two patrols or half-sections made up an eight-man section, two sections and a troop leader made up a 16-man troop (the troop commander and sergeant were each assigned a patrol). A degree of flexibility existed and the squadron depended on available manning rather than fixed personnel numbers. Missions could be carried out by anything from one man to a full squadron (in fact patrols of two, four, eight, or 12 men). Land Rover, Zodiac, Klepper, parachute, helicopter, and foot provided mobility available to reconnaissance and combat patrols. In addition to the fighting elements, a strong headquarters and base existed that had operations and intelligence, personnel and quartermaster, signals, medical, motor transport, and training functions along with managing a reserve of qualified men for surge efforts.

The SAS saw its role as "deep penetration" and destruction of "hard" targets (roads and rail lines, bridges, shipping, and key installations) by demolition. It could also overtly or covertly deploy into enemy territory and establish bases from which raids, ambushes, reconnaissance, and training of "local" dissidents could be conducted. In addition to classical war operations, the Special Air Service trained and prepared to assume the roles assigned to the infantry for anti-terrorist operations: military assistance to the civil power, urban and rural internal security, and counterinsurgency.

The SAS was important in the structure of special forces in Rhodesia because it became the point of departure for all other efforts that evolved from its example and personnel. This included the tracking and pseudo concepts discussed in following sections. The Special Air Service participated in every aspect of the terrorist war and was, as army headquarters recorded, "A tough, highly trained mobile fighting force … Keeping a watchful eye on Rhodesia's frontiers … moving in where the action is, by land, air and water."[28]

From the start, Prime Minister Smith played a direct role in special operations along with Central Intelligence Organization Director General Ken Flower, who funded and controlled the internal effort and overseas actions. In the prime minister's office as special advisor was Kenya's Ian Henderson.[29] The OCC formed a special operations subcommittee under a full colonel. Initially the army and air force service chiefs were included in the decision-making, until the subsequent advent of Combined Operations made them administrative force providers. By then, noted one SAS commander, "In many instances the army commander was outside this loop!"[30] The later Combined Operations headquarters had a special operations planning cell that also took part in command of operations.

The CIO had two main branches. Branch 1 (or DIN: Director Internal) was essentially the Special Branch (SB) of the BSAP, responsible for domestic intelligence to include combat information as the war expanded. Branch 2 (or DEX: Director External) was responsible for foreign intelligence, entailing disinformation, psychological efforts, and sanctions evasion which used the same players. A central registry, analytical desks, and administration served both branches. The Directorates of Military (DMI) and Air Intelligence (DAI) were eventually incorporated in the

CIO as Branch 3. Military capabilities that proceeded apace were excellent mapping, air imagery, and signals intelligence support.

Flower's Director Internal was William (Bill) Crabtree (Derrick Robinson from 1970); Director External was Ken Leaver with operations under Eric J. (Ricky) May from 1975.[31] Duties were shared based on the identity of their adversaries similar to the British intelligence and security services or the American Central Intelligence Agency and Federal Bureau of Investigation.[32] Domestic dissidents were tracked by Branch 1, even while overseas; Branch 2 was responsible for foreign threats including those inside the country. This division may not have been as complicated as it appeared, with the actual working relationship operating well within the intelligence and security institutions. Though separated for discussion, keep in mind that the internal situation was based upon external agitation trying to foment insurgency from the sanctuary of the Frontline States.[33]

Both the CIO and SB lacked full-time "action arms" and depended upon the military for unconventional warfare actions. These were people on the ground to conduct direct action or to "run" others for these tasks—Europeans, Africans, or foreign nationals. The SAS was used for external operations by the CIO (Operations Division) while the SB (Projects and later Department Z) focused on internal subversion, later using the Selous Scouts. The Selous Scout "operators" were also used overseas, along with ongoing CIO agent and SB informant networks.[34]

Internal operations as military assistance or aid to the civil power were brought on by various states of emergency in Southern Rhodesia from January 1959 and continued through the dissolution of the Federation in January 1964. The Central Intelligence Organization moved agents and supplies into Zambia across the Zambezi River and Lake Kariba from January 1964. Early activities were "compartmented" and outside of the military chain of command, conducted by the Special Branch Task Force, Central Intelligence Organization with a preference for ex-SAS members with overseas passports. These endeavors were security and intelligence in nature rather than military actions.[35] Though not its intended capacity, the SAS was assigned conventional border control operations from May 1964, under Major Coventry. According to army headquarters, "the SAS has taken its full share of border control and operations. The squadron is well acquainted with the [Zambezi] 'Valley' and many are the stories of the adventures and exploits there."[36] Early in the conflict the Special Air Service provided an immediate reaction force to terrorist incidents moving by air, parachute, or its specialized Land Rovers. Some of these initial episodes had a special weapons and tactics flavor, reflecting the nature of the terrorist threat. In July 1964, the SAS responded to the Oberholzer incident (the murder of a White farmer) by parachuting into the Melsetter area to search for the "Crocodile" gang. At dawn the day after the attack, "the sky was filled with billowing white parachutes, each one with a soldier swinging below it," according to an eyewitness.[37]

The OCC with its supporting Joint Planning Staff came into being as border control operations began in the Zambezi valley in October 1964, facing the Zimbabwe People's Revolutionary Army (ZPRA, also ZIPRA) infiltrating out of Zambia.

At UDI, 11 November 1965, two officers and six other ranks were in Great Britain. Subaltern Brian G. Robinson[38] was one of them, who had been with 22SAS, and returned with exposure to recent experience in Malaya and Borneo. Tactical innovations were being made by the SAS at this time. Naturalist and territorial officer Lieutenant C. A. R. (Allan) Savory, along with bush skills and "counter-gang" techniques, had advocated the use of trained trackers in rural areas during the Federal period.[39] Members of the SAS and Savory evolved rudimentary tracking tactics by 1965. The formation and use of combat tracker teams had been taught at the British Far Eastern Land Forces jungle warfare school. Visual and dog pursuit of guerrillas was urged in *The Conduct of Anti-Terrorist Operations in Malaya* and *A Handbook on Anti-Mau Mau Operations*.[40] Both the Rhodesian *MCP* and later *COIN* manual had detailed chapters and sections on tracking, tracking dogs, and tracking teams.[41] Tracking also fit with Rhodesian colonial experience. RLI Regimental Sergeant-Major Ron Reid-Daly felt both Savory and Robinson were "complementary," one an expert on bush lore and the other a disciple of special forces.[42]

Savory believed Europeans as well as Africans could and should be used for tracking duties.[43] He wrote, "guerrilla war is such a filthy tiring business that the greatest requirement for success is mental toughness and determination." As a result, he concluded people with motivation were better than those who were just good trackers. A certain amount of discussion between the army and district officers was conducted at an early phase as to which direction to take. It was thought by some that visual tracking expertise resided with Africans in the Rhodesian African Rifles and the Internal Affairs or National Parks Departments. Concerns existed as to how useful African trackers would be, were any ethnic groups better than others, and how could they to be recruited and sustained. One proposal was to recruit a standing force of "bushmen," but the army felt the use of Africans without military training was a problem. There was also a belief that Blacks were not suited for SAS-type training and operations.[44] The need and advantage of trained trackers was "not fully appreciated" at this date because terrorist threats were still limited in size and duration.[45]

In 1966, the United Nations Security Council voted mandatory sanctions on selected Rhodesian exports and imports. British Prime Minister Harold Wilson met Rhodesian Prime Minister Ian Smith in an unsuccessful bid to arrange a return to legality. The Zimbabwe People's Revolutionary Army stepped up fighting with Rhodesian security forces in April 1966, and the first of a series of ad hoc joint operations centers were stood up for border control operations.[46] As clashes began, Rhodesia's Central Intelligence Organization and Special Branch were successful with informants, infiltration, and exploitation of knowledge on various nationalist groups to the point that the military was excluded from active information-gathering. The SAS met CIO direct action needs in Zambia from May 1966 after the Viljoen incident (murder of a White farmer and his wife). At the time, efforts were limited to the so-called "secret seven" in the squadron while the remainder was on more orthodox infantry deployments.[47]

Captain Robert C. MacKenzie[48] understood the 30 to 40 men in the SAS "started engaging in across the border reconnaissance missions for the most part. Three or four chaps would sneak across the border, wander around the enemy countryside for a week or two and come back and report on what they had seen. In addition, there were a few not quite raids, a few small missions done to eliminate key personnel on the enemy side, to eliminate a few key facilities."[49] Historian Richard Wood pointed out "at this stage ZANU [Zimbabwe African National Union] and ZAPU [Zimbabwe African People's Union] only had a few hundred trained men," and early operations were economic targets inspired by the CIO such as blowing up Zambian coal dumps or the Luangwa bridge.[50] Eventually these included the reconnaissance of possible nationalist camps or crossing sites and attacks on specified targets. These early efforts had mishaps. Agents infiltrated terrorist groups moving into the country, but in some cases were killed by crossfire in the contacts with security forces.[51] On 12 October 1966, four Special Air Service and Special Branch men died when the explosives they were transporting went off. They had been en route to Zambia on a sabotage mission. The SAS's commanding officer, Dudley Coventry, was also injured.[52]

The concept of "pseudo gangs" also came from earlier Commonwealth experience in Malaya and Kenya where security forces fielded teams that dressed and acted like terrorists, including the use of real terrorists "turned" to the government's cause. Rhodesian security force interest in this first came from the Special Branch and Central Intelligence Organization, but they had to rely on the army for personnel and military skills.[53] Various unconventional techniques were visited as part of Operation *Reptile* in October/November 1966. Under Senior Assistant Inspector Ted "Oppie" Oppenheim, the BSAP Criminal Investigation Division and Special Branch conducted it with military participation from the SAS. The possible use of "pseudo gangs" to get at guerrilla groups was examined, but the main focus was on bushcraft and visual tracking. In retrospect, the employment stressed bush living, no specific guerrilla group was "mirrored," and Europeans tried to pass unconvincingly as Africans. Only the survival and tracking aspects proved useful until a real need for pseudogangs was identified.[54]

The end result was more emphasis on basic survival expertise in remote areas rather than on increased counterinsurgency skills. Reid-Daly, by then a commissioned officer, recalled events with the Rhodesian Light Infantry in this period where troops made bad navigation decisions in the Zambezi valley. He found "the younger soldiers had been the worst affected. It was clear that the older men had a tougher mental outlook and were much better able to cope with the considerable stress the situation had created." He decided that bush survival and tracking formed an important part of operational training for "confidence and self-assurance." Reid-Daly recalled Spencer Chapman's Malayan experience that "the jungle is neutral" to the knowledgeable.[55] A guide was published in 1967, based on the security force need "for a concise book on bush craft, couched in simple terms." The lesson was "Use your common sense—don't die in the bundu." Author Colonel Donald H. Grainger had an education and communications background rather than practical experience. Its subsequent use by the nationalists as instruction material caused consternation among the Rhodesians.[56]

In 1967, during Operation *Nickel* (August/September 1967), the need for skilled and determined trackers was conspicuous.[57] As infiltration increased, guerrillas left footprints or other signs which, if detected, could be followed quickly to contact, if correctly anticipated, similar to big game hunting. During *Nickel*, Rhodesian African Rifles Lieutenant Ian P. Wardle followed one group for 48 hours and 54 miles until killing eight and capturing six. Concluded Grainger, "Tracking represents the ultimate in bush craft skills," to keep police and infantry patrolling from being "a long walk and a perfunctory search," a view confirmed by Reid-Daly and others.[58]

Combined operations with the South Africans in Rhodesia and the Portuguese in Mozambique began in 1967. The September 1967 deployment of South African Police saw them used in company-sized bases along the border as well as integrated into the Special Branch ground coverage effort of the BSAP: "Generally they were used to fill a gap in ... areas not deemed operationally vital to the Rhodesian Army." Numbers ranged over time from 1,000 to 2,000 personnel, and had a sizable impact considering the low number of regulars and heavy use of reserves by the Rhodesian forces. They brought their own vehicle transport, light aircraft, and helicopter backing. This left the Rhodesian Air Force (RhAF), RAR, RLI, and SAS free to run down infiltrating terrorists before they reached objectives in the interior of the country.[59] The Rhodesian Air Force also began operating in Mozambique with the Portuguese as early as 1967, providing helicopters, photo-reconnaissance, defoliant-spraying, and attack aircraft. Alex Binda recalled, the Rhodesian Army needed Portuguese speakers and "I lost count of the amount of ops I was on acting as liaison for RLI and SAS tracking teams working with Portuguese troops in the Tete area" between 1968 and 1971.[60] Reid-Daly and Robinson provided fieldcraft and tracking expertise to the Portuguese forces, among others.[61]

Later Walls remarked on Portuguese efforts in Guinea, Angola, and Mozambique:

> Let me say here and now that I think some of the Portuguese soldiers that I have seen, and that some of our chaps have seen and worked with, were first class soldiers, so I would never criticize them for their military qualities in some cases. ... They were fighting a war in which they certainly didn't have their hearts. In many cases they just longed to get back

home at the end of their tour or commission or whatever they called it. We are fighting for our homeland. If I may go on with that one, they also were inclined, perhaps because they didn't have their hearts in it, to adopt certain orthodox deployments and measures where they were accused by FRELIMO [Frente de Libertação de Moçambique] of looking after towns and building themselves forts which they lived in, and leaving the countryside to be dominated by terrorists. [62]

Reid-Daly recalled both Robinson and Savory spent many hours passing their knowledge on to trackers, particularly those from the SAS: "The SAS suddenly became the trackers and bushmen of the army and nearly lost their true role," particularly after Operation *Cauldron* (December 1967–March 1968) when tracker teams from the SAS were in great demand.[63] Reconnaissance and tracking gave rise to the derisive "Special Air Safaris" moniker with a certain amount of frustration expressed by the SAS with finding the enemy, but having to turn the follow-up to units "less combative and effective than we were."[64] In this they "performed a great service to the army by teaching it to be aware of bush conditions and techniques. It provided confidence in combat that resulted in a greater casualty ratios with the insurgents."[65]

Another attempt to operate in Zambia took place on 30/31 December 1967 (Operation *Sculpture*), using a Cessna 206 aircraft to fly in three SAS operators (including Robinson) to Lusaka to attack the ZANU headquarters, but they had to abort because of faction fighting in the target area.[66] Reid-Daly observed that "Poor intelligence and a lack of experience" in paramilitary operations by the CIO were reasons behind these early troubles. Needed were careful planning and flexible minds, as these operations demanded "every ounce of professional skill and courage."[67]

Combat Trackers: Run the Bastards Down

In February 1968, Robinson and Savory ran an "aggressive bush craft for guerrilla warfare" exercise for the SAS and Special Branch at Buffalo Range, although the police eventually withdrew. It gave the mostly urban Whites and Blacks confidence that they could work in rural areas as combat trackers. After Operation *Cauldron* the practice was to send trackers to investigate "every guerrilla action, sighting, or even suspicion of terrorist presence."[68] This required three to four teams fully trained and available at any one time. The use of dogs with tracking remained a police and air force prerogative (the Rhodesian Air Force used dogs for security, including locating explosives). The capabilities and limitations of dogs were well documented.[69] Concrete results of these efforts were the formation of a specialized unit of trackers and a tracking school. The initial concept called for the SAS to administer both initiatives, but the army chief of staff noted, "I don't know enough of SAS classified activities" to judge if this was workable.[70]

A territorial Tracker Combat Unit (TCU) was formed by Savory to supplement full-time SAS, RLI, and RAR tracker teams.[71] Tracking skills were perishable and suffered from lack of use. This was one reason why Savory believed they were better placed with those who worked with these techniques daily, rather than the active duty forces. Savory felt that the normal military was not the best source of trackers and territorial and reserve volunteers "with considerable bush craft and tracking ability and experience" were preferred. Operating between 1968 and 1973, it eventually fielded some 90 members assigned to the various joint operations centers for use during border control operations.[72]

The United Nations established comprehensive mandatory sanctions against Rhodesia in 1968. Prime Minister Wilson softened the terms for return to legality but was rebuffed by Prime Minster Smith. Two referendums approved establishment of a republic and endorsed a new constitution in 1969. The Rhodesian government adapted a policy of parity calling for racial segregation through separate political development and a land tenure act that imposed classified land use.

To meet the broadened need for skilled and trained trackers a small group of instructors from the SAS, including Captain Brian Robinson, Sergeant André P. Rabie, and Sergeant Danny Hartman, established a tracking wing as part of the School of Infantry in March 1969.[73] Known variously as the School of Bush Warfare, the Tracking and Bush Survival School, or the "takkie wing,"[74] it was located at Kariba. The first pupils were regular soldiers from the SAS, RLI, and RAR who were taught a three-phase program: basic tracking, aggressive bushcraft, and a final exercise under operational conditions. On return to their units they became the nucleus of full-time tracking platoons or troops. Both tracking unit and school initiatives fostered a straightforward approach to eliminating terrorists as they entered the country.

Robinson believed that if a soldier had to operate in the bush environment "he had to become one with the bush; and the ability to track and anti-track was a vital need."[75] Taking Savory's bushcraft skills, Robinson knew a single tracker was vulnerable, but a four-man team provided security and the ability to move ahead in the chase. The resulting standard tracking team consisted of a tracker, two flankers, and a controller with a radio, the tracker and flank positions rotating within the team to ensure constant alertness while moving. The team moved some 100 to 200 meters ahead of conventional follow-up troops from the army or police. The Rhodesian Army compared the whole follow-up approach to Zulu *impi* tactics where the bull's head was the tracker group, flanked by the horns of two skirmish groups, with the follow-up force commander and radio in the center, with the reserve group as the "chest" of the bull.[76] Additional techniques developed to include backtracking, leapfrogging, and aircraft tracking to get ahead on "cold" tracks and to overtake the quarry.[77] Related efforts to give the pursuer an advantage included various efforts to use aircraft, motorcycles, horses, and even hounds fitted with transponders to be tracked from the air. But even these could go no faster than the tracking team's efforts to follow the signs.[78]

Tracking was taught based on first-hand study and experience. The approach used covered the "A to Z" of application appropriate to the requirements of modern low-intensity conflict. Understanding that training was no replacement for doing, this started with a history of tactical tracking and moved into individual attributes and proficiency. With this background, the specific techniques of the art were identified as well as the part played by each member of a tracking team: the controller, tracker, and flank trackers. After the basic and alternate methods of "running down" an absconder were covered, advanced subjects were addressed to include counter-tracking, command and control, and training.[79]

A proponent of tracking techniques with service in the Special Air Service, Tracker Combat Unit, and later RLI and Selous Scouts was Captain David Scott-Donelan.[80] His analysis introduced the subject, when pursued by practical tutelage, and served as an aide-mémoire for maintenance training. Scott-Donelan summarized his principles as: the tracker sets the pace; record the starting point; always know your position; confirm on aerial spoor; keep in visual contact; identify the correct tracks; never walk on ground spoor; get in the quarry's mind; and never go beyond the last known spoor.[81]

Tracking skills are as old as the Stone Age and as current as newspaper headlines. While others had focused on tracking for search and rescue or apprehension of migrants or poachers, combat trackers dealt with tracking those who were armed and dangerous. This competence was a throwback to other times and places where the same need was met through organization and the use of human senses rather than on technology that might not be available or did not do the job as well.

Methods took tracking from the realm of individual skill and made it almost a science—even though practice might teach otherwise. Reid-Daly wrote that once the basics of bushcraft, tracking, map-reading, camping and survival were taught, the various skills still had to be put into use "in the bush." This involved small teams under supervision completing a cross-country course by day and night, with obstacle-crossing, map-reading, finding water, and tracking.[82] His view was a timely reminder that technology does not always provide the best or only solution for the hunters and the hunted.

Continued border control and hot-pursuit operations between 1969 and 1972 called for the services of SAS tracking teams along with those of the RLI, RAR, and TCU. Trackers were put on the trail as soon as possible, and from that moment until contact was made or pursuit was no longer possible, the team leader was in absolute charge. Trackers moved by stealth and speed until the enemy was closed with, to allow the follow-up forces to launch an immediate attack, at which time the tracking team would resume the pursuit of any survivors.[83] If more than one tracking team was available, one could be used to follow up the direction taken by the terrorists, another could backtrack to find where the terrorists came from, and a third could be kept in reserve to get ahead of the terrorists if possible. It was soon found that the tracking team made and had to resolve contacts before support could be provided, either because they met the terrorists first or to keep them from fleeing. Scott-Donelan noted, "never let your support group slow you down." Actual contact time varied from 15 seconds to 36 hours with overall command varying from section to company level.[84] One advantage noted was that "we knew the area like the back of our hand, all the water holes, all the strategic routes, etcetera. ... The insurgents didn't. All we had to do was pick up the tracks, track them down and shoot them."[85]

Trackers looked for both ground and aerial "spoor" or "sign" that was unnatural or could be interpreted. The team's focus was on the possible number of terrorists being followed, the general direction, the age of the track, and the type of track followed (boots, shoes, bare feet).[86] Starting with a "confirmed spoor," or footprint, an estimate of number could be made by counting the prints in the space of an FN rifle's 40-inch length, counting complete footprints, for a total, and adding two if more than five. Confirmation on the number was continually looked for and other methods existed for estimates of 10 to 12 people or less. Direction was based on a compass heading from the tracks, as well as the lay of the land, and intuition as to what the enemy was trying to do. The age of the track depended upon observing the impact of weather, moisture, and experience. The tracks themselves might indicate whether men or women were being followed, what type of load they had, and how fast they were moving. A card with the distinct types of boot prints made by the guerrillas was provided for this.[87] Time of day had an impact on the light needed for tracking and the team had to be prepared to spend the night on the track when it got too dark to continue. Losing tracks required going back to the last known print and cross-graining: 360-degree or box-search methods were used to find the trail again (sometimes as much as five kilometers beyond the last confirmed sign). Efforts made to disguise the trail by deception or evasion were encountered, as well as ambushes, snipers, and booby traps to discourage security force pursuit.[88]

Commented one army officer, "Tracking requires intense concentration, stamina and an eye for detail." Trackers were forced to travel days without food and little water, under tremendous pressure at a fast pace.[89] In one example, an SAS team under Sergeant Joseph Conway tracked a gang who had murdered a farmer. This follow-up went for six days and covered some 100 miles over broken and rugged terrain in temperatures over 100°F (38°C) . After making contact, killing three and capturing the rest, one survivor remarked they had been "tracked down like dogs."[90] The army's leading tracker was an African Selous Scout who had personally tracked and killed some 80 terrorists. In addition, he had tracked twice that many that resulted in contact by following forces that were able to achieve surprise.[91]

Based on their function, the trackers soon developed uniform and equipment adjustments that saw running or track shoes (takkies) worn without socks instead of combat boots, shorts, cut-off shirts or T-shirts (with a spot of camouflage cream), and minimum personal equipment. Bare head or combat caps were preferred because these were less noisy than a bush hat. The goal was to move around rather than through vegetation, silently and quickly without being burdened to the point of fatigue. "Quick-kill" or snapshooting was also a necessity with well-rehearsed immediate action drills for when contact was made.[92] Asked about this unconventional appearance, an officer replied, "As long as a man feels comfortable and is able to use his weaponry without getting entangled in accoutrements, we turn a blind eye."[93]

The tracker unit and tracking school played a part in an ongoing debate on how best to counter terrorist incursions. This witnessed the RAR using a Malayan model of platoons or sections engaged in cross-grain patrols, observation posts, and ambushes to dominate terrain from 1967's Operation *Nickel*. The other approach from the SAS, RLI, and trackers was the use of small, light, and mobile follow-up forces to locate and run the terrorist groups to ground with fast pursuit and a focus on the enemy and not the ground from 1968's Operation *Cauldron*. With the addition of helicopter firepower and mobility, this solution prevailed in the end with Operation *Hurricane*. It was an approach that matured quickly with experience in Mozambique and the integration of helicopter and light aircraft support for both movement and observation.[94] It was pointed out that the war was mostly fought by small units (four to six men) on both sides. Former British SAS man Nicholas Downie, among others, considered this a "corporal's war" with the large number of small units operating about the countryside.[95] Walls added:

> We dominate all of it, although we have terrorists in certain areas. ... We operate as much by night as by day. We reckon that twenty-four hours of the day we've got to be in control of the situation, so there is no difference between day and night as far as our operations are concerned. ... I think if one uses common sense, one can see the sort of thing we are liable to do: to contact the terrorist, to cut them off from the local population, and to ensure the local population that we are there.[96]

There was a sense of relief expressed by SAS commander Major Peter S. Rich when the squadron was reassigned from border control tasks in 1969. It was "no longer a superannuated rifle company engaged on straight border duties, but [we] have reverted to our proper role."[97] This required some three months of retraining in advanced special operation techniques.[98] Along with an untimely rotation of commanders, the SAS squadron had difficulty in attracting and keeping European recruits, reaching 133 men at this time. MacKenzie recalled SAS strength dropped to 80 men by 1970, and then still less. This was attributed to the high standards required of a Special Air Service soldier.[99] There were subsequent joint-operation and brigade demands on the special forces, for example SAS tracking teams, met by Major A. B. R. Mulock-Bentley (the air marshal's son), and even emergency Fire Force duties occurred before other infantry units were fully parachute trained.

While skill and diligence by the infantry of the RAR, RLI, and RR at observation posts, patrolling, and ambushing were required, early on it was recognized that contact with the insurgents depended upon advance information. Lessons were applied from Malaya and Kenya for patrols and ambushes. Information came first from local informants, tracking skills, signals interception, and undercover work. The oft-repeated utterance was that killing the terrorists was not the problem, finding them was. This highlighted the differences between the military and police approaches over the need for combat information rather than processed intelligence (of forecast rather than analysis).[100]

Rhodesia declared itself a republic in 1970. By then, the Rhodesians were targeting ZPRA support networks in Botswana in addition to Zambian bases. The Ian Smith–Alec Home agreement proposed terms for settlement in 1971 as Bishop Abel Muzorewa formed the African National Council (ANC) to oppose the settlement. The Pearce Commission conducted hearings from January to March 1972 to ascertain public reaction to the proposed settlement with Muzorewa organizing internal African opposition. A new phase of guerrilla war opened with increased activity by the Zimbabwe African National Union from Mozambique. By early 1972, Special Branch Detective Section Officers Peter Stanton and Winston Hart reported that ZANU's military wing, ZANLA (Zimbabwe African National Liberation Army), was operating with FRELIMO in Mozambique in the Tete province. In March 1972, the SAS and RLI raided Matimbe base near the Rhodesian border, capturing prisoners and documents establishing a link between the two nationalist groups. Since this flew in the face of the CIO's stated position, the results were sidelined until December 1972 when farm and landmine attacks by ZANLA indicated the unexpected extent of the infiltration in the northeastern portion of Rhodesia.[101]

CHAPTER 3

A Question of Supporting Arms

Before going further, a look at the security forces' advantage in fire and air support is in order (including everything from mortars to artillery, armored cars to tanks, and rotary- to fixed-wing aircraft).[1] While the advantage of one outweighed the others, these provided a decisive edge to the Rhodesian ground forces over their opponents and it was the air force that made the difference. In a state where the prime minister was a former fighter pilot, it was natural that the air arm had a singular place.[2] As the smallest service, the Rhodesian Air Force felt it offered a distinct spirit, "The feeling of being treated as a valued, individual member of a small close family rather than just one of a crowd."[3] In fact, the air force's position was beyond challenge, either by the larger army or police. The following pages consider the use of aviation from the perspective of its unique ability to support a counterinsurgency effort, as well as the air force's approach to joint operations.

By 1951, the Royal Rhodesian Air Force (RRAF) provided two fighter squadrons for the British Commonwealth, as well as basing of a Royal Air Force training group. Between 1958 and 1963, fighter and bomber squadrons deployed to Aden and Cyprus under British command. In 1961, transport aircraft were used to assist the Royal Air Force during the Kuwait crisis and to move British troops in the Middle East. Relief operations were also conducted in Somalia at the request of the British government.

Units were based at Gwelo and Salisbury and the air force included its own Territorial Force, General Reserve and Volunteer Reserve to back up its regular establishment, including some pilots, but primarily for base and support activities.[4] At UDI, the 1,158-man air force supported some 71 fighter, bomber, transport, and utility aircraft. Of these, pride of place went to the racehorses of the stable, the fighters and bombers which had been represented in the United Kingdom air order of battle. The Cinderella of the service was the late-developing helicopter squadrons.[5] Air force strength peaked at 2,300 personnel and 132 aircraft, with direct augmentation in crews and planes from the South African Air Force (SAAF). Losses were 55 airmen during the conflict.[6]

Of this, Zimbabwean Air Vice-Marshal Hugh C. S. Slatter recalled as a junior officer:

> I do not believe any of us foresaw the dramatic changes … resulting from UDI in 1965, the escalation of the anti-terrorist war over the next 15 years, and the Lancaster House agreement leading to the granting of independence by the British government to the new state of Zimbabwe in 1980. … This period may have seemed a particularly difficult time in the history of the country—all too often we were numbed by the death of our colleagues who paid the ultimate price.[7]

Other leaders had political as well as military impact (H. Hawkins, A. O. G. Wilson, F. W. Mussell, Rob Gaunt, et al.) and airmen held key positions with the joint staff and combined operations during the conflict. Reputations were made in the full spectrum of military activity: strategic (Michael McLaren, et al.), operational (Norman Walsh, et al.), tactical and technical (Peter "PB" Petter-Bowyer, Christopher Dixon, Peter Briscoe, et al.), special operations (Basil Moss, Michael Borlace, et al.), and individual airmanship (Kevin "Cocky" Benecke, the most decorated serviceman of the war). As with the accounts about the police and army, the individuals mentioned are those available in the records without assigning merit other than the honors and casualties lists.[8] Air Marshal Michael J. McLaren understood this when telling a graduating class of airmen, "The lesson of history is that when difficulties are greatest and the set-backs most severe, the greatest performances are turned in. I cannot do better than point you to the example of those who have served, and are serving, in this force."[9]

Fire and Maneuver from the Air

The Rhodesian Air Force had four roles in order of significance: deterrence, air defense, tactical support, and aid to the civil power.[10] The Rhodesian *Financial Gazette* reported that the question of air defense retained great importance during the escalation of the bush war. The threat of attack by air, however remote, had to be faced. Throughout the conflict, the leaders of the Frontline States knew their capitals were within range of Rhodesian fighters and bombers. This was displayed on enough occasions to prove the fact with successful raids against terrorist bases in Zambia, Mozambique, and Angola.[11] As Zimbabwean Air Marshal Norman Walsh explained, "the air force provides a meaningful deterrent against external aggression."[12] This kept the air force's jet aircraft (Hunter, Vampire, Canberra) fully occupied with deterrence until needed for offensive air support in the mid-1970s.

The use of what was a conventionally configured air force in unconventional circumstances required modification of functions and tasks based upon a shift of assumptions for aircraft utilization. The roles remained, but the emphasis changed.[13] Air Marshal Archibald O. G. Wilson concluded:

> With Rhodesia facing, virtually alone, the unimpeded incursion of guerrilla factions on a large scale, the new generation of ground and air crews was ready and professionally more than able to fulfill both its tactical and strategic roles with consummate success. … Not only did the air

force remain cost effective, but actually also expanded its operational capability, including an improved radius of action in strike potential.[14]

Aviation historians Dudley Cowderoy and Roy C. Nesbit provide their interpretation of this, listing the innovative wartime effort as Fire Force, cross-border strikes, sanction-busting, strategic bombing, air transport, command and control, and communications.[15] The analysis here provides a more detailed perspective on this successful transition.

Tactical support emerged as the indispensable aspect of anti-terrorist operations. The air force's capacity in backing either the police or army was well defined, by means that tended to be with general rather than direct support.[16] "The Rhodesian Air Force today," observed the nationalists, "has a greater percentage pro rata of manpower and equipment in the operational area than any other branch of the security forces. ... The air force is organized along conventional squadron lines although aircraft may be dispersed throughout the country, or attached to joint units such as Fire Force units. Pilots spend up to eight months a year on operational duty, and on average fly troops into two contacts per day."[17]

Organization and Basing

The Rhodesian Air Force was structured on a Royal Air Force model, modified by local circumstances. The air force was organized with a headquarters staff, main stations, and lastly forward airfields. An examination of the structure of the force in terms of its aircraft and crews indicates what could be accomplished; a review of their actual employment shows what was undertaken within the conditions of the conflict.

The air force consisted of a Regular Force, Territorial Force, General Reserve, and Volunteer Reserve (including civilian, African, and female members). The commander and his chief of staff supervised directors of operations (air branch), supporting services (technical branch), and administration (administrative branch) piloting "mahogany bombers" from the "glass palace" of Air Headquarters at Dolphin House;[18] from which, recalled Zimbabwean Wing Commander Preller M. "Prop" Geldenhuys: "Command and control was rigidly enforced, and with set lines of communications—upwards, downwards, and sideways. ... Deviation from accepted norms was not tolerated ... and the tried and true methods employed by the military stood the test of time."[19]

Under the air branch were the flying squadrons, flying and parachute training schools, operations and intelligence staffs. Weapons and communications were shared responsibilities between the air and technical branches.[20] A general service unit conducted initial recruit instruction, which was followed by general service training, and subsequent specialist or advanced courses at Number 1 and 2 Ground Training

Schools. In conjunction with the provost branch, the later Air Force Regiment, it provided security for installations and aircraft, including low-level air defense, at main bases and forward airfields.[21]

When formed, the Air Force Regiment consisted of two infantry, two support, and two antiaircraft squadrons. Ground defense specialists were grouped into 201 Squadron at New Sarum and 202 Squadron at Thornhill. According to David P. Newnham, who commanded 202 Squadron and was the Staff Officer Regiment at Air Headquarters, this structure is somewhat misleading, as the antiaircraft capability was added later with detachments at Flyde using seized Communist Bloc (12.5, 14.5, and 20mm) weapons. "The squadrons formed at each main base were, in fact, composite squadrons consisting of an infantry squadron which included an armored car troop [manned by national servicemen] and administrative control of all other Black airmen employed on the base. While not strictly correct ... two infantry and two support squadrons probably accurately reflects the operational commitment."[22]

Basic flight training was in 6 Squadron, advancing to 2 Squadron, followed by operational assignment.[23] The goal was to produce pilots who could fly any one of the air force's aircraft on a planned three-year rotation. Wartime necessity circumvented this and about 20 percent of the aircrews came with outside experience from other air forces. The belief was that the general duty system "provides an ideal basis for economic manpower usage in peace-time but tends to fall apart in war when more and more officers are required to forsake their desks for cockpits."[24]

Over time, training remained a key to successful operations. The aim produced versatile air crews capable of operating with a high degree of autonomy. One instructor stated Rhodesian Air Force pilots needed to provide "direction and advice" to ground commanders and were completely familiar with tactical needs to "provide support to the army with the least possible prevarication." An official explanation of a joint operations center was "Reasonable men acting in reasonable cooperation with one another."[25] According to Group Captain Peter J. H. Petter-Bowyer, on occasion "pilots assumed the role of ground forces command when an army Fire Force commander was incapacitated or absent from the K-Car cabin. Control of forces in these circumstances was usually equal to the best the army could provide because pilots had been involved in more Fire Force actions than [the] recognized army commander."[26]

Training was geared to understanding the enemy and the purpose of revolutionary war. The methods to defeat the guerrilla were made part of the pilot's thought process in order to draw lessons and apply them.[27] Flight training emphasized low-level flying, navigation, and short field operations under all conditions. Weapons training emphasized quick, unpremeditated attacks on targets of opportunity in a variety of tactical situations. Squadron Leader Christopher J. T. "Chris" Dixon stated: "The idea is to teach them to think for themselves—to be flexible within the system."[28]

Refresher and continuation training took place at the squadron level.[29] The levels of stress varied with the type of flying; for example, helicopter or light attack pilots involved in relatively constant combat flying operated effectively only for three to four years. After which they were retrained to fly more sophisticated aircraft or as instructors under more routine conditions. Even this was demanding as Squadron Leader Richard J. "Rich" Brand observed, "A fighter pilot has to be fit … You're pulling 6g [six times the force of gravity] on a sortie and the more unfit you are, the lower your threshold of endurance."[30]

Experience taught the need for "well-maintained aircraft and thoroughly motivated and well-trained air crews." Because good training and high skill levels made up for shortcomings in hardware, it was a view in counterpoint to those who thought the future lay in high technology often purchased at the expense of training.[31] Air Marshal McLaren noted, "While the equipment may be vintage in some areas, the flesh and blood in the cockpit is young, skilled, and very dedicated and that counts for a very great deal, as hundreds of terrorists have discovered to their cost."[32]

Two permanent bases supported the air force, New Sarum at Salisbury and Thornhill at Gwelo.[33] These secure complexes afforded conventional support and servicing facilities to house aircraft and crews. New Sarum and Thornhill provided administrative headquarters and supply elements, "sited to facilitate rapid movement of spares, men and equipment to forward operational areas."[34] New Sarum shared runways with Salisbury international airport from which air traffic control was provided for the entire region.

Major expansion projects were undertaken as a result of Portuguese and South African regional defense agreements, with Wankie Main (northwest) and Fylde (central) strategic air bases developed away from the constant observation New Sarum and Thornhill were exposed to. This included hard runways of 2,000 meters, revetted parking space, control facilities, and fuel storage. Buffalo Range (southeast) was enlarged in this category, but work was still underway at the end of the conflict.[35]

"As with tactics and training, ground support is a vital aspect of the [counterinsurgency] air force," observed Zimbabwean Wing Commander Peter Briscoe. This lent itself to a more inherently flexible organization that moved where it needed to support the police and army, and was often located in close proximity to areas threatened by guerrillas. Some 10 forward airfields (FAFs) were established to back different operational areas. Wankie and Kariba were first in support of border control operations against Zambia and the police and army camp at Kanyemba served as well. With Operation *Hurricane* in 1973, area control counterinsurgency operations required expanded full-time backing along the eastern border with Mozambique. This was followed by the need to mount early external operations such as from Musengedzi and actually within Mozambique at Macombe.

Forward airfields were tactically sited, providing a chain of springboards to the enemy areas. A forward airfield was used only when required and was capable of activation on short notice with only a small caretaker element. At a minimum, it had a paved 800–1,000-meter runway, messing and accommodation for up to 200 men, and an operations center with radios and teletype communications. Along with fuel, a variety of aviation ordnance as well as small-arms ammunition was stockpiled.[36] The expanding war required direct air support needing additional bases. While these could be almost anywhere there was a sufficient runway, base development ensured adequate military infrastructure. Computerized lists were maintained of civil fields or strips and aviation fuel was staged throughout the country within 20 minutes of flying time for helicopters.[37] Fields were manned and run almost exclusively by air reservists. The guerrillas were aware of the value of aircraft and their vulnerability to attack on the ground. In particular, approach and retirement lanes were exposed during takeoff and landing. "A particularly obnoxious guerrilla tactic in Rhodesia was the planting of anti-tank mines on runways and taxiways," wrote one air force pilot.[38] Although, Petter-Bowyer recalled this happened at Mrewa, only one other mine was found at a forward airfield.[39] Mortar-proof revetments for aircraft and facilities were built (earth berms, sandbags, or fuel drums filled with earth and overhead wire nets strung on gum poles), that were "cheap and easy to construct and provide excellent protection." Though the air force and army had joint duty for forward airfield security, the air force commander was directly concerned with the protection of aircraft, crews, and vital facilities.[40] This required the use of mortars, armored cars, patrols, and close-in ambushes by Air Force Regiment personnel, duly shielded from being siphoned off for other ground combat operations.[41]

The air force deployed to the operational areas with a focus on the task at hand:

> When detached to the forward area in support of the army and police, the air force pilots did not see themselves as being from a different force but rather worked with the army as close team members. They concentrated their effort on the achievement to the goals of the mission. Many young officers went to great lengths to achieve these goals sometimes at great risk to themselves and their machines. ... The army in turn made this type of cooperation easy for us all. ... Many senior army officers went to great lengths to explain the operation and to educate the young air force officers in how the army operated on the ground. This education process was an extremely good investment in time and paid off handsomely.[42]

Procurement, Maintenance, and Sustainability

As a technical service, the air force's ability to operate after the rupture with Great Britain depended upon creative internal and external sources of maintenance and supply.[43] Portuguese and South African air forces provided training, basing, and direct backing, even participating in specific operational and logistical efforts, based as much on fraternal as self-interest.[44] One wing commander felt, "Western nations are notoriously fickle concerning policies of arms supplies to Third World countries. They supply them when it suits them, and are prone to cut off supplies when the customer becomes politically or economically expendable."[45] He concluded, "little help can be expected to be forthcoming from the West in the event of an emergency, either in men, material or ideas."[46]

The Rhodesian Air Force thought that aircraft required for low-level insurgencies did not have to be sophisticated. In fact, it preferred to have machines that were reliable and capable of operating under adverse conditions with minimum maintenance.[47] "It is essential, however, that the force be a balanced mix of transport [fixed and rotary wing], light ground attack, and that a medium ground attack/ fighter capability exist." Peter Briscoe added that sophisticated machines were also needed, in that "a well-trained air force operating a capable jet fighter and ground attack aircraft provides an effective deterrent to any neighboring state who might feel predisposed to joining any dissident element."[48]

In the local high and hot flight regime, spare power was essential. Aircraft needed high reliability for extended periods of deployment with ground forces without extensive maintenance facilities. Easy maintenance away from base with no ground support equipment meant engine, gearbox, and blade changes could be accomplished, based in part on maintenance data kept up to date with minimum effort. Ground support of aircraft at the forward airfields needs to be appreciated as seen in high serviceability rates. One pilot reminisced:

> At the airfield you would have one Lynx, one Dakota, and four to five Alouettes. Each had a mechanic and armorer for support, but more often just the pilot and mechanic. One would refuel while the other rearmed. Instead of the normal ... serviceability it was something like 90 percent! And this was without operational accidents. ... This same pilot and noncommissioned officer drank their beer together after hours. I learned to keep on the good side of the ground crew.[49]

The aircraft and weapons used were ubiquitous in nature and readily available on international arms markets to obviate the effects of sanctions. Aircraft came from countries with similar types, notably South Africa, Portugal, Spain, France, Italy, and United Kingdom client states. With an economy struggling to make ends meet, and precious little remaining for defense expenditure, it was imperative that the right aircraft were procured and that these aircraft were capable of fulfilling more than a single specialized role.

Air Vice-Marshal Harold Hawkins told the *Rhodesia Herald* on 20 July 1967, "The potential of Rhodesian industry was explored diligently during the year and a firm policy is to be adapted of purchasing wherever possible locally manufactured articles in preference to imported ones."[50] As part of the acquisition strategy, comprehensive spare inventories were built up to keep the air force viable.[51] Spares, petrol, oil, and lubricants traveled sometimes convoluted routes as the aircraft. And there was the need for constant awareness of alternative supply sources to preclude any catastrophic shortages as the result of changes in political favor.[52] Also, the relationship between the Rhodesian Air Force and commercial international air carriers (Air Trans Africa, Affretair, Air Gabon, etc.) ensured the balance of trade required to maintain the military air effort. At times these "civil" aircraft with reserve crews under air force colors flew cross-border military operations such as reconnaissance, deceptive flyover, airborne communications relays, and covert parachute drops.[53]

An overview of aircraft types follows, with some details on equipment by squadron.[54] Specifics for each will be discussed, providing the capabilities available for employment. These were the aircraft used at the height of the war, predated by others and were not necessarily those desired by a sanctions-strapped service.[55] Some indication of earlier aircraft are noted to show technical progression. Numbers are from postwar aggregates, with fewer on hand at any one time (75 percent available for operations was the maintenance figure).[56] Losses are both operational and combat and again are estimates, because references do not show whether aircraft were repaired, written off, or replaced. A South African air attaché, Colonel Jan W. Mienie, who flew with 4 Squadron during the war, noted that *Jane's* tends to be optimistic about speeds and radius of action. Contemporary speeds and ranges are for comparison without regard to maximum or cruising speeds, altitude, load, or maneuver conditions.[57]

Aircraft

Bombers ("Find and Destroy"): the Canberra B2 and T4 were jet "light bomber" and "photographic reconnaissance" aircraft. Tasks included tactical and strategic bombing, photo reconnaissance, and courier. Primary weapons were general-purpose high-explosive bombs. Secondary weapons were fragmentation bombs, later replaced by various cluster bombs. The Canberra's maximum speed was 6 miles per minute with a radius of action of 1,100 nautical miles, or less at low levels. [58] The power plant was 3,000 kilograms of thrust twin Rolls-Royce Avon 101 engines. The "Can" first entered Rhodesian service in 1958. A total of 19 were used, with seven lost during the conflict.[59]

Fighters ("Strike from Above"): the Hawker FGA9 Hunter was a single-seat jet "day fighter/ground attack" and "photographic reconnaissance" aircraft. Tasks included air defense, ground attack, visual and photo reconnaissance. Primary weapons were cannon and rockets; secondary use was made of general-purpose high-explosive or fire bombs. Air-to-air missiles were also available. The Hunter's speed was 8 miles per minute with a radius of action of 398 nautical miles, or less at low levels. It was powered by 4,600 kilograms of thrust Rolls-Royce Avon 207 turbo-jet engine. It first entered Rhodesian service in 1962. A total of 12 were used, with three lost during the conflict.[60]

The de Havilland FB9 and T11 Vampire were single- and dual-seat "day fighter/ground attack" aircraft. Tasks included advanced air weapons training, ground attack, and visual reconnaissance. Primary weapons were cannon and rockets; secondary use was made of general-purpose high-explosive, fragmentation, or fire bombs. The Vampire's speed was 5 miles per minute with a radius of action of 240 nautical miles, or less at low level. It was powered by a 1,520 kilograms of thrust Goblin MK35 turbo-jet engine. The "Vamp" first entered Rhodesian service in 1954. Replacements were from South African FB52s and T55s. A total of 32 were used, with eight lost during the conflict.[61]

Helicopters ("Anywhere and Everywhere"): the Aerospatiale IIIB Alouette (Lark) was a single-engine light "vertical support" helicopter. Tasks included command and control, forward air control, fire support, troop transport, cargo transport, and casualty evacuation. It was armed with machine guns or cannon. The Alouette's average speed was 1.5 miles per minute with a radius of action of 35 nautical miles with four troops and up to 50 nautical miles with two stretchers. It was powered by an 870-horsepower Turbomeca Artouste IIB turbine engine. The "Alo" first entered Rhodesian service in 1962. A total of 42 to 50 were used, with 27 to 36 lost during the conflict (cumulatives vary because of South African crews and aircraft).[62]

The Agusta Bell 205A "Cheetah" was a single-engine medium "vertical support" helicopter. Tasks included troop transport, cargo transport, and casualty evacuation. It was armed with machine guns. Its maximum speed was 1.8 miles per minute with a radius of action of 162 miles. It first entered Rhodesian service in 1978. A total of 11 were used, with four lost during the conflict.[63]

Light Attack/Utility ("Seek and Strike"): aircraft of this type included the long-serving Hunting Percival T52 Provost (22 total, with six lost). The Hunting Percival T52 Provost first entered service in 1954 as an internal security and training aircraft. It was armed with a machine gun, rockets, and fragmentation or fire bombs. It had a speed of 2 miles per minute and a radius of action of 100 to 200 nautical miles.

The Aermacchi Lockheed AL60 Trojan supplemented the Provost from 1967 carrying cargo and passengers. Eventually armed with rockets, its speed was 2.4 miles per minute, with a radius of action of 322 miles. A total of 11 were used, with five lost during the conflict. The Provost was designed as a military aircraft but had reached the end of its service life; the Trojan was not a perfect fit for the demands placed on it. Flight Lieutenant Edward H. Paintin recalled, "credit should be given for the work done by the Provost and Trojan aircraft during the first eight to 10 years of the war. Without these aircraft the results of the conflict would have been very different."[64] Even the follow-on Lynx was described as "a botched-up civil aircraft" used as a substitute for more desirable craft.[65]

The Reims Cessna 337G "Lynx" was a dual-seat "light ground support" aircraft. Tasks included ground attack, visual reconnaissance, courier, search and rescue, and casualty evacuation. It was armed with machine guns, rockets, paired high-explosive or fire bombs, flares, and teargas. The Lynx's speed was 3.3 miles per minute for a radius of action of 502 miles. Power plant was 225-horsepower twin Continental TSIO-360D turbo-charged engines. It first entered Rhodesian service in 1976 replacing older Provost and Trojan aircraft. A total of 21 were used, with four lost during the conflict.[66]

Training/Light Attack ("Aspire to Achieve"): the Siai Marchetti SF260 Genet was a triple-seat "flying training" aircraft. It was primarily a basic flight and weapons trainer with additional tasks of courier, reconnaissance, convoy escort, and light attack. It was armed with machine guns, rockets, bombs, flares, and teargas. The Genet's air speed was 3.1 miles per minute with a radius of action of 500 miles. "The Genets … although they could be armed, were even less suitable for the COIN role than the Lynx," observed one pilot.[67] It first entered Rhodesian service in 1977. A total of 31 were used, with two lost during the conflict.[68]

Transports ("Swift to Support"): the Douglas DC-3C "Dakota" was an "air transport" aircraft, a civil version of the World War II C-47A. Tasks included communications, sky-shouting, leaflet dropping, search and rescue, visual reconnaissance, casualty evacuation, troop transport, paratroop dropping, and aerial resupply. It carried some 30 passengers or 2,750 kilograms of cargo. The Dakota's average speed was 3 miles per minute with a radius of action of 300 nautical miles. Power plant was 1,200-horsepower twin Pratt & Whitney R-1830-92 radial engines. The "Dak" first entered Rhodesian service in 1947. A total of 17 were used, with three lost during the conflict.

The Britten-Norman BN-2A Islander was a light passenger and cargo aircraft. Tasks included communications, sky-shouting, leaflet dropping, search and rescue, visual reconnaissance, VIP courier, casualty evacuation, troop transport, paratroop dropping, and aerial resupply. Its speed was 3 miles per minute with a radius of action of 632 miles. Power plant was 260-horsepower twin Lycoming engines. It first entered Rhodesian service in 1976. A total of six were used, with one reported lost during the conflict.

Additional light utility aircraft included the Cessna 185, Cessna 421 Golden Eagle, and Beech 95 Baron. A number were used, with losses. These types were also employed by the police reserve and South African crews.[69]

General Aviation: Police Reserve Air Wing: in a region where distances were great and infrastructure lacking or subject to seasonal disruptions, the value of aircraft for movement, observation, and communications was obvious to the security forces. Even the BSAP and Internal Affairs acquired aircraft and airfields when travel by road became restricted and outposts isolated. From the example of the Malayan Auxiliary Air Force and the Kenya Police Reserve Air Wing, the police supplemented their efforts by organizing the Police Reserve Air Wing (PRAW). Civil aircraft and pilots served a limited air role by providing their own aircraft for security operations: observation, radio relay, and courier.[70] The BSAP had an arrangement to lease these for scheduled use and fuel was provided or paid for. Cessna 172s, 185s, and a variety of other general aviation types filled this role.

Control of PRAW aircraft was an issue for both the air force and army, as the police reserve crews lacked compatible training and radios. The Cessna 185s and Alouette IIIs that accompanied the South African Police to Rhodesia were manned by military or police crews and were easier to incorporate into the air control system. The army, lacking its own air corps, called on these assets when the air force was stretched thin for utility duties and questioned the "value and expense of recce flights" routinely conducted. An air force bathroom riposte was, "If God had meant the Army to fly He would have painted the sky brown."[71] It reached a point where the air force even considered using civilian pilots and "light civil aircraft in a courier role and crop-dusters can be used to defoliate no-go areas."[72]

Parachute Training School: From Above

With transport aircraft there was the ability to conduct the dropping of personnel and materiel by parachute. Military parachute training and equipment for the Rhodesian Security Forces was provided by the Rhodesian Air Force. This included the full range of static line (from 1961) and freefall (from 1967) techniques. The related air delivery of supplies by parachute was a Rhodesian Army Service Corps function of the Air Supply Platoon. The first operational jumps were made by the SAS in 1962 at Melsetter, with others following through 1974, with the creation of Fire Forces and the expansion of the RLI and RAR parachute component.

Initial concepts and equipment were derived from the British, but later South African techniques and equipment were followed.[73] The static line parachute was the Saviac Mark I (the American T10 type) parachute and reserve with quick-release harness and lowering lines (CSPEP: carrying straps, personal equipment, parachutist). Free fall parachutes were the American Para Commander and British Tactical Assault Mk 2. Training was conducted by the Parachute Training School (PTS) at New Sarum Air Force Base, with army troops being billeted with 2 Brigade. The army conducted screening and pre-training (selection, conditioning, battle school) followed by air force parachute jumping training (synthetic ground training, practical parachuting). Ground training included actions on exits, descent, and landing with mockups, apparatus, tower, and dragging drills. Practical training included care and fitting of the parachute, day and night descents and water drill. There were no exercise jumps and combat loads were added after the second training jump. After the basic course, soldiers were assigned directly to combat duties. "In some cases troops would finish paratroop training on Saturday and on Monday would be dropping in a para-Fire Force assault."[74]

The PTS had made some 10,000 training jumps by 1975 when the tempo of operations picked up to 8,000 jumps in the first seven months of 1976. Up to that time, the staff of six instructors had only failed eight trainees and had one refusal with a 1.39 percent injury rate. Some 64,000 training jumps were made by 1979. Then the injury rate in training was reported as .75 percent, in operations 1.77 percent, with a combined fatality rate of .0016 percent. Parachute packing and maintenance continued apace, going to a shift system in 1977 and crossing a

2,000-a-month barrier with a 100 percent safety rate. Squadron Leader Walter T. "Frank" Hales commented "that these percentages compare favorably with anywhere else in the world."[75] Parachute Training School's Squadron Leader Derek J. G. de Kock concluded "every soldier should be trained to use a parachute. It makes a better soldier of that man even if he is never used in that role ... [and] the parachute is no discriminator of color or rank or creed."[76]

Camouflage and Markings

Rhodesian aircraft marking schemes were patterned on British Royal Air Force practices of the 1960s, including the use of national insignia in the form of a roundel in red, white, and blue on wings and fuselage with a fin flash (changed to green and white in 1970). Serial numbers were black on light surfaces, white on black, and red on gray. These were removed with the start of cross-border operations. Rhodesian security concerns for aircraft operating outside of its borders began at UDI and increased with the war's escalation: tactical markings were muted or removed, wreckage was destroyed or recovered to prevent enemy photo opportunities, and air support could even be denied if the antiaircraft threat was too great.[77]

While livery was supposed to be based on aircraft category, images indicate as many departures as compliance ranging from temperate colors to desert "sand and spinach" finishes. Bombers had dark sea gray/dark green side and upper surface colors and light gray under surfaces. Fighters had dark sea gray/dark green side and upper surface colors and light or medium sea gray under surfaces. Transports had white and gray sides and upper surfaces with a blue mid-fuselage cheat line and light gray under surfaces. Helicopters had dark sea dark/dark green upper surfaces and light dark under surfaces.

The gloss paints of the 1960s and 1970s gave way to flat finishes as the conflict developed. These standardized paint jobs eventually became a universal overall dark earth/light stone, similar to army olive and dark green vehicle coats. In turn, special paints were developed to face the threat of infrared heat-seeking missiles and radars.[78]

Air Measures and Countermeasures

Squadron Leader Peter I. "Monster" Wilkins recalled events in the 1960s: "The guerrillas seldom looked too threatening in those halcyon days and we had most of it our own way. When they fired back, it was inaccurate, usually blindly, backwards over the shoulder whilst on the run! Their mistake was to actually carry weapons, as we knew exactly who to pick off—the guy with the rifle!"[79] Flight Lieutenant John S. Fairey, a Dakota pilot, noted later that "the only weapons used against aircraft by terrorists within Rhodesia were small arms. Very occasionally an RPG-7 was fired at an aircraft but the likelihood of an aircraft in flight being hit by an unguided rocket is extremely small. Therefore, apart from during takeoff and landing, there was no risk of being hit when flying inside the country provided one stay[ed] above 2,000 feet."[80] Flying Canberras, Paintin felt, "The operational flying was quite different than that on the ground attack squadrons as the action was remote. ... You really did not have the opportunity to understand what was happening on the ground. Even seeing tracer rounds as they passed seemed of little consequence, although once hit I was a little incensed they had the audacity to fire at us."[81]

Light aircraft and helicopters flew at heights that allowed protection from small-arms fire, normally 2,000 to 3,000 feet above ground level. The presence of heavy antiaircraft weapons or surface-to-air missile threats were countered by flying at lower level (below 200 feet) or at altitudes that were higher than optimum missile ranges (15,000 feet). One helicopter pilot observed:

> We were told, in fact, to fly at 800 feet or above if we were in the K-Car, *or* on the trees—not 400 to 300 foot, as that's very dangerous, they can see you and they can hit you. The higher you go, the harder it is to hit obviously. Or on the trees, they can't see you quickly enough, because one minute you're there and the next minute you've gone.[82]

A fixed-wing pilot pointed out that "flying low at 50 feet or just on top of the trees which was dangerous and therefore not done (certainly by me) unless absolutely necessary."[83] Takeoff, landings, and transition were the most vulnerable and flight profiles were aimed at making it hard for guerrillas to aim weapons rather than using flak-suppression methods.[84]

Experience led Briscoe to advise that "The progression from the ubiquitous AK-47 to sophisticated anti-aircraft artillery and even surface-to-air missiles can be extremely quick and planners need to bear this in mind."[85] Petter-Bowyer recalled, "True anti-air effectiveness within Rhodesia only developed after the Vorster–Kaunda detente led to a long ceasefire in 1975. This allowed ZANLA/ZPRA to regroup and consolidate on the lessons learnt from survivors who returned to Zambia. Once fighting resumed in 1976, it was clear that much attention had been paid to antiaircraft fire. From 1976, hardly any action took place without aircraft sustaining hits."[86]

As larger groups of better-armed guerrillas were met that were more willing to "slug it out" with security forces, fighting sharpened. Air Lieutenant Martin S. Hatfield was flying a Lynx from Grand Reef in 1977, when summoned to assist an ambushed convoy. On arriving, the insurgents moved east to higher ground:

> I commenced circling, slowly moving eastward when the call [sign] on the ground informed me that I was taking small arms fire from the vicinity of Gondo hills. I picked up the terrs' movement and positioned for an air strike. By now there was a fair amount of popping around my aircraft and I can remember cursing the terrs on each attack. Every time I called "turning in live," I told the troops to keep their heads down, followed by "the [fuckers] are shooting at me." (I was informed after I landed that my choice of language was interesting!) The terrain was hilly with thick vegetation so I attacked the areas where I saw muzzle flashes. On my third

or fourth run in, I took a hit through the cockpit. When I pulled out I could smell fuel, and I had no boost indication on the rear motor, so I shut it down and diverted to Chipinga Air Field about 10 minutes away. I had dropped two Frans [frangible tanks], and fired 30 SNEB and about 200 rounds of .303. As I left the contact area, a G-Car from Grand Reef was already on the way to assist.[87]

Rebel air defenses improved from small arms, to mobile antiaircraft artillery, and eventually surface-to-air missiles.[88] As guerrilla antiaircraft capabilities increased, particularly at cross-border base camps, and the demands of tactical flying evolved, so did Rhodesian active and passive countermeasures. The Rhodesians reacted with technical solutions to challenges without wasted effort as with countermeasures to both antiaircraft or landmine attacks. Responses were made including air filters for dust (removed in wet weather), cable cutters for obstacles, and evasive flying from the enemy. Where possible, pilots wore flak vests and aircraft had armored seats and integral armor installed to cut losses from small arms and machine guns (12.7 and 14.5mm range).[89]

There was an effort by the guerrillas to establish safe or "liberated" areas within the country to be defended with more determination (albeit Fairey interjected: "Terrorists never succeeded in establishing 'liberated areas' inside Rhodesia"). These in turn were supported by large training bases, weapons caches, transit and rest areas from the Frontline States of Zambia and Mozambique that were generally well constructed with established defenses and more sophisticated antiaircraft artillery (AAA) and missiles (SA-7s, or more improbable SA-2s and -3s).

Fairey wrote:

To the best of my knowledge the only occasions on which SA-7s were fired within Rhodesia were when the two Viscounts were brought down. ... Eventually all RhAF [aircraft] were painted with heat absorbent paint in order to reduce infrared radiation which could be detected by SA-7s. This measure together with the fitting of shrouds to engine exhausts made it impossible for SA-7s to lock on any RhAF aircraft other than Hunters and Canberras, the exhausts of which could not be shrouded.[90]

The Portuguese reported manpad SA-7s in their colonies as early as 1973, while the Rhodesians first encountered SA-7s in 1974 (when two aircraft were lost over Mozambique) and captured examples from ZPRA at Feira on the Zambezi in 1978.[91] Once the SA-7 threat was known, aircraft were "suppressed" with heat-absorbing matte-finish gray paint and "black hole"-shrouded exhaust (metal and fiberglass ducting to dissipate heat) with resulting loss of some lift.[92] Petter-Bowyer remarked, the:

SA-7 missiles sensed air targets which radiated sufficient infrared in the two micron band. For all air force aircraft, including jets, a camouflage paint which absorbed all light in this critical band was developed and applied because an airframe alone could provide sufficient radiated signal to attract the missile. The use of baffles and cold air shrouding, when applied to correctly painted airframes, made an aircraft "invisible" to [the] SA-7. In the case of jets, the exhaust pipes were impossible to render a missile's detection system worthless. This is why all SA-7s were launched once the aircraft was flying away from the launch point.[93]

Squadron Leader Anthony D. Oakley noted:

With regard to Strela, we simply accepted that we could not reduce our heat signature on the Hunter. Instead we relied on our speed and the lack of skill of the operators. We certainly had our fair share of Strelas fired at us without success—except one. We actually saw the Strela launch as an opportunity to pinpoint the [bastards]. Then we could stomp them nicely with cannon.[94]

Flying over Zambia and Mozambique was relatively safe "provided one avoided known trouble spots,"[95] which was not always possible in the course of conflict. By late 1979, strikes on enemy base camps met determined antiaircraft fire. For example, in Zambia in one incident:

As number two turned in, and before he was half way down his attack, the 14.5s on both ridges opened up on the Hunter. Red Lead delayed his dive, holding back about 15 seconds, and came in at a different angle. 'Okay. I've got the bugger,' he said, referring to the heavy weapon gunner on the main ridge. The enemy gunners were giving both Hunter pilots stick, as they in turn let rip with their 30mm Aden cannons. It was a pinpoint air strike and as the dust and stones flew everywhere, the weapons pit erupted and the weapon was momentarily silenced. Then the cheeky bugger shook his head, grabbed hold of the 14.5 and swung it around again, firing up at the Hunter as it pulled out of its dive. The red tracer followed the Hunter as the pilot flew off into the sunset.[96]

These situations required the most capable aircraft attacking with heavier air weapons: the Hunter, Vampire, and Canberra.[97] Commented Squadron Leader Oakley:

Anti-aircraft weapons became an increasingly serious threat as the war progressed, and 12.7 and 14.5mm weapons gave way to 20mm, 23mm, 37mm and 57mm guns and eventually the ZSU 23-4s. It was imperative to hit this weaponry first during a strike on a big target. A number of Hunters would be given one or even two AAA sites. Other aircraft would be dedicated to the target for the day. ... There were, however, some simple tactics that individuals followed depending upon the nature of the target, and they will probably seem highly irresponsible now. One tactic that I am sure everyone will admit to having used, was practiced on heavily defended targets. The trick was not to pull out after the attack, but rather turn away from the target with as many 'gees' as you could muster and keep heading for the deck. Very few weapons were good enough to get you at 20 feet and 500 knots.[98]

More sophisticated danger existed from the Frontline States. Zambia deployed British Rapiers and Mozambique reportedly had Soviet SA-2 missiles and control systems. Noted one airman, "The Rapiers possessed by Zambia were early ones ... They were never used in anger and were almost certainly non-operational."[99] Fighter threats were from Zambia and Mozambique as well as farther afield from Tanzania and Angola. On occasion, intercept radar was detected or aircraft made visual contact but never closed. The South African Air Force had similar concerns and operated in coordination with the Rhodesian Air Force on occasion to counter threats. A 1 Squadron commander noted "the fact [was] that we were fully trained in air combat maneuvers, even though we never had the opportunity to prove our skills."[100] The Rhodesians felt little qualms unless these aircraft were flown by foreign "volunteers," again an example of the "K-factor" bias.[101] In August 1979, an incident in Botswana involved an armed transport blocking a Rhodesian helicopter flight. In response, an Alouette gunship earned credit for shooting down an attacking Britten Norman Defender.[102]

Guerrilla Measures and Countermeasures

Characteristic of insurgency warfare is that rebels seek to neutralize government advantages in firepower, communications, and maneuver. Nationalists used a variety of methods to strike back in a one-sided fight against the Rhodesian Air Force. This saw guerrillas that habitually relocated, moving in the dark, mixing with civilians, and dispersing to avoid providing targets for air attack. Notebooks of killed or captured guerrillas made constant reference "that it was the air force who were their greatest threat."[103] Staying low in camp "is not very bad, but the problem is the air force. If you attack anywhere, it does not take time for the air force to come."[104] In the earlier days, the presence of aircraft warned the guerrillas of the proximity of security forces and allowed them to take cover or to split into smaller groups. One result was moving only at night and basing up in the heaviest cover available in the daytime. Unavoidable daytime movement would be from cover to cover, often dictated by aircraft appearance. They were not sure if they could be detected by an overflight, and of most concern was the aircraft's communication with ground forces.[105]

What the guerrillas did in response to aircraft depended upon the situation at hand. If walking through the brush and an aircraft was seen flying towards them, they would run for cover or stand still if already under adequate shelter. This might involve kneeling on the ground with the head covered so as to resemble stones or anthills or standing against a tree. In a base camp if aircraft were detected, immediate stand-to occurred, fires put out, reflective objects and loose clothing were concealed, and aircraft intentions were deduced. If the aircraft came in their direction and remained overhead for a long time, they assumed it had not spotted them; if it circled over several different areas, they also assumed it had not spotted them; but if it did a few circles overhead and moved off, they assumed they had been sighted and split into assigned pairs and vacated the base along a predetermined route. Any locals present would be sent away, with the possibility that civilian figures would divert attention from the fighters. If the aircraft began circling, especially before having time to move out, the twosomes would remain undercover until the aircraft's tail was pointing at them. This was part of guerrilla training and used in both internal and external camps in the summer when there is a lot of cover. Camouflage against air observation was also taught as a skill in Zambia and Mozambique.[106]

Prior to contact guerrillas avoided firing at aircraft, but once contact was made, they would divert a large part of their fire towards the planes. If engaged by aircraft, they were trained to fire indiscriminately in front of it to "frighten" and distract the pilot. Terrorist antiaircraft instruction appeared limited to using machine guns with tracers.[107] While specialized antiaircraft weapons were not deployed inside Rhodesia, rocket-propelled grenades were used as the vulnerability of aircraft on the ground and during takeoff or landing was known. Efforts were made to take out helicopters by booby-trapping landing zones with grenade traps that used a block of explosives to launch four stick grenades 30 to 60 meters into the air where they detonated.[108]

All aircraft were considered threats, but specific worry was first for helicopters and then spotter aircraft (utility types: Provost, Trojan, Lynx). Johnson Matongo, from Msama village, described the impact in the rural areas of the air war:

> In Shona, we call it *kemabemba*—the one with the bars [Lynx]. ... They usually fly over the TTLs [tribal trust lands] one at a time. It is very dangerous. When villagers see it they run for cover. It flies high and very fast. The boys say that it is well protected and hard to bring down. I used to see it maybe twice a fortnight ... It fires heavily ... It fires bullets from the front when it dives, and when it goes up it drops bombs.[109]

In some cases airstrikes completely demoralized the guerrillas with the loss of the will to fight and desertions. Prisoner interrogations found, "The fear of aircraft becomes very real after the terrorists have been subjected to, or witnessed, an armed attack from above. Prior to such occurrences they do not seem to have realized fully the dangers of air attack."[110] One insurgent leader recalled that:

> Fighter aircraft were really frightening although if you were dug in and resisted the almost overwhelming temptation to run, then you were usually okay. You had to be careful about leaving your hole to treat injured people. The enemy used delayed action bombs which were timed to blow up when everyone thought the attack was over. Control during an attack was very difficult due to deafness induced by the explosions and to panic which particularly affected the younger soldiers.[111]

Defense of fixed locations such as camps developed with time and experience, first adjacent to the border, then farther back and consolidated, and finally farther back and dispersed. ZANU's Operational Base 1 at Chimoio was a preferred target and had to adapt accordingly. During initial attacks, the most common option sent fighters running, often into security force killing zones. Guerrillas were disorganized, often unarmed at this point, and resisting as individuals. By 1978, this changed as security and intelligence cadre were "of the opinion that the trenches should be dug to encounter this type of warfare." Centralized command was needed to keep cadres from dispersing "in an unorganized way if the attack is to come at any time." The cadres argued that "when the enemy invades our bases we should not run away or retreat in passive way instead we should try our maximum best to stand the enemy within our base."[112]

The reality of an airstrike was quite different than the theory as the nationalists learned time and again. In October 1978, at ZPRA's Mkushi Camp in Zambia according to Martin Gutu, the camp logistics officer:

> The bombs came first. Two jet fighters came and bombed the parade square and HQ. It hardly took five minutes, and they were followed immediately afterwards by some Dakotas and helicopters in formation. ... The bombs didn't actually kill many people. They didn't use napalm at this stage, but another big bomb which opened a big hole right in the parade square. But then the helicopters came in battle formation, sweeping the whole area and firing, and the Lynxes firing from ... machine guns. ... A few minutes after the bombing the whole bush was burning and full of fire. There was a lot of noise all over, covering a radius of over four kilometers.[113]

Gutu and seven comrades moved some 200 meters away from the camp. "We remained at this same spot until about seven o'clock in the evening, watching them firing from helicopters. Their ground forces had already occupied our HQ. We didn't have enough ammunition and I saw that if we continued firing we would expose our position ... we didn't have any heavy weaponry, only small arms. So it was hard to combat the helicopters."[114]

To the nationalists the air threat remained a constant thorn to be dealt with, as "the Rhodesian Air Force has expanded its fleet out of all proportion as a result of a series of spectacular sanctions-busting transactions, and has acquired some of the most lethal counterinsurgency aircraft available on the international market."[115] But this advantage was eroded over time as the guerrilla forces received more sophisticated antiaircraft weapons, manifested in the rise of air force casualties in men and aircraft later in the war. One postwar analyst went as far to say if the conflict had continued, "the insurgent forces would have been in a position to defend their bases with zones of SAM-2/3 and mobile SAM-6 missiles. Further, it is probable that hand-held SAM-7 missiles would have proliferated among the insurgent forces, presenting a threat of major dimensions to helicopters." The arrival of MiG-19s and -21s in the theater increased air-to-air combat prospects.[116]

CHAPTER 4

Air Power from Internal Security to Counterinsurgency

Air Marshal McLaren summarized in mid-conflict, that:

> Air power is the key to victory is today universally accepted. The principle has been seen for decades to apply to what we call conventional war, but only very recently has it also applied to anti-terrorist operations. Indeed, the classic communist blueprint has designed all terrorist initiatives to negate the fire power advantage of conventional defense forces and particularly to make impotent their air superiority.[1]

Another air force officer acknowledged in hindsight that things were not that easy:

> All too often we, in the developed countries, confuse progress with technology, and in war it is seldom that technology alone can win e.g. Vietnam ... It is neither necessary nor desirable to use the most modern weaponry in [counterinsurgency] as logistical, reliability and maintainability problems can render the most advanced weapons useless and result in disproportionate effort and expense being required to get them serviceable again. ... In essence, what a third world country lacks monetarily, it may be able to compensate for by sensible acquisition policies, innovative tactics and attempts to remove the grievances that caused the insurrection in the first place.[2]

The Rhodesian Air Force had common background to draw upon with the army and police for counterinsurgency doctrine and experience.[3] They felt aircraft only assumed importance in this type of warfare after World War II, although early British examples "go back to the colonial era." While the Malayan emergency saw "sophisticated" use of helicopters, transport, and attack aircraft, the Kenyan experience witnessed the "singularly ineffective" bombing of the Aberdare forest. Similarly, the French and American experience in Southeast Asia produced mixed results, although the French were given higher marks in their employment of air power in Algeria. Experience closer to home was shared with Portuguese Africa, South Africa, South West Africa, and as far afield as Israel.[4] Wing Commander Geldenhuys noted that the Rhodesian Army and Air Force had overseas background, but the police had never been out of the country and did not have this fund of experience to draw upon. "They refused to accept the lessons of Malaya, and furthermore they were not attuned to trying new methods. In addition, the country's top level security council supported the view that the police knew best. IntAf on the other hand were a law unto themselves."[5]

Wing Commander Briscoe observed that air support varied with the stage of the conflict and compared this to the Maoist phases of revolutionary war. According to Briscoe, aircraft use divided into Phase I: psychological action, civic action, border control reconnaissance and light attack, transport, courier, special operations, and riot control; Phase II: all of the above, especially border control, area control, lines of communications, close air support, light and medium attack, transport; Phase III: all of the above, conventional warfare supported by guerrilla action.[6] Functions evolved as the conflict progressed, expanding or refining initial roles and adding others not first considered. The *COIN* manual acknowledged distinct internal and external requirements that could best be met with air weapons.[7] It was understood early that support for the civil power would be jointly with the police or army, for internal security operations.[8] The air force established detailed organization and procedures for the police and army to obtain air support and in time there developed a high degree of confidence in air power. Wing Commander Geldenhuys recalled:

> Internal Security Operations, or ISOps for short, were largely dictated by the civilian authorities— mainly the BSAP [British South Africa Police]—who were charged with intelligence gathering through their SB [Special Branch], and IntAf [Internal Affairs]. The primary role of the air force is the security of its air space, and in this theater of war Rhodesia was never seriously challenged, for they enjoyed total supremacy of the air. However, it was in its secondary role of 'to assist the civil power in the maintenance of internal security' that the air force contributed its fair share in all ISOps.

Counterinsurgency operations were another matter, with the army and air force in the lead during early border control operations. Geldenhuys commented, "Counterinsurgency lessons learnt in Malaya, and also applied in the Portuguese provinces were soon introduced into Rhodesia, like the PV [protected village]. ... Needless to say, much resistance was encountered from the civil authorities and the army and air force commanders often found it necessary to use bulldozing tactics to push their proposals through."[9] Briscoe felt the key to winning was "having the right men, with the right motivation, using the right equipment, in the right place, in the right numbers, at the right time."[10]

For air operations Rhodesia was divided into sectors corresponding with existing administrative divisions (Mashonaland North and South, Matabeleland North and South, Midlands, Victoria, Manicaland); in turn, each sector provided direct support to any police or army deployment from existing sector or forward airfields. By 1969, with the onset of increased fighting, the air force refined its organization for the conduct of border control and counterinsurgency operations. Two tactical air headquarters (TacHQs) were formed to provide coverage for the western and eastern half of the country, known as field force units (FFUs) under the staff officer operations of the Air Staff. The TacHQs, each under a wing commander, controlled all aircraft allocated for border control or counterinsurgency operations at the joint operations center at provincial or brigade level.[11]

```
                        ┌─────────────────────┐
                        │  Rhodesian Cabinet  │
                        └─────────────────────┘
                                  │
                        ┌─────────────────────┐
                        │  Security Council   │
                        └─────────────────────┘
                                  │
              ┌───────────────────────────────────────┐
              │           COIN Committee              │
              │ Chaired by PM + relevant ministers,   │
              │ heads of ministries,                  │
              │ commanders of services, police and    │
              │ Director, CIO                         │
              └───────────────────────────────────────┘
                 ╱                              ╲
┌──────────────────────────────────┐  ┌──────────────────────────────────┐
│ Operation Co-ordinating Committee │  │ Counter-Insurgency Civil Committee│
│               OCC                 │  │              COCC                 │
│            comprising             │  │           comprising              │
│    Chief of General Staff (CGS)   │  │   Heads of appropriate Ministries │
│     Chief of Air Staff (CAS)      │  │         and a Secretary           │
│     Commisioner of Police         │  └──────────────────────────────────┘
│         Director, CIO             │
└──────────────────────────────────┘
┌──────────────────────────────────┐
│      Joint Operations Centres     │
│               JOCs                │
│ comprising senior representatives │
│ of Army, Air Force, Police and    │
│ Special Branch and co-opted       │
│ District Commissioner             │
└──────────────────────────────────┘
        │                     │
┌──────────────────┐ ┌─────────────────────────────┐
│ Units in the field│ │ Aircraft at Forward Air Fields etc│
└──────────────────┘ └─────────────────────────────┘
```

Command and control, joint operation centers (JOCs)

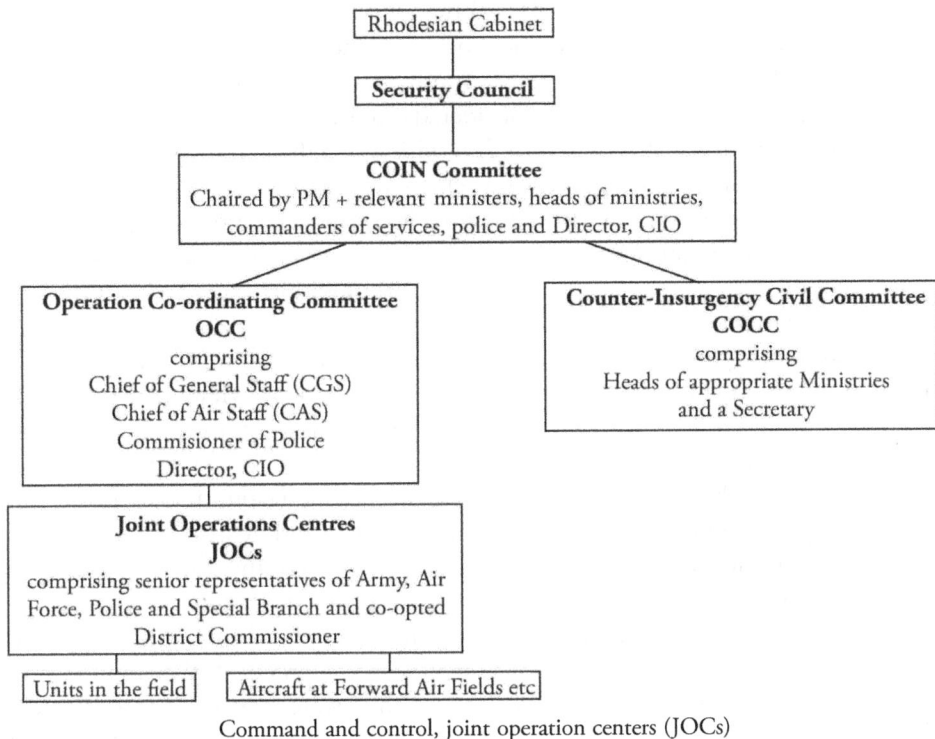

Finally, forward air support operations centers (FASOCs) were organized to deploy with headquarters below the brigade (sub-JOC at district/battalion level), if multiple deployments occurred. The FASOCs were "fully air-portable, mobile operations centers which will normally deploy with appropriate army formation HQ" with the air commander acting as the air advisor to the army commander. The forward air support operations center, forward airfields, forward air controllers (FAC), and ground liaison officers (GLO) provided air support needed to operations in progress.[12]

A squadron leader was assigned to command the forward airfields first at Wankie and Kariba who could also move to the designated joint operations center if located elsewhere, and a backup officer would take over the airfield. Made available at the forward airfield would be direct support in the form of one or two light attack aircraft, one or two utility aircraft, one or two transport helicopters, and PRAW aircraft. This allocation formula changed to include late-war allocations of Lynxes, Dakotas, and helicopter gunships. Successive cross-border operations could include every available aircraft and South African reinforcements as well.

By 1975, field force unit structure was required to support multiple operations from additional forward airfields at Centenary, Mount Darwin, and Mtoko. Group

Captain K. A. S. "Ken" Edwards released the plan from the Air Headquarters that aimed at constancy by eliminating ad hoc assignments of personnel involved in other duties. This placed full-time wing commanders at each forward airfield and at JOC Hurricane at Bindura.[13] It was considered essential that at any given level, only one air commander was designated to deal with a specified land commander. This mutual pairing of air and land forces was characteristic of the war and contributed to the centralized control of the air effort in support of ground operations.[14] Aircraft allocation, requesting, and tasking were made at the first level where an air commander was present, usually the JOC, although higher army, air force, and police headquarters coordinated other requests.

Internal security operations developed identifiable air–ground concepts that called for common land–air warfare tenets.[15] Air support was viewed, in general, as preplanned or immediate with ground and airborne alert options. Air procedures were codified and taught to the army and police. Emphasis was on standard request forms, helicopter characteristics, landing and drop zone layout and marking, and close air support procedures. An air transport organization existed with the air force providing movement control and the supported ground force providing an air transport liaison officer.[16]

It was noted that while aircraft had the advantages of flexibility, mobility, speed, and range, there were some restrictions on their employment. Other than adverse weather and light conditions, technical limitations were stressed. These included maintenance that fixed available aircraft strength to no more than 75 percent, weather could restrict operations, large amounts of fuel were needed, specific aircraft were best suited for specific tasks, and extensive transportation, supplies, and facilities were needed to provide support in forward areas.[17] Geographic distances and circumscribed assets were real considerations demanding economy of effort. The value of limited numbers of aircraft and pilots could not be taken for granted by supported units.

The Operations Coordinating Committee wrote: "It should be the constant aim in all [anti-terrorist operations] to make full use of the advantages that stem from the ability to use air power with little enemy interference. During [anti-terrorist operations] the air force can provide a quick reaction to requests for offensive air operations, casualty evacuation, and logistic support."[18] The approach was technology based, characterized as "the skills of the air force were being patiently applied" similar to "domestic chores well in hand."[19] The Joint Planning Staff noted air support for the ground forces "has been vital and employed in all but a few minor operations."[20]

The recognition of the value of air power was seen on both sides of the conflict. Rhodesian security forces concluded that "Although air power in itself does not guarantee success in [anti-terrorist operations], the tactical concept relies primarily on it for strategic and tactical movement, fire support and logistics support."[21] The nationalists recognized that the "importance of the air force to the regime's war effort must not be underestimated. It is unlikely that the security forces could mount a military operation of any size without air force support in reconnaissance, air-strike, casevac [casualty evacuation], trooping, resupply and other roles."[22]

Air Marshal McLaren concluded:

> The terrorist is supposed to be an invincible foe; difficult to find, hard to identify and impossible to destroy. Over the last 10 years, however, we have been able to demonstrate that air power is not only useful but is actually essential to combined anti-terrorist operations. Hundreds of terrorists have been found and identified, and destroyed from the air—and air support enables our ground forces to move rapidly around the operational area. Air resupply keeps them equipped and air rescue facilities boost their morale and save their lives.[23]

General Walls, as Rhodesian Army and then Combined Operations commander, expanded on this:

> I am personally extremely grateful for the unfailing gallantry, cheerfulness, and spirit of brotherly affection, shown by the pilots and their crews who work with us in the operational areas, and my feelings are shared completely by all ranks, in all units, of the army deployed in these areas. I would like to mention, in particular, the risks taken, frequently at night, in the deployment of troops and their redeployment, under fire, and, indeed, the willing and unhesitating response to all tactical demands made under hazardous conditions.[24]

Eight flying squadrons provided aircraft and crews for the most common tasks during the war. Air power was applied both to internal and external operations, with a major worry for irreplaceable aircraft and crews (there were, at times, more aircraft than crews to fly them) and the risk of cross-border flying. Some air assets remained on call for defense and deterrence, while providing direct air support when called upon.

Wing Commander Briscoe, as a senior air officer, commented:

> Numerous books, journals and papers have been written on the subject of guerrilla warfare, however, most of these writings concentrate on methods of combating the guerrilla or insurgent using ground forces. Comments and evaluation of the role and use of air power in counterinsurgency operations is normally restricted to a passing reference, probably due to the fact that most authors have been army, or possibly policemen.[25]

The following should balance that perspective. Rhodesian doctrine identified three key functions for air force support to internal security and counterinsurgency: transport, reconnaissance, and offensive use. Tasks consisted of delivering supplies and troops by landing and by parachute or free drop, as well as evacuation of material and personnel casualties; the conduct of either visual or photographic reconnaissance, followed by analysis and reporting; providing utility flights including the use of non-lethal or psychological devices; undertaking offensive support involving a variety of lethal weapons delivery used for "close air support," "interdiction," and "proscription."

Transport

The *MCP* stated the nature of a counterinsurgency or internal security campaign was such "that the operational value of air transport support is greatly enhanced while the scope of offensive air support operations may be limited."[26] Transport was the most common and useful form of air support during the conflict although, despite distance and poor road conditions, rail or motor transport was still the preferred method of moving men and cargo. Long haul was provided by fixed-wing transports, and helicopters afforded short-range movement.

One way to view this was larger transport aircraft carried cargo and personnel to the operational areas and light aircraft or helicopters moved them within these areas. An assortment of air force and police light aircraft were available that were comparatively economical to operate and filled the gap between the heavy transport and the scarce helicopters. While helicopter and light aircraft were invaluable for many tactical transport tasks, there were never enough of them, and their use had to be effectively controlled. This depended on well-organized air movement sections at the main and forward air bases to work efficiently.[27]

The helicopter, well suited for urgent resupply of water or ammunition, was considered a bonus if not needed elsewhere. Common tasks included tactical troop and infantry weapons deployments, resupply of supplies and material, casualty evacuation, rapid reinforcement, movement of units into inaccessible areas, follow-up actions and landing cut-off parties.

While a rudimentary airfield was required for takeoff and landing, the delivery of personnel and supplies could be delivered while in flight. Since water and ration containers did not always survive free drop, parachute delivery was often required.[28] Because small units could not recover parachutes and containers, a disposable system was developed. This was with the "parasheet" that delivered some 20 to 25 kilograms of supplies in a disposable wooden container. Water was dropped by this method in collapsible bags or frozen using Trojan or Cessna aircraft.[29]

A *Rhodesia Herald* reporter watched the delivery of some one and a half tons of supplies during a flight:

> The supplies were in 14 separate crates or 'shooks' each with a parachute attached. They would be dropped from about 300 feet, and would take only seconds to hit the ground. Liquids can be dropped to the troops in specially designed boxes and mealie [corn] meal can go out without a parachute. The air dispatch team stood by the open hatch as we closed in on the base camp. The crates were put on a conveyor of rollers, two at a time. As two men push the crates out, the others in the team haul the next crates to the conveyor for each drop. On this drop, all the crates were going out at the same base camp. With two shooks going out at a time, the Dakota would make seven circuits over the target, each taking about three minutes.[30]

As more units deployed during the course of the conflict, the need for air transport expanded. Beginning in 1968, when in April some 70,000 kilograms of freight was carried, transport sorties remained high throughout the conflict.[31] The guerrillas made an increasing effort to dominate conventional travel routes by use of landmines and ambushes to make travel difficult. To maintain the initiative, men and supplies had to be moved quickly and safely by air, while the need to maintain surface lines of communication was recognized. It became imperative for the security forces to retain flexibility of movement by these means; "Air transport operations are the only way of doing this, short of forcing ground forces to walk everywhere, or use time and manpower intensive techniques to clear lines-of-communications."[32]

Squadron Leader Wilkins recalled:

> The transport types did things that, even if one were allowed to write about them, would probably be denied by others who would claim that no one could perform such difficult missions without losing [airplanes]. These fellows, in their large and not too agile aircraft, supplied people in places where many other pilots of smaller aircraft would not think of going into, and then at night! When their number was called, the transport types would go, and go, and go … seemingly tireless, flying so much at night that they probably saw little of the countryside during a deployment to the bush, except for what was in the landing lights on short finals! On top of that, these were the kind souls who kept us all supplied with those precious commodities from home, particularly mail.[33]

With the increase in size and duration of engagements, air transport delivered reinforcements and resupply in the shortest possible time as well as providing medical evacuation. Emergency casualty evacuation requests were made through a JOC to the nearest helicopter base. Journalist Beverley Whyte wrote that "Casualty evacuation work, however, takes precedence over all other work" for the helicopter crews (at one time being primarily civilians injured by mines).

An Alouette carried two litters and if the patient's condition was critical a medical orderly or doctor went along. The final destination depended upon the type and degree of the injury, in general most being taken to the JOC for preliminary medical treatment.

One pilot, Squadron Leader Christopher P. Dickinson, recalled an incident in 1976 near Birchenough Bridge. Because of the enemy situation, he and technician Wally Wallace flew in at last light to evacuate a wounded soldier:

> I plotted the LZ [landing zone] on my map and decided on an approach for the night landing. As we came in, the call sign fired the flare and we landed without mishap. Other groups nearby provided covering fire to keep the gooks' heads down but it was pretty nerve-wracking having all that tracer flying around while we were coming in. The members of the stick carried their leader in his poncho and placed him in the back of the chopper … we got airborne—without lights—and headed for Chipinga. The mountains in the area are thousands of feet higher than Birchenough Bridge and in order to reach a safe height we had to do a spiral climb to well over 9,000 feet before setting course to Chipinga Hospital. The journey took us the better part of an hour … Unfortunately, the stick leader died shortly after arrival.[34]

By 1976, general practitioners were available at the forward airfields to supplement military medical personnel (resuscitation equipment, special inflatable stretchers, and mountain rescue stretchers were available at the fields). Flying on board transports or helicopters, they carried medical kits for immediate minor surgery and intravenous treatment.[35] Where injuries were critical and minimal movement was necessary, helicopter evacuation proceeded directly to Salisbury or Bulawayo hospitals. If possible, fixed-wing transport flew the casualty to these more distant trauma hospitals. Combat casualties could be more demanding to evacuate when conducted as part of pursuit or Fire Force contacts.[36] This ability to rapidly evacuate the wounded by helicopter and transport ensured a chance of survival that gave security forces an edge in morale that the nationalists lacked. General Walls felt "the frequent casualty evacuations by various aircraft, which often put a pilot and crew at considerable risk, but which they undertake cheerfully in the knowledge that speedy evacuation saves lives, and give a tremendous boost to the morale of the chaps who know they can rely on this back up."[37]

The versatility of helicopters made them particularly useful in counterinsurgency operations. Their ability to lift troops from anywhere and to put them down anywhere was exploited fully. Petter-Bowyer noted, flying with technician Ewart Sorrell, "I found for all my training, I had not been properly prepared for operations. To fit a helicopter into an opening among trees with no more than six inches to spare all around was fine in training; yet here I nearly fell out of the sky as I had a full load of police reservists and their operational equipment on board."[38] Helicopters were expensive to operate, vulnerable to fire at low altitude, and had short endurance (helicopters could fly for two hours as normally configured, but flying with troops reduced this to one hour aloft).[39] Range limitations could be due to a number of factors: "added weight of shrouds, armor, guns, ammo, starters, and refuelers. The altitude ... The up-and-down nature of the terrain and irregular flight paths needed."[40]

There were more demands for helicopters than air frames to go around, and if fixed-wing aircraft were available and could do the job required, then helicopters were not used. Air Lieutenant Dawson described typical Alouette flying tasks in the forward area:

> We'd get a call from the army saying, 'We need somebody resupplied at this location, loc stat [location].' And then the K-Car commander or the air force commander would tell one of the pilots to go and do it and he'd just get the stuff loaded in his airplane and he'd go off to wherever they were and drop the stuff and come back. Quite straight forward ... Tended to be, depends what they were doing. But it tended to be food and rations and that sort of stuff, you know ... [Radio] relay change, that was going out to a hill with some blokes and taking their supplies and them up to the hill and bringing the old blokes down with their supplies and bringing them back to base.[41]

Flight technician Warrant Officer Geoff Dartnell added he enjoyed the variety of helicopter effort, "although our basic work comprises taking troops into the operational area and bringing them out, as well as [radio] relay changes, there's the spotting role, the casevac role, the rescue work ... as a crewman, one's tied in with it all."[42]

Helicopters required ground forces to be well drilled in their use and lift capacity defined the basic tactical structure for both the army and police. While the Alouette III could carry up to six passengers, including the technician-gunner, fully loaded troops limited this to a more practical four plus the technician-gunner. This "stick" was ultimately made up of a small unit leader, machine gunner, and two riflemen in a classic "fire team" configuration. Initial techniques called for helicopters to land reinforcements behind friendly units and to conduct medical evacuations after any fighting was over. Although the terrorists could often see the aircraft, they would not fire until directly jeopardized. In the early days of Operation *Hurricane* situations were so relaxed that helicopter crews would sometimes deplane to form "fifth" sticks, where the crews from machines on the ground would participate in the action as ground troops.[43] Later operations were not so forgiving: in 1976, Flight Lieutenant Victor B. W. "Vic" Cook overflew a guerrilla section while en route to a medical evacuation. The Alouette was struck by small-arms fire, damaging the controls and wounding the technician, causing Cook to "crash land the aircraft." He came down among some 15 terrorists and, despite his own injuries, was immediately engaged in close combat using an AK-47 seized from the nearest "Freedom Fighter." His one-man war continued until help arrived.[44]

An early champion of helicopters in a direct combat role was Group Captain Petter-Bowyer. As a flight lieutenant, he had flown in the Sinoia incident on 29 April 1966 and had learned a number of lessons that were later applied in the development of both follow-up and reaction force operations. Observations included that "success of the operation was the direct result of good intelligence and flexibility made possible by airborne controlling." As combined air and ground operations continued with the conflict's increased incidence of fighting, some of aviation's approach to combat rubbed off on ground units: less formal radio procedures and a more flexible means of moving units around to deal with enemy contact.[45] Further lessons included that three was the minimum number of helicopters to use in an anti-terrorist operation, allowing for refueling and difficulties and that one in three should be armed with machine guns. Rapid deployment required ground troops to be staged in the operational area—some 150, a company-size force, was adequate—with a reserve nearby to avoid risks of redeploying units already in contact. The army's ability to fire and maneuver as units made them the obvious choice for air–ground cooperation involving fire fights rather than the police.

Control from the air was essential and distinct identification of ground forces from the air simplified this (starting with the use of fluorescent air panels inside of caps). Petter-Bowyer noted that the guerrillas would make "determined" efforts to shoot the helicopters down and that African soldiers or policemen should not be used unless visually distinct from the air (knowledge of enemy weapons and dress being essential).[46] As the conflict progressed, specialization took place that saw helicopters designated as "general purpose" (G-Car) or "killer" (K-Car), the first being the troop carrier and the latter the platform for a 20mm gun and airborne ground commander.[47] Inevitably the helicopter served as a battle taxi to bring the enemy to bay by pursuit or direct assault. When guerrillas heard the distinctive sound of blades overhead, they knew that avoiding a fight—and on unfavorable terms—was not an option. This eventually ensured a special effort to knock the helicopters out with all available firepower from rifles and rocket-propelled grenades or even heavier antiaircraft weapons. It also might explain the excessive claim made by insurgents for shooting them down or the stir when this did in fact occur.

Both fixed- and rotary-wing transports went from delivery of personnel and material to secure locations to direct combat assault (covered in detail in a following chapter). This was with Alouettes as gunships or troopships and Dakotas parachuting troops directly into action. Limitations on the load and range capacity of the Alouette were behind the expanded use of paratroops for larger employments and the acquisition of the Bell 205 "Cheetahs." Even with Alouettes from South Africa (withdrawn by 1976),[48] large operations required most helicopter assets until the Cheetahs arrived in 1978. With extended range and payload, the Cheetahs allowed external operations to be conducted without having to pull Alouettes from internal operations. These were well-worn machines and not enough to make up for the lack of decent numbers of helicopters.

The South Africans provided direct help using Hercules, Puma, and Super Frelon aircraft at war's end in their effort to support the interim government. This culminated with joint Rhodesian and South African operations in Mozambique in 1979 where "small arms fire, RPG-7s and 12.7mm AAA would come up from all over the place—even far from any villages." As the carnage in the Frontline States picked up, so were the demands made on transport utilization.[49] The Rhodesians, South Africans, and Portuguese together had as much experience as any gained by Americans and Europeans in flying helicopters under demanding and hazardous conditions including the range of antiair threats. In a postwar interview, SAAF chief Lieutenant-General James Kriel concluded about rotary-wing aviation, "This capability made it possible to cover a large area with a relatively small number of ground forces. It also made it possible to achieve a concentration of forces, economy of effort, surprise, and flexibility when needed."[50]

While dealing with more general-purpose operations to this point, special forces required dedicated transport support for success, particularly with clandestine ground operations in guerrilla-controlled areas.[51] Briscoe commented, "All of these operations require air support, be it high altitude low opening (HALO) parachute insertion, or close air support in the event of a contact," as well as the necessity to use dedicated helicopters to provide "hot extraction" for immediate troop "uplift" or casualty evacuation. Resupply was also a constant for these extended stays in hostile territory. Dakotas and Cheetahs supported external special forces operations, generally at night, with Lynx aircraft used for escort, assignments, again, where crew experience and stability paid off.[52]

Night missions were with instrument landing system (ILS)-equipped Dakotas or Cheetahs engaged in special operations insertion, resupply, or extraction.[53] Aircraft filling this role used a comprehensive navigation and communications system: the Bekker 2010 VHF radio and homing system, automatic direction finding (ADF), VHF omnidirectional radio range/distance measuring equipment (VOR/DME), global navigation system (GNS 200), and the later Omega worldwide navigational system. In a reality check, Fairey felt that:

> No RhAF aircraft were ever fitted with a global navigation system or night vision equipment. Omega had been fitted to some aircraft by the end of the insurgency but it was not in widespread use. The Canberras were fitted with Doppler which is a navigational aid which, like INS, is independent of ground stations. ILS is a precision landing aid which requires ground transmitter; Salisbury was the only Rhodesian airport equipped with ILS.[54]

Night vision for low-level flying with these missions was desired, but never implemented, with instrumentation, ground markers, and dead reckoning being used instead. Various options were considered: personal night vision goggles were obtained from American commercial sources, but did not prove useful for pilots also using instruments or dead reckoning within the cockpit. The South African "Cat Eye" project went into a night vision observation sight fitted to a weapons system that did not progress beyond the prototype stage, the so-called Alpha fit.[55]

Other tasks entailed dynamic and flexible employment of aircraft and crews because of the fluid nature of these demands. While considered separately, these were interrelated: reconnaissance, observation, communications, command, and control— the so-called "utility" missions.[56] The evolution of utility air support emerged with experience, aircraft type, and tactical necessity. It started with transportation of passengers and cargo, resupply in the field, radio relay, air observation, forward air control (with accommodation for leaflet drops and loudspeakers, flares, rockets), armed reconnaissance, airborne stop line, and finally close air support. The Lynx rapidly came into its own, although increased antiaircraft threats limited its utility on external operations.

These same aircraft switched rapidly to light attack or forward air control duties as well.[57] By January 1973, with Operation *Hurricane*, some 642 hours were flown by light attack and utility aircraft, more than twice the monthly average from previous years. By 1976, pilots of multi-mission aircraft (fixed-wing and helicopter) were spending an average of 295 days a year on "bush duty," three weeks out with one week back at base. Squadron Leader David A. G. "Dag" Jones noted: "The chaps have learned to adapt to operating in the bush and we're in among the kills pretty often. There's a very high level of cooperation with the Browns [army] on the ground and that helps get the job done too."[58] Wilkins observed that:

Light aircraft types never ceased to impress with their perseverance on difficult missions—always coming through. They flew missions longer than the aircraft were designed for, becoming experts at recce as well as flying for endurance! From such meager beginnings they progressed to the point where if a recce pilot told you there was a guerrilla camp, there certainly was one! They flew these long missions without complaint.[59]

Air Vice-Marshal A. M. "Raf" Bentley, an earlier air force commander, observed that the light aircraft had "consistently set a standard of inter-service cooperation which might well be the envy of other air forces in the world."[60]

Reconnaissance and Observation

There were two separate methods of "air recce," photographic and visual reconnaissance (air observation) in turn conducted by point or area surveillance. The *MCP* stated: "Air reconnaissance is a valuable form of air support in operations against terrorists, particularly in remote parts of the country where it will sometimes be the only reliable source of intelligence. Air reconnaissance secures a manifest advantage over enemy forces that are tied to movement on the ground."[61]

Available for high- and low-level reconnaissance missions needing speed and long range were two aircraft, despite being offensive types. A majority of these missions were with the Canberra B2 light bomber, and occasionally the Hawker FGA9 Hunter day fighter, as "photographic reconnaissance" aircraft with a radius of action in this role of 1,100 and 398 nautical miles respectively. This was along with the Joint Services Photographic Interpretation Service (JSPIS) at New Sarum who produced interpreted imagery, including detailed target files of the region.[62] Also, a relationship with the government surveyor general ensured continued practice in this technical field that contributed to updating maps of the same areas.[63] Light aircraft provided more limited hand-held photography, including use of Polaroid cameras for prompt exploitation.[64]

Group Captain Petter-Bowyer wrote that:

All photographic tasks involving potential targets were directed to the JSPIS by Air HQ who coordinated requests from [Combined Operations], the operations staff at Air HQ and all requests placed on Army HQ from field and special force units. JSPIS issued the photo tasks to the squadrons and took possession of films which were then processed by the Photographic Section at New Sarum and passed directly back to JSPIS for analysis. Photo interpretation reports with marked-up photographs were then submitted to Air HQ for distribution to the requesting unit. If [an] air strike was likely, the appropriate squadrons were given a full dossier to undertake preliminary planning. JSPIS maintained target files on every region and used government surveyor maps for such purposes. But the government surveyor was in no way involved with targeting or with JSPIS.[65]

Flight Lieutenant Peter Knoble recalled, "It is not generally appreciated what an extremely high standard of flying accuracy is required for aerial photography. Deviation in height, speed, aircraft altitude and navigational errors can all render the resulting film unusable."[66] Geldenuys added, "Cognizance needs to be taken that the navigator had to direct the pilot to the target area in the first place, roll the cameras at the right time, mark up the film, and often return to bomb a target hidden in featureless terrain."[67] Had it not been for the photo effort, many airstrikes and cross-border raids would not have been conceivable.

Already operating in close coordination with police or army to facilitate deployments and resupply, the Provost, Trojan, and Lynx aircraft were suitable for air observation as were planes of the Police Reserve Air Wing. This could be for a specific task or part of standing missions similar to ground patrolling. Ground commanders used these same aircraft to overfly areas of operation on visual reconnaissance flights for general familiarization or in conjunction with specific operations that required first-hand appreciation of conditions and terrain to be met.

In the initial stages of the insurgency, in 1966, flights were for border control and air observation over neighboring states harboring guerrillas (first Zambia, then Botswana and Mozambique). It was felt that pilots assigned the same areas over time would develop a feel for the local conditions, population, game movements and the detection of any changes that indicated guerrilla presence.[68] As Petter-Bowyer found:

> Flying at 1,500 feet above the ground, because it was considered to be high enough for safety from enemy ground fire, I spent hour after hour studying every pathway and disturbed area over hundreds of square miles of tribal territory. I watched people moving along pathways, found where women bathed and laundered clothing along rivers and even watched people move into cover near their homes to attend their toilet needs. Slowly I picked up similarities that helped me understand what I was seeing and how to use the sun to illuminate very faint pathways. Herds of cattle in the tribal areas were too great in numbers for the ground that supported them, resulting in hundreds of cattle paths which ran in parallel lines. Though clearly visible, they were not so well defined as human paths and had many distinctive shallow-angled linking lines—something like a railway center.[69]

A 4 Squadron pilot, Jan Mienie, recalled that "Petter-Bowyer was a legend in the air force, a technical innovator, and great instructor. He talked with the locals and came up with the 'crap pattern' that was used to visually locate terrorists."[70] Petter-Bowyer concluded:

> I developed visual recce and achieved many kills before instructing others in the art. My best protégé was Cocky Benecke who not only found terrorists bases by 'unnatural trails' and pathways but by fresh tracks too. He was responsible for the deaths of many hundreds of ters he found during recce. The only PRAW pilot who generated good Fire Force actions from Mark 1 eyeball recce was Hamie Dax. When Hamie called, the Fire Force never failed to take notice.[71]

Flight Lieutenant Paintin remembered:

> It is possible to discern the location of a terrorist camp by the pattern of small paths [tracks] that develops as a result of the biological function of the group, particularly where the bush is not overly dense. It is possible to notice the way the long grass is flattened when a group crosses the grassland against the natural fall of the grass due to wind, etc. This is not to say this

method can be compared with following tracks on the ground using trackers. It was never the less a method used and some pilots like Cocky Benecke and others were particularly good at this type of reconnaissance.[72]

There were also those who believed routine air reconnaissance was no more successful than random ground patrolling in turning up guerrilla units. Wilkins provided some insight: "We worked a lot with the recce pilots who flew low and slow Cessnas and Trojans and there is no way you can spot tracks like that—they go by trends and patterns in the bush—signs of new or unnatural trails, etc., but not tracks!"[73] But Petter-Bowyer felt these views were a helicopter pilot's about SAAF recce pilots in South West Africa and Angola, rather than from any experience in the Rhodesian context.[74]

After 1972, as the insurgency intensified, border control flights remained and expanded to include area control and coverage of internal lines of communications (roads, bridges, railroads). Demands expanded to include the need for armed reconnaissance, light ground attack, and the airborne forward air control of heavy ground attack jet aircraft. A sighting, contact, or detection of a border crossing would be countered at once when air observations were carried out by armed light attack aircraft instead of passive reporting that delayed a response until after the enemy had moved on. There was also an increased dependence upon air couriers for movement of critical persons and items. This became more difficult as operations stepped up, resources became stretched, and the risk of casualties became greater as guerrilla preparedness and weapons improved.[75]

Airborne systems also contributed to more specialized signals intelligence. The army provided radio intercept operators to man a Central Intelligence Organization ground monitoring facility at Hatfield and smaller mobile stations. These intercepted long-range low frequencies but not those that were short-range line of sight in the upper bands. While South Africa provided airborne surveillance over Mozambique, attempts were made to fit a Rhodesian aircraft with radios and recorders to accomplish this, resulting in the AL-60 "Aardvark." It lacked endurance and other means had to be found to accomplish this monitoring task. Combined Operations required intelligence support for cross-border operations that used an airborne communications and signals-interception platform based on the DC-3, called the "Warthog." Deployed in 1978, an intelligence officer and four intercept operators monitored and recorded on tape ultra, very, and high-frequency radio traffic from the various nationalists. Radar signals were also detected and identified. Teletype communications were with the defense headquarters in Salisbury's Milton Building which allowed early warning of air-to-air and antiaircraft threats to be passed directly to the forces involved through a command and control aircraft.[76]

Flight Lieutenant Fairey flew these missions. In September 1979, this was in support of Operation *Uric* in Mozambique:

> I and Flight Lieutenant John Reid-Rowland flew the Warthog from New Sarum to Buffalo Range. We landed at 11:30AM and were told that the operation had started and that we were to get back in the air as soon as possible. … While all this excitement was going on, John and I cruised sedately back and forth over the Kruger Park between the Limpopo and Phalaborwa while the operators in the cabin monitored communications and hostile radar in Mozambique which tracked us throughout the sortie. Once we saw a SAAF DC-4 [Spook] which was obviously engaged on the same sort of mission as ourselves.[77]

Command, Control, Communications

The police, air force, and army depended upon complex communications schemes to exercise control of often-dispersed forces. Each service had its own radio, wire, and messenger systems that needed to be integrated, particularly in the operational areas. The air force was tasked with part of this, to include operating a network that involved Combined Operations and Air Staff headquarters, various fixed bases and forward airfields, and army ground and air force airborne radio relays. Security concerns multiplied, with the danger of radio intercept, wiretapping, and just careless voice procedures.

Utility aircraft often provided mobile radio relay for ground forces under the nickname "Telstar," particularly during external operations (for example, two Lynxes provided relay, spaced some 160 kilometers apart). Ground commanders could control operations from the Lynx with more endurance time (three hours) than provided by the Alouette (one hour), which was used more for internal operations.

The examples of airborne command and control provided by use of the Alouette and Lynx (often in tandem during Fire Force operations) was expanded. Combined operations required command and control for cross-border operations based on the DC-3, called the "Command Dak." Created in 1978, it served as an airborne command post for the Commander, Combined Operations (a lieutenant-general) and the Director of Operations, Rhodesian Air Force (an air commodore). Voice radio allowed communications to air and ground commanders, often airborne themselves in Alouettes or Lynxes. Both the Command Dak and Warthog operated out of New Sarum and would assume a racetrack flight pattern and orbit near the scene of action while operations were underway. Teletype allowed communications with the defense headquarters in Salisbury's Milton Building and voice communications with tactical units or aircraft.[78]

Fairey also flew the Command Dak during Operation *Uric* with Reid-Rowland:

> Since the main activity of the day was to be air strikes and there were no major operations involving ground forces, General Walls did not fly. His place was taken by Air Commodore

Norman Walsh. We flew twice and were airborne for a total of nine hours, most of which were spent orbiting the Admin Area. The aircraft would have been a 'sitting duck' for enemy fighters but, fortunately, the Mozambican Air Force did not intervene.[79]

Utility Missions

The *MCP* summarized: "Aircraft can be usefully employed for special tasks such as the dissemination of propaganda, liaison flights, and the protection of road convoys."[80] Teargas, leaflets, flares, and parachutists had been previously deployed by air in the Federal period for internal security. Riot control during civil unrest was an early "non-lethal" use of the air force in support of the civil power as far back as the 1950s. Dakotas, Alouettes, and Provosts were used to "show the flag," drop leaflets, broadcast, inspect public utilities, deploy police and army troops, drop dye, teargas, and flares, photograph rioters, and carry out visual reconnaissance of threatened areas.[81]

Aid to the civil power included moving magistrates, registrars, and police for continuity of government services. Related civic action missions were the flying of medical and veterinary services as tangible antidotes to nationalist promises. Briscoe commented, "as the cause[s] of wars are usually rooted in some form of perceived injustice or discrimination, these actions serve to demonstrate the government's good faith."[82]

Psychological action (psyac or psyops), particularly in the early stages of the insurgency, were leaflet drops and loudspeaker "sky-shouting" using native speakers. This warned rural populations of the presence of guerrillas with offers for information or punishment for harboring them. Initial efforts used light aircraft or helicopters using one or two 100-watt loudspeaker amplifiers and a control box. A microphone or tape recorder would deliver a 30- to 50-second message. This worked best from an orbit or hover at 1,000 to 2,000 feet in good weather. Simultaneous "fire power" demonstrations by attack aircraft were given to demonstrate government will and power to both locals and guerrilla supporters.[83]

In 1979, a comment described the later sky-shout as a bank of powerful speakers:

> Used to talk to crowds or people suspected of harboring guerrillas. This device was a great improvement over the original one that was used with the Dakota and even tried on the Alouette. The older one consisted of two massive speakers, one mounted on each side of the Alouette, or on one side of the Dakota ("one loudspeaker mounted on the forward bulkhead of the cabin"). The new one contained lots of smaller speakers and was much more powerful, yet much clearer, so easier to hear on the ground. There were safety regulations about how close it could be used and though I can't recall the figures, I know it was dangerous in that it could damage the ears if used too close to people.[84]

Peter Briscoe thought that airborne surrender appeals were only effective if combined with ground action against any "hard core" terrorist. He cited Lieutenant-General Sir Frank Kitson that: "Unless the terrorist is in imminent danger of being killed, or of starving he will probably laugh and will certainly lose any vestige of respect that he might otherwise feel for the government."[85]

Fully instrumented Dakotas, Alouettes, Cheetahs, and Lynxes were available for night operations such as medical evacuation, resupply, radio relay, and flare drops. In the latter example, response to farm attacks had a Lynx arriving over the homestead in communications with the police who were in contact with the farmer through the Agric-Alert system. The Lynx's first flare went out over the target and adjustment would be made for wind drift with subsequent flares. The 18-kilogram Recco magnesium parachute flare would be dropped from 3,500 feet with a five-minute burn time at 600,000–800,000 candlepower. "Normally when the first flare was dropped the attack would stop," but magnesium flares also started grass fires.[86]

Police reserve aircraft and crews flew similar missions with increasing frequency during the war.[87] At first organized to support their own service needs, particularly PATU and Support Unit, later "more emphasis was laid on cooperation with ground forces and with the … Rhodesian Air Force who had always served as a guide, mentor, and inspiration to [PRAW]."[88] For example, in 1977 some 22,000 hours were flown by 180 pilots and observers. With similar concerns for the antiaircraft threat, they remained unarmed and unarmored until the end.[89]

Offensive, Direct, and Close Air Support

The *MCP* stated: "Aircraft in the offensive role will be armed mainly with anti-personnel weapons for use against groups of enemy whose position is known, but who cannot be seen. Aircraft may also be employed in air-pin operations where the enemy is pinned down until the ground cordon has been completed."[90] To be effective, close air support had to, 1) be readily available (quick reaction), 2) on call at all times, and 3) weapons delivery should be extremely accurate, with 4) weapons-to-target matching very good.[91] Available weapons and their use within the borders of Rhodesia expanded over time with the escalation of the conflict. Concern for the principle of the minimum use of force was expressed by Air Vice-Marshal Hawkins, as well as noting the waste of ammunition to kill a single terrorist at Sinoia.[92] In retrospect, Petter-Bowyer noted, "Sinoia was the first operation in Rhodesia against armed terrs. It was the first time [the] air force had fired in anger inside the country but this resulted in the first terrorist kill by any force." Technician George Carmichael's shooting of a MAG from an improvised mount with no sighting system from the moving aircraft, flown by Murray Hofmeyr, at a running target, dropped the terrorist in four bursts. Petter-Bowyer closed: "Even when we had improved mountings and decent gun sights, 176 rounds to down a single target would have been considered good shooting."[93] This first internal use of guns was in 1966, with rockets, bombs, and napalm following in 1967. Covert external air operations followed in Portuguese Mozambique thereafter. As the war progressed and external enemy targets were more removed and better defended, air attack became the preferred and often the sole means of engagement.[94]

To obtain offensive air: "The system in general works this way: ground or air forces locate the intruders, and when necessary, call for air support. Within a very short time the aircraft are there swooping in with cannon and rocket fire, and bombs if these are required."[95] The goal was to get the guerrillas to take cover until they could be taken under fire by ground forces. Too strong an air response might split the guerrillas up and was reserved for when ground forces already had them pinned down. Immediate air support was available at all times on one- and two-hour standby with standard loads of ordnance; preplanned air support could reduce this to 15-minute strip alert or even airborne over the target area.[96] High-speed refueling and rearming ensured a quick turnaround. Including refueling, checks, and arming, this could be accomplished within 18 minutes for fighters. In contrast, loading four Canberras with bombs could take up to five hours, with three hours being the record.[97] But this may be misleading and reflected conventional weapons under peacetime conditions. As Petter-Bowyer noted, "When loading 300 Mk II fragmentation bombs [the Alpha bouncing bomblets], our technicians could turn a formation of four Canberras around in 40 minutes."[98]

Abbreviated procedures existed that could speed up support, but these were also more restrictive because of the preplanning required.[99] The jet fighter and bomber squadrons worked closely together. Squadron Leader Jacobus F. "Randy" du Rand felt that "at any time, we can do a strike together without lengthy briefings. ... As a rule, a mere telephone call suffices, to arrange position in formation and the geographic point at which we'll join up."[100] The extensive effort that went into joint operations briefings were exceptions.

Terminal air control was by ground air controllers (GACs, any small unit leader in practice) working through airborne forward air controllers (AFACs). Needed was positive identification of the forward line of troops (FLOT) and target using panels, smoke, and flares. A radio-activated marker system (RAMS) used with the special forces allowed offset bombing or cargo drops at night.[101] Forward air control for Canberras, Hunters, and Vampires was provided by slower light aircraft that could provide suitable target marking with smoke rockets as well as pilot briefings. This fell to the pilots and aircraft of 4 Squadron who in turn were either future or former pilots of the fast-movers in 1, 2, and 5 Squadrons.[102] Positive control of air weapons and the difficulties of target recognition were a factor. Even if visual sighting occurred, the *COIN* manual noted "chances of misinterpreting the situation will be high."[103] Squadron Leader Oakley noted in regards to jets:

> Target acquisition was a very serious problem and sometimes strikes would have to be postponed because of bad weather. Even when there was little or no cloud cover, the haze and smoke made it difficult to identify targets in the bush. We were usually armed with a photograph that was the wrong size to manage in the cockpit and seemed to bear little resemblance to the view we had of the ground.[104]

Doctrine was that great care should be taken in planning and delivery of air weapons: "Not only must it be certain that friendly forces are not in danger, but because there will not normally be a definite theater of war, consideration must be given to the property and lives of innocent persons."[105] Air Lieutenant David A. D. Bourhill described an airstrike in Mozambique that went astray in 1978:

> We had been tasked to suppress [anti-aircraft] and cause general mayhem on the ground. The attack was to commence at the magic hour of 0800 as this was when the gooks would be lined up on parade for roll call. Officer commanding No 1 Squadron, Vic [Wightman], and Alf Wilde were leading sections of Hunters tasked to bomb from high dive profile. As it was the end of the dry season, the haze was a thick dirty yellow below 12,000 feet. Vic identified his target, turned in and dropped his two Golf bombs, but unfortunately it was the wrong hill and an SAS call sign, Trooper [Steve M. G. Donnelly], was fatally injured. So a "Stop Stop Stop" went out and the attack was called off. [In turn, Bourhill's Blue 2 was hit by a Strela].[106]

Briscoe explained that mixes of light or medium attack aircraft carried out close air support, depending upon the enemy threat and the target. When the guerrillas took the initiative after 1972, fleeting contacts between them and the security forces required "air power to give ground forces the best chance of inflicting substantial casualties." Under these circumstances all types of aircraft, except for dedicated transports, needed to carry appropriate mixes of ordnance. Each aircraft was fitted with radios compatible with those of the army and police, as well as for long-range communications. Navigational aids, which allowed night and bad weather recovery landings, were essential.[107]

There were advantages to the use of light aircraft: the Provost, Trojan, and Lynx. They could operate from short semi-prepared airfields and thus were based in the operational areas. These piston-engine propeller aircraft were easily modified to reduce infrared signatures. Their low speed was not a problem, as in counterinsurgency operations many targets were visually acquired and provided targets of opportunity impossible to see at high speed. With contacts often of short duration, during the early stages at least, the Provost, Trojan, and Lynx were valuable assets.[108] However, as fighting increased in intensity these light aircraft proved slow and vulnerable to antiaircraft attacks, and jet aircraft were used with appropriate air-to-ground ordnance.[109]

The value of anti-personnel weapons over other air ordnance led to refinements during the conflict.[110] Early experience indicated against open targets, "Air strikes of a heavy nature have caused terrorists groups to fragment and scatter, thereby extending operations."[111] It was found, "The traditional iron bombs and 3in or 68mm rockets have limited abilities, particularly over large areas, and cluster sub-munitions delivered from high speed, low level profile will be required to inflict meaningful casualties on the enemy."[112] Progress by the air force plans directorate and technical branch followed accordingly in the production of local ordnance.[113] Petter-Bowyer, who worked with these improvements, felt that the ordnance developed and manufactured in Rhodesia provided "highly effective, ultra-low cost" weapons that replaced various high cost imports "that were totally unsuited to bush warfare."[114]

The development of specialized ordnance took place in the 1976/7 period with Wing Commander Petter-Bowyer as Staff Officer Planning and Squadron Leader Ron Dixon as Senior Staff Officer Air Armament. The projects were in conjunction with local engineering firm in consultation with John de Villiers and Vernon Joynt from Pretoria's Council for Scientific and Industrial Research (CSIR).[115] Project Alpha was an improved fragmentation bomb for the Canberra; Bravo and Delta were the 37mm rocket white phosphorus and TNT boosters for the Lynx; Echo was the 16-gallon NapGel fire bomb for the Lynx and a 50-gallon version for the Hunter; Foxtrot was a fuel air explosive high-pressure bomb for the Hunter using ethylene oxide; and Golf was the high-pressure bomb for the Hunter using Anfo. Project Hotel was another weapon for the high-speed Hunter using a flechette dispenser. Flechettes were basically a six-inch nail fitted with plastic stabilizing fins to keep the point falling first. Because of international concerns, use was restricted to within the country's borders despite notable success. Project Juliet was the Mini-Golf bomb to arm the Lynx with a device similar to that for the Hunter.

Other projects included turning 20mm cannon over to the army for vehicle use, night vision devices for gunships, work on a chemical agent dispenser, and cable-cutting bombs to demolish bridges.[116]

Guns proved the most accurate and most often used air-to-ground weapon. These were the Hunter's 30mm Aden (armament development Enfield) gun (with 540 rounds), the Vampire's 20mm Hispano-Oerlikon gun (with 300–600 rounds), and .303 Browning machine guns on the Provost and Lynx (with 1,200 rounds each). Gunnery attacks were made in a shallow low dive, similar to the run for the firebombs and these could be used in conjunction with each other. The Lynx would do this from 1,500 feet at a 12-degree dive to a pull out as low as 100 feet. The progressive arming of the Alouette transformed it from a transport with a flexible 7.62mm MAG to a valuable weapons platform by 1974. Matra MG 151 20mm cannon (with 240–480 rounds) and dual or quad Browning Mk 2 .303 machine guns (with 500 rounds each) were later mounted on helicopters to make them gunships that were precise and "most effective against enemy in the open and have a high demoralizing effect."[117] This was in a left-turn orbit at a relatively low 800 to 1,200 feet.[118]

Rocket projectiles followed next in precision and usage. Rockets were "delivered more accurately and, therefore, more effectively" than bombs, particularly when "boosted" with fragmentation, hollow charge, and smoke marking heads. The high-speed French SA Matra 68mm (2.68in) rocket used either six or 18 projectile pods. Older 3-inch rockets were fired in arrays of six, eight, or 12 depending on the aircraft (Vampire or Hunter), mounting either armor-piercing or squash heads.

The low-speed French TDA SNEB 37mm (1.46in) rocket used an 18-projectile pod. Wielded by the Provost, Trojan, and Lynx, it lacked punch when used for anything other than marking targets and various modifications were made. There was also a 25 percent failure rate caused by faulty fins or warheads. The more powerful 68mm rocket was considered, but was heavy and needed a higher launch speed than could be obtained by the light aircraft, making them somewhat inaccurate. The only solution was to carry as many 37mm pods as possible and rely on quantity over quality. The Lynx delivered rockets from 1,500 feet with a 15-degree dive to as low as 300 feet.

Frangible tanks (Frantan) were fire bombs "used with great effect against terrorists in the open" and thus in high demand. A plastic resin canister that held 16 to 20 gallons of locally produced napalm (a less common version held 50 gallons of jellied gasoline for jet fighter delivery). Since the canister was fitted with fins, it could be aimed with greater accuracy than similar North Atlantic Treaty Organization and Communist Bloc weapons. Dropped short of a target, it spread its flaming contents forward with a 45-degree swath. It not only destroyed what it hit, it was also demoralizing and resulted in surrenders. One pilot observed, it was "used with outstanding success against a variety of targets, including caves."[119]

More effective than general-purpose bombs were multiple 20-pound (9kg) fragmentation bombs for most common targets. These locally produced weapons also proved hazardous. A Canberra accident in 1974 with locally manufactured fragmentation bombs preceded development of the highly successful Alpha bomb.[120] Alpha bombs were a cluster bomb designed for the Canberra bomber. An aircraft carried some 300 sub-munitions in a hamper for delivery at 300 feet at 350 knots. According to Petter-Bowyer, "An Alpha bomblet consisted of a 100 gravity activating pistol encased within the explosive charge of a central 6mm core which was held inside an outer 4mm steel case by hard super-rubber balls that caused the bomblet to bounce off any surface."[121] A delayed action (.6 second) mechanism caused detonation at six to 12 feet above the ground, dispersing a lethal fragment per square yard in a 15-foot radius. These were delivered in pattern of 100 by 1,000 meters. Four Canberras in formation could cover some 105 acres, larger than the area of early nationalist camps.[122]

Another fragmentation device designed specifically for the Hunter were flechettes. Some 4,500 of these darts were carried in a dispenser. Dropped in pairs at 450 knots flying a standard gun attack profile, a burster charge then opened the dispenser, and the darts were spread by air pressure. This produced a high-density swath some 80 meters wide by 900 meters long. Used internally towards the end of the conflict, they proved successful. In one case, a directed daylight strike killed 26 of 26 guerrillas and all high-ranking ZANLA staff members.[123]

Golf bombs, were designed for the Hunter in the attack role, as "Air bursts are preferable against enemy in the open" to shock and confuse them into staying in place. The air force designer concluded, "Not only was the Hunter's punch greatly enhanced, the country saved millions of dollars and could provide replacements of these high-blast weapons immediately without regards to problems induced by sanctions."[124] An aircraft carried two bombs for delivery at a 60-degree angle. Further design followed with paired bombs, one delayed by fins (later a drogue parachute) resulting in a two-bomb spread. Each of the 5 foot by 18 inch bombs weighed 1,000 pounds (450kg) and had a 3-foot extension to detonate it just above the ground. An Amatol charge sent some 80,000 fragments out with an effective casualty range of 400 feet (200 feet for blast and 200 feet more for fragments). Described as having a "stunning effect," although its six-second time of flight could result in drift, very few malfunctions occurred with the fuse probe. After their success, a smaller version was developed, the Mini-Golf bomb for use with the Lynx. Initially, a cruciform parachute was used to retard the bomb and a cable deployed from the nose to detonate it at 12 feet above the ground in a vertical position (at first there was a high failure rate and even premature detonations).[125] Squadron Leader Brand recalled developing a flight profile for delivery of these blast bombs in early 1978, "In order to create a situation where the enemy would not hear the aircraft approaching, this called for an approach at 10,000 feet above ground level and 10 nautical miles out, throttling back, and gliding to the target, ending with a 60-degree dive to deliver the bombs." At this point, "unless someone saw the aircraft approaching, the first [time] they could hear the aircraft (if they could hear) was after the bombs had been dropped and the aircraft was departing."[126] Conventional "iron" bombs were only found useful in those limited situations where there were fixed defensive positions, but were less capable of accurate hits. These were costly imported weapons wielded with care. Medium-capacity high-explosive bombs ranged from 250 to 1,000 pounds (115–450kg).

Aircraft and flights carried mixes of weapons depending on the mission. Hunters and Vampires carried guns and paired rocket pods, Frantan, or Golf bombs (Sidewinder AIM9B missiles were available from South Africa, a simple low-cost air-to-air weapon against non-maneuvering targets). The versatile Lynx carried two 18-rocket pods (three smoke, the rest high-explosive projectiles), either two Frantans or Mini-Golf bombs, and guns. The Canberra first carried a variety of conventional ordnance (250-, 500-, 1,000-pound general-purpose bombs in various mixes of sixes and nines), then 96 fragmentation bombs, and the later Alpha cluster bombs. Air strikes combined aircraft and weapons to maximum effect: on externals this would be with Hunters going in first from a high-altitude 20,000 feet and diving onto the target area with Golf bombs then going back to "top cover" with guns, followed by Canberras at a low-altitude 300 feet with Alpha bombs, at which point Alouettes would arrive over the target to strafe with 20mm cannon. In 1974, these tactics accounted for an estimated 300 ZANLA in Mozambique; in 1977, for another 1,200 ZANLA; in 1978, for an estimated 1,500 ZPRA casualties in Zambia.[127]

The delivery of air weapons began as the least likely option for air support in counterinsurgency, but became an essential element of combat power as the war expanded within and without Rhodesia. Analysis of airstrikes passed by the Air Staff included, where possible, that aircraft should operate in pairs, particularly over Mozambique; that the enemy in camp would run "as far and fast as possible" when hearing jet aircraft; if the enemy was surprised, then the first targets should be antiaircraft weapons; when operating within Rhodesia, positive target identification was needed because of problems involved with mistaking the enemy for African or special forces troops; helicopters needed to be kept more than three minutes out because the sound would carry and alarm the target; terrorists would often have "a go at shooting down a helicopter." It also seemed intelligence reports were reacted to without confirmation, hitting "empty spaces;" that it would be better to confirm with air reconnaissance and an intelligence buildup and only then follow up with an air attack when most likely occupied.[128]

Even the part-time PRAW flyers armed themselves, against the air forces wishes, for escort or reconnaissance duties that demanded more than just passive reporting.[129] Police reservist Arnold Woolley recalled flying with the Marandellas PRAW in 1978, that:

> The gun was laterally behind the front seats, firing from port side ... Ours was a .303 Browning, recycled to take 7.62mm. Floor mounted with limiting pegs to prevent over-exuberant gunners shooting bits out of tail or wing. The method was to find the target, establish a tight orbit centered on the target and then let fly. One-in-five tracer let the pilot [Dave Pritchard] adjust angle and orbit for best effect. The gunner was there to keep the bullets streaming. Brownings were notorious for not liking vibration. If flown and not used for a while they tended to fire one shot then jam, because the safety catch had slipped half on. Gunners learned to be damned quick at clearing jams! Once over any initial jam, they were pretty reliable. The pilot had only his armored steel "butt-plate" in case anything nasty came too close. The gunner had nothing but an open doorway between him and any opposition.[130]

Air Lieutenant Dawson recalled that the police air wing were "all right," but "there again, they were old buggers, a lot of them, and they were sort of reliving the Second World War, a lot of them. ... But a lot of the blokes were like that, because they were sort of getting into the spirit of things, I suppose, which was good. It's better to have that than nonchalance and couldn't-care-less attitude, I suppose."[131] Dawson, who flew helicopters from 1974 to 1978, remembered an incident where:

> I nearly had a mid-air with one of those fuckers in Darwin! He'd spotted these gooks and when he got us in, I was in K-car, he wouldn't go away. I looked up, and he was so close. If I hadn't avoided I would have hit him. I was literally speechless! He had radio [problems] so he couldn't receive anything; he could transmit though, so he was fucking jabbering away like this and obviously couldn't hear anybody else trying to talk.[132]

Flight Lieutenant Paintin felt Dawson's comments were in poor taste, as:

> The PRAW pilots were all volunteers, many of whom gave up most of their time in order to play their part. Most were good pilots and did their job to the best of their ability. Many were never recognized for their dedicated service. ... The incident related could have happened to any fixed-wing pilot ... [making] little sense to castigate the entire air wing over one incident.[133]

CHAPTER 5

Provisional to Brigade Joint Operations

In December 1972, Operation *Hurricane* was established in Centenary (moving later to Bindura and finally Salisbury) for counterinsurgency operations in the northeast facing the Zimbabwe African National Liberation Army (ZANLA) arriving from neighboring Mozambique. This marked a shift from border to area control, and an important transitional period occurred between when the first full-time joint operations center was started until the ensuing creation of a national joint operations center.[1] With the commencement of *Hurricane*, the need for something more effective than combat trackers was revealed by the lack of information on the terrorists in the region. This was because government informants "on the ground" had been eliminated and the British South Africa Police and Internal Affairs failed to replace them. These habitual sources of information were eliminated by the arrival of ZANLA cadre who used selective and arbitrary terror to persuade the tribesmen away from the government cause. The populated tribal areas were not conducive to the previous border control methods of follow up on explicit trails previously left by infiltrators. The extensive use of landmines by the guerrillas added to the problem.[2] To some extent, the Rhodesian security forces had to go back to square one.

Tracking terrorist incursions was not the Special Air Service's true role and in fact was a hindrance to its evolution. When Operation *Hurricane* began, trackers were no longer able to follow insurgents that were mingling with local populations. But captured terrorists provided a fairly good picture of the bases and routes being used to enter Rhodesia. It was necessary to block internal terrorists from their external bases with small patrols operating for long periods in any type of terrain.[3] The Operations *Hurricane* commander Brigadier John S. V. Hickman[4] worked out a plan with SAS Major Brian G. Robinson to deploy forward into Mozambique to locate and destroy ZANLA infiltration groups.[5] This was done by pulling SAS tracking teams out of the operational area and sending them across the border. It was the SAS's external functions in Zambia, Botswana, and Mozambique that began to absorb its full attention.

Under Robinson, from early 1973 until mid-1974, the SAS operated out of Macombe, Mozambique. This involved the air force and army in six-week

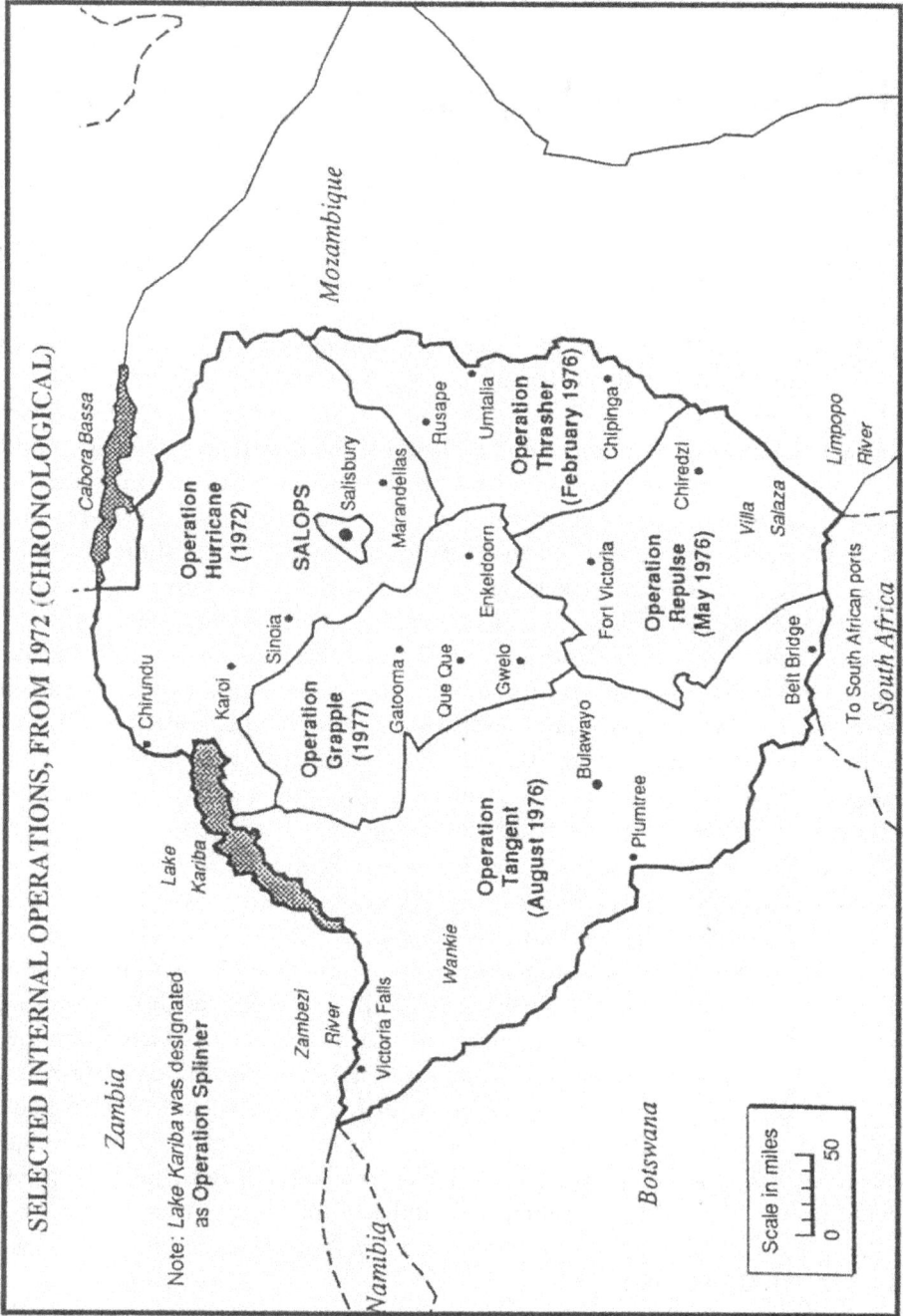

SELECTED INTERNAL OPERATIONS, FROM 1972 (CHRONOLOGICAL)

Note: *Lake Kariba* was designated as **Operation Splinter**

Scale in miles

0   50

Selected internal operations, from 1972

deployments followed by a 10-day stand-down and then return. Ground forces were provided by the SAS and RLI ostensibly in conventional support of the Portuguese with a covert role to verify the presence of ZANLA with FRELIMO and to ambush or attack them if the opportunity arose. Also provided were insights into the deteriorating situation in Portuguese East Africa. Enhanced was the value of helicopter and light aircraft support of small units on the ground. The experience marked a change that came to maturity later in the war. But there were too few SAS and too much ground to be covered to be really successful.[6]

For the SAS, internal and external deployments had similar preparation and support, although larger demolition or base attacks required a "full court press" including headquarters and reserve personnel. An SAS troop or squadron TacHQ deployed as part of border control or counterinsurgency operation to establish a forward operating base (FOB).[7] A cover story was provided for its movement and an area of operation would be "frozen" at the joint or combined operations headquarters to prevent mishaps with other security force units. An Alouette III would be on standby for routine or emergency insertion, extraction, casualty evacuation, and resupply—later two aircraft were available for this (Operation *Parker*). A TacHQ consisted of the squadron commander, squadron sergeant-major, a signals detachment, cooks, mechanics, medics, and a reserve team or troop for base defense. With a squadron headquarters were some 14 men with fuel, water, stores, and heavy weapons managing the efforts of some 10 "call signs" or four-man "sticks" sent out in rotation. Any patrols at base concurrently conducted training, maintenance, and resupply.

Patrols first deployed in the border region before moving into neighboring states as the need to operate in "enemy" territory became obvious. Missions were initially confined to observation and reconnaissance. Robinson recalled these were "recce only. Tasked to remain totally clandestine for periods of six weeks at a time, reporting on enemy movement in host country locations, establishing enemy base camp positions with close-up recce, and observing enemy transport."[8] The patrol radio was the 14-pound (6.35kg) TR28 with an equally heavy battery using either a whip or long wire antenna. Skip distance and radio relays had to be planned in, as well as security using anything from one-time pads to frequency hopping.[9] Patrols would use high-frequency Morse code to the tactical headquarters, while the tactical headquarters used high-frequency Morse and teletype. Local communications were by VHF voice A63 radios. The tactical headquarters kept a radio listening watch 24 hours a day seven days a week with patrols reporting in three times daily on a rotating morning-noon-and-night schedule. Both airborne and fixed radio relays were used for communications. The TacHQ submitted a daily situation report to the SAS headquarters including any administrative or logistic requests. At the time, security was ensured through the use of verbal orders, without telephone or facsimile, and one-time pads while deployed. Later a unique SAS code was provided to communicate with headquarters.[10]

The army magazine *Assegai* detailed a November to December 1973 SAS deployment.[11] A patrol of 20 men from A Troop went into the Zambezi valley on the northeastern border with Mozambique. The patrol was to locate enemy base camps and supply lines. They were briefed that the "Locals may support and sympathize with the terrorists and often tell when security forces are near, but mostly they just prefer to be left alone." Enemy weapons and supplies were moved from point to point with civilians forced to provide food and porters.[12] The terrorists were extorting the local African population but a need for security kept them on the move and based away from villages and settlements. Sentries were posted outside their camps to warn of the approach of security forces. "When there is cause to flee, the exodus is rapid and much equipment is abandoned in the flight," noted a patrol member.[13]

A night parachute drop concealed the patrol's presence by eliminating a cross-country move into the area. The patrol soon found an unoccupied terrorist camp and established an observation post to monitor it. After this dramatic start, the routine of patrolling for 30 days became a reality. Moving several kilometers in the morning, halts were made during the heat of the day for food and rest. The patrol moved again in the afternoon until nightfall, established communications and cooked a meal, then moving again to bed "down in a tight little circle, each man taking a turn at guard."[14]

Reconnaissance patrols were usually four-man teams, combat patrols were larger (eight to 12 strong)—often with a senior leader and less experienced troops under his direct control with little call for independent action. There was a learning curve that began in the border control days and progressed through deployments that saw patrols expand from two- or three-day walkabouts upward to 10–14 days or longer with resupply. Movement was now by night with lay-ups in the hours of daylight. These matured into ambushes, mine laying, and camp attacks as the offense was taken.[15]

Experience showed that 10 days maximum could be tolerated without resupply, but food and eating were always a problem. Loads carried on patrol focused on ammunition, claymores, batteries, medical kit and water. Every effort was made to reduce weight, including cutting down spoons and blankets. The South African Council for Scientific Research provided solutions to camouflage cream ("black is beautiful") and nutritional food supplements (Tarzan bars) that required no cooking to eat. Food and water were necessities, with two water bottles on the Bergen rucksack and two on the belt with emergency rations and gear.[16]

Time took on a different meaning in the bush, regulated by dawn and dusk. As a result, individual attitude was vital and could fluctuate with boredom and this was as much an enemy as the terrorist. The first 10 days were the hardest, with subsequent days becoming a blur of routine activities, interrupted by the very real chance of catching the terrorists off guard marked by the "chatter of machine guns and AKs shattering the silence."[17] The valley's humid heat sapped strength and energy, requiring water for relief—even if mixed with mud, algae, and larvae. Some 10 to 15 pounds were lost after a month of tea, coffee, bully beef, braised steak, and rice rations. Air-dropped supplies came in every 10 days including a tin of orange juice and beer per man, with casualty evacuation on call if needed. The end came with a message to select a landing zone for helicopter extraction. This resulted in a return to base and additional patrolling of enemy camps at Courrie, Moses, and Rudodo by helicopter with mixed results. Finally, there was a Dakota flight back to barracks in Salisbury for rest and refitting.

Special Air Service commander Robinson felt, "Any reasonably fit Rhodesian who wants to get into the squadron will walk the selection course … He must be able to act as an individual on his own initiative, certainly—but also as a member of a team."[18] The army expected candidates to be, "enthusiastic, intelligent, of reasonable physical ability, and above all keen to join this fine unit."[19] Grace under pressure, often seen in humor, was an unstated trait desired, but "if he is not keen he will not pass."[20] Desired outcomes were, "At the point of exhaustion can he recall all he's seen and done, and how has he got on with his fellows?"[21] The goal was to demonstrate the logic, stamina, fitness, endurance, and initiative of candidates. Preferred traits were compatibility, positive and quick thinking, and those who would not give up. MacKenzie believed identifying self-reliance "was the main thing the SAS selection course did."[22] Journalist Barbara Cole wrote the lesson from selection was "that their minds would carry their bodies through bad times and they would find the energy if they had to."[23] Deputy Garth Barrett recalled, "everyone had a compass, heliograph, matches, and 12 feet of parachute cord." For example, one SAS man became separated from his patrol without a radio but kept his head and headed for the border. After five days he was spotted from the air and picked up by helicopter.[24]

Also apparent were the limitations of Whites fighting a war where black faces were needed.[25] This led to the use of Africans for access to the local population and the guerrillas in a new and forceful manner. Brigadier Hickman recognized the need for effective pseudogangs to locate terrorists who were within Rhodesia's borders and, by January 1973, past survival, tracking, and pseudo experience was revisited.[26] Interest in the use of pseudo techniques existed but nothing came of this in Rhodesia until nationalist subversion of the country's northeast eliminated existing informer networks and access to Mozambique dried up with the collapse of Portugal's control. Citing Policia Internacional de Defensa de Estado (PIDE) and Flechas (Arrows) experience, CIO's Flower stated this was called for to deal with the infiltration and politicization in the northeastern tribal areas. Both Robinson and Reid-Daly had worked with the Flechas in Mozambique. Other Portuguese counterinsurgency units were more ruthless, such as former big-game hunter Daniel F. Roxo and his "Column of Fire," dressed and equipped as insurgents, which killed or captured more rebels than the Portuguese expeditionary force.[27] Flower believed this provided an "African solution to an African problem" but sought agreement from the Portuguese and South Africans to implement the concept on a larger scale. Of note was Flower's desire for operations to be in Mozambique rather than within Rhodesia, but events decreed otherwise.

The police and army fielded ad hoc pseudogangs in the Operation *Hurricane* area with some success and failure.[28] Police Superintendent Tommy Peterson was directed to field an African pseudoteam, prepared in part by Stanton and Hart, for use in the subverted areas. Sergeants André Rabie and Alan Franklin were brought in from the army with their SAS and tracking backgrounds. A "new dynamic dimension" began as information began to flow about the impact of nationalist subversion in the northeast. These "pseudoterrorists" substituted for the collapsed Special Branch and Internal Affairs networks.[29] What was disturbing was the anti-government viewpoint of the local population rather than the actual presence of guerrilla sections.

Selous Scouts: Together as One

An expanded pseudo approach was sponsored in November 1973, using security force personnel tasked by the Central Intelligence Organization and funded through the Prime Minister's office. By year's end, this saw the organization of a group of army-based operators. This resulted in a different kind of special force that brought previous uncoordinated efforts together. Captain Michael F. "Mick" Graham worked on this effort with JOC Hurricane's Special Branch representative and was even offered a post in the new unit which he declined in order to stay with the SAS.[30]

Its first commander was Major Ron F. Reid-Daly who had been recalled by the army from retirement for this assignment. Police Superintendent M. J. P. "Mac" McGuiness was his Special Branch counterpart in the venture.[31] Reid-Daly soon learned that most useful initiatives during the conflict came from the bottom and had to overcome resistance at the upper levels to meet to Smith's demands for progress in defeating terrorism. Army General Walls wanted to hold off on expanding his forces due to the lack of resources to meet increased demands despite the call for pseudo-terrorists by JOC Hurricane's Brigadier Hickman. Opposition came from the SAS and RAR who felt the new unit took away from their mission and personnel – one consisting of very conventional African soldiers hard pressed to expand and the other the racially exclusive SAS that had certain limitations in Black Africa. Flower rued what he saw as a military rather than a police initiative. The army tracking wing and trackers formed the nucleus of the unit with the Special Branch providing existing experimental teams of "turned" terrorists. The unit was named the Selous Scout Regiment after Frederick Courteney Selous, a legendary explorer and hunter who died serving as an intelligence officer in World War I.[32]

The unit's charter from the prime minister to the Director of the Central Intelligence Organization presented a concept for "the clandestine elimination of terrorists/terrorism both within and without the country." The Selous Scouts were "Tasked to carry out operations of a clandestine nature wherever it may be called upon to serve, drawing its manpower from the combined services and other less obvious channels while receiving instructions from the Operations Coordinating Committee, the Director of the Central Intelligence Organization, Service Commanders and Joint Operations Commands." Reid-Daly trained, equipped, and deployed forces in coordination with the army and joint operations commanders. McGuiness recruited "turned terrorists," provided direction of employment, and disseminated the intelligence collected.[33]

On paper, roles included those assigned to the SAS, with the addition of providing combat tracker teams to follow guerrillas and to undertake "special reconnaissance" tasks. Tracking functions were a cover for the unit's real purpose, which at the time would "never be officially" acknowledged. This meant its actual mission was not known to most of the security forces, resulting in resentment and misunderstanding. A multiracial structure unique to the stratified Rhodesian society had to exist where rank and recognition existed on merit and performance in the field (the regimental motto was "*Pamwe Chete*" or "Together as One"). As a result, the members of the unit enjoyed a special and possibly unique relationship as a basis for success.[34]

The Selous Scouts comprised African and European regular or territorial soldiers, all of whom were volunteers required to pass a common selection course.[35] The trackers had to be reorganized and the training group was made responsible for curriculum and territorial member management. Under this system it conducted the selection, tracking, and survival courses for the Selous Scouts and for other security force requirements.[36] According to Reid-Daly, the training produced a group of men with speed, stealth, and efficiency as trackers. Both Black and White lived together, subsisting off the bush and locating the terrorists. The rigors of selection and training ensured they could exist indefinitely no matter how bad the conditions. After the first month designed to break any but the strongest spirit, one candidate concluded: "Our main task is to kill terrorists and with a unit like this you know you are with the best fighters in the world. You can count on them completely."[37] Perhaps this individual bonding was the main goal obtained.

The regiment's Inkomo Barracks was named after Sergeant André Rabie, the SAS soldier and tracker. He had pioneered pseudoterrorist techniques until killed on operations in a "friendly fire" incident. Where possible, the customs of both races were incorporated into organization and parade procedures. For example, infantry colors were not used and a standard was carried instead with symbolic significance meeting the African custom of totems. A stylized osprey, a bird of prey, was the unit badge. Regimental colors were green and brown, the dominant hues in the bush.

Initially a group of some 120 men, formed into 29-man troops consisting of three nine-man sections of two four-man combat tracker teams each (or some 33 men in headquarters and 87 men in the field with a ratio of two Europeans to eight or nine Africans). The term "operator" was used for individual scouts as it was for the SAS trooper. Like the SAS, the basic Selous Scout unit was the four-man half-section or tracker combat team but in practice it copied the terrorist "ANC" section.[38] These were led by White troop and section leaders with Africans serving up to the rank of color sergeant, supplemented with turned terrorists in varying numbers.[39] A robust headquarters group and base structure was set up to provide necessary staff support, including intelligence and operations, administration and logistics, signals, motor transport, medical, and training. By May 1974, the Scouts totaled 270, with a headquarters and six troops of 40 Europeans, 180 African soldiers, and some 50 "turned" terrorists. But ambiguity of structure and purpose caused continual problems.

Unique was a 12-man Special Branch element that gave both tasking and exploitation of deployed call signs. A byproduct was the continued need for captured terrorists and their equipment to keep current with ever-changing guerrilla authentication procedures. Keeping information flowing to those that used it was solved through direct liaison teams to the various headquarters (Scouts made good intelligence analysts), but the "need to know" security effort engendered hard feelings in police and military circles.[40] There was an inherent conflict between intelligence and combat operations, where a balance was needed between locating and eliminating terrorists as soon as possible or using them to get more information later on (a military and police dichotomy). Scout troops were designated by color and provided numbered call signs for operations. At peak strength some 420 operators could be deployed, but smaller numbers (200 or so) were more representative.[41] These call signs, the pseudoterrorist gangs, were controlled through Selous Scout "forts" established in the various provinces at Bindura, Mount Darwin (moved to Rusape), Chiredzi (at Buffalo Range), Bulawayo, and Fort Victoria.[42] Special Branch elements were headquartered out of Bindura while the military headquarters was at Inkomo. From there, teletype communications went to Central Intelligence headquarters and South African intelligence and security agencies. Special Branch "liaison officers" controlled tasking from these provincial fort location.[43] Special Branch officer Henrik Ellert recalled that access to facilities was strictly controlled, although usually adjacent to police or army camps for physical security. Each forward operating facility included an enclosed helicopter pad and vehicle parking area, a radio and operations room, special branch office, medical clinic, armory and storeroom, living quarters, and detention cells. Forts were linked by secure telephone, VHF and HF radios (A63s and TR28s), and kept a 24-hour-a-day, seven-day-a-week listening watch. A helicopter and crew were usually kept on standby for emergencies (again Operation *Parker*).[44]

The Selous Scouts provided pseudo forces developed from previous SAS and Special Branch trials within the designated internal operational areas. This was an aspect of counterinsurgency similar to law enforcement—the use of informants and "sting" methods to penetrate and disrupt criminal or subversive organizations. In both police and military pseudo operations there is a conflict between immediate and long-term exploitation of this method, seen in demands for combat information versus continuing intelligence. To some extent results are determined by what superiors value the most. In wartime Rhodesia, this was often a favorable kill ratio or "body count" that masked real measures of success or impending defeat.

The goal was to step into the guerrilla infiltration chain or local village base arrangements and identify subverted populations to locate guerrilla sections. A pseudoterrorist "gang" would be inserted into a populated area, establish a hide and observation point, make contact with real terrorists through the locals, and attempt to ambush them at the hide, a village, or even political rally.[45] The only way to pass as guerrillas was to use terrorists who had been "turned" to the government side and Whites kept to the background in the face-to-face encounters that were used. Reporting information from recent captures allowed the police or army to respond for the kill. Selous Scout call signs would attempt to remain in the game and direct fighting would give them away. This led to the famed Fire Force tactics of helicopter-borne assault forces used to eliminate the nationalist fighters. Success was measured in that some 68 percent of the guerrillas killed or captured were due to Selous Scout efforts.[46] To paraphrase Reid-Daly, killing insurgents was simple, finding them was not. He created an organization that was a successful master of pseudooperations, the military version of an intelligence and police game.

A South African military observer, Major Jakkie K. Cilliers, summarized the basic pseudo method in a postwar study:

> Depending on the specific circumstances that enabled a pseudo team to enter an area as insurgent forces, pseudo methods and the deception employed varied widely from one area to the next … the role of the Selous Scouts was to infiltrate the tribal population and terrorist networks, pinpoint the terrorist camps and bases and then direct conventional forces in to carry out the actual attacks. Then depending on the skill of the particular Selous Scouts' pseudo group concerned, their cover should remain intact which would enable them to continue operating in a particular area [usually indefinitely].[47]

The preferred areas for Selous Scout deployments were the tribal trust areas through which the guerrilla lines of communications flowed and whose population provided the "sea" in which the terrorist "fish" swam. These were graphed out: "People are predictable. They do the same things over and over again, even terrorists." This analysis showed what they were doing and when.[48] The terrain in the northeast was most suitable for pseudo teams (to infiltrate guerrilla networks, leading to ambushes or Fire Force callouts) with its broken and covered terrain that provided excellent observation and concealment, while the flat and arid southeast required the use of hunter-killer teams that often times had to locate and quickly eliminate more fleeting targets without the aid of infiltration or observation points leading to Fire Force use.

Other variations included stings or "Q" cars based on analysis of local terrorist incidents involving tribal trust land stores and bus services in the northeast and northwest. Two bus lines were being hit consistently, one more than the other that was having their buses burned. One of these was owned by a European, the other had a mixed-race (Colored) owner, while bus lines not being targeted were owned by Africans. A subsequent pseudoterrorist-staged robbery determined collusion with the terrorists to transport weapons, supplies, and fighters. A solution was to build a bus carrying Selous Scouts dressed like locals and to drive the bus route until terrorist tried to stop them. After the sixth trip, a terrorist section was waiting in the road. Nineteen were killed and the detachment leader captured, leading to further contacts based on his information.[49]

Mistaken identity with the other Rhodesian security forces was a complication, particularly when seen from the air and methods to "freeze" an area for operations were taken. Centralized control of pseudo efforts prevented further problems within the security forces as pseudo tactics appeared to have value at various levels. Captain John C. Cronin[50] provided an example where an RAR company commander, another American, in the southeast dressed his men up in captured guerrilla uniforms and weapons and sent them into an area in which both ZANLA and ZPRA operated. Since they lacked contacts and bona fides, everyone knew they were not the real thing. This spoiled the opportunities for real penetration for some time.

Grey's Scouts Ride Again

In July 1975, an experimental mounted infantry unit under Major Alexander Fraser-Kirk was created by the Rhodesia Army. On 26 March 1976, it was named after a historical predecessor. This was referred to by Frederick C. Selous in 1896, when in Bulawayo "Mr. Grey got together 23 good men and rode back to Tokwe the same evening. These men formed the nucleus of the force which had done splendid service in the suppression of the present rebellion under the name of Grey's Scouts," to put down the local Matabele and Mashona. A regimental song, "The Grey's Scouts Ride Again," characterized Rhodesia's foremost mounted unit (although the police and Internal Affairs all had horse-mounted elements). It was manned by regulars, territorials, and national servicemen. They fought from horseback and were often in action on the Rhodesian border areas.[51]

Based at Inkomo Barracks, the regiment began with a single squadron, expanding to battalion size with 800 men organized into a headquarters, support, and three combat squadrons (A, B, and C) with some 450 men and 400 horses at full strength. Each squadron had three troops consisting of four eight-man sections (again the basic four-man patrol or half-section). The support squadron included reconnaissance, mortar (60 and 81 mm), and tracker dog (foxhounds) sections. Normal headquarters and support elements were provided, including motor transport that had both "hardened" mine- and ambush-protected (MAPV) and "soft" horse-carrying vehicles (HCVs).

Starting with a four-and-a-half-month selection and training course, horse and rider were kept together to develop and keep "affinity and trust," including "gun proofing." Riders were desired that were 160 pounds (72kg) or less and most successful were trained soldiers taught to ride rather than those with riding experience who needed to be made into soldiers. Mounts were from various sources, with the majority being "smallish" mature horses from South Africa (crossbreeds of Bossiekops and Basuto ponies were preferred). Various camouflage efforts were tried with the horses with sometimes visually astonishing results. Pack horses carried stores, ammunition, and crew-served weapons with weights up to 300 pounds (140kg). For example, a mortar tube was strapped to a pack frame, balanced on the other side by ammunition, with the base plate mounted on the pommel. Furnishings were of local manufacture including a McClellan-style saddle and pack frame.

The role of the Grey's was long-range reconnaissance, patrolling of rural areas, tracking, and follow-up on horseback, deep penetration in support of armored cars, and serving as dismounted infantry when needed. It operated in those areas where the terrain limited vehicle and foot mobility, such as along the eastern and southeastern borders, often in parallel with the border minefield cordon—much of the regiment's deployments supported the engineers on the boundary cordon and patrolled the border, although occasionally it provided support to the units engaged in external operations. [52] Patrols lasted up to 10 days, with "self-supply" using local fodder and concentrated horse pellets. Two sections would work together and could cover up to 40 kilometers in a day. A horse and rider could alternate a 7 kilometer an hour walk with a 12 kilometer an hour trot (although the trot was found to be uncomfortable and tended to dislodge equipment) and a canter at 18 kilometers an hour could be attained. Horses, unlike vehicles, moved relatively silently through the bush. The horses placed the rider well above the high savannah grass and meant that the section, equipped with radios, could spread out to cover a wide front, making ambushing them difficult (and a startled horse would simply burst out of an ambush).

Paraphrasing commanding officer Lieutenant-Colonel Mick McKenna, vehicle-drawn horseboxes allowed the Grey's to be quickly inserted into areas, to follow up on tracks, and to pursue retreating groups. An American observer remarked that the unit was used "on border control and sweeps that resulted in successful contact situations for the Selous Scouts."[53] The speed of the horse allowed running men to be overtaken. Like the Special Air Service and Selous Scouts, the Grey's suffered a degree of notoriety during the war but this did not stop them from continuing after Zimbabwe's independence as a mounted infantry unit for border control and antipoaching operations.[54] The Grey's Scouts finally served under Lieutenant-Colonel Chris J. Pearce.

The Combined Operations headquarters regarded the Grey's Scouts in the same way it did the Special Air Service, Selous Scouts, Fire Forces, and the border cordon which was under its direct control. There can be some question as to this status, as the standards of the Grey's were not comparable to either the more exclusive Special Air Service or Selous Scouts. Still, the unit was a special response to a specific situation and often operated where the other special forces were not as successful. Instead of technology, biology was used to provide mobility. If they could not run the terrorist down with personnel and helicopters, then adding horses to the mixture would solve the problem over men on foot in broken terrain. Thus was the value of a mounted infantry unit that was employed throughout the country to augment more conventional counterguerrilla forces spread thin over "MMBA" (miles and miles of bloody Africa).[55]

Other Initiatives

Several topics mentioned in passing deserve more coverage than given here, including mine- and ambush-proof vehicles, border minefield and obstacles, the consolidated and protected village effort, the need for protection forces by African and European civilians, and psychological operations. Mine- and ambush-protected vehicles (MAPVs, now mine-resistant, ambush-protected) were developed to counter the effective use of landmines by the guerrillas. These increased from 20 incidents (mines detonated or detected) in 1973 to 2,089 incidents in 1979. It was observed that this had its initial impact on the police and farming community that often had to travel by road in isolation from the security forces and were most vulnerable on these rural routes. This saw technical responses that spawned a minor industry in Rhodesia and South Africa where automotive manufacturing took place.[56]

"Going fast won't miss the blast"

According to RAND, "mine-protected and mine-resistant vehicles were among the most successful countermeasures of the war." In 1972, the guerrillas began a road interdiction effort using landmines. This was a factor throughout southern African due to the availability of Communist Bloc material, notably the TM46 anti-tank mine. The dependence on dirt, gravel, or tar-covered roads made this easy to accomplish without the need for skilled personnel in ambush. The Portuguese, South Africans, and Rhodesians used various responses to counter this threat. This ranged from remaining off the roads, to using physical counter-measures, and developing technological responses. Expedients were first made that included searching for mines by foot patrols, using sandbags and conveyor-belt material to "harden" vehicles, and avoiding the roads if air transport was available. "Some of the earlier attempts at mine protection look crude," noted an army observer about this early period. There were obvious problems with increased weight and cost: "The attention and effort directed at mine and ambush protection has not only been a necessity, but the results have been a resounding success." The Rhodesians could not afford the foreign exchange to purchase available South African products and had to resort to local purpose-built vehicles as well as continued improvisation, so that: "Apart from the marriage of civilian engineering techniques and military planning, the vehicles represent a totally local manufacture both in material and assembly."

The desire for a self-contained technical response came from police and Internal Affairs personnel who traveled throughout the rural areas on their own in long-wheel-base Land Rovers. The South Africans were working along the same lines on using Ford F250 trucks. The results were the Camel, Hyena, and Rhino. This effort expanded to include modifying Toyota Land Cruisers and International one-ton trucks. Army developments followed that resulted in Bedford-, Datsun-, and Nissan-based engines and chassis, resulting in the Leopard, Cougar, Puma, and Crocodile vehicles. Full seat harnesses, encapsulated cabs, roll bars, V-shaped hulls, monocoque components, and angled armor reduced casualties and allowed continued road movement despite guerrilla efforts to hinder traffic.

Experience indicated that "seldom are any injuries sustained in a landmine blast when a combination of three factors exist in a MAP. They are: (a) traveling at the correct speed [18–20 miles per hour] on all road surfaces and under all conditions; (b) all passengers and drivers are properly strapped in with safety belts; and (c) no loose objects left lying on the floor of the vehicles, e.g. mineral bottles, tools, etc." Other expedients included filling tires with water instead of air and using protected convoys for civilians and well as military travel. One result that contributed to the effort was a mobile mine detector, the Pookie. Civilian engineer Ernest Konschel deserves the credit for this unique vehicle that allowed roads to be checked and cleared at speed, up to 50mph (80km/h). Electronics allowed the detection of metal mines, and non-metallic devices were found by locating the hollow in the road surface. [57]

Locally Produced Mine- and Ambush-protected (MAP) Vehicles in service, c. 1979

- MAP Troop Carrying Vehicle (x 4-wheel axles)
- MAP Troop Carrying Vehicle (x 6-wheel axles)
- MAP Troop Carrying Vehicle with MAG turret
- MAP Weapons Carrier (81mm Mortar, 106mm Recoilless Rifle)
- MAP Cargo Carrier
- MAP Towing Unit and articulated trailers
- MAP Wrecker

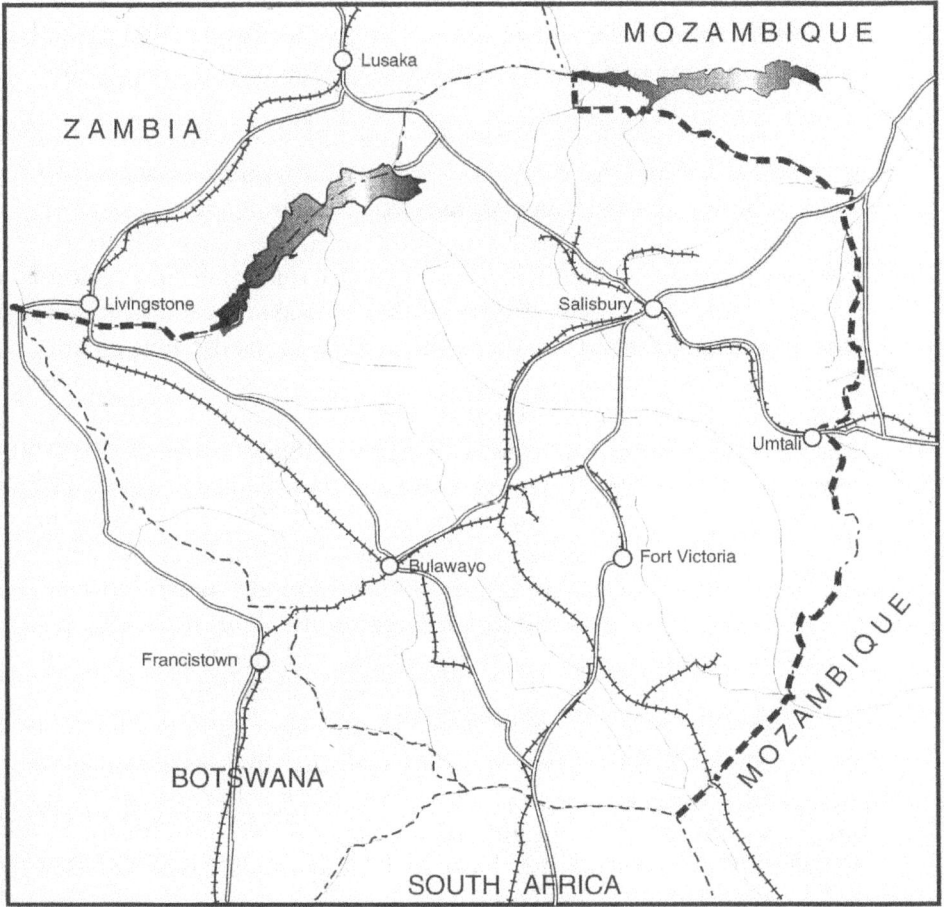

Legend

⌒‖‖‖‖⌒ = railway lines

⌒⌒⌒ = roads

= rivers

Cordon Sanitaire (CorSan -----), c. 1979

The Cordon Sanitaire (CorSan) began in the northeast, where border minefields and barriers were constructed by army engineers, and were later expanded to other areas with threatened borders.[58] While not covered by forces in its entirety, national service and territorial independent companies, artillery, and armored cars defended key locations. According to Wing Commander Briscoe:

> Cordons Sanitaire were used in Algeria, Malaya, and Kenya in conjunction with proscribed areas where anything that moved was deemed a target. In Rhodesia too, the Mozambique border became a cordon, unfortunately though it did not achieve its purpose as infiltrating guerrillas could transit through it in a comparatively short period of time and disregarded casualties suffered in breaching it. A far more effective strategy is to channel the guerrillas into predetermined killing grounds.[59]

This was intended to isolate the guerrilla on security force terms as opposed to reacting to incidents and fleeting contacts. These were in the tribal trust lands or abandoned agricultural areas and with judicious movement of conventional security forces around these areas and unconventional infiltration in them, it produced a "target rich" environment for the airborne reaction forces.[60]

Walls commented on the population and resources effort that began in 1973:

> This protected village scheme is really part of the civil administrative effort to defeat terrorism. I think that in the security forces we probably did a lot to extol the advantages, such as they are, from the protected village scheme, and we may have, to a certain extent, pushed this idea along. Some of the Internal Affairs chaps we deal with say security forces were asking for it to be pushed along too fast. But what we were trying to do was separate the law-abiding citizens, who need protection and who have a desire to carry on a normal way of life, from the terrorists. ... So by introducing the protected village scheme we were merely separating the terrorists from the local population.[61]

Consolidated (centralized housing without security) and protected villages (centralized housing with security) were intended to control populations within the areas where subversion or terrorism was taking place.[62] This required the local people to be concentrated in one location in order to provide security and services under direct supervision of the Department of Internal Affairs, but this needed more resources than were provided. Walls continued:

> What I can say most emphatically is that the protected village scheme has worked to a marked degree. In the areas where you have protected villages you still get the odd terrorist and we still have to look after those areas, but we know for a fact that we've been pretty successful in cutting off the terrorist from the locals. The consolidated villages are, of course, not as effective a measure as protected villages, but nevertheless better than nothing. They are also the first step toward a protected village, which is a good step, and we have started introducing them already.[63]

One defect with the consolidated and protected village program was the lack of protective forces in the form of local militias needed for self-defense. Commercial farming in rural areas had received similar considerations as part of the BSAP use

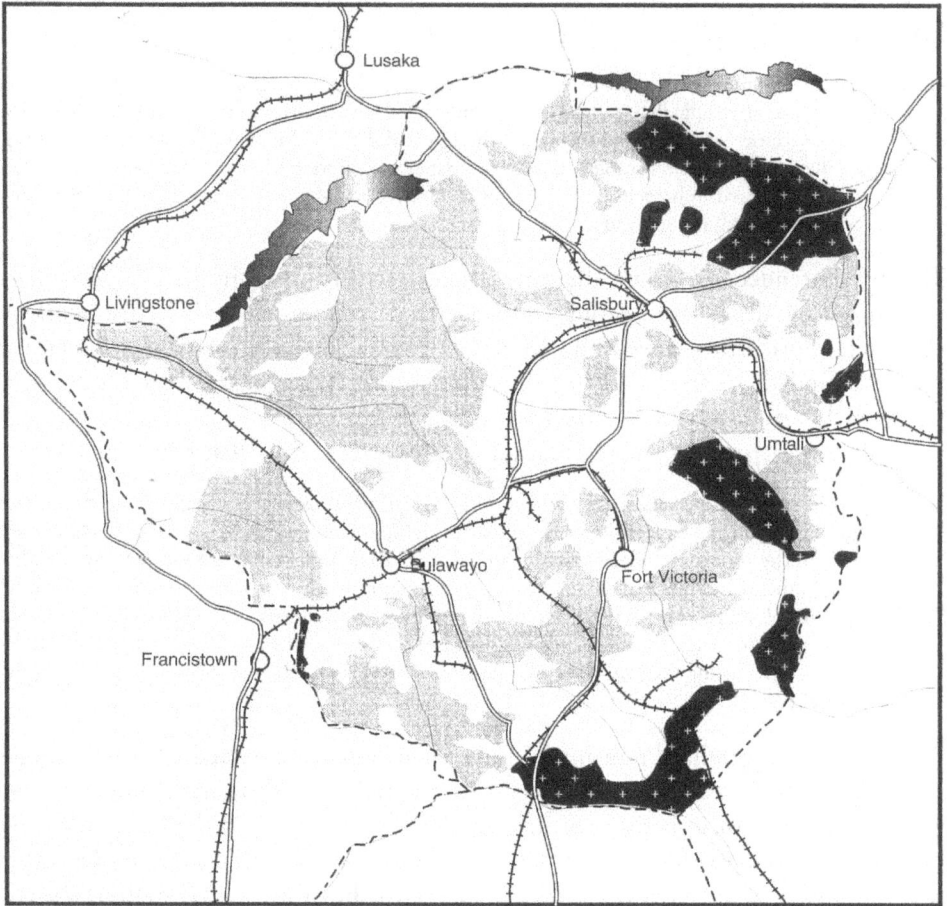

Legend

꜀꜀꜀꜀꜀ = railway lines

〜〜〜 = roads

= rivers

■ = Areas where the local population had been concentrated in PVs.

▨ = Tribal Trust Land where the PV programme was not implemented.

Existing or planned protected and consolidated villages (PVs & CVs), c. 1979 of a variety of reserve protection schemes involving static or mobile security and for population and resources control. From 1975, variations were met with security from Internal Affairs or the military-controlled Guard Force, Rhodesian Defense Regiment, and Security Force Auxiliaries to support the settlements and the civil administration. Again, they were limited by available resources and a prejudice against "arming the natives."[64]

While there was the recognition of the needs for a "hearts and minds " approach, other voices argued for harshness. Minister of Defense and Foreign Affairs P. K. van der Byl warned in July 1976:

> If villages harbor terrorists and terrorists are found running about in villages, naturally they will be bombed and destroyed in any manner which the commander on the spot considers to be desirable in the suitable prosecution of a successful campaign. ... Where the civilian population involves itself with terrorism then somebody is bound to get hurt and one can have little sympathy for those who are mixed up with terrorists when finally they receive the wrath of the security forces.[65]

Psychological operations or action included defining a cause at odds with the opposition, but never seemed to get off the ground further than rewards and punishments.[66] In regards to drawing the line concerning interrogations, searching *kraals*, and so on, Walls felt:

> I think interrogations aren't really my side of the house, but I think that one can say quite definitely that any actions, whether interrogations or shootings, or anything else, have got to be in good faith. Anything that a soldier or security force member does, has got to be in the cause of eliminating terrorism in general. It's got to be completely impartial and just. The chaps are answerable to me for doing anything that does not come within those lines. ... Where it is necessary to take disciplinary action against somebody who has not kept within the bounds that we've laid down, we have taken that disciplinary action. And I'd rather not go further than that, but this is why I don't bother two hoots about the accusations of the Catholic Commission for Justice and Peace [CCJP] and so on, because my conscience is absolutely clear. Where it has been necessary to take disciplinary action, we have taken it.[67]

Responding to Rhodesian CCJP charges, [68] Walls stated:

> I perhaps should make it clear that as far as I am concerned if we're in contact with terrorists and there are people actively helping them during the contact, they are terrorists. The security forces generally, have been absolutely outstanding, incredibly good, in trying to sort out in some of these skirmishes who the terrorists are, the armed terrorists, in order to shoot only at and or capture them. And in many cases, local civilians have been incredibly lucky. They've gotten away from a skirmish when they've been right in the middle of it and this is what annoys me when you get these accusations, from well-meaning people no doubt, but accusations none the less, that we have carried out atrocities. The soldiers have been absolutely magnificent about dealing with the terrorists and not the civilians who happen to get in the way.[69]

By the end of 1976, the Joint Planning Staff had reached a number of conclusions: the need for a joint military headquarters (not what they wanted to hear); a Fire

Force was required for each operational area; Special Branch and Selous Scouts had to coordinate with JOCs and provide timely information; trackers were at a premium and the Selous Scout-run program was too demanding to produce them in numbers; Selous Scouts should balance utilization of pseudo and hunter-killer teams; that "freezing" an area tipped the insurgents to pseudoteam employment; the cordon sanitaire compensated for lack of manpower; external operations up to 20 kilometers were needed to dominate border areas; Selous Scouts would continue to have internal and external tasking; there was added value to targeted leadership kills rather than quicker low-level kills in greater numbers; and concluded that "The military war will be won externally."[70]

Contact Report Analysis

The Rhodesian Intelligence Corps and Army Data Processing Unit produced research reports that analyzed the results of Rhodesian security force actions with the Zimbabwean guerrillas between 1972 and 1979 (the army, police, and air force all used a standardized report form for enemy "contact").[71] While admitting the data was somewhat incomplete, it was felt enough information was available to make some conclusions. These included 1,519 contacts of all types (army, air force, police) distributed with 595 in the area of Operation *Hurricane*, 429 in *Thrasher*, 295 in *Repulse*, 143 in *Tangent*, five in Salisbury, and three in *Splinter*. Off these totals, 428 involved the use of a Fire Force reaction, while another 77 were considered as part of external operations. The breakdown by nationalist affiliation indicated 205 contacts were with ZPRA forces and 1,266 contacts involved ZANLA forces. The casualties incurred were 629 (156 killed, 473 wounded) on the Rhodesian side as opposed to 3,391 (2,892 killed, 499 wounded) on the nationalist side. In addition, 544 guerrillas were captured.[72]

In turn, the contacts were divided into those initiated by the security forces, those initiated by the "communist terrorists," and those which were "spontaneous." The security force modus operandi was seen as consisting of ambushes, follow-ups, observation posts, intelligence lead-in, road runner (radio bugs), air reconnaissance, foot or mounted patrols, single vehicle or convoys, and sweep generated. Guerrilla actions considered were ambushes, landmines, deliberate attack, flight or "bombshell" (scatter in all directions), withdrawal by groups, lying low, foot patrol, or in the course of a robbery or abduction. Subsequent actions were also taken into account in the studies.

As the most winning counterinsurgency technique available, the Fire Force actions received a detailed look from Rhodesian Intelligence Corps data collected between 1974 through 1978, the majority of which came from JOC Hurricane, Thrasher, and Repulse operational areas. Of these, 43 percent were contacts of 100 percent success, 17 percent were contacts of 80 percent success, 23 percent were contacts with less than 20 percent success, and 18 percent were contacts with guerrilla presence that were not successful. A combination of gunship effectiveness, well-organized stops, and effective sweeps were credited with the contact going to the security forces. I would add a superior ratio of troops in contact had an effect as well. There was a minor riff between the RLI and RAR over who had the highest "score," with the RAR in the lead more from remaining on the ground overnight as part of its follow-up.[73] An expanded examination of these actions follows.

Reactive Attack, Air–Ground Task Forces

By mid-conflict, the fighting had changed from that confronted previously by the Operations Coordinating Committee and Joint Planning Staff. Lieutenant-Colonel Brian Robinson summarized the previous status quo: "There were mainly three routine methods of making contact: 1) most successful, intelligence produced by the Selous Scouts by captures or locals, 2) observation post locations manned by Selous Scouts or conventional troops, 3) location of tracks and follow-up by tracker combat teams—this being the most common type of operations."[74] With the enlarging war, a decisive shift from border control to area-oriented counterinsurgency, and external operations, Rhodesian security forces had to come up with ways to meet Prime Minister Ian Smith's demand for "revolutionary thinking" to fight the nationalists flowing into the country.[75]

Revised methods were needed, as expanded by Air Force's Peter Briscoe:

> The main problem facing any commander in a counterinsurgency campaign is very basic. How do you force the guerrilla into confrontation situations (contacts) on your own terms, given the fact that the enemy's tactics and training make him adept at avoiding these situations? He is inherently mobile, albeit mostly on foot, he mixes with the population for concealment and protection, knows the area and will not stand and fight under any circumstances except for those where he has overwhelming numerical or weapons superiority. Army actions alone (ambushes and fleeting contacts) seldom result in the guerrilla suffering significant casualties and follow-up operations on foot using trackers are also of dubious value, as the tracker must, of necessity, move slower than his quarry and stands little chance of catching up with him. Air power used in isolation is similarly ineffective. In order to locate the guerrilla and force him to fight (or surrender), the peculiar attributes of ground and air forces acting in concert are required. Employed in the appropriate manner, they provide the best possible chance of inflicting heavy casualties, and combined they provide a formidable fighting force.[76]

The dynamic use of helicopters and ground forces, including fire support and troop positioning, evolved from tracking follow-ups in the Zambezi valley, the Macombe deployments in Mozambique, and what were known as "hunter-killer" operations. Fire Force drills were added to existing helicopter techniques to include observation post and callout procedures described in the narrative and communications coordination was continually emphasized. Some mentioned the example of the Vietnam War: "The Fire Force was based upon the American Vietnam air cavalry model with more modest assets," according to John Cronin, himself a veteran of

Vietnam. Others, Mark Dawson for one, disputed this, claiming Fire Force was a unique Rhodesian development.

This development brought air and ground efforts together in what was regarded as the most successful, or celebrated, response to guerrilla intrusion. It was a technical solution more on the side of killing rather than conversion and was a direct product of the JOC Hurricane example, where ground forces and air assets were brought together for quick response. While air–ground cooperation is inherent in modern forces, conventional or unconventional, certain elements enhanced its application in this case and allowed a steep learning curve to be reached. When the JOC Hurricane (under a brigadier and wing commander or group captain) was strengthened in mid-1973 and moved to Bindura, it left sub-JOCs (under lieutenant-colonels and squadron leaders) at the forward airfields at Centenary and Mount Darwin. The infantry commandos and companies of the Rhodesian Light Infantry (RLI) and Rhodesian African Rifle (RAR) regular battalions and the helicopters of 7 Squadron remained at these locations. While initially helicopters ferried about whatever troops were on hand, it became apparent that a more dedicated system was needed.[77] The 50 or 60 men available at any one time were put on standby, with a third on immediate call, a third on 30-minute call, and the remainder available as needed for a quick reaction force.[78] Named Fire Force in January 1974, its first recorded use was in February when a terrorist group was eliminated using airborne fire support and infantry alone.[79]

Selous Scouts' Ron Reid-Daly recognized that: "The Fire Force enabled the Rhodesian security forces to bring the same characteristics as the tank: firepower, mobility, and shock action—to their bush battlefield ... The advent of Fire Forces allowed the security forces to neutralize to a large degree the advantage that the insurgent normally has."[80] According to Robinson, who was later with Combined Operations:

> A Fire Force produces instant stop lines to cut off the enemy line of flight. In my humble opinion special forces should be deployed in four-man call signs. They should move only by night and dominate the high ground in [observation post] positions and carry out silent hunting. Any sightings should result in a Fire Force deployment initially using half-mile sticks in a box around the enemy position. Thereafter gunships of every description. The gaps in the para sticks are then filled by [helicopter] troops who rope in. Unless there are jagged rocks, paratroops can be dropped anywhere by day or night. Conventional [drop zone] requirements went out the back door 20 years ago. The troops wear day-glo colored inserts in jungle hats which are reversed so that the airborne commander can see where all the sticks are positioned. Steel helmets remain with the parachutes. Special forces then disperse and start again. ... The other method of closing with the enemy is by using human tracking skills. Once again a Fire Force should be deployed when the tracks start getting hot.[81]

A 4 Squadron pilot summarized:

> There were three distinct types of Fire Force operations: preemptive strikes, Fire Force callout, and rapid-reaction Fire Force. Preemptive strikes were mounted usually as a result

of intelligence gained from captured terrorists or collaborators, SAS reconnaissance teams, or aerial reconnaissance by … Canberras or Hunters; these were usually well planned well in advance and normally initiated at first light. A request for Fire Force assistance generally came from ground troops in a clandestine [observation post]; there would be little time to plan the operation, normally no more than 30 minutes from call to airborne. A rapid-reaction mission would be mounted if ground forces or civilians were under attack, and the Fire Force would brief over the radio while en route.[82]

J. R. T. Wood broke this development into three phases from 1974 to 1976, 1977 to 1979, and into 1979. Phase one in the evolution of the technique, was when:

> The tasks of the observation post were to spot the enemy, take a bearing, call Fire Force and give the exact grid reference and description of the target, a suggested route for contour flying to mask Fire Force from the enemy, numbers of insurgents, what clothes they are wearing, likely escape routes, etc. Once the Fire Force was airborne, the observation post would brief the commander again, updating his information so that he could make any necessary adjustments to his plan. As Fire Force approached, the observation post would "talk" the K-Car gunship over the target so that it could be marked. Thereafter, the observation post would continue to observe and draw the Fire Force commander's attention to enemy movements and the like.[83]

Other ingredients followed as experience was gained. Between February and November 1974, the air force put more effective helicopter gunships into service. These now mounted a 20mm cannon, had a bench and communications for a ground commander, fitted with armor plating, rope descent arms, low radiation paint, and heat-dispersing shrouds.[84] Leading the Fire Force in, the K-Car would fly directly over the target, mark it with white smoke, and then pull up to orbit at 800 feet and to command the air and ground attack. As soon as the enemy position or the enemy themselves could be seen, the K-Car would open fire with the potent 20mm cannon. The Matra MG 151 20mm cannon was calibrated to fire at 800 feet from an aircraft traveling at 65 knots. Because each 20mm round cost Rh$35 (roughly US$50), the gunners restricted themselves to bursts of three shells. The weight of the ammunition carried was also a factor because it affected the endurance of the aircraft. The gunners had trays of 100 or 200 shells. Waiting to be used, a light attack aircraft orbited the contact at 1,500 to 2,000 feet. To keep the heads of the enemy down, while the stops and sweep line were put into position, the Lynx put in a rocket and Frantan (napalm) attack. It could restrike the target with its twin .303 guns, mounted on the top wing.

The G-Car troop carriers, led by G One carrying Stop One, would orbit the target in a wide left-hand circle, waiting for the K-Car to order them to put their stops down. This was a somewhat cumbersome procedure. The time wasted was used by the enemy to escape and aircrews had to remember to look outside the orbit for signs of fleeing men. Pilots had to remember to widen the orbits constantly as the enemy were able to move at a rate of 500 meters every minute. As soon as they could, the insurgents "bombshelled" to regroup at a prearranged rendezvous. They knew that if they stood and fought, they would be annihilated. The purpose of the guerrilla was to strike and run, to disrupt and to survive, so that they could fulfill their political function of influencing the tribesmen.

G-Cars would make dummy drops to confuse the enemy as to the number of stops being placed in cut-off positions. G-Car One, having dropped its stop group, would depart to pick up further sticks from the approaching "land tail" (i.e., the remainder of the company, mounted on trucks which would also carry helicopter fuel and ammunition). Reinforcements from the land tail or second wave would be brought to join one of the stops as a sweep line or would be placed to block other avenues of escape.

After dropping off its stop group on an escape route, G Two would fly off to the land tail to bring in reinforcements. Thereafter, the G-Cars would land in a secure place—such as a hilltop—to conserve fuel but still be on hand to move stops or to remove casualties. G-Car Three, having put down its stop group, would orbit low on a flank to spot escaping enemy, to drive them to ground with its .303 or 7.62 machine guns, and to be available to evacuate casualties or to relocate stop groups. The K-Car commander would keep at least one G-Car back in case problems developed with the K-Car and he might have to transfer from it."[85]

In June 1975, the Operations Coordinating Committee published basic Fire Force doctrine for the security forces, calling for the employment of only "well-trained troops" such as the RLI or RAR to ensure success.[86] The committee also believed that in areas where the population had already been subverted and was actively supporting the guerrillas, then scrutiny of the area by covert observation posts by the Selous Scouts was more effective in finding terrorists than other methods, most notably infantry patrolling and air observation (as supported by Rhodesian Intelligence Corps studies).[87] The *COIN* manual defined a Fire Force as the "immediate reaction to a reported terrorist presence by helicopter-mobile troops in conjunction with appropriate air support."[88] This avoided the drawbacks of vehicle-mounted responses by avoiding mines and ambushes and reducing the response-time factor. Contemporary accounts described it as:

> A number of air force aircraft (helicopters and fixed-wing) and personnel who cooperate with a number of army personnel (troops and paratroops). They form a quick reaction team, completely mobile and self-contained, who are able to provide fire power or assistance immediately on request. ... The advantage of a Fire Force is that the entire operation can be packed up and moved to a new base within 24 hours.[89]

In July 1975, in response to demands for improving ripostes to guerrilla incursions, the army proposed using paratroops and transport aircraft to augment helicopter forces, and parachute training of regular infantry units began in August 1975 (while military parachuting had been available, to this point it was only used by special forces resulting in the SAS serving in a Fire Force role). At the time, it was envisioned that the dropping of "troops by parachute will be very rare, being used only when normal infantry cannot be deployed by helicopter."[90]

In January/February 1976, the air force acquired Lynx aircraft to replace aging Provosts and Trojans as a more capable multi-mission light attack airplane to support Fire Force deployments. Helicopter and parachute troops were teamed up and all the major components associated with the fully developed Fire Force were then in place.[91] The first integrated parachute support of a Fire Force was documented in April 1976 and this function was accelerated by the unexpected diplomatic withdrawal of South African helicopters and crews in August 1976.[92]

Originally, Fire Forces were controlled by the various brigade chiefs. Operation *Hurricane* had provided a prototype but these methods were more symptomatic of strategic and even operational decline leading to the ultimate frustration of the military struggle. Combined Operations and General Walls had to take charge of the fighting in 1977 for a coordinated military effort rather than the previous independent actions by the brigade commanders in their own areas. This left the joint operations commanders with national servicemen, reservists, protection forces, and police in a defensive role to consolidate the "frozen" areas the various special and reaction forces had worked over. The joint operations commands had to respond to larger threats outside their immediate control. Combined Operations now was in control of the special forces: Selous Scouts, Special Air Service, Grey's Scouts, and the Fire Forces (in effect the RLI, RAR) when employed. The key military components that emerged were the internal air–ground task forces (Fire Forces), cordon sanitaire, and external cross-border raids. These were critical to tactical success, but, despite notable efforts, they were again initiatives more of necessity rather than skill.

By 1977, jet aircraft were being used in support of Fire Force, including Canberras, with improved and heavier anti-personnel weapons. Also in this year, a variation on the theme used Grey's Scouts in a Fire Force role, integrating horse mobility, air reconnaissance, and fire support. This witnessed, according to Wood, the second phase of development:

> The tasks of the observation post on the hilltop remained the same. He was to report any sighting and to guide Fire Force onto target. The Fire Forces preferred to fly in behind him if possible in order to see the target from his angle so that no time was wasted. K-Car marks the target then pulls up to 800 feet to command the air and ground maneuver, and to put down 20mm fire. Once the attack began, the insurgents "bombshell."
>
> G-Car One, having put down its stop group on a preselected potential escape route, orbits low on a flank to spot escaping enemy, to drive them to ground with its .303 or 7.62 machine guns, and to be available to evacuate casualties. After dropping off its stop group on a preselected potential escape route, G Two flies off to the "land tail" to bring in reinforcements. G-Cars Three and Four, having dropped their stop groups, depart to pick up further sticks from the approaching "land tail."
>
> A further duty of the standby G-Car could be to examine the dropping zone, transmit the precise QNH altitude reading of the drop zone to the Dakota so that it could set its altimeter for a precise above ground reading. When the K-Car called for paratroops, the G-Car would talk the Dakota in. The Dakota would be loitering at an interim point four minutes' flying time away, ready to react but out of earshot.

At the command of the Fire Force commander and talked on to the dropping zone by the K-Car or a G-Car pilot, the DC-3 "Para-Dak" begins its run in at 90 knots, watching the wind drift so that its 16 paratroops would land in the drop zone, close together, ready to form a sweep line. The dropping height was between 600 and 300 feet, too low to use the reserve parachute. As the last man left the door, the first man's feet would touch the ground.[93]

General Walls asserted "operational command" while passing "operational control" to their respective joint commanders to support the various JOCs in *Hurricane, Thrasher, Repulse, Tangent,* and *Grapple.* In January 1978, these air–ground units were allocated and Fire Forces established at Mtoko (Fire Force A), Buhera (Fire Force B), and Shabani (Fire Force C). This was to meet the threat from some 4,800 terrorists estimated in Rhodesia with more to come, "both in numbers of CTs [communist terrorists] and in the area affected." This trend was expected to continue during the rainy season "whilst the foliage cover remains good."[94]

By early 1978, there was some concern that the productive "kill" ratio was being reversed, leading to a further spate of self-analysis. Brigadier Herbert Barnard, Director General of Operations, Combined Operations, brought representatives from all services together to King George VI Barracks that May to review the state of the art and to benefit from Rhodesian Intelligence Corps operational analysis.[95] Combined Operations headquarters analyzed the results from Fire Force and concluded it was the most effective means of dealing with terrorists, defined as killing the enemy without incurring friendly losses. Two K-Cars became the norm with backup for the airborne leadership. In 1978 a .303-caliber quad-gun with improved optical sights was used as a gunship supplement. Even though the .303 provided more effective target coverage, the 20mm gunship was still preferred. Expanded Fire Force elements were eventually assigned each operational area, known as Fire Forces A, B, C, D, E, and F including those stood up by the South African Defense Force in active support of the Muzorewa government (later designated Z, Y, X, W, etc.).[96]

While this addressed most contacts, later groups of 100 or more guerrillas made it impractical to use a Fire Force alone. In these cases combined Fire Forces could be used, "however, on many occasions this was just not possible due to distance and urgency," but more likely a heavy air strike by Hunters and Canberras would be called for, using guns, rockets, fragmentation, and high-explosive bombing directed by an airborne forward air controller. If Fire Force was added to this mix it became a "free for all" with a high risk of air-to-air collision (despite the risk, only one collision actually occurred).[97] A Combined Operations "Jumbo" Fire Force was formed by bringing two or more Fire Forces together for a specified area, truly becoming the regime's "killing machine." Operating for six months between March and October 1979 (although stood down in August and September because of the demands of external operations), it killed, wounded, or captured some 1,005 enemy.[98] This required Selous Scout saturation of the designated area with observation posts, but by then resources were not available for subsequent consolidation of the civilian population and the guerrillas returned.

This was the third and final phase of development according to Wood:

> The Jumbo Fire Force comprised the aircraft of two Fire Forces. Thus the Jumbo would have two K-Cars, six to eight G-Cars, a Lynx and a Dakota. If the target warranted it, there might be a pair of Hunter ground attack fighters in support.[99] In this case, seven minutes out from the target, K-Car One, followed by K-Car Two, would pull away from the formation of helicopters. Once over the target, neither K-Car would pull up, as before, but would open fire and then might call in an air strike to stun the enemy further. Talked in by K-Car One, the Hunters would bomb the smoke of the marking grenade. Supporting Hunters could be used at the outset to attack the target with the devastating blast and shrapnel of Golf bombs. K-Car One would then climb to direct the ground operation while K-Car Two roamed over the area at treetop height, shooting at will (K-Car Two, with Alpha Fit Dalmatian with four .303 machine guns, acted purely as a gunship). The high number of G-Cars allowed the quick and effective sealing off of the target area.[100]

An RLI trooper provided an overview of the tactic that resonates with experience:

> The initial Fire Force contact strategy is primarily determined by the terrain and viable escape routes. ... Fire Force maintains the initial employment of surprise and shock and induces confusion and suppresses the immediate movement of terrorists by use of ... air support during the helicopters' arrival at the contact area to drop the blocking and sweeping sticks. The low and fast helicopter approach suppresses rotor blade noise until it is too late for the terrorists to effectively react. ... Fire Force maintains the initial employment of surprise and shock, induces confusion and suppresses the immediate movement of terrorists. ... By encirclement with helicopters, confusion sets in with enemy as to what escape route is viable ... an enemy rapidly moving away from the initial contact area can be pursued and re-engaged by the same ground forces again and again until killed or captured. Exhaustion and mental fatigue soon overtakes even the most highly mobile enemy and destroys their willingness to continue to flee or fight. ... Fire Force becomes a terror weapon against the terrorist, psychologically demoralizing the very person or group that is attempting to be the terrorist. They quickly lose their momentum by being on the defensive. ... Simplicity makes Fire Force work. Surround, contain and aggressively engage. Pursue and re-engage relentlessly.[101]

CHAPTER SIX

The Killing Machine

With evolution and growth by war's end, Prime Minister Ian Smith recalled: "Fire Force deployments, once limited to perhaps twice a week against five-strong guerrilla groups, increase to three to five a day against groups of 50, 60 or more."[1] With this, some idea of operations will be detailed as one of the bush war's distinctive ordeals. What follows is a composite view of the experience, in effect an oral history of Fire Force operations, taken from selected first-hand accounts.[2]

Fire Forces were stationed at any forward airfield with at least a 1,000-meter runway in an operational area located near the JOC and Selous Scout fort. The "op" area also had army sub-JOCs, BSAP stations, Internal Affairs district offices, and other elements of the government engaged in counterinsurgency operations.[3] With Rhodesian Air Force detachments, both the Rhodesian Light Infantry and Rhodesian African Rifles were assigned Fire Force duties in six-week spells. Journalist Nick Downie observed that Rhodesia's best troops manned these reaction forces, generally with two commandos from the RLI and two companies from the RAR at any one time.[4] A basic Fire Force consisted of a reinforced rifle company of 120 men divided into a command element, helicopter "stop" groups, parachute "sweep" group, and a "reinforcement" group to be moved by either helicopter or truck.[5] The air force component was made up of helicopter, light attack, and transport aircraft with minimal flight and ground crews. Included were command and control gunships (K-Cars) and three or four transports (G-Cars). The gunship air crew and ground commander wore "turtle shell" one-piece body armor that was heavy (8 kilograms) and restricted movement. The seats were later armored to protect from bottom and side hits. The ground commander had a leather flight helmet headset and control switch (push-to-talk, intercommunication, and hot-mike) for ground communications while the pilot had the air nets. The pilot flew on the right-hand side of the K-Car, with the aircraft gunner immediately behind him with the flight deck taken up by the 20mm cannon firing out the left-hand side. The ground commander sat on the left next to the pilot on a jump seat looking out the left-hand side of the helicopter. This meant that gunships flew a left-hand turn as opposed to the natural right-hand pull desired by the pilots (it was mentioned that helicopters flew counterclockwise and fixed-wing aircraft flew clockwise concentric orbits.)

Notional Fire Force Communications

While airborne, aircraft formation numbers and call signs were used. Once landed, units reverted to normal unit call signs. Voice call signs were used with the prefix of the Fire Force alphabetical designator, i.e., Fire Force A would use "Stop Alpha One" or "G-Car Alpha One." For effective control purposes the nets were not cluttered with excess traffic.

Communications networks included:

Command, three voice nets at base:
ComOps, JOC, RLI or RAR headquarters (HF)
the commando tactical net (VHF)
air force headquarters (HF), with telephone and teleprinter backup where available.

Air (UHF):
K-Car, G-Cars, Dakota, Lynx; Lynx, fighter, bombers.

Ground (VHF):
Ground commander in K-Car, troop commanders, stick commanders (primary radio and spare) in G-Cars, Dakota, land tail, forward operating base.

The G-Cars carried a pilot, technician-air gunner, and a four-man infantry stick (the so-called stop group). As mentioned, while the Alouette could administratively hold six passengers, this had dropped to five with the need of an air gunner, and then to only four with fully loaded troops and the demands of practical flight time. Each stick had a junior leader carrying an A63 (later A76) radio and medical pack, a machine gunner with an MAG58, and two riflemen armed with FN automatic rifles and spare ammunition. On board aircraft, stick leaders had headsets available to listen to air radio discussions and carried their own tactical radios on the ground frequency for immediate use on landing. Standardized seating had the stick leader and one rifleman in the left front facing to the tail alongside the pilot. The MAG gunner and the other rifleman sat in the right rear facing forward allowing them to cover the side of the aircraft opposite the helicopter technician's gun. (This configuration was to change in 1974—the stick leader switching from the front to center back.) In addition to standard trooping drills, procedures were refined to move casualties, machine gun, and mortar teams.

For example, an RLI commando or RAR company commander (usually a major) controlled Fire Force ground elements from the air through troop or platoon leaders on the ground with the stops or sticks. These compact, self-contained, units with greater than normal firepower (a light machine gun with every fourth trooper) and helicopter gun support were an optimum structure as opposed to earlier infantry section or even platoon deployments. The *COIN* manual felt that 10 sticks (40 men) was optimum, but no less than four sticks (16 men), and helicopter backing; a second wave was desirable "where possible" along with fixed-wing air support. The standby or second wave of the Fire Force under the unit deputy or quartermaster, moved by vehicles as the "land tail" carrying backup sticks, fuel, ammunition, and medical supplies. If needed, helicopters could ferry them into the contact as well.[6]

The exact configuration was subject to study and debate and could vary widely in practice due to circumstance.[7] Aircraft and troop arrangements changed and much attention was paid to strength ratios as a factor of success in combinations of troops and aircraft. Rhodesian Intelligence Corps studies found that a Fire Force of three to four G-Cars, a K-Car, and Lynx was most successful against groups of terrorists of 10 to 11 or less. A pilot with 4 Squadron ventured the opinion: "On Fire Force missions the Lynx would usually operate with up to three 'K-Cars' … and as many 'G-Cars' … or Cheetahs … that could be gathered together."[8] Four G-Cars, a K-Car, Lynx, and Dakota were best able to handle groups of 12 to 15 terrorists.[9] Correspondent Thomas Arbuckle added that even with being airborne in eight minutes, and a maximum of 75 minutes' flying time, the most lucrative Fire Force situations were within 15 minutes of flying distance from the forward airfield, thus giving the guerrillas a radius to stay clear of.[10]

According to Pat Lawless, with a specific example by Support Company, 1RAR:

> The plan was a fairly standard Fire Force deployment. The officer commanding would lead from K-Car One, followed by K-Car Two, and four G-Cars each containing a four-man stop group. I was to command the first wave of stop groups. If necessary, the G-Cars would return with a second wave commanded by Lieutenant M, while it was Lieutenant R's turn to command the paratroopers who were held in reserve at Mtoko until called forward by our Lynx light observation/ground attack aircraft if needed. We had to keep a reserve in case any other operational emergency developed elsewhere in the "Op" *Hurricane* [area].
>
> The company sergeant major, Warrant Officer II T, would lead the land tail of six Rodef 7.5 troop-carrying vehicles, each containing three four-man stop groups; and a number of Rodef 4.5s carrying Avtur and 20mm ammunition for the K-Cars. We also had a 106mm recoilless rifle and some 60mm mortars "just in case."[11]

Arriving at Mtoko with 3 Commando, 1RLI, Color Sergeant John Coleman described their experience: "Because of the constant threat of callouts, the commando sergeant-major [CSM] wasted no time organizing our commando into two waves of heliborne stop groups and a complement of 16 parachutists to act as the sweep line on the ground." Noted Coleman, "A stop group is a four-man team or stick, generally commanded by a lance-corporal or a corporal which is inserted by helicopter on previously determined escape routes. A sweep line is an extended line formation which moves through the contact area, clearing it of terrorists either by shooting them or driving them into the stop groups."[12]

This was further expanded upon by Support Commando, RLI Trooper Anthony Rogers:

Each stick/stop group was led by a stick leader/radioman who was responsible for an A76 set, codes, maps, mini-binos, compass and a pencil flare. He and two troopers would be armed with 7.62mm FN rifles, for which they carried a minimum of four [generally six to eight] magazines apiece. The fourth trooper, a gunner, was equipped with a 7.62mm MAG and a least 300–350 rounds of link. Extra ammunition for the gun was distributed among the stick [150 rounds]. We carried our own choice of grenades. These were invariably a mix of [high-explosive] hand and rifle grenades, [white phosphorus] and colored smoke—the latter used for calling in choppers for resupply or casevac. … Some troopers liked to carry a handgun. Para-trained individuals were entitled to draw the issue 9mm Star pistol. A few owned captured weapons. Others—those who could afford them—sported privately purchased pistols and revolvers. … Each stick was equipped with a well-stocked medic's pack. Some of us also wore around our necks a syringe of sosegon or morphine, and most carried an extra saline drip … virtually any combination of suitable clothing and web equipment was permitted in the bush: I had a one-piece camouflage "jump suit." In the event of a callout I could quickly pull it on over boots, shorts and T-shirt that I usually wore on the base.[13]

While not used in the early days, later a 3 Squadron Dakota (Para-Dak) added a further dimension with paratroops dropped for rapid augmentation, multiplying from 16 to 40 troops total (or from four to 10 sticks) on the ground. The improved speed and number of groups available gave a decisive edge against guerrilla aggregates. This was as much from necessity as practicality, with the withdrawal of South African helicopter support and the subsequent lack of helicopter lift capability.[14] With the advent of the SA-7 threat and loss of lift due to the weight of countermeasures in the form of paint and exhaust shrouds, the numbers were reduced from an administrative 24 to an operational 16 parachutists (four sticks). Robinson, thought it better to "Consider the Dak troops as stop lines or sweep lines as opposed to sticks."[15] Like the land tail, the Dakota also carried additional fuel and supplies for air delivery. After dropping troops, the same aircraft could also deliver follow-up ammunition and weapons (60mm and 81mm mortars, bunker bombs and breaching explosives, 3.5-inch or RPG rocket launchers, and landmines).

The Parachute Training School recommended a parachute stick sequence of rifleman (with FN and normal ammunition), stick commander (A76 radio, whistle, instant light grenade, with FN and normal ammunition), machine-gunner (with MAG and 200 rounds of ammunition), and rifleman (with 200 rounds of ammunition for the MAG, FN and normal ammunition).[16] It was also cautioned that they "must carry rations and bedding to cater for follow-ups, ambushes, etc." Each stick had a radio, map, compass and protractor, mirror, mini-flares, and smoke.[17] In addition to the normal scale of weapons and ammunition, Fire Force members carried a pistol and wore full denim shirt, trousers, smock, or jump suit. Boots were preferred to "takkies" or light shoes (parachutists occasionally added gloves, goggles, and helmet).[18] The jumpers carried "skeleton" order without packs and little excess equipment with only one to two days' rations, water, and ammunition. A so-called Fire Force vest was

THE KILLING MACHINE • 119

developed that allowed personal equipment to be arranged and available in one place. The training school noted: "It is strongly recommended that all troops … should be as light as possible, i.e. they should carry minimum equipment. This will facilitate quick [rendezvous] after the drop and, if the terrs are still around, they may be attacked quickly."[19]

Life on Fire Force varied from the routine to the absurd, as is often the case in wartime. Color Sergeant Coleman wrote about the Rhodesian Light Infantry at Mtoko: "We quickly settled into normal camp routines: muster parades, physical training (PT)."[20] Coleman recalled, "a good part of our days were centered around normal bush routine: volleyball, cards, test-firing and retraining. However, we were never able to relax completely because the callout siren was manned from dawn to dusk, ready to send us out."[21] Or from Support Commando, RLI: "Amazing that we stayed at country clubs and golf courses a good share of the time. Everyone wanted us around because the terrs never hit them while we were there. Tough to have to tear yourself away from the swimming pool when the alert horn sounded!"[22]

An air gunner in 7 Squadron woke at first light on a day when:

> Nothing was planned for this morning. … I got up, pulled on a jumper over my bush shirt and wandered out into the cold African morning. I made my way across to my machine and busied myself with the endless minor tasks that kept it in working order, then cleaned the cannon (which I had given a thorough cleaning the previous evening, but once more would not hurt) and did a quick check of the equipment. I then wandered back to rouse the rest of the sleeping crews.[23]

Adding:

> I started my preflight ritual, checking that the oil reservoirs were full, the panels secure and that there was plenty of ammo in the bin. I made sure that there were flak jackets for myself and the pilot, and that my survival jerkin and weapon were ready in the event of a forced landing. Finally I began the tedious business of cleaning the dew off the windscreen.[24]

A 1RAR stick leader recounted:

> At 0400 hours the sentry woke me up from inside my [basha]. I got up and rolled up my sleeping bag and fastened it to my webbing. I then took my towel and washed my face with cold water before taking my rucksack and kit bag to the stores truck for safekeeping. It was still dark but it was one of those nights when the moon decides to set before the sun comes up and as a result it was still hanging up there in the western sky. So by the light of the moon I checked my area and satisfied myself that the [company sergeant-major] would have nothing to discuss with me when I came back—you see he does not normally like to see bits and papers lying around. By the time I finished checking my section area the east was red, the time was 0445 and I took my mug and went to the kitchen. The cook was in a good mood despite the early hour and I got a full mug of tea. The whole platoon was there in the kitchen this morning and they were talking in low tones, joking and laughing quietly. We had been briefed the previous evening and everyone knew what he was going to be doing today.[25]

From Support Company, 1RAR's Lawless continued:

> We were based at a pleasant, relatively modern forward airfield at Mtoko, which provided a secure base for the Fire Force and resident Selous Scouts/British South Africa Police Special Branch (SB) detachment. ... The first few weeks of the tour went well. We had several very successful engagements, then all went quiet. The Selous Scouts, deployed in covert observation posts, and often operating as "pseudo terrorists," suddenly found their intelligence had dried up. This situation persisted for about a week, interrupted by the occasional "lemon" [false alarm or abortive operation] which increased the sense of frustration amongst all members of the Fire Force. ... One night, the officer commanding got his platoon commanders together over a few beers to see if we could do something positive about the situation.[26]

Subjective accounts of the Fire Force mission profile and experience follow using the breakdown the Combined Operations had for after-action evaluations.

Observation Posts

The first problem was for the security forces to "locate the guerrilla on your own terms."[27] Briscoe concluded what made the Fire Force successful was that it was a "reaction to security force generated incidents."[28] Thus, "Fire Force operations require the prior clandestine deployment of observation posts with good communications to the operational [headquarters] where the troops and helicopters are located."[29] Lawless felt, "The role became more aggressive and changed from reacting to incidents to hunting out and killing terrorists."[30] This was with a three-phased approach: identifying through the various intelligence agencies the different areas into which guerrillas would be expected to move, receive support from the population for food or assistance, or in establishing bases; the insertion of regular or reserve security force units to establish observation of these areas (normally four men); and the reaction of Fire Force units to observations reports.[31]

The Selous Scouts were best at this covert ingress and were credited by Combined Operations Headquarters with involvement in some 68 percent of the enemy killed or captured within Rhodesia. When Selous Scouts deployed in an area, it was "frozen" to other security force actions, with the army, police, and Internal Affairs being restricted to roads and stations although air reconnaissance would continue. The Scouts' biggest concern was being mistaken for guerrillas from the air, previous "own goal" incidents having taken place.[32] The guerrillas were channeled at the border along likely avenues of approach in part by the border minefields of the cordon. Continued overt observation and patrolling by regular forces in adjacent areas also ensured guerrilla sections were kept on the move and driven into the "killing grounds" of the tribal areas.[33] Some locations were already known as sites for the enemy: "From past experience, this area looked like Indian Country: plenty of water, covered escape routes down a thickly grassed stream and high, rocky ground protected by clumps of trees,"[34] or "The Wedza [tribal trust land] was ideal ... and

THE KILLING MACHINE • 121

we had many hard contacts in its dense scrub, rocky terrain and numerous caves."[35] Contacts took place in the tribal areas, where the guerrillas were held up near water and food, along streambeds near villages.[36] Terrorists moved into the villages only at night or during the rainy season.

Clandestine observation posts were set up on high ground by African villages and these looked for "feeding patterns," the sight of women carrying bowls and buckets or bringing empty containers back to a village. African Selous Scouts were extremely adept at interpreting signs, even if there appeared to be no visible terrorist activity and, according to Cronin: "If they called, something was there."[37] Lieutenant-Colonel Reid-Daly observed his Scouts only called out Fire Force for an "actual sighting" rather than "behavior" pattern, unless otherwise qualified. He also noted that African Scouts needed consideration for speech disparities and for good judgement from intimate knowledge of the ground: "If one becomes frustrated, harsh speech only serves to confuse [African servicemen] further."[38] The Joint Planning Staff's Lieutenant-Colonel John C. P. McVey cautioned JOC commanders that "opportunities to eliminate terrorists must not be inhibited by inflexibility in the use of Fire Forces where those on the ground may be better positioned to deal, in the light of all circumstances, with the situation," bearing in mind the limited number of assets and the best chance for success.

Fire Forces could be dispatched on intelligence "tips," including a Special Branch scheme that allowed the guerrillas to "liberate" transistor radios from stores in the tribal trust areas that had homing devices installed (Road Runner). When activated, aircraft direction finding systems could obtain a location. This worked well in areas where the terrain was unsuitable for observation posts, such as the arid southeast of the country. In this terrain greater use was made of alternatives such as air reconnaissance, Selous Scout clandestine "hunter-killer" teams, or mounted patrols of Grey's Scouts.[39] But the Rhodesian Intelligence Corps, according to Wood, concluded that Fire Forces called in by competent observation posts still had the greatest success.[40]

Callout Procedures

A brigade JOC would contact the nearest Fire Force to an observation post sighting or in response to intelligence tips, with the Fire Forces coordinating as needed, and the National Joint Operations Center adjudicating any conflicts.[41] The JOC would approve the callout, with the Fire Force and requesting agency having a three-way discussion. "The Fire Force is required to be airborne and moving to the target area within minutes of a report of a terrorist presence being received" stated the *COIN* manual.[42] Journalist Peter Younghusband related, with the Rhodesian African Rifles:

> The alert crackled just after sunup. "Call Sign Three to Acorn. We have six terrorists visual, moving away from us, distance 300 yards." An officer moved to the radio. "Acorn speaks," he

barked. "You are copied. Fire Force is coming. Maintain contact." He touched a button and a mournful bleat howled across the orderly rows of tents. Cursing troopers ran out of canvas shower stalls and latrines, struggling into jungle fatigues and grabbing automatic rifles as they raced for their helicopters. In minutes they were airborne.[43]

Wrote RLI trooper Rogers:

> Approaching a group of wooden huts, the men slowed to a walk and began to disperse. Those carrying para-helmets entered one of the huts, while the rest continued towards several Alouette III helicopters parked in protective enclosures constructed from 44-gallon oil drums packed with earth. ... As [NCOs] hurried away to the briefing's hut opposite the chopper pens, the men relaxed, sitting or standing around as they waited for their "stick" leaders to return from the briefing with a few details scribbled into note books. It was not at all unusual at this stage, for the callout to be cancelled.[44]

Without going to extremes, the more time spent on planning a Fire Force deployment, the better the end result achieved and it was felt "Time spent on good briefings produced the best results."[45] Briefings were standardized with an approved aide-mémoire and all participants using a joint operations room.[46] Initial planning and briefing of participating air force and army units included the location of the sighting, circumstances in which the sighting was made, location, call sign, and radio frequency of friendly forces making the sighting, number of sticks and helicopters needed, possible air support requirements including deception,[47] direction of approach to the contact area, call signs of aircraft, sticks, radio channels, and any authentication procedures used.[48] Pat Lawless noted, the "company commander, in consultation with the senior helicopter pilot, would be making a quick map appreciation. ... A good direction of approach might mean the terrorists might break into a good killing zone."[49] Weather conditions over the target area were critical if different from that at the forward airfield.

Journalist Dick Pitman watched:

> There was less of a briefing, and more of a discussion, in the operations room. There were large-scale [1:250,000] maps, laid on a table, showing fine detail of terrain and surfaces. "If we come up around the back ... we can funnel through those hills." "We'll have a long run that way. How about the west?" "Wouldn't it be better to come up the road? Then we've got all this high ground protecting us"—indicating a feature on the map. I studied the faces, mannerisms. There was drama, certainly, but subtle, more an undercurrent of expectancy. There was an atmosphere of calm competence; of people who knew their jobs, and who did them.[50]

At Mtoko, for example, 1 Commando, RLI, and 3, 4, and 7 Squadron aircrews were briefed by Major Piet V. Farndell along with Selous Scout Captain John Cronin, and helicopter flight leader Lucio Mantovani. Lynx squadron commander Peter Briscoe recalled the briefing:

> "OK guys, [Selous Scouts] Call sign 86 Bravo has got about 20 gooks visual at this grid reference," Farndell pointed to the map and to the callout board. "They seem to be dressed mostly in civvies, but there are a few in rice-flecked cammo." He paused as he went down the list the operations staff had written up. "They're carrying AKs [assault rifles], AKMs [assault rifles], at

least two RPDs [light machine guns], two RPG-7s [rocket-propelled grenades], and a mortar. It's probably safe to assume they're fresh from Mozambique as we're so close to the border, and [Special Branch] have 'int' [intelligence] that quite a few groups have recently left Chimoio.

"Anyway, they're probably full of all the normal propaganda bullshit and we should be able to give them a good coming-home present." Smiles creased the suntanned faces of the troops.

"As we see it on the map, after we make contact, they will only run up or down the re-entrant, so we'll preplan the drop. As the K-Car pulls up I want [helicopters] Yellow One and Two to drop Stops One and Two either side of the re-entrant, here"—he pointed out a spot about 400 meters north of the terrorist position— "and Yellow Three and Four drop Stops Three and Four here," this time pointing to a position 400 yards south of the target.

"We'll hold the paras in reserve for the time being. I'll be in K-One, usual call sign One Nine, and Captain [Richard J.] van Malsen will be in K-Two. If there are any changes we'll let you know en route. We'll be on Channel 23. Any questions?"

"Yes sir," said a young corporal holding up his hand. "When we're down, do you want us to move forward or hold our possy [position]?"

"No, I want you to get into a good ambush position and only move when and if I tell you to. Also, once you're down and settled, put out your day-glo panels so we can see where you are. Any more questions?"

Everyone shook their heads. They'd all gone through this drill many times before.

"OK, Lucio, do your thing," Farndell said, stepping aside.

"Startup taxi and takeoff will be [standard operating procedures]," he said. In fact one of the first things a pilot did when he arrived at a [forward airfield] was to be briefed on [standing operating procedures] to prevent any unnecessary delays during a callout. "I estimate we'll be on target about 28 minutes after takeoff." He turned to me and asked, "Where are you going to hold, sir?"

"I'll be at the big bend in the Ruenya River just west of Elim Mission," I replied. "Call me when you're five minutes away."

"Roger," he acknowledged. Turning to the helicopter pilots, he continued, "Drop per the major's briefing and once you've dropped, go into low orbits and keep your eyes open for 'runners.' If you see gooks drop an orange smoke grenade to mark the target and start firing. Stay in the area for about five minutes or until I tell you to go and refuel. There's fuel at Elim Mission, and after you refuel maintain a listening watch so I can get hold of you. If I run short of fuel, K-Two will take over."

He turned to the Dakota captain, Wing Commander Rob Gaunt. "I want you to hold about three minutes out and I'll call you in if I need you."

Turning to the sky-shout pilot, he said, "Hold three minutes out high above the contact area and I'll let you in once things settle down."

"OK guys, I want radio chatter kept to a minimum, especially if we have a contact. Any questions?" There were none. "Let's go."[51]

According to Rogers:

The men's orders were simple and to the point. First, four-man "stop groups" would be flown in by helicopter. If they could deal with the enemy themselves, all well and good; but if difficulties arose, the paratroopers would be called in. It would be the paras' task to sweep through the bush, acting like beaters at a pheasant shoot, and cause the terrorists to break and run in the direction of the stop groups.[52]

After concurrent briefing, drawing relevant 1:50,000 maps, and putting on equipment, pilots and stick leaders "scrambled" to their respective aircraft. With visual contact and thumbs-up by the pilot of the already turning helicopter, the four-man stick approached from the right front and split to the port and starboard for their seating. The stick leader had an aircraft headset on the air frequency and his own radio on the ground net. Parachute sticks took longer to get ready, involving putting on the parachute over combat equipment, the rifle or machine gun over the shoulder (strapped in down the right side of the body) and muzzle down, with radios slung under the reserve parachute.[53]

Loading was in reverse sequence so that troops would exit the aircraft in the order desired on the ground.[54] "The commander should position himself in the middle of the stick for control purposes; leading from the front did not come into contention," according to Robinson.[55] An RLI color sergeant wrote "Sitting as the first man, starboard stick, gave me the advantage of listening in on the action, as well as landing in the center of the sweep line once we hit the ground."[56] Again, headsets on an extension were provided by the aircrew to the stick leader for the air nets, to be discarded on standing up, in addition to the radios carried for ground communications.

Two or three air force parachute jumping instructors (PJI) or army assistant jumping instructors (APJI) served as jumpmaster in lieu of the normal flight technician. These would be at the jump door or by the forward cabin having contact with the Dakota pilot. Jumpers hooked directly up to overhead cables while sitting down in case of an immediate assault or bail-out from a damaged aircraft. Jump commands and procedures were streamlined with safety checks carried out on board en route to the objective. Each individual jumper checked himself or his fellows. Helicopter and parachute sticks rotated duties, but remained together in stick order over extended periods (bush trips of six to eight weeks) and remained in the same units (two to five years). With multiple callouts in the same day from dirt airstrips, then recovering sticks to a major airfield for equipping and arming immediately for another assault, made this seem a normal procedure and they could concentrate on their actions on the ground rather than the tension of the flight. Individual strengths and weaknesses were known and commanders could interchange, as well as sticks themselves if needed for replacement.[57]

Based on relative air speed, helicopters launched first, followed by light aircraft, and then the parachute transport. Pitman recounted:

> The engine RPM [revolutions per minute] came up, the rotors began to turn, slowly at first, then accelerating into a blur. The helicopters taxied to the runway and lifted off after a short takeoff run—less strain on engines and gearboxes than lifting off vertically with a full load.
>
> After the noise, the silence was scarcely broken by a Lynx; it backtracked, opened the throttles, and took off. Spindly undercarriage legs wavered, hesitated, and finally disappeared into the fuselage.
>
> Lastly, a Dakota, doors closed, engines running. The engine note altered slightly as the pilot checked his magnetos. He too, backtracked. The Dakota rolled, slowly at first. Then the tail lifted, the machine gained airspeed, and the noise became deafening as it roared past at full throttle; at the side of the runway, we were buffeted, hard, by the tip vortices. The noise fell away, abruptly; the Dakota lifted off and was soon out of sight.[58]

Move of Fire Force to Area of Incident

It was now the air force's job to get the Fire Force to the contact location, defined as a 1,000-meter grid square. This was best left to the pilot with the army commander taking over only after the target was pinpointed. Where possible, the K-Car approached from behind the observation post heading towards the target at a low level. The observation post talk-on was prepared in advance and a different approach caused confusion and was not done without notifying the observation post. A stick leader with the African Rifles described his flight:

> Up there the wind was cold and crisp and it blew on my face from the open side of the chopper. Down below the trees were green and some turning grey, but they all seemed to be of identical height, so that looking down one was reminded of those advertisements for carpets. ... I have enjoyed riding in a helicopter ever since I was a recruit and right now I was enjoying myself looking out there below as the world slid past.[59]

From a 4 Squadron pilot's perspective:

> The lead K-Car, as overall Fire Force commander, would transit to the target with the main force of K-Cars and G-Cars following in a loose gaggle five minutes later. The Lynx would be briefed to orbit at low level five minutes out from the target, with the "Para-Dak" and "Sky-shout" orbiting still farther out. When the lead K-Car reached a point five minutes from the target he would make a "five minute!" call, signaling the other helicopters to make their own way to the rendezvous. He would also begin communicating with the [observation post] in order to gain updated intelligence on the target, including clothing details, location of the terrorists, and what they were up to (feeding, sleeping or in transit). Two minutes out the lead K-Car would pull up to orbit height of 245 meters [800 feet] and attempt to mark the target with a smoke generator. This was the most critical point of the contact because the K-Car had then to contain any attempted breakout by the terrorists. If such an attempt was made the Fire Force commander would order the G-Cars to drop their troops at preplanned positions and the Lynx to drop a Mini-Golf, which would usually send the terrorists to ground.

The tactical situation dictated the height and direction of approach, if the K-Car wished to channelize the enemy's line of flight it flew high or flew low if surprise was desired.[60]

The K-Car followed terrain to mask the sound of its approach and flew directly over the observation post on a bearing towards the enemy and then climbed to an orbit of 700–900 feet. It would then be talked over the enemy position to drop a smoke marker, to confirm the correct location with the observation post. The pilot flew counterclockwise to keep the gun and army commander oriented on the target. A 7 Squadron pilot felt:

> It became obvious that the first two minutes of the attack were the most important. Once the gooks began to scatter, it was very difficult to contain them. ... it was essential for the Fire Force leader, usually the pilot of the K-Car, to map read accurately and achieve surprise. The best plan was to mark the target immediately with smoke grenades and smother it with Frantan and firepower from the fixed-wing aircraft and the helicopters.[61]

After the initial stage:

> The observation post or lead G-Car would find a suitable [drop zone] for the Para-Dak to drop his troops, who would then be uplifted to the contact zone by the G-Cars. Once all the troops were down, the G-Cars would disappear to refuel. The K-Cars would then sweep the area to clear out all the possible hiding places and for obvious reasons it was always a case of "shoot first, ask questions later." When the lead K-Car was running low on fuel he would frequently hand over the reins to the Lynx pilot, upon whose shoulders a fair amount of responsibility rested. He always flew solo and so had no-one with whom to discuss the situation, whereas K-Car captains had the luxury of a crew and always had at least 600 hours in command of a G-Car before going on to gunships.[62]

Talk-on Procedure

While special forces provided the preferred observation posts, Fire Force callout and subsequent talk-on was by any security force unit including the territorials and reservists. Richard (J. R. T.) Wood, of the Rhodesia Regiment recounted, "My experience ... was as an [observation post] calling in Fire Force onto a distant line of men running many thousands of yards away. My men went into silent convulsions at the sight of 'Doc' trying to remember to press the pressel switch when talking while trying to hold binoculars to his glasses, all with the shakes!" His training had come from being in follow-on waves and having a lieutenant demonstrating by running in circles with his arms out making engine noise while having his troops maneuver him with simulated radio traffic.[63]

Target indication had to be "immediate and accurate" for the Fire Force. While a positive and "troopie proof" means of target marking was desired (rifle grenade, flares), the use of a signal mirror proved the best to identify the observation post location. The K-Car would also drop smoke on a given grid reference and corrections were then made using "add," "drop," "left," and "right" system with the direction of flight being 12 o'clock. Visual means of identifying the various helicopters from the ground reduced confusion such as colored stripes on tail booms or even smoke grenades on the landing gear.

According to helicopter pilot Peter Wilkins:

> Some of the troops were fairly basic in their approach to things and had an even more basic level of usable grey matter. Some funny things were heard over the radio at times, like "No, not that left, the other left" or the other west or east etc.! These calls normally came at times of duress, such as when there was a "contact" (firefight) on the go and they wanted your assistance [as soon as possible]. Bear in mind that "Charley Tango," or CT, stood for "communist terrorist," recce aircraft were always called "Four" for the [Rhodesian Air Force] squadron number, as choppers were called "Seven," Dakotas "Three" etc. and the army ground commander was usually "Sunray."[64]

Jan Mienie, flying with 4 Squadron, felt the battlefield communications differences between ground and air forces had an impact:

The commanders and pilots were often from other countries and had terminology and cultural differences that did not translate well. Communications between observation post to observation post was okay, but the effort to talk in third world English to a first world airplane was a stretch! ... The brush and *kopje* made it difficult to redirect forces easily as the guerrillas moved out of an area.[65]

Fire Force Contact Techniques

Fire Force aircraft could be heard up to four minutes before arriving, allowing the enemy to move at 500 meters a minute, or one and a half kilometers, and continuing for every minute required to find them.[66] On arrival, reaction had to be swift and the helicopter troops were needed to block guerrillas on the run or to flush them from cover for the gunship. "The helicopter gunships would concentrate on the described targets and try to pick up movement while the troop-carrying helicopters would fly low around the periphery looking for motion undetected by the observation post," related one pilot. "We were circling an area of fairly thick brush which spread out for about 10 kilometers between two *kopjes* when the major and I spotted smoke from a cooking fire. 'Contact nine o'clock!' The pilot maneuvered so that the smoke was in the center of our orbit. At the same time I made out individual figures dressed in a motley assortment of camouflage, blue overalls, and civilian clothing," remembered a helicopter gunner. He added, "This was the critical time. The guerrilla's tactic was to 'bombshell'—scatter in all directions, enabling us to apprehend or kill a small percentage of the total number. So we had to contain them."[67]

If a sighting was made, the helicopter would open fire and drop smoke, notifying the rest of the force that there was contact. "Although troopers could fire from the aircraft," commented Brian Robinson, they "would *never* open fire on any target of opportunity unless specifically ordered to do so by the pilot, not the stick commander. Pilots tend to become unhappy when the MAG gunner puts a burst through the main rotor blade during a 30-degree bank in an orbit around the target."[68] An RAR officer recalled:

> An old military adage suggests the best laid plans rarely withstand the first contact with the enemy! ... Within minutes, the Fire Force wheeled 90 degrees to the left, and the K-Cars opened fire with their 20mm cannon on small groups of terrs barely visible through the treetops. After that my memories become somewhat disjointed ... the Lynx passing *beneath* our helicopter to drop a Frantan canister near the top of a prominent *dwala* [granite dome] ... then our pilot signaled we should prepare to deplane as he was about to land.[69]

The commanders in the gunship would take over in an effort to "read the battle," with the air commander normally calling for an immediate Frantan strike from available 4 Squadron aircraft (this could just as well be a Mini-Golf bomb).[70] "The napalm detonation resulted in a huge flash and plume of smoke which enabled the ground troops to orient themselves once they deplaned from the helicopters," recalled

Peter Briscoe.[71] It also kept the guerrillas occupied and slowed them down or made them take cover as the stop groups deployed. The G-Cars orbited until called on to deploy their stop groups by the airborne army commander to landing zones along egress routes. Some used a standardized employment based upon the clock system to set sticks down in sequence from a wider orbit flown around and in the same direction as the K-Car, hopefully trapping a rapidly dispersing enemy—this could be an area up to half a mile wide.

Helicopters would approach using terrain masking, put down their stick (with the stick leader hopefully leaving the aircraft headset behind) and then move out to a holding pattern, set down, or even refuel. On order, these same helicopters could redeploy sticks, conduct medical evacuations, or fill in for the K-Car. The G-Cars could also pick up reinforcements from the land tail at a rendezvous point or from the forward airfield. One army commander related,

> I had just given these orders when a more frantic cry came over the radio, "K-Car, you are under heavy fire!" Tracer bullets flashed past my window and up through the helicopter's blades. Luckily, this gave away the enemy's location, so within seconds Hoppy [the tech-gunner] was sending a stream of cannon shells down on them. ... I ordered the other helicopters to unload their troops and go and collect more men.[72]

The Para-Dak closed as part of the lead element, using the same formations and principles used for the helicopter. The Dak did not drop its troops until a contact was properly underway. "The paras, once committed, could only be moved with extreme difficulty," observed one trooper, and often conditions were dry with brush fires resulting during the contact, which further complicated decisions ("Parachutes were expensive and had to be recovered," noted one army commander). It also meant the paratroopers did not have to do the "tremendous amount of humping to clear the brush" that the stop groups did or spend the occasional night on the ground.[73]

An RLI jumper, William Norris, described the experience: his commando's sergeant-major, Warrant Officer II A. F. S. Edwards:

> ... was probably the only person aboard the aircraft—including the pilot—who made any pretense at all of wanting to be there. As the Dakota bobbed and weaved through low-level turbulence, he sat or stood by the open door, an intense little troll, concentrating on the voices in his headset. The 'vomit comet' would drop, lurch starboard, lunge and drop. Hurricane wind and engine noise screamed through the cabin.
> News of the chopper sticks, already deployed, would arrive over the headset. Edwards would blink at the interesting parts, nod and pass back information through sign language, while his audience sat like thawed wieners, stirring only occasionally to make doggy noises into brown paper bags. Grenades and cocking handles would dig into ribs. The Dakota would circle and circle, sometimes buffeting about over the target area for hours, waiting for the call.
> "Helmets on!"
> "Omigod, can't we go 'round again?"
> "Stand up! Hook up! Check equipment!"
> Helmet, reserve, quick-release box ...

"Action stations!"

Desert-dry mouths and unpredictable knees as the aircraft plunged to operational jump altitude of 500 feet.

Red light on. "Stand in the door!"

Unbelievable noise, wind, numbness … seconds now …

Green light! "Go! And go! And go!"

The fact that the paras had jumped meant contact: "Hey someone is shooting at us!" From this point on, a full-scale Fire Force action would be instituted.[74]

Another RLI jumper observed:

The operation began smoothly as stop groups were deployed without incident and, a short time later, the DC-3 "Para-Dak" was called in and kept on standby. Circling the drop zone (DZ) time and time again, the men inside the cramped fuselage sat and fidgeted, smoking cigarette after cigarette endlessly.

Suddenly, one of the three air force dispatchers stood up and faced the seated troopers, frowning as he concentrated on the ground troops' radio messages that echoed tinnily inside his headphones. The double row of 16 anxious men studied the dispatcher's expression and waited patiently for him to pass on any snippets of information.

"There's been a contact," he shouted to make himself heard above the roar of the aircraft's engines. "The K-Car is taking flak … Seven-Nine is requesting a paradrop." A pause of several seconds followed, during which helmet chinstraps were tightened and cigarettes were stamped out.

The ancient Dakota now began to drop down to below 400 ft, thereby rendering the paratroopers' reserve chutes totally useless in the event of a malfunction of the main canopy—a fact not widely advertised!

"Looks as if you're going to jump," shouted the despatcher. "Yes … Okay men, we're going to drop you in one run-in so get out as fast as you can. It's a good [drop zone] but there's a strong cross-wind, so be prepared for it … Okay … All sticks stand up, hook up."

The 16 men rose unsteadily to their feet, clumsy in their cumbersome parachutes and equipment, their movements restricted by the FN rifles and FN MAG machine guns strapped to their sides. They snapped their static lines to the double overhead steel cables and automatically checked their equipment and that of the man in front. The Dakota lurched violently, jolting the troops against each other.

"Remember men, as fast as you can … Action stations!" yelled the dispatcher, and immediately the paras shuffled forward. The leading man halted near the open doorway, right hand over the reserve chute strapped low on his chest, while his other hand gripped the door above his head to help steady him against the buffeting and rocking of the aircraft.

"Stand in the door" came the order. A quick step forward, left hand down to grasp the outside edge of the door above which a small red light had flickered on. All eyes were riveted to that spot as the three dispatchers prepared to shove the double line of men out of the plane as speedily as they could.

"Have a good jump, lads," said one, as the red lamp blinked off and beside it a green one immediately snapped on.

"Go!" screamed the dispatcher.[75]

Jumpers went out at 500–700 feet above ground level (a few combat jumps were recorded at a not always desirable 350–400 feet; Cronin had a friend "who went out at 200 feet and hit the ground almost as the parachute opened").[76] There was "the general chaos of a fast stick and the sporting chance of … having a mid-air collision," according to Robinson.[77] The low altitude reduced time in the air and the possibility of being shot at on the way down, "although the guerrillas were terrible marksmen."[78] Once on the ground, the parachute sticks went straight into contact or were repositioned by helicopter if some distance from the fighting as could be the case with a parachute drop. Having the Para-Dak to drop its sticks onto their stop position was more efficient than repositioning them by helicopter once they were on the ground, but this depended upon the terrain for available drop zones. Robinson commented, "Regrouping on the ground takes a hell of a long time so it is far easier to get out of the harness and provide an instant stop or sweep line without having to go through an [rendezvous] procedure. The K-Car commander would normally have observed the drop" and provided control.[79] Jean-Michel Caffin, a stick leader with RLI Support Commando, recalled that the first stop group positioned on the ground, or in contact, was often placed to effectively control the others, regardless of rank making this a "corporals war" in most cases.[80]

Briscoe observed, "Once all the troops were on the ground, it became a matter of winkling the guerrillas out from cover. The guerrillas' attention was divided between air and ground forces and hence they became more vulnerable."[81] The ground commander and his men had to contend with a number of situations in which the enemy either ran as far and as fast as possible or went to ground in cultivated fields, along streambeds, in caves or huts. Each situation required a variation of techniques to solve. Fire and maneuver depended upon the terrain and situation, with no real formal division of stop and sweep duties existing between G-Car and Dakota sticks (though it is recorded the helicopter groups served as stops while the parachute sticks conducted sweeps). It was similar to the "stand and drive" approach used in hunting game. In this an RLI officer said, "The troops were good and knew their business and were alert to the danger of friendly fire. They listened on the radio to what was going on, but kept off the air unless called upon."[82] "We carried the minimum to allow us to run and outflank the enemy," remembered one RLI trooper:

> The combat in a proper contact is close and sometimes results in a checkerboard of friend and foe. This prevents the terrorists from utilizing heavy weapons support elements of their own. When a clear shot presents itself, friendly fire must be minimized. Flanking movement by ground stops and [helicopters] and aircraft support must consider lines of fire and friendly troops' positions, and the Fire Force commander was the best at moving us out of the way quickly so he could use the cannon, the quad [machine guns], or call in the Lynx propeller-driven air strikes without losing track of the foe.[83]

By way of initial considerations, the first helicopter stick on the ground or in contact set the pace for the deployment of the other helicopter sticks to find and fix the enemy. When this occurred, the parachute sticks would be dropped to provide the sweep line to finish the job with their own fire, that from the gunships, or stop groups. "The commandos had the advantage of air support, but the enemy was usually well concealed and frightened. In a sweep line, you met each obstacle one on one. The first hint of danger was often a glistening eyeball."[84] Noted an RLI stick leader, "sweep lines were dangerous and did not work against dug-in forces" who stood and fought.[85]

The observation post had to keep track of the Fire Force rather than the other way around (John Cronin knew of only one instance where a pseudo operator was shot by friendly troops during Fire Force). While the observation post location was a given, the army commander in the K-Car had to track the stick locations on the ground and be available for fire support. Terrain orientation rather than map work was necessary for this. Air panels or map sheet was used to mark positions, with smoke and flares available on demand. Cronin recalled one case "where a good commander had 25 sticks to manage at one time."[86]

The gunships were used to move or fix the enemy, and even shoot at individual targets. Noted one RLI trooper: "When in a tight situation, it was most reassuring to hear over the radio the familiar words, 'Stand by, K-Car firing!' You knew then all you would have to do was move forward and pick up the pieces—literally!"[87] Lieutenant-Colonel Robinson observed, "I believe that most of the Fire Force damage was done by the 20mm K-Car. The troops in the main did the mopping up after the Lord Mayor's show." The army commander and air gunner both faced in the same direction and could position the pilot on target or the air commander could see the target himself and fly accordingly.[88]

Norris of the RLI chronicled:

> "One-Nine, One-Nine … One-Two."
>
> "One-Nine … go."
>
> "Roger, One-Nine … I've got a contact in the reentrant to my front … Four, maybe more … Confirmed, one RPD … Can you give clearing fire? Over."
>
> "Affirmative, One-Two … Give me a mark with the phos … Over."
>
> "Roger, One-Nine … Marking."
>
> "One-Two, I see your mark … One-Nine firing," followed by the 20mm's crack.
>
> [Norris] judged [that] in the Fire Force chess game, "K-Car was Queen—and King—able to strike anywhere with greatest force, able to command all the powers of the pieces."[89]

A mix of high-explosive incendiary (HEI) and armor-piercing (AP) rounds were used at a ratio of five to one: the HEI could kill the enemy without needing a direct hit while the AP was called on to break through any cover or concealment. Wing Commander Briscoe still felt that there was "a balance between the technical and technique" and it was "often the Mark I eyeball and the Mark I grunt getting in there and doing the killing."[90] This was when friendly casualties could and did occur.

An air gunner wrote his pilot directed him to fire at the base of a *gomo* (hill) and work upwards:

> I took aim and fired short bursts, no more than three rounds at a time; any more would have pushed the chopper sideways and meant us losing our orbit. Then I saw the first slight movement below, and once my eyes had focused onto it I picked out first one terr, then another, until I eventually had a number of them in sight. … I was able to impede their progress by firing

ahead of them and slowly bringing my bursts back towards them, and one or two went down, but not from direct hits, I thought—more likely form shrapnel and ricochets.[91]

In another incident:

Several terrorists fell over. Some would not be getting up again, but others were playing possum until the chopper overflew them, when they would open fire on our unprotected rear. They were starting to scatter already, running with their weapons, firing back over their shoulders—a far more effective tactic than you might think. A couple of them just standing, weapons at their shoulders, emptying their magazines in our direction.[92]

Air support also came from accompanying light attack aircraft, or fighters and bombers if a contact was really intense. The Lynx carried machine guns and had bombs, napalm, or flares for use as the first responder. If heavier close air support was justified, the Lynx served as an airborne forward air controller and marked targets with white phosphorus smoke rockets. Air support was controlled by the Lynx pilot, with the important part being positive target identification and marking by the K-Car. Air panels, maps, and day-glo in caps were all used by "friendlies" on the ground to indicate location. Sometimes forces would have to pull back when fixed-wing air support was called. This delayed closing with the enemy and was felt to contribute to the escape of some. Overall it was felt "A better knowledge of air support was needed, particularly the characteristics of the different weapons employed and the time delay needed when jet strike aircraft were requested."

One 4 Squadron member recalled:

The Lynx pilot was entirely responsible for all his weapons and could attack targets independently. It was absolutely essential that he should keep a complete and constantly updated mental picture of the tactical situation in order to avoid scoring "own goals" with his weapons. He would usually position behind the troops and hold, waiting to be called forward to attack. This was made in front of and parallel to the front line of the friendly troops, who would engage the terrorists to keep their heads down until the Lynx opened fire. This allowed the Lynx pilot to concentrate on his task without fear of being hit by friendly fire or ricochets. During the attack strict radio silence would be maintained so that if the Lynx fired upon friendly troops the action could be aborted on the command "Stop, stop, stop." Sometimes the rules were bent slightly and the Lynx attacked from behind friendly troops, or within the safety distances of their weapons, in order to save lives. At times the Lynx would expend all its ordnance in the first few minutes; if this was the case it would return to the [forward airfield] and quickly refuel and rearm, which more often than not was a 10-minute affair if "all hands were on deck."[93]

"Monster" Wilkins added this about the benefit of air support in the follow-up after contact:

It was late afternoon when the fixed-wing pilot, "Cocky" Benecke, in a Provost spotted the guerrillas. They were also exceptionally tired, having been on the run all day long and looked to Cocky as if they were busy setting up an ambush for the following troops, who were not far behind at that stage. He immediately rolled in and dropped both Frantans (frangible tanks, like napalm) on the guerrillas. They were fairly well grouped at this stage, not "bomb-shelled" or split up as they usually would be when under attack. This must have been due to having seen the Provost and Alouette gunship all day long, without being attacked, so they had relaxed a little and settled on a plan of sorts to take the troops off their tail.

That was a mistake on their behalf, for Cocky's Frantans were spot on and eight of the 12 guerrillas had burns to attest to his accuracy.[94]

Light infantryman Rogers reminisced:

> During Fire Force operations, advance to contact was extremely nerve-wracking for anyone unaccustomed to local procedures. After deploying by helicopter, each stick would begin to sweep through an area. The stick leader listened in on his radio and advised his troops when the K-Car warned that they were nearing the enemy. Sometimes the K-Car could not see where the guerrillas were, in which case the element of surprise lay with the enemy. Either way, the troops had to press on until contact was initiated, usually at very close quarters. Often, guerrillas would break and run, hopefully towards the waiting stop groups. Although that was the theory, both the sweep line and stop groups could become embroiled in their own little battles, with the operation developing into a series of individual contacts—a nightmare for the commander trying to direct events from above. However, superior training and firepower usually prevailed and the few guerrillas who survived a firefight would try to surrender. But not always.[95]

Additionally from the RLI:

> In theory, a well-constructed Fireforce [sic] action left no avenues of escape. Certainly it worked out well enough on paper at the School of Infantry. The classroom is so tidy, though, and war is such hell. Nasty details arise in the field, details that would hardly be worth half-points in a theoretical exam. Details like boulder-strewn hillsides, caves, thickets as dense as cold porridge.[96]

For those engaged in these drills, "It is frightening to have a hidden armed aggressor watching you, and even more so when you have to go in and find him. Such an exercise almost always resulted in killing of the enemy, but he was likely to be desperate and doubly dangerous."[97]

To control the expenditure of ammunition, rifles were used on semiautomatic fire with only the machine gun in the automatic mode. Journalist Downie observed, "the men depended on good observation and fast reactions ... they will fire perhaps five or six aimed shots, or, in the case of a machine gunner, a one-second burst."[98] South African Cobus Claasens described "Drake shoot" field firing techniques used to overcome terrorist opposition:

> We believed in firepower. When most armies carry one or two spare mags [magazines], we carried 10 to 12 with a double [magazine] in the weapon. On the first contact, if it was a heavy stand, the soldiers would drop prone. They are trained to cover a narrow area in front of them. We fire at real or potential targets sweeping from right to left. You shoot at the enemy and where you think the enemy is hiding. Even when you can't see the enemy you keep shooting. We'd shoot straight through mud walls into bushes to kick up stones and chips. We worked in teams. You are number one and your number two is on your right. Your number two fires slower so you are covered when you change magazines. Our style is to shoot, observe, then yell, "changing mag." That means dash down, crawl to the side a little, observe, and fire. Then you yell "buddy, buddy, advance." That is the signal for you buddy to get up and repeat.[99]

Elaboration followed:

> You had to gut shoot the African to kill them, head shots did not always work. I saw an RPD [light machine] gunner with half his head blown away kill five guys and blind another with single iron sight head shots at 200 meters in one hour, he was eventually shot dead, but it took 150 men from 1 and 2 Commando and 6 Rhodesia Regiment to get him.[100]

In these circumstances, mistakes could and did happen that resulted from shooting first and asking questions later. An RLI Support Commando trooper clearing a village was surprised by an African moving quickly from cover in front of him: "Before I realized she was a civvy [civilian] I had put a round into her backside (her own fault for doing what she did). Anyway, I think I must not have hurt her too badly because she did not stop and we didn't see her again—not a bad instinctive shot from the hip I thought."[101] There were grimmer repercussions, again with Support Commando, RLI as:

> We both opened fire at the same time—another gook bit the dust—we were still trying for a captive so we went over to see how bad he was. Again, unfortunately for this fellow, though still alive, he was not healthy enough according to my boss so I was told to dispatch him. Although it may sound a bit morbid, we all had a bit of a laugh at the way he kicked his leg—just like in the movies when someone raises his leg and gives the shake as he kicks the bucket.[102]

Support Commando, RLI[103] had a representative incident one morning around 1100, when the parachute sticks Eagle One to Four:

> ... were airlifted by choppers to a nearby kraal and were told to flush out one gook who was hiding in a thick clump of bushes left of the kraal. We (Lieutenant Walters, Corporal Salzmann, [Trooper Michael A.] Mike Moore and myself [Trooper Anthony Rogers]) fired several rounds into the bush and I walked up and threw a [high-explosive] grenade into it whereupon, following a further bout of firing, myself and Carl Salzmann were detailed to run along a track in a flanking movement on the right of the bush, which we did, taking up temporary positions while Lieutenant Walters and Mike were ordered by the K-Car (Major Nigel Henson) to run across a cleared mealie field directly into the bush.
> They began to do so and seven or eight feet from the edge of the thicket ran straight into a burst of automatic fire from one, possibly two, weapons. Both men fell flat while bullets hit the ground all around them. Immediately following this incident, I saw a figure running back through the bush past me, 25 feet away, and I opened up but do not know whether or not I hit him. I then doubled back to some rocks as I was lying in open ground—temporarily leaving a magazine behind in the event—and firing one-handed towards the bush behind me. I met up with Carl who told me that Mike had been hit and was still lying in the mealie field. After Lieutenant Walters had joined us, we learned that Mike was, in fact dead, hit in the head and chest. We then called in a couple of more sticks to help clear the bush and these duly arrived (one chopper recovering Mike's body on the uplift). Following several Frantan strikes by two Lynx aircraft and machine gunning from a G-Car plus much firing and grenade throwing by us, the bush was eventually cleared. No gook was found.[104]

In another RLI example:

> Then we began firing into the dense undergrowth and tossing grenades into caves, never knowing where the enemy might choose to hide.

Suddenly Lance-Corporal Graham Gilbert shouted, "Check, check, check!"

I was just in time to "check" two figures armed with AKs who had broken cover a hundred meters to our front.

We all opened up simultaneously, six FN rifles and two MAGs, sending a hail of deadly fire towards the unfortunate terrs, who quickly dived headlong into some long grass.[105]

Again from Rogers:

Our stick—now reinforced by Koos Basson [to replace a casualty]—was detailed to sweep across a fairly bushy area in search of a wounded gook. Before long, I found a blood-stained shirt and webbing in a dried-up riverbed. While I debated whether it could be booby-trapped, Koos and Carl [Corporal Salzmann] began to clear a bush by firing into it. They immediately received return fire and Koos ran past me, one hand clasped to his neck and shouting he had been hit. As he took cover up on the riverbank, I knelt down and placed several rounds in the direction where I presumed the gook was—this being only a few feet from where I knelt. For a few seconds I thought I had hit him, but when the dust and smoke had cleared, I saw that I had only "killed" several large stones. I then patched up Koos—who had luckily only been grazed by the round—and we again called up reinforcements. Koos was casevaced and we continued our sweep, sometimes crawling flat on our bellies, our nerves by now quiet taut. It was "Binny" [Corporal Peter Binion] who finally flung a grenade at the gook who was subsequently shot up by several men and killed. We were uplifted at dusk.[106]

In another case, several hours after initial deployment, 2 Commando, RLI was following a group of four evading terrorists, according to Trooper David S. Armstrong, when:

The combined [Territorial Army] patrol/10 Troop stick was ambushed in a narrow, twisty, overgrown riverbed, or *donga*. ... The [TA] patrol, 10 Troop stick had come around the first bend and thus exposed themselves to the terrorists, who opened fire. The sergeant of the [territorial] patrol [Temporary Warrant Officer II T. G. Bain] and a member of [Corporal M. J. "Jannie"] de Beer's stick, [Rifleman E.] Hennie Potgeiter, were both killed. Ken Lucas, the gunner in Cpl de Beer's stick was wounded in the legs.

It was into this situation 7 Troop arrived. [Major] Meyer deployed [Lieutenant Johannes M.] du Plooy's stick and another to sweep through the area, as at this stage no one was sure whether the terrorists were still there or not. The bodies of the two men in the riverbed were seen by this sweep line and [Lieutenant] du Plooy ordered John [Corporal John A. Coey] to see whether or not he could help them. As John climbed down into the riverbed, he was shot by the terrorists who were still in their hiding place—right under du Plooy's feet!

During the rest of the afternoon, several attempts were made to get at the terrorists in their position and this [is] where they used the strength of it to their advantage. As I said before, anyone attempting to assault the position was clearly exposed without in turn being able to see into the target area. We suffered two more casualties, one of whom was [Lieutenant] du Plooy. Also, any grenades thrown at the target simply bounced off the tree roots fronting the position and exploded harmlessly on the sand of the riverbed. ... Shortly after dark, the four terrorists broke out and in doing so managed to kill Cpl de Beer and wound another of his stick. Again, no one [was] sure whether the terrorists had continued with their breakout or had returned to their position.[107]

In my opinion, one unusual circumstance and two mistakes occurred which contributed to this fiasco. ... The unusual circumstance was that the terrorists were well led and prepared to fight it out (the RLI was definitely not prepared for this). The first mistake was too many people were in the riverbed initially and that there was no flanking protection for the tracker. ... The second mistake was [Lieutenant] du Plooy's in sending John into the riverbed without completing the sweep of the area. ... In the section which we are concerned [about] there were two sharp bends about 20–25 yards apart. In the outside bank of the second bend, there was a washout fronted by heavy tree roots. It was in this extremely strong natural position that the terrorists had taken position. They had two major advantages, and these were that it [was] very difficult for anyone to see into this washout without exposing himself in full view to enemy fire. In fact, it was more than difficult; it was impossible. The second major advantage was the fact that the floor of this washout was about two feet above the level of the riverbed.[108]

Hut-clearing prompted procedures such as not standing silhouetted in front of openings, starting rather at ground level when going in, and having another rifleman or machine gun in position to fire directly into the entrance in a personalized version of fire and movement. Robinson provided the straightforward solution practiced by the SAS:

> I am unaware of any standard drill. A white phosphorus grenade would be tossed into a cave which would generally have the desired result. A hut would normally be of mud construction with a thatched roof and no windows. After a command in the local language, a match in the thatched roof normally did the trick. In case of enemy fire coming from a hut we would have used an RPG-7. We also carried "Knock Knock" charges made of [plastic explosives]. This would demolish the hut.[109]

A trooper whose stop group went after a guerrilla seen running into a hut, related:

> It was my turn to clear the hut so I ran to the back (no windows) and set fire to the thatch, then positioned myself so as to be able to shoot anyone running out the door. The thatch was burning well by now and still no one came out. My stop leader indicated to me to kick the door in (we were trying to capture him, not kill him). Anyway, I kicked the door in and jumped to the side of the doorway—no firing from inside. By this time it was starting to get a bit warm with the roof on fire, and with smoke inside the hut nothing could be seen inside so I put three rounds inside hoping to scare him out. Still no-one came out, but this time movement was spotted. To cut the story short, unfortunately (especially for the gook) I had hit him with one of my shots—we managed to get him out of the hut before the roof collapsed but he died shortly afterwards.[110]

Hut clearing was described in a contact with Support Commando, RLI:

> We joined Stop Three and started clearing a village. This meant clearing out each hut by working in pairs. Myself and another chap called Nigel ... had cleared two small huts and were in the process of clearing a third which was large by African standards. It had two rooms, I was in the main room on one side of the doorway to the bedroom and Nigel was on the other side. It was Nigel's turn to go first and he had just pulled the curtain on the doorway aside when he suddenly jumped back and started firing into the bedroom. He had done this because as soon as he had looked inside, he had spotted an AK assault rifle sticking out from under the bed. Fortunately, that was all we found there. Because of this, we set fire to all the buildings in the village.
>
> The next hut was my turn to go first—there was nobody inside but I also found an AK plus two sets of communist webbing and three grenades. The reasons we burned the village were 1) punishment for harboring terrorists and weapons and 2) because a common practice is for

weapons and ammunition to be hidden in the thatched roofs. The latter proved to be correct for we had no sooner fired the last hut when ammunition in the roofs of the other huts started to explode.

We continued going through three–four other kraals, clearing as we went, finding more equipment and therefore burning all the kraals we went through. ... Once again my stop (Number One) was up-lifted and taken by chopper to a kraal where a terrorist was seen running into a hut. We were dropped about 150 meters from the kraal and started towards the hut where the terrorist (gook) was supposed to be. ... To try and cut this tale short again, we swept through another couple of kraals (burning as we went). The other stops got a few more gooks, but we did not shoot anything else except for a civvy who suddenly sprung up from some bushes in front of me. ... In that contact we culled seven gooks and captured three. One of the captives was the chief executioner of that area—this bloke is the fellow who decides which targets are to be hit and he personally stabbed to death 12 Africans he suspected of being "sellouts."[111]

Trooper Rogers wrote:

There then followed hours of hut clearing. I cannot say how many were shot up or burnt out. Several locals were "questioned" as to the whereabouts of the gooks but to no avail—one seemed to have a fit during interrogation, another was beaten unconscious. During the clearing of one kraal, following several warnings for the inhabitants to come out, Corporal [Peter] Binion flung a [high-explosive] grenade into a hut. On kicking the door in it transpired it held a nanny and a piccanin [child] ... [who] came out wailing and screaming and covered in blood. We just left her and carried on. During much of this time, Fran' strikes and firing was going on in the distance. The sky was filled with smoke from burning kraals.[112]

Cave clearing provided a unique situation in itself,[113] as when 1 Commando, RLI was deployed from Grand Reef with a K-Car, three G-Cars, and a Dakota (seven sticks totaling 28 men on the ground). According to Trooper John Foran:

We had an unknown number of terrorists on this mountain. It was raining quite heavily and continued to rain all day. Three stop groups were deployed. We were dropped behind the mountain. Climbing the rear side, we began to sweep down the terrorists' side, 16 troopers in extended line. This mountain was honeycombed with natural caves which we had to clear on the way down. Approaching the base camp we had our first contact. Two terrorists broke cover and tried to bolt for it. We got one of these. We swept on through the base camp area, securing it and clearing a massive cave alongside the base camp. Lieutenant Paul Courtney and myself proceeded along this ledge, approximately 30 meters wide, to check it out. Midway along the ledge we came under fire from automatic weapons. We retreated to cover and marked the cave with a white phos' [phosphorus] grenade for the Lynx aircraft. We moved back to allow him to drop a Frantan bomb but he hit the wrong target, so we climbed up and over the ridge to come at them from the other side. The rain continued to belt down. On the way down the other side, I found myself directly above the cave entrance. From my position I could see the lower portion of one terrorist's leg standing at the cave entrance. Informing Paul of this, I prepared to toss in two grenades, a [white phosphorus] and a [high explosive]. The white phos' was a mistake as in the heavy rain it hung there like a smoke screen. One terrorist escaped in this, despite the bullets and grenades we put in there. They still refused to come out [after] a failed frontal assault [which] saw Lieutenant Courtney killed. The fight dragged on. I fired at least a dozen teargas bombs into the cave along with HE grenades. We were about to use a bunker bomb when they called out they wanted to surrender. I moved to my old position above the cave. The terrorists were instructed to come out with their hands up. The first one emerged with his hands behind his back, trying to locate the voices. I shot him from point blank range. He did have a grenade in his hands. The next one came out with his hands up. Upon questioning him he admitted one more terrorist remained but was very badly wounded. He was sent back in to bring him out. When this was done, I entered the cave to check it out. It was deserted. Three AK-47s and one SKS [carbine] lay on the floor. The wounded terrorist died. Night fell, and Christmas Eve was spent on a muddy, wet mountainside with one dead troop commander, three dead terrorists, one prisoner. It was a very sad, very cold, wet and hungry Christmas Eve. We were uplifted at first light.[114]

In another example, RAR officer Lawless said:

I pulled my stop groups back from the cave, and called in an air strike from a Canberra armed with 200 Alpha bombs (small football-shaped bombs which bounced, armed, then detonated at about waist height), which had been scrambled from Salisbury and was orbiting the contact area. The first box of 50 bombs fell well short, the second landed beyond the target … and the third landed on my sweep line! Miraculously, nobody was hurt, and the Canberra pilot, obviously embarrassed by his performance so far, made no mistake with the fourth box, which landed short and bounced into the cave, shredding the luckless terrs inside.[115]

Richard Wood recorded fundamental tactical rules primarily looking at the efforts of Support Commando, RLI under Major Henson: first, never sweep uphill—always downhill; second, never sweep into the sun; third, always sweep from cover into open ground—never from open ground into cover.[116] Some disputed any fixed rules, stating that every situation was different and examples cited provide the exceptions (i.e., troops being moved towards each other or moving uphill rather than down). Flexibility was required as once in Cronin's experience they were left on the ground with a single G-Car overhead, while the remainder of the helicopters returned to base to pick up the land tail to take them to another contact in the opposite direction.[117] Robinson felt "Nothing was cast in stone. … Indeed, flexibility was essential and every single battle differed. The plan was formulated by the K-Car commander who directed the troops and the K-Car pilot who provided the air support. The success of the mission depended upon two reasonable commanders working together, discussing the situation and formulating a sound plan."[118] One RLI trooper felt "an experienced K-Car commander often made use of his sixth sense and added the unexpected. In other words, he played chess."[119]

Color Sergeant Coleman believed that soldiers serving on Fire Force duties required two qualities: "a healthy instinct for survival and a lot of luck. It took only a few hot callouts to develop the first; but luck came and went at its own whim throughout all of our bush trips."[120] He then added, "However, as on every callout, you went in with the idea of staying alive, which meant hard, aggressive action once you hit the ground."[121] Another veteran noted:

We were beyond being afraid … we were in a constant state of numbness. Of course that's when you got it … when you did not care anymore and did not fear … I stood at the edge of a clearing while a terr [terrorist] fired his RPD [machine gun] at me and an Aussie friend [Corporal Peter Binion]. … I watched him fire burst after burst at us while I leaned on my rifle, smoked a cigarette and Binny and I both muttered something to the effect of "look at that [fuck] shooting at us." I can still recall the sound of the bullets cracking by me. In a split second the Lynx took him out with Frantan.[122]

Lieutenant-Colonel Reid-Daly, pragmatic as ever, believed what was needed in a Fire Force solider was "a. To be highly aggressive. b. To have a high standard of snap shooting. c. To have initiative." Slow or hesitant reactions and poor shooting just wasted the effort of everyone involved in putting sticks on the ground.[123]

Post-contact/Deployment Procedures

Finally, an airborne sky-shout or loud speaker appeal from a Cessna 185 Kiewit utility aircraft was used to warn off local populations and also to capture more guerrillas, so "overwhelmed by their Fire Force experience" that they volunteered information or even came over to the Rhodesian side as "tame terrorists."[124] A Lynx pilot felt, "Normally when activities had quieted down, the helicopters would land and leave the Lynx to coordinate the mopping-up operations. Once all was complete the Lynx would return to base, its pilot awaiting further instruction—generally in the swimming pool if there was nothing on the go."[125] Lawless observed: "A Fire Force could deploy for periods from three hours up to two days, and often dealt with two or three sightings in a day. This brought inevitable strain to bear on all members of a Fire Force unit, both physically and mentally."[126] It was often necessary to conduct detailed searches of the contact area, including alongside riverbanks, in caves, and huts. "In these circumstances all locals should be apprehended and screened by appropriate intelligence agencies. It has been found that children are the most informative" for purposes of instant information.[127]

During a late-day RLI Support Commando callout that started slowly, "all we found were a lot of old and middle-aged Africans coming home from a beer drink. Regardless, we made a hasty roadblock (so to speak) and started rounding up all the Africans in sight (regardless of sex or age)."[128]

A major drawback to Fire Force operations was its limitation to daylight hours, because of difficulties in flying and in accurate observation. The tendency of Fire Forces to withdraw before dark was observed and the need for follow-up on the ground overnight with ambushes was recommended by Combined Operations even if remaining units were left shorthanded. Also recognized was a reluctance to deploy Fire Forces at last light.[129] If contact was not made directly, patience and moving sticks through the area could stir guerrillas up and the ground element could be left overnight to ambush remaining guerrillas. Although this was not popular with keyed-up RLI troopies, the RAR *askari* often had better results this way.[130] Throughout the experience, there was a competition between the regulars of the RLI and the RAR for "body counts." By the standards of the day, Major Henson's Support Commando, 1RLI and Major André Dennison's A Company, 2RAR stood out.[131] "If RLI are the Incredibles, RAR must be the Phenomenals" concluded one staff officer reviewing statistics.[132]

Robinson felt, "After a Fire Force contact the survivors would normally 'bombshell.' Tracker combat teams and follow-up troops would then conduct the follow-up until they eventually tracked to contact (I believe that the ability to track the enemy using both Black and White military-trained trackers proved to be the most important aspect of counterinsurgency operations)."[133] The Operations Coordinating Committee noted, "A common pitfall is the tendency to leave an area too quickly. … Thorough follow-up/search operations and flooding the area with troops must always be carried out when necessary to ensure that maximum terrorists are accounted for."[134] But the needed follow-up troops (intelligence personnel, trackers, tracker and search dogs) were not always available as contacts increased in number and intensity.

An RLI commanding officer commented that his men developed bad habits if left on Fire Force duties too long—they forgot bush skills, the need for stealth, became lazy from operating only in daytime, and developed a "kill or be killed" nature not conducive to "hearts and minds" efforts. The RAR soldiers adapted much better to changing roles without loss of skill.[135] Units on Fire Force duties could and did more routine patrolling and ambushing, but this was more often left to other army units, the national service Independent Companies, the part-time Rhodesia Regiment, and BSAP full-time Support Unit or part-time PATU units.[136] The Fire Force soldiers felt "they put us on endless patrols of no strategic use" as opposed to leaving this to others while they "got so many kills" as an air–ground task force.[137] This was an argument heard in other places where wars were won or lost in the populated areas for "hearts and minds." Consolidation of tribal areas fell to the Internal Affairs security units, the Guard Force, and late-war Security Force Auxiliaries. [138]

Tension dropped off as the chance of confrontation departed: "With any immediate threat taken care of, the men now took the opportunity to relax and wait for uplift. It had been a long and active day, resulting in the death of 12 terrorists and the capture of four prisoners, the final captive being taken by a lone stick on the other side of the *gomo*."[139] The *Rhodesia Herald* reported an incident when some 10 terrorists were killed by an RLI Fire Force and another 17 "were accounted for" over the next two days:

> The helicopters fly out the bodies, captured equipment and personal belongings. The troopies at the rendezvous point search the bodies and strip them of webbing [one of those killed was a women wearing a green uniform with webbing]. Tucked inside a magazine is a letter from a girlfriend. They carry cigarettes, charm beads to protect them from death, and spare clothing. This particular battle is over. The men are flown back to the rendezvous point for the long ride back to base. Their parachutes are being collected. They look like a line of dead bodies—there is no comment. They have been out here for five hours and their faces record the strain. Then someone reads an entry on one of the captured documents: "We were never told about the power of Fire Force on the other side," the terrorist had written. The troopies laugh.[140]

Being picked up prior to nightfall, an RAR noncommissioned officer wrote: "As the chopper lifted off, I looked down on the contact area, now so peaceful. We climbed high and sped back to base, the wind blew on my face and, I thought, that was the life, never a dull moment. Then I got to thinking of that cold beer waiting for me and I settled back. Today was good and gone, tomorrow was out of sight."[141] Even aircrews would get caught up in the desire to return to base as sundown:

When the sun started to drop in the sky and the light began to fade, we formed up in echelon formation and returned to base camp at the end of another long, hot, dry, dusty day to rearm, refuel and clean both helicopters and weapons. Then grab a bite to eat, and if we were lucky there might even be some water left for a much needed shower. Then bed, ready for the next day's 4 a.m. start.[142]

An RAR Fire Force commander ended his day's action with:

Soon we were back over our home airfield. After a sharp turn to the left we touched down. Servicing by the ground crews started immediately, and I went to the ops room to make my final report. We had been in the air for eight and a half hours. ... I had a much needed shower, a drink, and the first meal of the day. Then I received my orders for the following day. These included: "Long lie-in tomorrow; you need not take off until 0600 hours!"[143]

Related by the *Newsweek* account that began this section: "The patrols chased the two guerrillas who had escaped earlier until the next day, but could not find them. That did not seem to bother the [RAR] colonel: 'Four out of six isn't too bad,' he said. 'It's time for a drink. Fabian, bring me a whiskey-soda.' The trouble is, a four-out-of-six score will not win the war against the guerrillas," concluded the journalist.[144] As a standby force, "Occasionally, nothing happened. Particularly when the rains came, filling out vegetation and rendering areas' observation posts less effective. The periods of inactivity allowed the troops time to settle back and lick accumulated wounds."[145]

Rhodesian Light Infantry's John C. LaDuke with Support Commando and Fire Force Delta late in the war recalled:

As the last chopper sat down one day, I walked over to look at the 206 bodies laid out on each side of a makeshift runway in a tribal trust land I have since forgotten the name of. I know there were that many because I counted them. I drank a Lion beer as I slowly strolled down that airstrip, filthy dirty from the camo cream, the ever present dust of the bush and the sweat of fear and exertion of battle, watching Black police officers fingerprint those dead men, women and children, sometimes kicking bodies no longer capable of response. My mind was numb and my ears were still ringing at the results of 13 hours of fighting that had started at four in the morning. ... This was more than I had seen before, so many bodies that the police had separate piles, one for arms and one for legs ... some of them were civilians caught in the fire zone and cut to pieces by the K-Car quad machine gun.[146]

This allowed for rest and refitting, in which "All officers and [noncommissioned officers] must take an interest in the men, or their effectiveness will be impaired" recalled an RLI medic, "In the meantime we sit and wait, practice [physical training] and quick-kill shooting, and I give lessons on medics and first aid. It seems I have heard that tune before."[147]

Trooper Norris reflected the more subtle impact of the effort:

> No one liked caves. No one liked the way so many guys got shot in front of them.
>
> No one liked mango trees, with their dense canopy of dark green leaves. Clearing a mango grove meant dashing from trunk to trunk, peering stupidly up into the highest-quality concealment on the African continent.
>
> No one like reentrants. A walk single-file down a narrow reentrant was like a 3D afternoon at a horror movie.
>
> No one like female terrs. They were the ugliest, meanest, most seriously belligerent ball-busting bitches in the southern hemisphere. They looked better dead than alive.
>
> No one liked windowless huts. Anything could be lurking in those darkened rafters, and often was.
>
> No one like *mujibas*, the little kids, usually male, five to ten years old, used as couriers, spies or early warning for the terrs. They were impossible to detect and disturbingly effective in their pint-sized dedications to their "heroes of the revolution."
>
> No one liked dragging out gook bodies for uplift and identification by Special Branch ghouls. [This fell away later in the war, when escalating body counts rendered the study of individual remains impractical.]
>
> No one liked checking a buddy for a pulse.
>
> No one liked corned beef.
>
> No one liked to hear they were losing the war.[148]

Guerrilla Techniques to Counter Fire Force

To adapt to Fire Force, the guerrillas positioned air sentries whose only function was to listen for aircraft. If Fire Force aircraft were perceived, then the terrorist group would disperse in twos and threes. If the aircraft passed by, they would regroup. If the aircraft reacted to their position, then the guerrillas moved to a predetermined rendezvous. Depending on the terrain, weapons would be hidden to look like locals or advantage would be taken of undergrowth to move away. The amount of ground a running terrorist could cover was surprising and often underestimated.[149] One ZPRA fighter recalled, "Normally a turbine engine is quite easy to hear but when they came in at treetop height and from downwind, they could be on top of you before anyone heard a thing. ... It was very tempting to run like hell on these occasions but most of our casualties were caused by people gapping it in pure panic."[150]

The guerrilla response varied between "fight, flight, or freeze."[151] If they heard the aircraft early, they would "bomb shell" in different directions or if surprised they would "go to cover." Those caught in the open just stood there or opened fire with the weapons at hand. While fire was often limited to small arms, heavy machine guns and rocket-propelled grenades could suddenly change the situation.[152] "It is a common tactic for the terrorists to hide in thick cover or in huts and not to run. ... Where terrorists have been sighted in a kraal complex, they sometimes hide their weapons and become locals."[153] If the terrorists were observed moving, the K-Car would proceed directly to the target area as time was the utmost, with the troopships following. If terrorists were pinpointed or running, the gunship would engage them immediately followed by stick deployment. If no terrorists were seen then the sticks would have to deploy to flush them out. Reid-Daly felt most terrorists evaded the "cull," despite claims for Fire Force success, and that only about 10 percent of the guerrillas were thus killed or captured.[154]

Another option adapted was to counter the security force observation posts by compromising their locations. Group Captain Petter-Bowyer felt that by 1978:

> ZANLA relied on *mujibas* (locally trained terrorists and local youth spies) to provide them with early warning on Rhodesian security force positions and movement of Fire Forces. *Mujibas*, often posing as common cattle herdsmen, drove cattle through likely [observation post] positions. Their abnormal practice of driving cattle over high features clearly identified active *mujibas* who were counted as communist terrorists when caught and were either captured or killed.
>
> In most ZANLA-affected areas high features abounded. *Mujibas* used these to establish an early warning system in which whistled messages were passed from one high point to the next along the line of Fire Force and ground patrol movements. … A Fire Force flying at 90 knots could not hope to outpace the whistled warnings that passed ahead of their flight line at the speed of sound … At one point *mujibas* had started denuding high features of all natural vegetation in an attempt to deny hidden [observation posts] but the practice was dropped when they realized they needed the same cover themselves. … Visual recce from the air could not assist in these counter-*mujiba* operations because it was impossible to differentiate between security force [observation posts] and *mujiba* path patterns. … So troublesome was this warning system that selected troops moved into high points at night to kill *mujibas* when they took up their positions at dawn.[155]

One RLI veteran recalled:

> Stealth is next to impossible to maintain in remote third and fourth world tribal areas and exhaustion has diminished the fighting capabilities of the unit by the time they are in positions to contain or attack the terrorists and hopefully annihilate them. In Africa, those cute little pickaninnies (tribal children) hadn't stumbled into our midst—they were looking for us. I am sure all the candy bars and bags of sugar we gave them to get them to tell us about the terrorists did little more than encourage all the pickaninnies to find us. We found if you had two-day-old aftershave on or smoked cigarettes, forget it. They walked right to you from the village. If the birds stopped chirping, started chirping, or flew out of a tree within sight of them they knew you were there just as they had learned their centuries-old enemies had stalked them and were ready to attack.[156]

On 28 December 1979, a final Fire Force was dispatched from Grand Reef forward airfield in response to fire received by a PATU patrol on Ruombwe mountain south of Rusape. Two K-Cars, two Cheetahs deploying seven 1RLI sticks, a Lynx, and a Trojan responded and arrived at 1445. An inconclusive engagement in broken and rocky terrain continued until police and army forces withdrew at dusk, after killing some 15 insurgents. At midnight, the ceasefire went in to effect.

CHAPTER 7

Cross-border Attacks

No Sanctuary

Rhodesian cross-border, or "external," operations were variously denied, considered hot-pursuit, or known as column attacks. Of direct interest were incursions conducted into the Frontline States of Zambia, Botswana, and Mozambique that provided support, basing, and access to Rhodesia for the nationalists.[1] These started against ZPRA in Zambia as early 1966. In 1967, operations along with South Africans within Rhodesia and with Portuguese armed forces in Mozambique began. By 1970, ZPRA was being targeted in Botswana with direct action to follow. To this point, external operations were clandestine or covert and kept hidden. External operations in Zambia and Botswana were run for the Operations Coordinating Committee by the CIO and by the military with the Portuguese and South Africans. This changed in 1973 with JOC Hurricane activities from Mukumbura and Macombe of a more autonomous nature against ZANLA in Mozambique. While the efforts directed at Zambia and Botswana were against supposed neutrals and fellow Commonwealth members, the 1974 exit of Portugal from Mozambique was seen to create hostile territory open to unilateral action by the security forces. Activities were put on hold for a time as an attempt was made through 1975 to secure an agreed-upon ceasefire with all parties. Infiltration from Mozambique increased as ZANLA's support by the Marxist independence government became a major factor. A new phase began in 1976, after the guerrilla staging areas closest to the border were pushed back by the Rhodesian policy of "hot pursuit." This remained the case until the camps extended in size and area that could no longer be effectively contained. The result was expanded air attacks and switching to transportation or economic targets. From 1977, cross-border raids were conducted by Combined Operations of a joint or combined character which were often complex and large scale, with significant political or diplomatic impact.

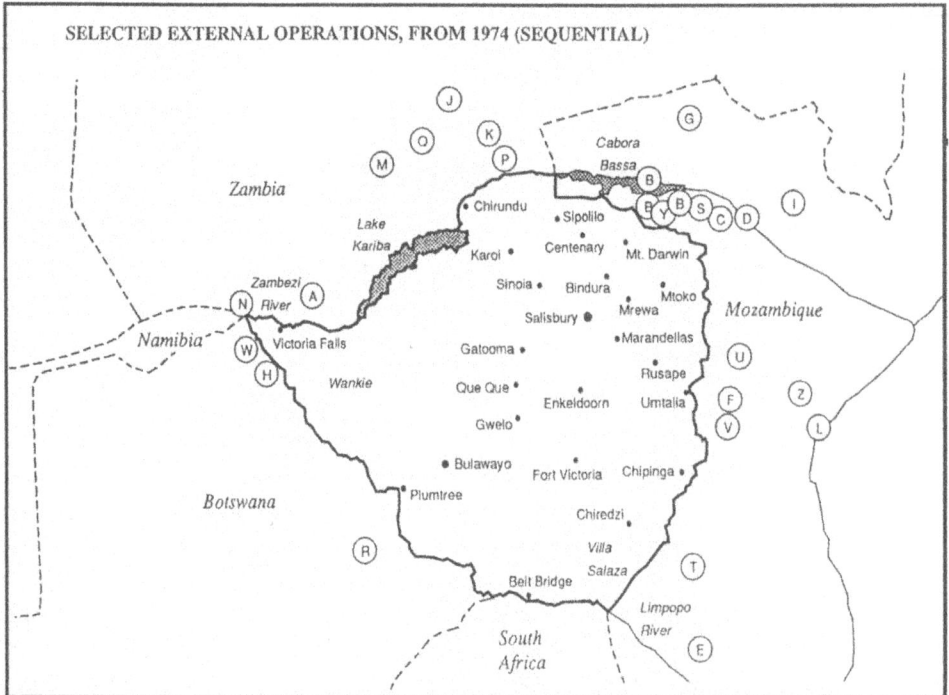

Selected external operations, from 1974

The details and context of these actions were used to shape this account. For example, the major cross-border raids needed to be considered as general purpose rather than special operations. Some actions were target specific while others were area focused, resulting in either fixed or prolonged sojourns in other countries. While together they had a cumulative effect, they have been discussed separately based on the aims for which they were undertaken. These should also be incorporated with outside diplomatic and political events to give a fuller understanding of their significance. Not included were sanctions-busting and intelligence activities of a non-military nature. Professor Richard Wood identified some 500 named operations conducted during the 1964 to 1980 period. Of these, some 41 were considered worthy of discussion with senior Rhodesian security force leaders in postwar interviews by David W. Arnold, a BSAP superintendent. These were used for a study by the American RAND Corporation and are examined here. A brief listing with essential details of these actions is provided.[2]

Selected Special, General-purpose, and Air Force External Operations, 1974–9

When (month, year), Where (country), Who (SAS, SS, GPF, AF, foe), What (combat, recon, unconventional warfare), Why (operation, objective), map location shown by letter in sequence vice alphabetical.[3]*

March 1974	Botswana, SS/ZAPU recon (Francistown) – R
August–October 1974	Zambia, SAS/ZAPU combat (*Big Bang*) – A
September 1974	Botswana, SS/ZAPU recce (Francistown) – R
March 1975	Mozambique, SS/ZANU combat (Caponda) – Y
January 1976	Mozambique, SS/ZANU combat (*Underdog*) – C
April 1976	Mozambique, SS/ZANU combat (*Traveler*) – Y
May 1976	Mozambique, SS/ZANU combat (*Detachment*) – T
June 1976	Mozambique, SS/ZANU combat (*Long John*) – E
August 1976	Mozambique, SS/ZANU combat (*Eland*) – U
October 1976	Mozambique, SS SAS GPF AF/ZANU combat (*Mardon*) – E
November 1976	Botswana, SS/ZANU combat (*Ignition*) – R
January 1977	Mozambique, SAS/ZANU combat (*Cockleshell*) – B
March, May 1977	Mozambique, SAS/ZANU combat (Chicoa) – C
May–June 1977	Mozambique, SS/ZANU combat (*Aztec*) – E
October 1977	Mozambique, SAS/ZANU combat (Chicoa–Tete) – D
October–November 1977	Mozambique, SAS/ZANU combat (Gaza) – E
November 1977	Mozambique, SAS GPF AF/ZANU combat (*Dingo*) – F, G
January–June 1978	Zambia, SAS/ZAPU combat (*Elbow*) – A
February 1978	Botswana, SAS/ZAPU BDF combat (hot pursuit) – H
May 1978	Mozambique, SAS/ZANU combat (Tete) – I
October 1978	Zambia, SAS GPF AF/ZAPU combat (*Gatling*) – J, K
December 1978	Zambia, SS/ZAPU combat (*Vodka*) – north of map
December 1978	Mozambique, SAS/ZANU combat (*Inhibit*) – E
December 1978	Mozambique, SAS AF/ZANU FPLM combat (*Shovel*) – L

---

* Note: operations marked with an asterisk, e.g., (Operation *Virile**) are not listed in the RAND study as above.

January 1979	Mozambique, SAS MNR/FPLM u/w (Mavuze power plant) – V
February–April 1979	Botswana, SS/ZAPU combat (*Petal*) – W, R
February–March 1979	Mozambique, SAS AF/ZANU combat (*Neutron*) – F
February 1979	Angola, AF/ZAPU combat (*Vanity*) – north of map
March 1979	Mozambique, SAS MNR SADF/FPLM u/w (Beira fuel depot) – L
April 1979	Zambia, SAS/ZAPU combat (*Bastille*) – M
April 1979	Botswana, SAS/ZAPU combat (*Dinky*) – N
June 1979	Zambia, SAS/ZAPU combat (*Carpet*) – M
June 1979	Zambia, SAS AF/ZAPU combat (*Chicory*) – M
September 1979	Mozambique, SAS GPF AF/FPLM ZANU (*Uric*) – E
September 1979	Mozambique, SAS MNR/FPLM u/w (*Norah*) – Z
September 1979	Mozambique, SAS MNR SADF/FPLM u/w (Beira dredgers) – L
September–October 1979	Mozambique, SS GPF AF/ZANU combat (*Miracle*) – F
October 1979	Mozambique, SAS/FPLM ZANU combat (Tete rail bridges) – I
October 1979	Zambia, SAS/ZANU combat (*Cheese*) – north of map
October 1979	Zambia, SAS/ZAPU combat (*Tepid*) – P
November 1979	Zambia, SAS/Zambia ZAPU combat (*Dice*) – K, P, north of map

A Selous Scout reconnaissance and a prisoner snatch against ZAPU in Francistown, Botswana on 29 March 1974 marked the start of expanded cross-border effort. An eight-man team (four Whites, four Blacks) infiltrated Francistown and captured four staff members from the ZPRA headquarters and returned them to Rhodesia for interrogation.[4] The SAS was in combat with ZAPU in Zambia from 9 August to 6 October 1974 (Operation *Big Bang*). With Brian Robinson ill at the time, the effort was led by his deputy Garth Barrett.[5] This cumulated in the "largest and most successful external raid up to that time," when the SAS launched a 43-man attack on ZPRA's Pondoland East "A" Camp designed to inhibit infiltration from Zambia.[6] The raiders crossed the Zambezi by boat and approached on foot. The effort killed nine insurgents, but captured or destroyed a vast quantity of ordnance and supplies impacting on planned ZAPU infiltrations for some time. Success was marred by a guerrilla attack on the operation's forward operating base in Rhodesia.[7] In September 1974, the Selous Scouts conducted reconnaissance and a prisoner snatch against ZAPU in Botswana. A subsequent return trip was made to recover passports, weapons, and radios left behind in the confused action.[8] African nationalist leaders were released from prison to attend the Lusaka conference in October 1974, but as diplomacy and negotiation stalemated, external operations stepped up with the approach of independence for Mozambique and the Portuguese departure.

The Selous Scouts went into combat with ZANU in Mozambique in March 1975. A 20-man party made a 24-hour approach march to reach the Caponda Camp some 34 miles inside Mozambique. They found the ZANLA transit camp deserted due to a cholera outbreak.[9] As the Victoria Falls Conference failed in August 1975, the African National Council split into two wings loyal to Abel Muzorewa and Joshua Nkomo, while Robert Mugabe consolidated his leadership of ZANU. The diplomatic and political powers took time to decide on what to do next. The need for cross border military operations became more obvious with the collapse of Portugal's African provinces and the reality of a Marxist regime in Mozambique. In part, Reid-Daly believed, because "the Rhodesians gave FRELIMO a two-year respite to get their house in order."[10]

At that time, August 1975, the Rhodesian special forces considered their respective abilities for external operations with the risk of competition for tasks that could have been resolved with centralized planning. Special Air Service capabilities were reported by its wartime commander Major Brian Robinson to the Joint Planning Staff as having a strength of 50 to 55 "bayonets" or operators capable of forming some 12–13 four-man patrols. Robinson further broke this down into 10 trained divers for five independent two-man underwater demolition teams, and eight two-man Klepper canoe teams (capable of carrying up to 24 men for short distances). All were trained for static-line parachuting and 41 trained for freefall parachuting (either high altitude, low opening or high opening) but limited by available number of parachutes and aircraft range. In addition, 32 were qualified medics, 19 were demolitions experts, for nine independent two-man general demolition teams, and 12 were trained trackers.[11]

Robinson stated the capabilities and limitations of the available SAS patrols: a minimum of a week was necessary for planning; missions were either short range or long range; the effort employed against individual targets depended upon the nature and extent of damage required; each soldier could carry 60 pounds (some 30kg) of gear, and would need carriers, caches, or resupply for extended missions;[12] insertion and extraction could be by parachute and foot with helicopter and fixed-wing support (depending upon the degree of enemy air defenses);[13] external positioning and recovery was needed for Zodiac craft seaborne efforts, involving submarine and warship support.

The Selous Scout commander, Major Ron Reid-Daly, summarized his unit's capabilities to the Joint Planning Staff as well. The European strength of the Selous Scouts was comparable to that in the SAS at the time—deployment of European members with the more numerous Africans was essential, with limitations (but no mention was made of the number of Africans in the Scouts). External deployment was by foot or helicopter. Parachute training was sought for all ranks, with limitations then being aircraft range and enemy air defenses. Ten days' worth of rations could be carried; extended operations required caches or resupply; elements could also live entirely off the land making full use of food from the local population and resupply unnecessary. Reid-Daly emphasized the unique intelligence gathering by his unit through the ability to "infiltrate enemy ranks." A limited number of his operators spoke Mozambican dialects, although Chishona was widespread in central Mozambique.

Reid-Daly went on to list a number of other capabilities to include conventional attacks on terrorist bases or camps adjacent to the border, demolition of unsophisticated targets (small bridges, power lines, or buildings), and kidnapping and assassination.[14] Deep-penetration operations were aimed at harassment by ambush, mining, and raids or by fomenting ill-feeling and friction within the terrorist factions. Like the SAS, these were characterized as being undertaken by either overt or covert means and a real capability for clandestine means existed. Significantly, the unit had the potential for forming three 30-man mobile "Chindit" columns for external operations of up to six weeks. These external missions were seen by some as an expansion of the regiment's original role, but not when considering the Special Branch responsibility for internal dissidents when overseas. Reid-Daly also added, "The Selous Scouts are adverse to joint operations with C Squadron SAS and prefer to operate on their own."[15]

As the Scouts succeeded internally, mission expansion followed as well as competition with the SAS for covert external operations. Robinson was incensed that the Scouts got the SAS's external tasks, although his deputy Barrett believed "there were more than enough assignments to go around."[16] Both organizations presented appraisals to the Operations Coordinating Committee and Joint Planning Staff for missions that created friction with each contending for limited resources as well as tasking. The exclusively European SAS could not compete with use requiring African participation and was always relatively small in numbers. Selous Scout reconnaissance and combat patrols crossed the Zambian, Botswanan, and Mozambican borders into the Frontline States, escalating to the use of mobile columns. To this point, external operations were clandestine or covert and deniable. These raids broadened cross-border activities to a level of conventional operations in size and scope. Afterwards, there was no turning back in the efforts to eliminate the nationalists in their "safe havens."

A major factor was the increase in internal counterinsurgency operations, as guerrilla infiltration and subversion was not stemmed. This stretched the general-purpose forces of the police, army, and air force to new limits in the conduct actions along the Operation *Hurricane* model. Joint Operations Center (JOC) Ranger stood up in September 1975 in Bulawayo as a result of ZPRA guerrillas from

Botswana infiltrating Matabeleland. A short half-year later, by February 1976, major infiltration by ZANLA guerrillas from Mozambique saw the need for JOC Thrasher in Umtali on the eastern border, and JOC Repulse in Fort Victoria stretching to the southeastern border. To take the pressure off, more cross-border raids were called for of an increased intensity and daring.

External operations continued with Selous Scouts in combat with ZANU in Mozambique on 17 January 1976 (Operation *Underdog*). The 15-"operator" raid on Chikombedzi Camp was undertaken. After insertion by helicopter, the force destroyed the ZANLA transit camp without incident in the night attack.[17] The Scouts continued to make Mozambique its hunting ground, when on 27 April 1976, they again went into combat with ZANU (Operation *Traveler*). This was a return to Caponda after a year's absence. A 20-man patrol hiked to the objective, attacked, and killed or wounded 23 terrorists although several Scouts were injured.[18] Selous Scouts were in combat with ZANU in Mozambique from 13–25 May 1976 (Operation *Detachment*). This attack took place at Chigamane Base, some 67 miles inside Mozambique. Twenty European and African Scouts traveling in four trucks were dressed as FRELIMO forces. The attack was made with mortars, rockets, and machine guns with no casualties to the attackers. Roads were then mined on withdrawal.[19]

The use of mobile columns became the hallmark of external operations. "The concept grew from a lack of alternatives," wrote an assault group second-in-command. "The Selous Scouts ... were so successful in this type of engagement that its subsequent use in Mozambique and by the SAS in Zambia became a regular feature of proximity cross-border operations." These were reasonably close to the border (roughly 15 to 20 kilometers); deeper objectives could not be reached with a chance of taking the enemy by surprise. Because speed and stealth was essential, seldom were more than a dozen Mercedes Unimog vehicles used in a column and 80 to 90 men. The SAS conducted similar columns in Zambia on a more limited scale.[20] In another example, between 18–26 June 1976, in Mozambique the Selous Scouts went into combat with ZANU (Operation *Long John*). This involved a mobile column attacking Mapai Base 77 kilometers inside Mozambique. Some 58 Scouts in four trucks and two armored cars again traveled disguised as FRELIMO soldiers. On entering the town, an armory was seized and 13 vehicles were destroyed. An airstrike was made after the raiders departed. Reportedly 37 terrorists were killed or wounded with one of the raiding party killed and several wounded.[21]

The committee approach of the OCC proved a limiting factor as the conflict expanded and military proposals were delayed or diluted by civil members.[22] As debate continued, JOC Tangent stood up in Bulawayo (incorporating the previous JOC Ranger) as ZPRA and ZANLA increased efforts in Matabeleland, infiltrating from Botswana, South Africa, and Mozambique. Border control and area counterinsurgency would not to be the solution to the increasing problem. Reid-Daly's experience in using a mobile column to hit Mapai, a transit camp in Gaza province, in June 1976 led him to feel larger targets were practical and would pay off in nationalist casualties and disruption. He pressed the army commander, General Walls, over the objections of CIO Director Flower to make a major cross-border foray. The attack marked a change in direction for special forces and cross-border operations with Operation *Eland* by the Selous Scouts.

In response to multiple attacks on the Ruda police camp and the Burma valley in Rhodesia from Mozambique, a reaction was authorized for a major cross-border response. Intelligence indicated that the source of these attacks was a ZANLA base on the Pungwe and Nyadzonya rivers. This information came from captured terrorists and air photo reconnaissance, which indicated several thousand nationalists would be in residence. The Nyadzonya raid was planned for 9 August 1976 as a covert operation (air support would be limited to helicopter gunships and emergency medical evacuation). The objective was a major ZANU base area 60 miles inside Mozambique, occupied by 5,000 individuals, of whom 3,000 were considered trained terrorists. A mobile column of 10 trucks and four armored cars carried 74–84 raiders disguised as FRELIMO soldiers. These would move cross-country then by road into the camp.

The motorized strike force departed from Umtali on 8 August 1976, eliminating a combined ZANLA and Tanzanian outpost of trained guerrillas before moving on to the main camp as it was assembling on the parade ground at 0520. With complete surprise and heavy machine-gun and mortar fire, the attack was completed at 0650. The attack by fire killed an estimated 1,350 terrorists. Fourteen important captures were made and an ambush by a covering party killed a further six ZANLA leaders. Four Selous Scouts were slightly wounded in the attacking force. The Rhodesian raiders destroyed several bridges on their return on 10 August with captured documents, prisoners, and material. Mozambique responded with rocket and mortar attacks on Umtali on 11 August, followed by similar strikes on Vila Salazar and other Rhodesian border posts.[23]

While a military success, plausible deniability for cross-border operations of this scale was no longer possible. Nationalist claims and Rhodesian counterclaims flew as to whether this was a humanitarian refugee camp or guerrilla training base, often being one in the same in the context of the war. The response varied—the international community abhorred it and the Rhodesian public reveled in it. The South Africans withdrew their helicopters and crews in protest. One sidebar was that the SAS regarded it as a personal challenge. Major M. F. "Mick" Graham, then second-in-command of the Special Air Service, felt "we in the SAS were disappointed and rather bitter about our exclusion" from the raid.[24] This was "puzzling" to Reid-Daly, because at the time the SAS could hardly put 90 men in the field and had no Black soldiers. Besides, there were then some 10,000 terrorists spread over 3,000 kilometers of territory.[25] As a result Brian Robinson would plan to get at least a thousand terrorists in an operation leading to the later open attacks of Chimoio and Tembué.

The Patriotic Front (PF) was formed from ZANU and ZAPU as an all-party Geneva conference was convened in October 1976, as a new phase began on the ground. After guerrilla staging areas closest to the border had been pushed back by the "hot pursuit" policy, according to one analyst, "The result was all sorts went over the border, the Territorial Force from 2, 5, 8 Rhodesia Regiment recce platoons, the Grey's, the RAR, and RR kept the Mozambique front quiet for long periods with patrols ... part of defense in depth: SAS in deep, 2RR in shallow; behind them within Rhodesia Fire Force and Shangaans."[26] Additional information was received at the time of Operation *Eland*, that FRELIMO was using the railway to move forces into the Malvernia area in support of ZANLA. As a consequence, a number of small sabotage teams were used to damage the line and rolling stock. Later two objectives were selected for more extensive destruction: Jorge do Limpopo on the railway and Massangena on the Sabi River crossing.

Selous Scouts, SAS, RLI and air forces went into combat with FPLM and ZANU from 30 October through 3 November 1976, in Mozambique with Operation *Mardon*. This was a series of attacks made under the codename. It involved mobile columns attacking to disrupt logistics and communications. Preliminary reconnaissance was from two teams (one of three men, the other of two). From Chiredzi two mobile columns of some 80 vehicles moved on the target areas in Gaza and Tete provinces in Mozambique on 30 October, taking longer to arrive than planned, on the 31st. On crossing the border a circuitous route was used, and although the closest target was only 57 kilometers from the border, some 350 to 400 kilometers were covered with the round trip (objectives were in fact some 100 kilometers beyond the border and 250 kilometers apart). A succession of attacks was made and road and rail routes were left mined as the column passed. In addition, the two reconnaissance teams were recovered on the return to the border. With air support, the columns successfully arrived back were they started from. A FRELIMO garrison had been destroyed, as well as a number of ZANLA camps and arms dumps, two trains derailed, telephone lines cut, and a reservoir demolished before returning to Rhodesia. [27] Meanwhile in Botswana, the Selous Scouts went into combat against ZAPU from 9 through 11 November 1976 (Operation *Ignition*). The raiding party hit the ZPRA headquarters in Francistown to destroy sabotage materials stockpiled there. The building was destroyed and at least five terrorists were wounded.[28]

General Walls commented about developments, the most critical since 1974 being, "Probably the collapse of the Portuguese and the Angolan episode combined the two most significant events as far as the conduct of our counterinsurgency war is concerned, yes." And by 1976, "Again, I prefer not to deal in numbers. I believe it gives you a completely false picture. I don't think there's any likelihood of a D-day. We've already had D-day. They've already, in the past, made an effort; they're still making an effort." He continued, "How effective have the terrorists been in cutting our rail links to southern Africa? I would say we're not worried about our lines of communications. All of which must illustrate we're pretty much on the ball."[29] South African support went without comment by Walls, although police units and pilots were withdrawn in 1976, while the South African Defense Force continued covertly after that. South Africa also had an active conflict in Angola and South West Africa underway at the same time.

Walls provided the rationale for operations, particularly into Mozambique:

> For a long time we have indulged in hot pursuit where we have considered this to be in the interests of the people living in Rhodesia. We did not just start it the other day, although some South African newspapers said, at long last that the Rhodesians have started in hot pursuit. But, at the same time, our government's policy, and therefore that of the security forces, is that we would like to co-exist with whoever is running Mozambique. In the old days, it was the Portuguese, now it's FRELIMO, one day it might be someone else. For the foreseeable future it's FRELIMO. We'd like to live with these chaps. We'd like to be friends with them; we have absolutely no aggressive intentions against them. Therefore, perhaps we've been putting up with a fair amount [the rockets and shelling of Vila Salazar, according to Venter], to prove our good faith in this respect. And I believe that so long as it's our government policy and ours, to get along with these chaps, we will put up with it as long as we can, in the hope that they will come to the same sort of feeling about us.[30]

He added:

> Nobody likes getting shot at, and everybody would like to shoot back when they are shot at. But fortunately, by contrast perhaps to the people on the other side, we have extremely well-disciplined troops. I think my instructions and those of my colleagues in the security forces are perfectly clear in this respect. Wherever there's danger to life and property along the whole border, they know exactly what they can do about it. I'm not worried that chaps don't understand their orders, and won't comply with them, and I think we have a pretty good record of controlled discipline. I think we've gone out of our way to show our good faith on all our borders. ... I hope I've made it clear that whenever we think it necessary we indulge, and will indulge in hot pursuit operations. We would rather that our neighbors behaved as good neighbors and made hot pursuit entirely unnecessary by not allowing terrorists to operate from their territory against Rhodesia.[31]

In regards to the overall situation in the northeast (JOC Hurricane) and east (JOC Thrasher) of the country at the time, Walls felt:

> There's no problem that we didn't expect and plan for. I don't think they were caught with their pants down. [Venter's source] may have been one of those enthusiastic young chaps who wishes everything was absolutely ideal; and this is fine because this is what we must all strive for. But I think perhaps you are quoting from something I said at Wankie when I was giving a bit of a boost to civil defense. I must admit to seeing that something was moving and I was giving it a bit of a pat on the back. But I would take issue with anybody who said that nothing was being prepared, because some of the civil measures, anti-terrorist measures, and some of the facilities available to the security forces and the civil population could never have been, if people had not been preparing.[32]
>
> I haven't had any great evidence of people evacuating the area—I'm sure they'll flow back as our measures bear fruit. But naturally the determination that I saw down there recently is

very encouraging from our point of view. I believe that in spite of what I've said about being prepared every time a new area opens up, there will be some initial successes on the part of the terrorists because we have tried not to make normal peace areas into operational areas until we've had to. But the measures we've taken now should be successful.

There is a difficulty in the east which didn't apply in the north inasmuch as the terrorists are able to hit and run, which they couldn't do up at the top [of the country, i.e., the northeast]. Because they've got Mozambique from which to operate and then bolt back to, they can build up their logistics there, and so on. This perhaps is slightly different. There have been a lot of instances of hit and run raids in small activity which didn't apply in the northeast.[33]

At this juncture, General Walls evaluated the nationalist situation:

There have been recent further examples of dissidence in the terrorist ranks and even between partners in crime, you might say. They've turned to fighting each other. The local population, who are no fools, see this. I think we can win simply because we are law and order trying to stamp out criminals. That's what it is in simple terms ... The Chitepo incident is a very good example. But take for example Bishop Muzorewa. He trundles around Africa, as somebody said to us the other day, trying on and ordering new uniforms in each capital he visits and trying to pose as the leader of the terrorists. I think it is pretty evident that he is not accepted by anybody, including I would say, possibly the African Presidents, as the leader of the terrorists operating in Rhodesia now. You've got Mr. Nkomo who is trying to negotiate with the Government. He himself would have to concede that he doesn't command the support of everybody who at the moment is carrying out acts of terrorism in Rhodesia. You've got Ndabaningi Sithole, Chikerema, Mugabe, all of these at some time or other have claimed to be the real leader. I don't think any of those I've quoted there and then can be said to be the leader. In fact, none of them has the support of the terrorist in the field. ... There is no man who stands out and there will be no man. If one comes to light between the time I'm talking now and the time you print this, if he stands up as the leader, within a few months it will be proved he is not the leader. This is quite definite. This is the whole pattern of their setup.[34]

The SAS started the New Year in combat with ZANU in Mozambique from 16 January to 19 February 1977 (Operation *Cockleshell*). Some 12 SAS men used kayaks operating from the Cabora Bassa reservoir. The group operated for six weeks, paddled 540 kilometers, and ambushed or mined lines of communications. They also raided several ZANLA and FRELIMO installations and bases. In this, they killed some 20 guerrillas and the FRELIMO commander, second-in-command, and political officer for Mukumbura. There were no SAS casualties. Further SAS and Selous Scout external operations continued using the same methods.[35]

Combined Operations

Combined Operations (ComOps) headquarters stood up, along with the National Joint Operations Center (NatJOC), in Salisbury in March 1977. With General Peter Walls as supreme commander, ostensibly in charge of army, air force, and police operations (although still no more senior in rank), this resulted in external operations expanding with a common headquarters that was a more receptive audience. It now had control of the air–ground reaction forces, border control, and external operations

Prime Minister

CIO
Central
Intelligence
Organisation

COMOPs : Combined Operations HQ
(Milton Buildings - Salisbury)

Commander (Lt Gen G.P. Walls)
+
Joint Staff - Army, Air Force, Police, Special Branch
Communications Centre & Ops Rooms

Special Forces

SAS
Selous Scouts
Greys Scouts

Army HQ

Air Force HQ

Police General HQ

Retained indirect command
Admin command of their units only

JOCs

Op Thrasher Umtali Manicaland	Op Repulse Fort Victoria Victoria Prov	Op Hurricane Salisbury NE Mashonaland	Op Tangent Bulawayo	Op Grapple Gwelo Midlands	Op Splinter Kariba Lake Kariba	Sal Ops Salisbury Salisbury City
3 Brigade	4 Brigade	2 Brigade	1 Brigade	2 Brigade	2 Brigade	2 Brigade
Sub JOCs at Risape Grand Reef Chipinga	Sub JOCs at Buffalo Range Rutenga Shabani	Sub JOCs at Mt Darwin Bindura Mtoko	Sub JOCs at Wankie Victoria Falls Gwanda	Sub JOCs at Gokwe Gatooma Enkeldoorn	Sub JOCs at Mt Darwin Bindura Mtoko	

Fire Forces

Alpha
Bravo
Charlie

Later
Delta
Echo

Army and other
Combat Units

Rhodesian Light Infantry
Rhodesian African Rifles

Rhodesia Regt
Independent Coys
TF Batts
Reserve Batts
Artillery, Engineers,
signals
Police Support Unit
PATU, Guard Force etc

Allocated to the JOCs on a
roster system

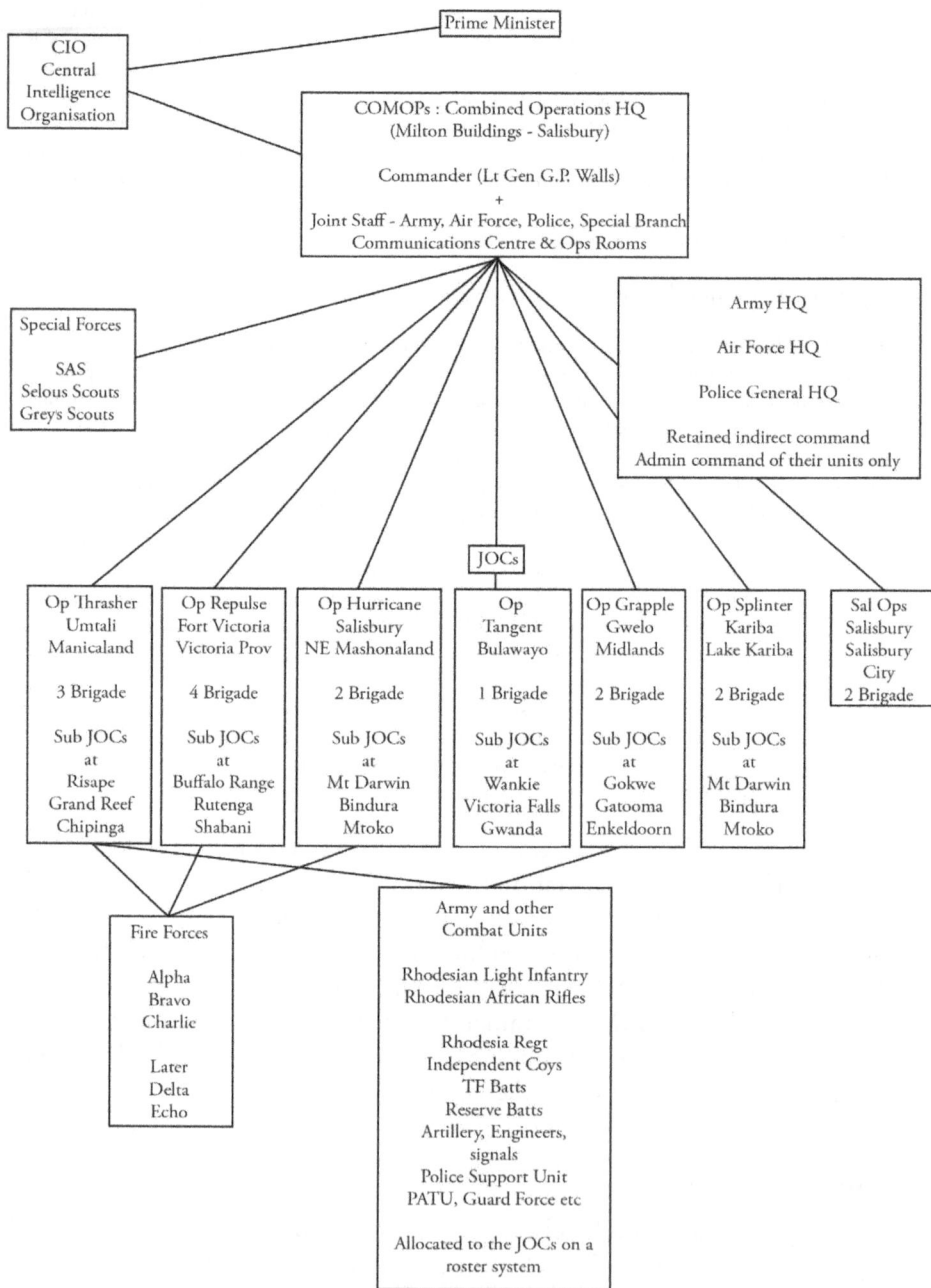

Command and Control, Combined Operations (ComOps)

while the brigade JOCs concentrated on the counterinsurgency effort in their own area of operations. From then on, cross-border raids were conducted of a joint or combined character which were often complex and large scale, and had significant political or diplomatic impact. By now, special operations were fully integrated into the full matrix of border control, counterinsurgency, and cross-border operations.[36]

For some time this centralized military control had been called for. Ron Reid-Daly felt the advent of a supremo "had done much to stabilize the military, who welcomed a strong hand." There were those that felt Walls was not decisive and failed to control the Selous Scouts as one example of this.[37] Personality clashes continued between the police, army, and air force commanders who felt Combined Operations should formulate higher policy and strategy and leave the execution to the service commanders and Walls, who believed the purpose of Combined Operations was to fight the war through the various JOC commanders, control of Fire Forces, the cordon sanitaire, and special operating forces.[38] With this, the Fire Forces kept the internal guerrillas moving, dispersed, and fragmented. The "CorSan" delayed, disrupted, and channelized insurgent entry into Rhodesia. Finally, external operations pushed the enemy back from the border, interdicted and destroyed supply or support infrastructure, and eliminated Patriotic Front leadership.

Brian Robinson convinced Walls that the command and control of the SAS "had to be at the highest level" and that a senior coordinating officer was "a must." "This was essential to avoid blue on blue contacts and duplication between the Selous Scouts and ourselves," he noted.[39] Special forces commanders continued their own planning, and then presented concepts for final clearance to Walls, Flower, and Smith. Robinson recalled, "Plans always seem to come from the bottom up" and not the other way around.[40] Garth Barrett felt: "This was multi-level and by that I mean there was planning at unit level from our own intelligence, from CIO level from their 'int,' and from air force 'int.' There was then discussions or direct tasking for operations; the Joint Planning Staff did not normally come into this process in my experience."[41] The special operations planning team that evolved would eventually include Robinson, and Group Captains Norman Walsh and Peter Petter-Bowyer. From the special forces perspective, it made it easier to obtain air support, photography, and other intelligence.[42] It also increased the number of people aware of the special operations outside of the units involved with a resulting security risk that plagued special forces to the war's end.[43]

The nature of Selous Scout deception-based technique required that its use be kept secret. Like signals intelligence, this usually meant its accomplishments were not publicized. While effective at their assigned task, unwanted publicity caused in part by extreme security measures, made them vulnerable to nationalist charges of atrocities created to look like guerrilla actions. An unintended result was that nationalist disinformation about murder, poaching, and unlawful activities was never adequately countered. Joshua Nkomo told the press from Lusaka that

"Freedom fighters are told not to molest civilians, to concentrate only on military targets. Our people are being killed in their hundreds by the Selous Scouts to make the people hate the freedom movement."[44] In a British Broadcasting Corporation interview, Mugabe stated, "we are fighting a progressive war which is aimed at mobilizing all the democratic forces capable of lending support to the revolution and all along we have been working harmoniously with all the church organizations."[45]

After a series of attacks on missionaries were blamed on the Selous Scouts (the Lupane, Honde valley, and Musami mission killings being incidents cited), the Rhodesians had to go public to present its cover story of being a "tracking" unit that ran guerrilla sections down by these means. In March 1977, various media representatives were taken to see training and meet individual Scouts who emphasized their multiracial nature, hard training, and bushcraft expertise. The use of enemy uniforms, weapons, and tactics were denied and no former terrorists were shown. How effective this was is difficult to gauge, as operations continued with a degree of notoriety.[46] By then, Reid-Daly claimed to have eliminated 1,205 terrorists with the loss of 10 of its own: "I wouldn't say we physically cut each bloke's throat, but our tracking resulted in these kills."[47]

The SAS was in combat with ZANU, March and May 1977, in Mozambique. ZANLA had established a major base near Chicoa in the Tete province. It was well built with a network of protective trenches and bunkers. An attack was launched on 24 March, with the 22 raiders carried in by three helicopters in two waves from Marymount mission police camp. On landing, there was an 11-mile approach on foot to the target. Demolition charges were used on the barracks, followed by a sweep through the objective. "It was a well-planned and executed operation and the garrison was never really reoccupied," according to one observer. Some 38 terrorists were killed with the loss of one SAS man. In May, after ZANLA moved into Chicoa town, a force of 16 SAS returned to the area to conduct ambushes and mine laying. Later that month, with 12 more SAS parachuted in, an attack was made on the town. In total, another 24 enemy were killed for two friendly wounded.[48]

Joint operations continued against ZANU from 22 May to 6 June 1977 with Operation *Aztec*. A mobile column attacked several bases as far as 222 kilometers inside Mozambique, to include those at Jorge do Limpopo, Mapai, and Madulo Pan. This was another effort to stop the ZANLA infiltration from Mozambique into southeastern Rhodesia. The three-pronged attack called for a battalion from the Rhodesia Regiment to eliminate staging sites along the border up to 10 kilometers beyond the border; a Rhodesian Light Infantry force would be moved by helicopter to attack the Rio Complex on the Nuanetsi river while another group would be parachuted in to attack a base at Madulo Pan. A Selous Scout mobile column would move along the railroad line as far as Jorge do Limpopo, then attack Mapai on the Limpopo River. The border was crossed on 28 May 1977, involving 110 vehicle-mounted Scouts dressed as FRELIMO, against resistance eliminated with the use of airstrikes. On 31 May, a Dakota aircraft was lost at Mapai during a supply mission, but despite this, the operation continued 200 kilometers south to Mabalane. After six days, on 2 June, the ground forces pulled back with captured material after major destruction to the rail and road lines.[49]

Smith rejected the Anglo-American initiatives in August 1977 and his government instead sought political settlement with internal groups. The Land Tenure Act was amended to open White rural areas to Blacks. At the same time JOC Grapple was formed in Gwelo for the Midlands, and *Salisbury* Operations (SalOps) formed at the capital for counterinsurgency operations that unrelentingly continued to spread internally despite all the external efforts. The SAS was in combat with ZANU, October 1977, in Mozambique, in an operation along the Chicoa–Tete road. When radio intercepts indicated terrorists would be returning to Mozambique from Rhodesia, 12 SAS men were inserted by parachute some 50 kilometers from an ambush location. After a wait of 10 days, 21 of 22 guerrillas were killed with no friendly casualties.[50]

Despite these successes, there was another story. To make up for debilitating personnel shortages, rather than continual recruiting from the rest of the army, particularly from the RLI, or by the more radical option of integrating Africans, the SAS came to rely on very junior soldiers led by far fewer more experienced operators.[51] According to a troop leader, "They came straight from school into the big camp attacks and thought nothing of it."[52] According to one officer, while the troops "had the badged SAS personnel ... there were signalers, motor transport, and service corps personnel, even African civilians. Plus the old, invalid, and those who had failed selection. Color was no bar, but no success was met in recruiting Africans."[53] Other factors were at play, as the pseudo terrorist efforts cost the squadron some of its best personnel to "poaching" by the Selous Scouts. The SAS squadron had a headquarters and six enlarged troops by 1977, but was only about 150 men strong at full mobilization. This formed the basis for cross-border raids that began to take on a life of their own. The SAS had started operations in the northeast, but were reassigned a portion of the southeast for its own "hunter-killer" patrols. This left the Selous Scouts operating in the northeast and eastern border regions. There was continued overlap and need for coordination.

The SAS was in combat with ZANU and FRELIMO, October to November 1977, in Gaza province, Mozambique. Replacing Selous Scouts in this area, the SAS disrupted lines of communications with Mapai from Maputo, over 80 kilometers inside Mozambique. In October, 22 men were dropped from a civilian DC-7. Four men were injured during the jump and left on the drop zone while the rest ambushed a three-truck convoy, killing 20 terrorists and destroying one truck. Three SAS men were wounded. An air force Hunter destroyed the remaining vehicles as they tried to escape. In November, a 16-man SAS patrol was parachuted 120 kilometers inside Mozambique for another ambush of the Mapai–Maputo road. The ambush site was compromised by a security patrol as the mixed ZANLA/FRELIMO convoy arrived. The lead truck hit a landmine and blocked the road as the remainder of the force took up defensive positions. The SAS withdrew in the night after calling for an airstrike the next day. Some 21 vehicles and 50 personnel were accounted for by Hunter aircraft controlled by a Lynx airborne controller.[54]

The special forces and intelligence staff picked up on the reports that after the destruction of Nyadzonya in Operation *Eland*, a new location was being used by FRELIMO and ZANU as the base for supplies, training, and infiltration into Rhodesia's eastern border. SAS Captain D. M. "Scotty" McCormack visited the Special Branch at Umtali, the Selous Scouts, and the CIO to find out all he could about Chimoio Base, the so-called "New Farm." The camp and its location was confirmed with air reconnaissance and photography, and estimated to hold some 9,000 to 11,000 residents of whom 4,000 were trained terrorists. Lieutenant-Colonel Robinson and Group Captain Walsh believed an attack was possible and worth the gamble of success. It took some 12 presentations to Combined Operations before authorization was granted for a bold and complex operation. This was against ZANLA personnel and material concentrations in the west and northwest of Mozambique. The largest of the identified focus of nationalists of all ages and sexes was located 90 kilometers from the border of Rhodesia and the city of Umtali.

All the previous cross-border attacks indicated that more could be achieved to stem the influx of ZANLA guerrillas from Mozambique, in support of the internal settlement. Earlier actions had caused the nationalists to pull back their bases from the border, and with FRELIMO's support, a major complex of bases was established in the Chimoio–Vanduzi–Pungwe area, 90 kilometers across the border. This was the reported location of Robert Mugabe, Rex Nhongo, and Josiah Tongogara's command post. Another camp was located farther north at Tembué, 225 kilometers inside Mozambique in the Tete province. FRELIMO provided logistics support as well as security with armored forces in the form of T-54 tanks and BTR-152 armored personnel carriers. Chimoio became known as Zulu-1 while Tembué was known as Zulu-2 for an endeavor known as Operation *Dingo*.

Robinson and Walsh, assisted by SAS Captain Grahame Wilson, put together and executed the scheme that pooled the resources of available air and ground forces for an overt "main event." The plan called for an air and ground attack. This was supported by forward arming and refueling points inside Mozambique. Preparations included briefing and mustering available forces, establishing two forward bases in Mozambique, and using an airborne command post.[55] According to SAS second-in-command Graham, maps and photographs were transformed into three-dimensional models of the target area. After which, syndicates would consider the various aspects to be accomplished and return with solutions in a final plan. According to Graham, "Our routine in such cases was to start with a 'think evil' session, initially with some of our own officers. We would then bring in the air force and go through the same routine. ... The final stage was always a briefing to the men from the same model, without disclosing our plan."[56]

A forward base in Rhodesia was established at Lake Alexander, as well as an admin base for refueling and ammunition inside Mozambique. D-day was 23 November 1977, preceded by a distracting flyover of Chimoio by a DC-8. Hunters and Canberras then conducted initial airstrikes using rockets and bombs, followed by further fighter and helicopter gunship support throughout the day. The scheme of maneuver called for a Fire Force effort writ large. Some 97 SAS and 48 RLI paratroopers were dropped on two sides of a "box," a 47-man RLI heliborne force was on the third side, while fixed-wing fighters and helicopter gunships closed the open end.[57] Command and control came from Robinson and Walsh in a helicopter while ComOps commander Walls flew in a command Dakota in touch with Prime Minister Smith. The troop assaults were a success and sweeps of the area were conducted. By the time these were completed, an estimated 2,000 total causalities were inflicted (as high as 5,000 by some calculations). After fighting that lasted all day and into the night, large quantities of supplies and records were captured for the loss of one soldier and one airman killed (and aircraft lost) with eight others wounded. Facilities, equipment, and infrastructure were destroyed, dealing ZANU its most striking blow to date.[58]

On 26 November 1977, the Tembué attack was launched from Mount Darwin, using two admin bases inside Mozambique. The formula of the previous raid was followed, with the somewhat less spectacular results. The second camp, Zulu-2, housed some 4,000 insurgents most of whom escaped prior to the attack. The previous warning and extensive distance to get to Zulu-2 all contributed to this. The raiders were able to destroy a large amount of material with no friendly casualties as weapons and documents were returned to Rhodesia for exploitation. No comment was made in regards to any prisoners. The nationalist response was to claim these were unarmed refugee camps and resorted to efforts to disperse or rotate the use of camp sites. These raids were followed post haste by a Selous Scout operation into Mozambique on 27 November 1977, after being delayed by the Chimoio and Tembué assaults (Operation *Virile**). A motorized column dropped five bridges in order to block access to the south in order to force the guerrillas to enter Rhodesia to the north in the Rusape area where terrain was more conducive to pseudo and Fire Force actions.[59]

Brian Robinson must be given the credit for the model standard of planning and preparation for external operations.[60] The examples of vertical envelopment came from Chimoio and Tembué with "two major base areas containing a total of 11,000 terrorists plus using 250 men. In order to deploy this force we used every single aircraft in the air force. We killed over 2,000 terrorists. If I had [American] resources we could have killed 8,000. The Fire Force method of vertical envelopment works!" To him, external camp attacks were efforts to use tactical containment. But the camps would now extend in size and area and would no longer be effectively contained, as the Rhodesians would find out to their cost. The result was switching to transportation or economic targets and an increase with air attacks.[61]

Robinson always felt more offensive operations were needed: "Deep penetration ambushes in small patrols (four men) to shoot and scoot, attacks on enemy external base camps, using air and vertical envelopment tactics, offensive landmine operations on communications roads, bridge destruction in depth, attacks on enemy shipping/fuel farms in Mozambique, and deep penetration kayak operations mining and harassment."[62] He went on to conclude "As our war developed I believe we added additional dimensions to the SAS modus operandi. We certainly used every skill for real and added a few for the SAS."[63] Special operations that appeared to have succeeded best were those comprising parties of between two and eight men moving on foot and at night to mine roads and bridges used by the guerrillas, to sabotage communications, and ambush convoys before the patrol melted back into the bush. Ambush and mine laying became an interdiction specialty of the SAS and Selous Scouts. It involved imagination and a standardized mine-laying drill, with detailed location logs used to ensure a record of where these occurred in case security forces had to pass through them later. All mine types were available for use but, in general, differing in targets rather than sensibilities. The so-called "rose" or "cake" landmine derived from the need of the special forces to have a mine that could be used that could not be lifted by the conventional means the Zambian and Mozambican engineers possessed. Mines could be placed anywhere, but most were used in the center of the road along with anti-personnel mines or additional explosives to "boost" their effects. The logic was that the injured required more care and resources than the dead, and an emotional inhibition to free movement was created, "It slowed the war and killed the enemy."[64]

Acting either as counter-guerrillas on one side of "the fence" and guerrillas on the other, much of the work by special forces on both sides of the border was still close reconnaissance done by four-man teams. These remained in concealment by day, keeping watch from a distance, and moving close enough to the target at night to obtain specific information with the help of night-vision devices. Some teams succeeded in remaining on station, doing this stealthy work for weeks at a time, constantly feeding information back to Cranborne or Inkomo without discovery. "We sometimes hit the jackpot and returned elated. On other occasions we found only a 'caretaker' group was in camp when we hit it, the real prize having flown the nest between the time of our reconnaissance and the assault. ... It's the sort of thing which happens to all soldiers, some of the time." The results of attacks on terrorist camps that followed these arduous preparations were, as one involved observed, sometimes a matter of chance.[65] Captain Rob J. Johnstone commented after one SAS raid near Cabora Bassa turned up an empty camp and one sick guerrilla, that it was "the most money he had seen spent and the farthest he had come to burn down a collection of grass huts."[66]

Special forces needed insertion, resupply, visual reconnaissance, extraction, and "hot extraction" support from the air force, in addition to surface and airborne radio relay. Call signs from both the SAS and Selous Scouts in Zambia and Mozambique depended upon helicopter support for this within the limits of the Alouette IIIs. Later in the war there was conflict for internal and external support, particularly after the South Africans withdrew aircraft and aircrew as political leverage.[67] This required helicopter assets to be pulled from internal operations to external support efforts. The Parachute Training School supported this throughout, although by 1977 the Selous Scouts recruited parachute jump instructor American John Early to run their air operations while the SAS used British W. T. "Frank" Hales. The airborne delivery system used a blind drop technique. A small "pathfinder" team would go in first to locate a DZ, by either freefall or surface means. According to Captain Early:

> I used aerial photos if I could get the air force to fly photo missions. I would usually have to use air photos that were two or three years old. When I found a drop zone, I'd check it for two or three days, and I'd always maintain 24- to 48-hour surveillance on a drop zone before I brought anyone in. Then I would make radio contact with our airborne forces standing by at a launch site, and tell them the date and time to bring them in. It worked fine for us every time.[68]

The aircraft carrying the main body was briefed on a dead reckoning heading and location to fly. As the aircraft approached the designated point and was heard, the pathfinders would indicate it was on time and target. At two or three kilometers the aircraft was ordered to flash its landing lights. The aircraft would be given an altimeter setting and be brought down to 300 or 400 feet and slowed to 70 knots to be talked over the release point when overhead.[69] Pathfinder procedures, the steps taken by those on the ground to receive a resupply or reinforcement drop, were also developed by the Parachute Training School and the special forces. Squadron Leader D. J. G. de Kock warned "it is not as easy as it seems and errors up to 2,000 meters are not uncommon."[70] A drop zone was selected that was a large open area. The pilot was contacted by radio as soon as visible and put in a holding orbit. The pathfinders would then send the magnetic bearing of the run-in down the long axis of the drop zone, preferably into the wind. Taken into consideration were the altitude of the drop zone above sea level; wind speed and direction; the length of the stick to be dropped, based on 50 meters per jumper plus 200 meters at either end for a safety margin; and finally the nature of the drop zone—free of stumps or rocks, power lines, and if wooded. The pathfinder would stand in the DZ where he wanted the first man to hit (based on the assumption that dropped from 1,000 feet, a man will drift 200 meters per 5 miles per hour of wind). After estimating the wind speed, he would calculate the drift, and walk the appropriate distance into the wind. If possible, an initial flyover would be on a reverse leg parallel to the run-in heading.

After going well past, he would bring the aircraft around and fly it straight towards him. From this location, he would talk the aircraft in with "go left," "go right" and "steady," using the navigation lights to keep oriented (red light on the left, green on the right, with white on the tail as facing the oncoming plane). At one and a half kilometers he would give "stand by," then "red light on" when roughly at 45 degrees and "green light on" when directly overhead.[71] This method dropped 500 kilograms in three seconds or less, spreading it out no more than 200 meters. Troops could be brought in the same way, getting 25 fully equipped jumpers out of the aircraft with the same dispersion. The first half of the stick would steer towards the direction of flight; the second half would steer back towards the first so that all hit the ground as a group. As a way to reduce malfunctions, jumpers only carried essential water, ammunition, medical supplies, and radios for two days. Rucksacks and the other equipment would be dropped last or by a separate aircraft. On landing, all they had to do was drop their canopy by busting their Capewell fittings and cocking their weapons. Despite the goal of being up and running within 10 minutes, the problem was rendezvousing, particularly at night. "The men dropped are invariably disoriented, and virtually the only way to [rendezvous] quickly is to make a lot of noise and show bright lights."[72]

The SAS was in combat with ZAPU, 12 January to 19 June 1978, in Zambia (Operation *Elbow*). A ZPRA camp located in southeastern Zambia on the Zambezi river was attacked by the SAS in January (Siajumba Camp). Some 27 insurgents were killed and additional Zambian casualties were caused by mines laid on surrounding roads. The camp relocated farther inland to be attacked again ("DK" Camp). By June, it had move 20 miles from its original location (Muchingwa Camp). An ambush patrol of 12 SAS operators was flown in by helicopter and after an 11-day wait, ambushed three trucks carrying ammunition, fuel, and recruits, killing 69. Casualties from subsequent road mining included senior ZPRA commander Alfred Nikita Mangena.[73] In Botswana, February 1978, the SAS was in combat with ZAPU in a hot-pursuit operation. An SAS patrol was attacked just inside Rhodesia and a 28-man force went in pursuit of the ambushers that led to a combined ZPRA and Botswana Defense Force camp near the Kazungula ferry crossing. An attack was mounted that netted 17 to 24 Africans with no SAS losses.[74]

A quadripartite executive council under Smith, Muzorewa, Ndabaningi Sithole, and conservative Chief Jeremiah Chirau headed the transitional government in April 1978. In the next two months, JOC Splinter was formed at Kariba for operations against ZPRA coming from Zambia and JOC Salisbury became a BSAP-controlled joint operation for the capital region.[75] Externals continued, with the SAS in combat with ZANU during May 1978, in Tete, Mozambique. Kayak operations on lake Cabora Bassa resulted in eight SAS operators mounting a demolition attack on the Battariao barracks in Tete town. Timed explosives charges were set, killing an unknown number of ZANLA, while the SAS suffered no losses and the team was evacuated by helicopter.[76]

Lieutenant-Colonel Brian Robinson moved to Combined Operations and was succeeded in June 1978 by Lieutenant-Colonel Garth J. M. Barrett who commanded the SAS through the end of the fighting. Also in June 1978, the SAS became 1 (Rhodesian) Special Air Service Regiment (1SAS) at Kabrit Barracks with three 60-man "Sabre" or operational squadrons (A, B, and C) of three troops each for a total of about 120 regular and part-time members.[77] Maximum strength was reached with up to 200 being available if all reserves and former members were present. Squadrons remained around 60 strong (averaging more like 35) with three 16-man troops and the rest on headquarters duties. Group photographs indicate 18 officers and some total 129 members in 1979/80. Commanders included Captains Robert C. MacKenzie (A Squadron), Colin B. Willis (B Squadron), and Martin F. Pearce (C Squadron). The South Africans provided a D Squadron from their Reconnaissance Commandos. After operating with the Rhodesians at first, they were given an independent area of operations under SAS regimental control.[78]

Routine missions like reconnaissance and ambushes were assigned to individual squadrons. At this time, "Ninety percent of SAS operations in the Rhodesian war were conducted in either Zambia or Mozambique," observed a squadron commander.[79] Zambia usually had one or two squadrons deployed, Mozambique always one squadron, while Botswana never reached squadron level. A rotation found squadrons operating out of Mabalauta, Kariba, Umtali and Victoria Falls (although it seemed A and D Squadrons ended up mostly in the southeast on the "Russian" front).[80] Zambian and Mozambican civilians would always report Rhodesian presence, unless the government and nationalists had alienated the locals in some way. Zambia and Mozambique also had the same intensity and "juicy targets," but Botswana was never a real threat. While assigned a broad length (200–300 kilometers), depth was limited by the range of available aircraft using fuel staged by air drops. Reconnaissance patrols would find the tracks and routes used, and in turn locate the enemy camps, as a camp attack (if surprised) killed more than an ambush. Interdiction missions were based upon the volume of traffic on the routes of communications. The squadrons were kept compartmented from each other, using separate communications systems to the regiment. Squadrons had a rest and refit cycle of 12 days or less before redeploying; during this time lessons learned were briefed, particularly about specific areas and targets.[81] Retraining after operations refreshed personnel on weapons handling, medical procedures, communications procedures, demolitions and mine-laying procedures, physical fitness, bushcraft, and tracking. Journalist Cole noted, "they would rather be deployed … than stay in base" with these demands.[82]

Special missions were Barrett's call and augmented by regimental headquarters and any squadrons in barracks. As noted, "Operating in Maputo or Lusaka was a different situation than hitting base camps on the border." Picking and choosing from all available sources allowed the right skills mix (pathfinders, demolitions, languages, medical) to be used. "I would analyze the requirement then put together a team with the right skills and personalities and assign the mission to my deputy (Major Grahame A. Wilson) or do it myself." From his experience, "these special tasks might be officer heavy, allowing the new personnel to operate under more experienced hands." The system of command was either from the air or ground with Barrett and Wilson alternating, in order to "be best placed to read the situation" with the "other placed to coordinate" support.

In most cases this involved establishing an administrative base in enemy territory to refuel, rearm, and to provide medical and logistical support. Barrett said, "You set up an airstrip in the middle of nowhere in a threat environment and there is a need for security. ... This was met with headquarters, training, and 'sick-lame-lazy' personnel." Combined with training injuries, this provided manpower for a protection unit using captured weapons (12.7 and 20mm guns). Minimal local security was used: "One time in Zambia, the six SAS men carried the load while the assigned RLI were dead weight," possibly being an example of age and experience being needed rather than youthful enthusiasm.[83]

MacKenzie wrote, "Sites were usually 20 to 30 kilometers from the intended target. In a deserted part of the countryside, the sites were preferably in low brush or elephant grass, without big trees, and near water when possible."[84] "Doctors were at the admin base and the medics had done three months at a trauma center so they wouldn't faint at the sight of blood."[85]

Tempo of operations was a factor, with a dozen operations going on at one time in three or four different countries ("We forgot more than we remembered"). Barrett believed special forces played a dramatic role in the war, "and their effectiveness was, in my opinion anyway, remarkable." However, in terms of employment by higher headquarters "in some ways this was excellent but in many ways poor. However, a lot of poor employment was in some cases internal military politics, governmental politics, and in some cases poor leadership (command and control). There were many instances where decisions were made not to act, which would later cause us grave problems" as "the situation never got better with time." At the strategic level, free thinkers were needed in special forces because special operations had effects larger than the actual impact of the mission. "The action has to have more than a tactical impact," he concluded.[86]

Despite differences, both the SAS and Selous Scouts recognized the need for shared intelligence and coordination of their efforts to prevent duplication and conflict. This started with enemy information which the Selous Scouts and their Special Branch had to excess, but lacked the facilities to process and disseminate (or saw reports purposely withheld from those that needed this information in some cases). In an effort to pool assets and improve the process, it was proposed the SAS would handle all external intelligence and the Selous Scouts would direct all internal intelligence for use by their respective regiments.[87] When the Directorate of Military Intelligence was approached for needed staff, the whole concept was shelved with the protest of CIO and SB. This was revisited in another dissatisfying effort to oversee special forces operations.[88]

Headquarters Special Forces

On 1 July 1978, a headquarters (HQSpecForces) was created to oversee special operations for Combined Operations. Proposed to provide the higher direction of these activities, it was intended to return the control of the special forces to the army, but this was objected to by Walls and Flower. The SAS and Selous Scouts, who had started this ball rolling, later opposed this when they found an RAR brigadier without special forces background put in command (Robinson, among others, had hoped he would be selected to head this effort, including supervising the Selous Scouts).[89] First under Colonel John C. P. McVey and then Brigadier F. G. "David" Heppenstall, its role was to formulate strategy; plan, execute, and coordinate operations; command and control special forces; and coordinate training.[90] In reality, it never served in the capacity for which it was created because of turf battles within and without the security forces, and finally was used to administer the Security Force Auxiliaries (SFAs).

The cross-border war continued undiminished. General Walls told the *Rhodesia Herald* in September 1978, that "There is no single day of the year when we are not operating beyond our borders," with anywhere from a one-man reconnaissance to brigade-size strike. For the big efforts, Combined Operations exercised airborne command and control using the Command Dakota manned alternately by General Walls, Brigadier Herbert Barnard, Lieutenant-Colonel Robinson, or Air Commodore Walsh.[91] The continual problems of helicopter support eased in the autumn of 1978 with the arrival of a dozen venerable AB 280 "Cheetahs" (the American "Huey") which were used primarily for external lifts, leaving the remaining Alouettes for Fire Force duty.

Using an SA-7, on 3 September 1978, ZIPRA shot down a civilian aircraft, Air Rhodesia Viscount *Hunyani*, with 58 passengers and crew. Some of these survived the crash landing, only to be killed on the ground by guerrilla terrorists, while eight survived to be recovered by a reaction force dispatched from the SAS. In the aftermath, Nkomo publicly claimed personal responsibility for the action.

In retaliation, on 20 September 1978, a major air attack was made on Chimoio (Operation *Snoopy**). While the main ZANU/ZANLA camp was lightly held, antiaircraft fire was met from a new location which was then attacked. Hunters and Canberras followed up the next day despite thick ground haze and a certain amount of chaos as an area of 30 by 40 kilometers was found to contain dozens of small camps disbursed for mutual support.[92] The SAS, general-purpose, and air forces retaliated against ZAPU, from 19 to 21 October 1978 in Zambia with Operation *Gatling*. The objectives of these attacks were Nkomo's main camps which were located near the capital Lusaka, and farther from the border in Zambian territory. Included were an air attack on Freedom Camp ("FC") just north of Lusaka, air and ground attacks on Mkushi Camp some 125 kilometers northeast of Lusaka, and at Communist Guerrilla Training Camp 2 ("GCT") some 100 kilometers east of Lusaka. Forward arming and refueling points were established inside Zambia.

The Rhodesian forces mustered on 19 October, including a command and control aircraft with General Walls and Group Captain Norman Walsh. The first target was Freedom Camp, 15 kilometers from Lusaka, with some 4,000 ZIPRA forces in training. The air attack was made by a mixed force of two Hunters, four Canberras, and four Alouette gunships. Of concern were Zambian air forces with MiG-17s and -19s and Rapier antiaircraft missiles. A commercial airline pilot queried Lusaka tower during the attack to ask who had priority. The tower replied: "I think the Rhodesians do!" This was the famed "Green Leader" incident that documented the attack for posterity. Squadron Leader Chris Dixon observed: "Bombs gone. They're running. Beautiful! Jeez! You want to see all those bastards." Once successful, the next attack was launched on Mkushi and its eight surrounding camps with 2,000 ZIPRA a further 125 kilometers northeast from Lusaka. This would be from the air (again Hunters, Canberras, and Alouettes) and an SAS assault force arriving by parachute and helicopters from New Sarum and Mana Pools. This put 165 SAS men into the area with machine guns and mortars. Large amounts of material were captured or destroyed and some 600 guerrillas were killed at the cost of only friendly wounded and an accidental death. The final target of the day was CGT Camp-2, about 100 kilometers east of Lusaka, again with another 4,000 ZIPRA. The airstrike (fighters, bombers, helicopter gunships) preceded the ground attack by RLI heliborne troops from Kariba and Mana Pools. The camp had been warned by the two earlier attacks, and so 51 insurgents were killed as most had fled with the news that the Rhodesians were coming. Conservative estimates put the total guerrilla losses at 1,450 to 1,650.[93]

Prisoners and information gathered, including from logistics chief Martin Gutu, led to further air attacks on 2, 3, and 5 November 1978 near Lusaka. Other actions took place in November through December 1978 at Mulungushi, 100 kilometers northeast from Lusaka. On 19 November 1978, a two-man Selous Scout reconnaissance patrol was inserted 40 kilometers away that was in position to observe the objective by 26 November 1978. Some 270 ZIPRA were present in a fortified camp hemmed in on one side by a reservoir. It was decided an airstrike would be the best means to attack, which took place with Canberras on 22 December 1978 (Operation *Pygmy**). According to radio intercepts, there were 33 killed and numerous wounded. The reconnaissance patrol was recovered without incident.[94]

A Selous Scout two-man reconnaissance patrol was inserted on 28 November 1978 to locate ZIPRA's Mboroma Camp 140 kilometers north of the Rhodesian border. It was during the rainy season and the patrol started some 25 kilometers from the camp that was reported to hold security force prisoners and dissidents. Some 100 prisoners, 60 guards, and 14.5mm antiaircraft positions were spotted by the time the patrol returned on 16 December 1978. A plan was made from air photos and a model that would see a Selous Scout attack launched on 22 December 1978 (Operation *Vodka*). A Hunter strike preceded a 42-man parachute assault that killed 18 guards and freed 32 prisoners (the remainder were away on work details). A Dakota transport was used to fly the personnel back to Rhodesia.[95]

On 11 December 1978, a ZANLA attack on Salisbury's fuel depot burned through 19 December 1978. The SAS was in combat with ZANU, 12 to 30 December 1978, in Mozambique (Operation *Inhibit*). A 20-man patrol was dropped into southeastern Mozambique to ambush vehicle traffic between Maputo and Malvernia. With the ambush, a running fight developed with ZANLA forces, killing 47 of them, for the loss of an SAS man.[96] The SAS and air force were in combat with FPLM (Forças Populares de Libertação de Moçambique, FRELIMO's armed wing) and ZANU, 15 December 1978, in Mozambique (Operation *Shovel*). A ZANLA prisoner pinpointed a large ammunition dump in an airfield hangar in the town of Tete, through which all insurgents were armed prior to entering Rhodesia. A Hunter destroyed the dump with a single rocket. Further ground operations followed in the same area. This involved the destruction of a railway bridge on the Moatize–Beira line in the Tete province. The SAS dropped 20 men to demolish the bridge, which occurred as a train was crossing. Another 12-man SAS patrol ambushed a ZANLA truck column, destroying the lead vehicle and turning the rest around. The next day an RhAF Hunter strike destroyed most of these.[97]

The SAS and MNR (Mozambique National Resistance) launched an unconventional operation against FPLM, January 1979, in Mozambique. A hydroelectric power station at Mavuze, located 40 kilometers within Mozambique, was destroyed by a stand-off attack with a 75mm recoilless rifle.[98] The Selous Scouts were in combat with ZAPU, 2 February to 21 April 1979, in Botswana (Operation *Petal*). An ambush was laid to capture the senior ZPRA intelligence officer in Botswana, Elliot Sibanda. This succeeded and was followed by an effort to kill or capture the entire ZPRA Southern Command in Francistown. This was accomplished by a mobile column of Scouts disguised as Botswana Defense Forces who "arrested" the Zimbabweans at their headquarters and carried them back to Rhodesia.[99]

Another airline was shot down by nationalists. On 11 February 1979, ZIPRA used an SA-7 to shoot down Air Rhodesia Viscount *Umniati*. All 59 passengers and crew were killed. Retaliation soon followed in Zambia, Mozambique, and as far afield as Angola. The air force was in combat with ZAPU, on 26 February 1979, in Angola (Operation *Vanity*). A long-range bomber strike was made on a ZIPRA base in Angola, at Luso near Boma. Four Canberras with fighter and search and rescue escort launched from Victoria Falls. The concern was for reaction from Angolan MiG-17 and -21s with Cuban pilots. After approaching at 39,000 feet, the final attack was made at treetop level through a rain shower. All target buildings were hit and an estimated 174–192 Angolans and Zimbabweans were killed with another 533–987 being seriously wounded.[100] The SAS and air force were in combat with ZANU, 14 February to 21 March 1979, in Mozambique (Operation *Neutron*). A two-man SAS reconnaissance team entered to locate ZANLA logistics bases at Chimoio Circle and Vanduzi Circle. The reconnaissance patrol estimated 400–1,000 ZANLA were in the area. On 17 March 1979, an air attack was called for, without the complication of ground troops. Hunters, Canberras, and helicopter gunships were all used in succession despite antiaircraft guns and missiles. The FRELIMO follow-up recognized that a patrol was in the area which witnessed its hasty withdrawal. The team left by helicopter in a hot extraction with one man wounded in the leg. Two month later, this same scenario was replayed on the camp housing 150 guerrillas.[101]

By February 1979, the Selous Scouts had expanded to a regiment organized into three operations groups (a fourth was formed later) with a headquarters and three troops each. A 100-man assault group (used for the motorized "Chindit" columns) was primarily composed of European reservists, along with a 14-man reconnaissance troop, and mortar troop.[102] This was with 516 attested Scouts and 800 "turned" terrorists in 1979 and up to a total of 1,500 including three Rhodesian Women's Service by the end.[103] Efforts were made to recruit from the Shona terrorists of ZANLA, expanded to include the Matabele of ZPRA with somewhat less success.[104] By this time, pseudoterrorist gangs, hunter-killer teams, Q-car, and mobile columns were being fielded inside and outside Rhodesia. John Cronin recalled that although seven joint operational areas existed, only three were assigned groups on a permanent basis where the infiltration was heaviest (northeast facing Zambia, southeast meeting Mozambique, and southwest covering Botswana), each typically deploying three troops of four- to five-man call signs at a time with a four-man control element directing their maneuvers by radio.[105]

One officer at Combined Operations headquarters, Group Captain Petter-Bowyer, observed that it now became apparent through Rhodesian Intelligence Corps analysis that the cross-border raids were more cost effective in killing the enemy than internal Fire Force operations. In the January/February 1979 period for example, some 262 terrorists were killed internally, compared to some 277 externally, but at a higher cost in time, men, and machines. The conclusion was the cost per terrorist killed (wounded numbers were not available) was a third less on externals than the internal cost (dropping to a quarter in the next 10 months). These figures were qualified in that the months examined were relatively quiet and the foliage was at its thickest, providing effective cover to the guerrillas. Also, during this period the focus of the Fire Forces was shifted from the tribal areas to "vital ground" coverage.[106]

The SAS, MNR, and SADF participated in an unconventional operation against FPLM, 22 to 23 March 1979, in Mozambique (Beria fuel depot). This was carried out by the SAS some 300 kilometers deep into Mozambique, under the cover of MNR participation. A team was landed from South African strike craft and attacked fuel storage tanks with rocket-propelled grenades and machine-gun fire. As the force withdrew, it left evidence that the attack was by Mozambican dissidents coming overland. The resulting fire was controlled ironically with South African help.[107]

On 10 April 1979, air attacks took place on ZIPRA headquarters near Lusaka and at Mulungushi to disrupt command facilities (Operation *Liquid**).[108] At the same time, the SAS went into combat from 12 to 13 April 1979, in Zambia. After the failure of the Selous Scout Operation *Aspect*, the SAS came up with a scheme to kill or capture the leader of ZAPU, Joshua Nkomo, at his quarters in Lusaka at the same time a major ZPRA armory was being attacked. For Operation *Bastille*, some 42 operators in Land Rovers disguised to look like Zambian army vehicles drove cross-country to the target. Although the house and armory were demolished, Nkomo escaped (apparently through a bathroom window). The group lost a number of vehicles and returned with two wounded.[109] The SAS was also in combat with ZAPU, 12 to 13 April 1979, in Botswana (Operation *Dinky*). Because the Kazungula ferry was being used to move war materials from Zambia to Botswana, 12 SAS men were deployed to sink the ferry without incurring civilian casualties. A 115-kilogram explosive charge was laid in the docking area and detonated by remote control. The aim also appeared to counter a potential conventional attack by ZPRA mechanized forces.[110]

The UANC won a majority of parliamentary seats in the April 1979 election. From 17 through 21 April 1979, Prime Minister Bishop Abel Muzorewa and President Gumede were elected to form a transitional government. Under the internal constitutional agreement, the country was renamed Zimbabwe Rhodesia. The 3 May 1979 election of conservative Prime Minister Margaret Thatcher in the United Kingdom gave hope that a settlement could be reached that would be in Rhodesia's favor with international recognition to end the conflict. The new Foreign Minister, Lord Carrington, consulted with the Commonwealth and European and American allies before making any policy announcements or changes. The Land Tenure Amendment Act of 1977 was repealed and an internal settlement constitution established Zimbabwe-Rhodesia in June 1979. But no international recognition was received.

On 26 June 1979, the SAS mounted a raid on ZAPU's intelligence headquarters ("The Vatican") near Lusaka with Operation *Carpet*. Planned by Lieutenant-Colonel Garth Barrett, it was executed by Major Grahame Wilson. Believed to be present was Nkomo's second-in-command, Dumiso Dabengwa, and his deputy, Victor Mlambo. The assault force staged out of Makuti, where they flew out at daybreak, with fighter and bomber air cover. A diversionary airstrike was conducted at Freedom Camp outside Lusaka and Mkushi Camp, 125 kilometers north. An airborne command post monitored any enemy response (Zambian MiG-19s were scrambled but did not close with the Rhodesians). The 28-man helicopter assault force was taken under fire as it landed on the objective, but the raiders continued. They neutralized the guards, breached a perimeter wall, and cleared the buildings before destroying them. By 0730, a single prisoner and documents were taken, for the loss of one wounded and one dead (Captain Martin F. Pearce, the assault leader). On withdrawing, the helicopters refueled at a dump in Zambia staged on their exit route.[111] A follow-up result was a 1 July 1979 strike on a major ZIPRA arms storage site. The SAS and air force were also in combat with ZAPU, 26 June–4 July 1979, in Zambia (Operation *Chicory*). In a further effort to reduce ZPRA's conventional capabilities, 50 SAS men raided "JZ" Camp near Lusaka. This involved preceding and subsequent airstrikes with a ground assault to destroy equipment and kill personnel. This was accomplished without casualties.[112]

A Commonwealth conference took place in Lusaka in August 1979. This resulted in the Lancaster House Conference that convened on 10 September 1979 in London, in an effort to resolve the conflict based on a set of proposals by British Foreign Secretary Lord Carrington. The 11-point plan had to be accepted by Zimbabwe-Rhodesia (Muzorewa) and the Patriotic Front of ZANU (Mugabe) and ZAPU (Nkomo). At Lancaster House, from September through November 1979, the internal parties and the Patriotic Front continued to negotiate with the British-proposed constitution and ceasefire plan. As direct rule was established, United Nations sanctions were ended, as the conflict continued at an even more desperate pace. The level of violence increased during this period as each side sought to determine events on the ground, particularly in the Frontline States.[113]

The SAS, general-purpose, air, and South African forces were in combat from 1 to 7 September 1979 in Mozambique with Operation *Uric*. The road and rail links in Mozambique from Maputo to Mapai were part of the critical continued FPLM support to ZANU. The operation aimed to forestall a FRELIMO-supported ZANLA invasion by demolishing five road and rail bridges between Malvernia and Barragem. In addition, Mapai was to be destroyed, as well as the Barragem irrigation system. It would require forces to operate 350 kilometers across the border to within 140 kilometers of the capital city, Maputo.

Despite the risks, the benefit of disrupting these links was apparent to Combined Operations. A full-court press required the use of 28 helicopters, 12 transports, eight fighters, six bombers, and six other light aircraft, as well as all available SAS and RLI troops. A forward refueling and rearming point was established in Mozambique. Targets were first hit by airstrikes, and then some 360 men were deployed for demolition tasks (a sizable force of South African troops and aircraft took part, in what was known to them as Operation *Boot Lace*).

D-day was set for 2 September 1979, but bad weather pushed this back for three days. On 5 September, the bridges at Barragem were hit following an air attack by Hunters. The 48-man demolition team was landed and had to overcome

Most of the African population lived in rural areas or designated tribal territories along with commercial European farms and agricultural industry. A mixture of Internal Affairs, police, and missionary institutions administered there. (IntAf)

European inhabitants clustered in urban areas and settlements that were economic and manufacturing centers along the means of communication that tied the country together. A pair of women patrol officers work off Cecil Square in Salisbury. (BSAP)

The Right Honourable Ian Douglas Smith, Rhodesian Prime Minister throughout the conflict. His leadership was both political and military as the war progressed. (GP&S)

General Peter Walls, the army and Combined Operations leadership paradigm of the counterinsurgency conflict. His commentary is an important part of this narrative. (RAA)

Other senior leadership came from police forces, in this case Ken Flower, the Director General of the Central Intelligence Organization. This made him another leg of the security force stool. (BSAP)

Lt-Col Brian Robinson greets Prime Minister Smith. Robinson was a pioneer of combat tracking, commanded the racially exclusive Special Air Service, and was a special operations planner in Combined Operations. (RAA)

Lt-Col Ron Reid-Daly also came with a special operations background and commanded the covert multiracial Selous Scouts. (RAA)

Rhodesians across the board provided personnel to British Empire and Commonwealth conflicts, particularly the post-war insurgencies such as Malaya. This gave the rank and file exposure to counterinsurgency methods in a colonial context. (RAA)

Rhodesia Regiment stick leader dressed for the field. The bulk of "boots on the ground" depended upon conscripts, reservists, and territorials who were the backbone of operations by the "brown jobs." (J. Cowper)

Rhodesian African Rifles on internal operations included patrol, helicopter, and parachute deployment. The bulk of the regular infantry were these volunteers from tribal backgrounds. (RhAR Regt Assoc)

The Rhodesian Air Force provided support to the security forces across the spectrum of operations, the "blue jobs" represented by regular and reserve aviators such as the esteemed Gp Capt Peter "PB" Petter-Bowyer. (P. Petter-Bowyer)

A Police Special Branch detective interviews a "tame" or "turned" terrorist taking advantage of a surrender offer. This could result in security force recruitment or lawful imprisonment. (N. Russell)

Nationalist guerrillas in Mozambique displaying typical "ANC" section weapons and clothing. ZIPRA provided well-trained "cadre" but ZANLA fielded untrained numbers in the African populated areas. (RAA)

Nationalist guerrillas with a heavy machine gun used for base air or ground defense. Internal operations depended upon small arms, including rocket-propelled grenades. Any external Rhodesian operations had to deal with heavier antiaircraft weapons in numbers. (RAA)

Border control in the Zambezi valley with a mixed police and army patrol deployed by an air force Aerospatiale Alouette III helicopter. Differences in operating procedures for the three services needed to be worked out to reduce confusion or difficulties early on. (BSAP)

Forward airfields provided support and communications for otherwise landbound units and a degree of needed command and control by cooperation. Here an AL60 Trojan utility aircraft takes to the air flanked by a pair of armed T52 Provosts on standby for border control. (RhAF)

Army and police patrols, supported by ground coverage, engaged with the local population in efforts to identify and locate terrorist infiltrators from Zambia. Both the army and police used patrol and guard dogs in this effort. (BSAP)

Police Support Unit engages in an anti-ambush drill as part of the effort to move safely by road and to respond to efforts to hinder ground movement in operational areas. Early actions relied on standard motor transport with minimum protection. (BSAP)

Internal Affairs and later Guard Force outposts were relied on to provide a presence in tribal areas and for protected villages as a population-control measure. Resources for this were never enough to prevent subversion or attacks. (IntAf)

Army and police trackers developed flexible and effective measures that would lead to the creation of the Combat Tracking Unit and Selous Scouts counterinsurgency groups. (Selous Scouts)

The barrier obstacle created by the cordon sanitaire used minefields, patrols, observation, and fencing to channel entry into the country, particularly from Mozambique. The sign reads "Beware Mines." Minefield maintenance became a Corps of Engineers' load through and beyond the end of the conflict. (RAA)

Artillery, a 25-pounder in this picture, from key points was used to counter indirect fire from guerrilla rockets and mortars fired from sanctuaries in Zambia and Mozambique, in the border "jitter" campaign. (RAA)

Daimler Ferret armored scout car and crew, replaced by the more lethal Panhard AML90. Mobile firepower existed if needed, along with covertly acquired T-54/55 tanks. These reinforced specific locations and provided mobile defense to roads and airfields. (RAA)

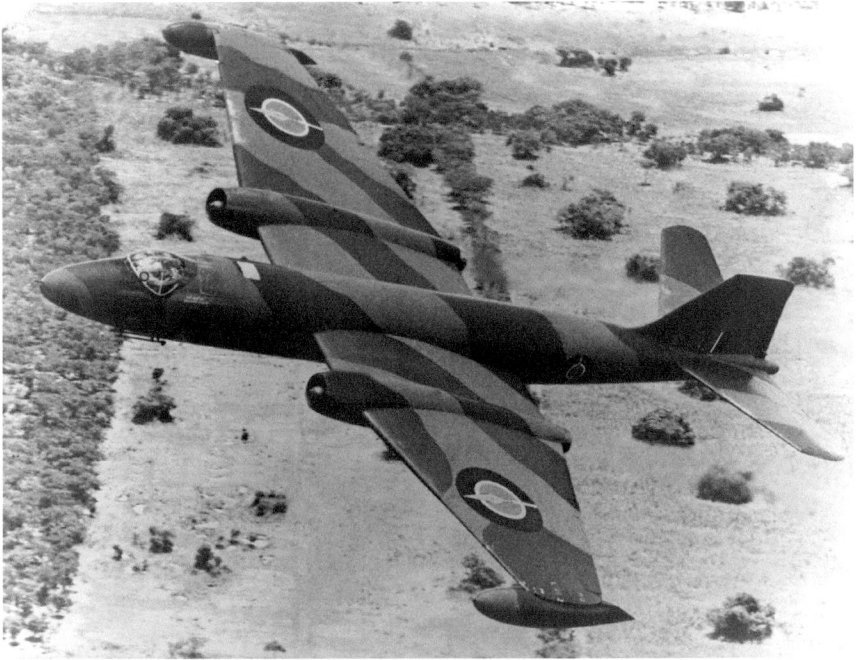

Strategic reach came from the air force B2 and T4 Canberra jet bombers that reminded neighboring supporters of the Nationalists that the Rhodesians could respond with a means they could not counter. (RhAF)

Fighters came in the form of FGA9 Hunters and FB9 and T11 Vampires that reflected a range of modern air-to-air and air-to-ground ordnance capabilities. These were expanded with local improvisations and illicit foreign trading. (RhAF)

A Hunter airborne in its natural element. In addition to combat air patrols and bomber escort, it could also provide attack and close air support to hard targets integrated into an effective air control system. (RhAF)

Utility aircraft for transport and communications early on came from BN-2A Islanders (as above) and DC-3 Dakotas. (RhAF)

Light attack, command, and control were the mission of the Reims Cessna 337G "Lynx," integrated as part of the internal Fire Force effort. (RhAF)

Static line and freefall parachuting was taught by the Rhodesian Air Force to the Special Air Service, Selous Scouts, and the Rhodesian Light Infantry and Rhodesian African Rifles. This had to be augmented by training in South Africa to meet the demand. In the center are the two air force PJIs who ruled the roost: Capt John Early (left) and Sqn Ldr Frank Hales. (RhAF)

Landmines were used from 1972 by terrorists and guerrillas in the operational areas, becoming the main offensive device that the Rhodesians had to counter: above are a landmine and trigger device typical of the ever-present threat. (D. Scott-Donelan)

Army Land Rover landmine incident shows the impact on an unprotected vehicle. (D. Scott-Donelan)

Landmine episode with a South African Police Hyena mine- and ambushed-proof vehicle. A Special Branch police officer indicates the depth of the detonation crater. (D. Scott-Donelan)

A variety of mines and munitions from Nationalist base camps demonstrating the extent of their external support. (D. Scott-Donelan)

A number of commercial mine- and ambush-resistant 4x light vehicles were developed for police and civil use. (C. Smith)

Army Puma mine- and ambush-proof vehicle (MAPV) 4x cargo carrier: this was one of several that evolved to counter the threat to ground mobility in operational areas. (C. Smith)

Innovative Pookie mobile mine-detector on display, which could find metallic and non-metallic landmines. (C. Smith)

Army, air force, and police conscripts or reservists at ease on internal duties, as these continued to back up both regular conventional and special forces. (RAA)

RAR riflemen at ease on internal duties. As Europeans crossed borders, the actual bulk of the army consisting of African volunteers filled reactive Fire Force commitments with their own distinctive capabilities. (RhAR Regt Assoc)

A forward airfield required aircraft to marshal and take off in fixed sequence to arrive over the designated contact area on time and target. Fire Force management started on the ground. (RhAF)

RLI commandos load a Dakota prior to a parachute drop from Grand Reef. As this is a practice jump, a "fun jump," the paras are "clean fatigue," that is without weapons, webbing, or packs. (Giles Gillespie)

RLI sticks boarding Alouette IIIs for Fire Force deployment. By this time, a set drill to save time and effort. (RLIRA)

Lynx aircraft head to a contact armed and equipped with communications to control the event from the start. These locally modified planes could talk to the observation post, mark targets, and provided firepower to pin guerrillas until the assault forces arrived by helicopter and parachute. (RhAF)

An RAR machine-gunner on the ground as part of a Fire Force containment and sweep. The MAG was an integral part of each stick, providing an essential base of fire. (RhAR Regt Assoc)

Ground contact required nerve and patience to successfully contain guerrillas that would hide and fight until killed or captured. (RAA)

An Alouette III removing captured spoils during operations in Operation *Repulse*, in part to supply local needs. (RAA)

Air Force Agusta Bell 205 "Cheetah" helicopter used by Special Air Service, Selous Scouts, and RLI for external operations into Zambia and Mozambique. (E. Pomeroy)

Special Air Service on an external parachute operation into Zambia in an air force Dakota. (E. Pomeroy)

Rhodesian soldiers with captured ComBloc material that was recovered and reused by the resource-starved security forces. Mop-ups had to carefully secure and search the contact area for anything left, particularly with external operations. (RAA)

Communist Bloc antiaircraft artillery captured at a sanctuary base camp. (M. Mason)

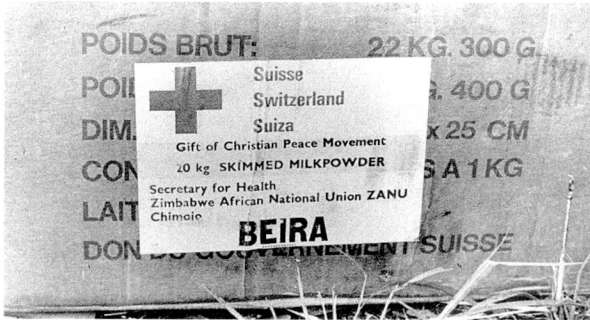

Captured material found foreign support to the Nationalists, viewed as military rather than humanitarian aid. The deeper and more prolonged the incursion the greater an impact on general economies and support for the Nationalists. (RAA)

Selous Scout mobile column in Mozambique to disrupt transportation, communications, and basing. (M. Mason)

The Selous Scouts on parade. (Selous Scouts)

Villagers undergo drill by guerrillas, aimed at radicalizing them rather than providing any military skills. (RAA)

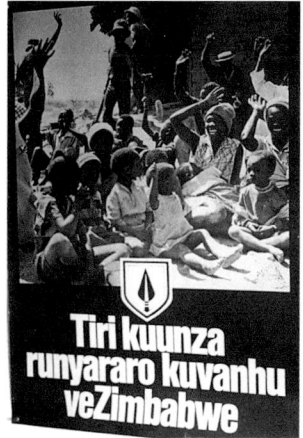

Internal settlement brought militias on board in rural areas as Security Force Auxiliaries. (C. Smith)

ZANU propaganda poster to indoctrinate local populations: "Correct ideological education, permanent armed struggle and work … these three, forever!" (C. Smith)

External targets included Nationalist leadership, such as military commanders Nhongo and Tongogara, identified for "kill or capture" by the Special Branch and Central Intelligence Organization. (RAA)

A threat from the early years, urban terrorism reached a peak with response to attacks on Nationalists overseas with the 11 December 1978 sabotage of the central oil storage depot in Salisbury. It destroyed 25 million gallons of fuel and took six days, with South African support, to extinguish the blaze. (RhAF)

further resistance before damaging the bridges, as well as those at Chicacatem, Folgares, Canicado, and Mezinchopes. Security force losses included a helicopter that overflew enemy positions. The next day, Mapai was bombed by Hunters and Canberras, hitting communications, radar, and fuel storage. Air defense (ranging from 12.7mm to 57mm antiaircraft weapons) was heavy and effective, with the loss of a South African Puma helicopter with all 14 troops and three crew on board. A major set-piece battle occurred at Mapai. The heavy air and ground defenses were impossible to overcome and the Rhodesians withdrew, having destroyed various headquarters, facilities, and mining the roads. One result was foreign Communist Bloc advisors withdrew from the forward areas.[114]

Combined Operations conducted joint efforts with the Mozambique National Resistance (MNR) against the FRELIMO government that indicated there was a lack of popular support for the Marxists in the countryside.[115] This allowed Rhodesian action to be taken that was also deniable within the cover of local resistance. An SAS and MNR unconventional operation was undertaken against FPLM, 12 to 18 September 1979, in Mozambique (Operation *Norah*). Penetrating 215 kilometers into Mozambique, a mixed MNR and SAS force attacked a communications microwave site on Monte Xilvuo. The aim was to force FRELIMO and ZANLA to rely on radio communications which could then be intercepted. The SAS element was flown in by helicopters and a two-day approach march was made with MNR guides. The station was damaged, and the attackers withdrew under fire with a heavy pursuit. A swift FRELIMO mechanized response blocked the withdrawal of the raiders and prompted a response by the Rhodesian Air Force. Three SAS and MNR men went missing from the emergency extraction which exacerbated Combined Operations concern for compromise and resulting diplomatic awkwardness. The three were eventually recovered 12 kilometers away from where they were left.[116]

Also in September 1979 in Mozambique, an SAS, MNR, and South African force conducted an unconventional operation against FPLM at the port city of Beira. Several targets were attacked at one time, including a telephone exchange and shipping. The telephone exchange effort was abandoned and the ship to be attacked was not there, but two dredgers were sunk with the same results of blocking the harbor channel.[117]

The month ended with Selous Scouts, general-purpose, and air forces in combat with ZANU, 21 September to 6 October 1979, in Mozambique with Operation *Miracle*. This was a set-piece battle involving air, artillery, armor, and ground forces. ZANU's Chimoio Circle remained a threat and it was attacked there repeatedly. Ground and air reconnaissance indicated a sprawling defended base area. Despite these efforts, it continued to expand to include the New Chimoio complex on the east side of the Chimoio–Tete road, with some 2,000 combatants in five locations. Soviet and East German advisors were believed to be present, along with support from FRELIMO armor and infantry.

A ground attack was conceived, supported by heavy airstrikes to eliminate enemy held high ground at "Monte Cassino," Hill 805, Hill 761, and Hill 774. An assault force of 100 Selous Scouts in 10 Unimogs trucks along with a troop of Eland armored cars from the Rhodesian Armored Car Regiment staged at Ruda Base Camp and crossed the border on 26 September 1979. A hundred men of the RLI were parachuted 10 kilometers from the objective to serve as stop groups to ambush any attempt to flee or reinforce the base. The column was delayed at the Gaeresi River and did not make their "Madison Square" assembly area before the planned Hunter and Canberra airstrikes. The assault force had to hole up for the night, while further airstrikes were called for the next day. Some 1,200 ZANLA were well dug in and fought for two days. By dint of heavy fighting, the defended positions were taken, followed by the withdrawal of ZANLA forces on D-day+2. Among the dead were senior Russian advisors. A FRELIMO reaction force of six T-34 tanks approached but did not close with the Rhodesians, who withdrew on 30 September 1979. Subsequent ZANLA and FRELIMO efforts to mount a counterraid on Ruda Base were met by Hunter and Canberra airstrikes, with the loss of two aircraft and crews.[118]

The SAS was in combat with FPLM, during October 1979, in Mozambique. This was a follow-up to previous bridge demolitions in the Tete province. Three bridges were dropped by three groups with the only casualties from bee stings.[119] The SAS was in combat with ZAPU, from 10 October to 6 November 1979, in Zambia with Operation *Cheese*. This was another effort designed to disrupt lines of communication from Tanzania to Zambia. The Tanzam Railway connected Zambia with Dar es Salaam. Built by the Chinese, it was essential to the Zambian economy after the closure of the rail route through Rhodesia. In September 1979 plans were made in Rhodesia to disrupt this vital link by dropping the rail bridge across the Chambezi River along with the adjacent road bridge. With the targets being some 500 kilometers from Rhodesia, the SAS had to freefall in a pathfinder team of four men, who marked a drop zone for the 12-man demolition team that followed. The initial date was scrubbed due to ground haze, with a successful drop being made on 3 October 1979. The demolition team arrived on the 8th and three days later the bridges were blown. The withdrawal to the border was conducted using hijacked vehicles along with a further demolition of seven bridges along the way. Recovery helicopters out of Mount Darwin staged at Musengedzi with additional fuel supplies to get them to reach the SAS team at first light on 13 October. The end result was Zambian copper being stranded and some 18,000 tons of imports being left at Dar es Salaam, much of it perishable. "This was one of the most successful operations of the war," according to one journalist.[120]

The SAS, general-purpose, and air forces were in combat with ZAPU, 16 to 23 October 1979, in Zambia with Operation *Tepid*. This was a set-piece battle 65 kilometers from Kariba on the Zambezi river and 50 kilometers west of Chirundu.

Intelligence revealed a battalion-size ZIPRA base southwest of Chirundu and north of Siavonga along the main road from Lusaka to Kariba. Photo reconnaissance confirmed this and a raid was planned to disrupt this force. Hunters and Canberras conducted a pre-attack airstrike on 18 October 1979. The assault force was then flown in from FAF 2 at Kariba, and parachuted on either side of the base. Air strikes continued in an effort to burn the cover from the entrenched positions. An airborne command and control team (Air Lieutenant Trevor A. Jew and Captain Robert C. MacKenzie) reported a lack of enemy response and called for the assault force to remain on the ground overnight to be taken out the next day by helicopters. Heavy contact was made that night with a ZIPRA force that included heavy machine guns, rocket-propelled grenades, recoilless rifles, and mortars. Fighting continued through the next day and additional airstrikes and reinforcements were required from the SAS and RLI. Despite rain showers, on 21 October 1979, nine waves of 72 men were flown in across Lake Kariba. This addition of two RLI commandos put Lieutenant-Colonel Ian Bate in charge, along with Lieutenant-Colonel Garth Barrett. The ZIPRA force of some 244 men withdrew under cover of darkness after a heavy mortar bombardment to break contact. The Rhodesian force secured their objective after ZIPRA withdrew. A Lynx command and control aircraft was hit by fire and forced to make an emergency landing.[121] In another effort to forestall a conventional border crossing by ZAPU, on 2 November 1979 a staging location in the Kabanga mission area south of Kalomo in Zambia was attacked. Air strikes were followed by RAR ground troops who returned with prisoners. A follow-up was conducted two days later in the same area in what was heavy ground combat.[122]

Operation *Dice* brought the era of cross-border attacks to an end as ZAPU had assembled and prepared a mechanized brigade in Zambia with the intent to move this force into Rhodesia via Wankie and Kariba, supported by fighter and transport aircraft flown by Libyan and ZIPRA pilots, with the eventual goal of Salisbury itself. Planned for 16 through 20 November 1979, *Dice* was the last major operation outside of Rhodesia. Demolition and ambush teams from the SAS were flown in by helicopter and landed on the objectives, followed by planned withdrawals. Three teams were to accomplish this. In response to the possibility of an air and ground conventional coup de main, major bridges on the lines of communications were cut on the roads from Lusaka to Kafue, Lusaka to Chirundu, and Lusaka to Livingstone. Subsequently, additional teams destroyed road and rail bridges south, east, and north of Lusaka, severing communications with Tanzania and Malawi. A final bridge was dropped near Lake Kariba, all with no casualties. Air support included fighter bombers and transport air drops.[123]

At war's end there were six active internal operational areas, closely linked to the provincial division of the country.[124] Each consisted of a brigade joint operations center, and approximately 18 sub-JOCs (battalion headquarters), and a number of company bases. The number of armed personnel in the country on both sides was substantial. Including part-time reserves, some 125,700 personnel carried arms in officially formed bodies. As well as the two guerrilla armies of the Patriotic Front (ZAPU and ZANU), there was the Rhodesian security force's army, air force, and police (still called the British South Africa Police) and their reserves. Any ceasefire was complicated by up to 25,000 government auxiliaries from the Internal Affairs Department and the political parties, and many private armies which also existed for security and protection. These figures did not include renegades who had broken away on their own and others still in Zambia or Mozambique.

With the Lancaster House bargaining reaching an end, impacted by the continued cross-border operations, on 22 November 1979 all external action was halted. While Bishop Muzorewa agreed to a ceasefire; the Patriotic Front held out until 5 December, after which pressure from Zambia and Mozambique resulted in an all-party agreement. The ceasefire was signed on 21 December 1979, going into effect on 28 December. Zimbabwe-Rhodesia had come under direct rule under a British governor, Lord Soames, in Salisbury. Zimbabwean post-colonial independence had arrived.

CHAPTER 8

Unconventional Warfare: Third Forces

Security Force Auxiliaries: Operation *Favour*

Operation *Favour* is discussed to indicate its origins and relationship with special operations forces. It had strong psychological elements aimed at winning hearts and minds to the internal settlement then expanded and used as a population and resource control measure. The internal settlement of March 1978 included amnesty programs that were expected to bring both ZPRA and ZANLA fighters in from the bush. Despite CIO and SB indications that this was not likely, moderates Muzorewa and Sithole needed to have the appearance of support from the Patriotic Front. The Combined Operations staff turned to Assistant Commissioner Mac McGuiness for help because of his knowledge of the guerrillas and his relationship with the Selous Scouts, so in April 1978 Operation *Favour* was unfolded. It used pseudo techniques and some 10 Selous Scout operators acting in support of the UANC in the Masana and Masembura tribal trust lands south of Bindura. Sithole-ZANU was represented by more than a hundred of his loyalists returned from Uganda and based near Enkeldoorn. In August, the public at large was introduced to "Comrade Max" and then "Commander Lloyd" from the ceasefire zones with some 100 Scouts and turned terrorists. It was hoped both these efforts would fool the real terrorists into coming over. Only some 50 actual amnesty takers were known compared to the 2,000 auxiliaries claimed by ComOps during this period.[1] Unintended consequences followed, despite the efforts of Special Branch liaison officers and ceasefire teams. Both moderates hoped the funding and weapons provided would allow them to develop an armed internal base of support rather than a real amnesty program. The Rhodesian public felt betrayed by this apparent deal with the enemy; neither the UANC nor Sithole-ZANU had any real support among the guerrillas, and they both soon lost control of their party militias.[2]

An expanded phase in September 1978 included the creation of Security Forces Auxiliaries to stabilize areas of low importance to the security forces but with large rural African populations. Beginning in November 1978, this effort was regularized under the army who provided uniforms, arms, training, and support to Africans primarily recruited in the urban areas. The 1POU took over the propaganda aspects to create the "Spear of the People." Selous Scouts and Special Branch personnel were still used as "coordinators" for this effort under the control the Special Forces Headquarters. The Special Branch transferred the Security Force Auxiliaries to full army control in July 1979. What had begun as a political effort became a security bid.[3]

Mozambique National Resistance: Operation *Bumper*

Special forces were involved with the Central Intelligence Organization's raising of a guerrilla body in Mozambique to counter Samora Machel's Marxist government because of FRELIMO's support to the Rhodesian nationalists, particularly ZANU.[4] The Rhodesians first made contact with anti-communist dissidents in Mozambique in 1969 in the effort to identify and report on nationalist infiltration during the Portuguese dominion. The Resistência Nacional Moçambicana was known to the Rhodesians as the MNR or Mozambique National Resistance movement. It came into being from a disinformation effort known as the Voice of Free Africa that broadcast from Rhodesia in June 1976, funded in part by Portuguese expatriates. Broadcasts were by Portuguese-speaking Europeans and not necessarily successful and the Rhodesians were somewhat unprepared when African dissidents responded.[5] It formed around FRELIMO defectors and other reactionaries, some freed from the Sacudzo reeducation center by the Selous Scouts.[6] This fostered a genuine, if savage, civil war in Mozambique that ended only much later.[7]

The group was first led by André Matsangaissa, and after his death in 1978 by Afonso Dhlakama. It operated from bases in the Gorongosa area, where it was sustained and advised by the CIO and the SAS. Special Air Service personnel established communications, coordinated the delivery of supplies (weapons, ammunition, food, clothing), and conducted training. The Rhodesian goal was, according to an SAS man, "to keep Machel and FRELIMO so busy they couldn't devote time and attention to supporting ZANLA."[8] Petter-Bowyer, who worked air force support from ComOps, recalled that in December 1978 the SAS was deploying from a forward operating base in the Odzi farming area east of Umtali, and the "Air force would be needed for resupply and other minor supporting roles. Surprisingly, when the time came for the first para-supply by Dakotas, it was to deliver maize and vegetable seed with only small amounts of ammunition and comforts." They were capturing all the ordnance they needed from FRELIMO.[9]

Those used to train the dissidents had no special credentials or language skills for this, although they were better instructors than the Selous Scouts. One member recalled his group was all non-Rhodesians ("An 'A' team we were not"—"listen up, you bloody baboons!" was the approach.). They wore unmarked uniforms and set up drops zones for unmistakable South African C-130s that "peppered the area with stuff that took days to police up."[10] The four SAS personnel with the MNR were changed regularly without difficulties, although in one case when moving towards Chipinga, the MNR leader, fearing abandonment, insisted the departing team not leave until the incoming team had arrived (the normal practice was for the four-man SAS team to walk well clear of the guerrilla base area for a helicopter pickup).[11]

The Rhodesian intent was to use intimidation and counterterror to weaken FRELIMO infrastructure and support for ZANU. This was accomplished by autonomous MNR mining, ambushes, and raids. It also provided cover and assistance to unilateral Rhodesian covert operations, several examples of which have been examined. A final operation took place in December 1979 with an attack on the Chibavava refugee center. The movement had reached a strength of 800 by then.[12] In 1980, with the settlement in Rhodesia, the MNR, now known as RENAMO, was turned over to the South Africans for continued backing. Flower was astonished that RENAMO accepted South African support.[13]

Dirty Tricks: Disinformation and Destabilization

Dirty tricks were defined as "special operations of an extremely sensitive nature." These involved eliminations, ambushes against persons of importance, carrying out of sensitive operations as ordered, and the gathering of intelligence as required to execute these operations, which included targeted killings, captures, and disinformation designed to split the nationalists with either negotiations or attacks. Also included was the accomplishment of certain special security tasks: the monitoring of sources or agents, conducting security penetration tests, and the elimination of those who posed a risk by revealing the actions of the special forces and ensuring the actions of these units were kept secret. These activities, labeled "funnies," often involved individuals rather than units. Research in this area is speculative and the line between sanctioned and unsanctioned actions is impossible to prove.[14]

This discussion is included with special operations, but these were not necessarily actions incumbent with special forces. The last SAS commander, Garth Barrett, cautioned, "You can't have regular soldiers participating in Special Branch operations."[15] As one Selous Scout operator remarked, "we did things we should not have been ordered to do."[16] This was a realm that witnessed both the intelligence, security, and military establishments going beyond accepted norms with "ends justifying the means" being carried to extremes to identify, locate, and neutralize (kill or capture) the terrorists. At a certain point in the conflict the identification, capture, interrogation, and execution of terrorists became a justified extra-legal method.[17] This was a logical byproduct of internal conflicts that failed to distinguish friend from foe in the pursuit of success. No ethical judgement is implied, as in war killing the enemy by deception or treachery is accepted practice with ambushes, snipers, and booby-traps.[18]

Legitimate attacks on nationalist leaders occurred when the opportunity was presented, although successes were debated.[19] For example, the Rhodesians got Herbert Chitepo, Jason J. Z. Moyo, Alfred Nikita Mangena, and Ethan Dube but did not kill Josiah Tongogara. The SAS built, although did not deliver, the Chitepo and Moyo bombs, that "created doubt and dissention, the epitome of special operations."[20] Operations *Bouncer*, *Milk Float*, *Aspect*, and *Bastille* reflected the special forces efforts to go after leadership targets when given a chance.[21] At the time of the April 1979 election, the SAS drove their decade-old Land Rovers to Lusaka to kill Nkomo. General Walls stated, "There is no question of us having been striking at Nkomo. I don't mean to sound boastful, but I would like to suggest that our record shows that if we wanted to kill Nkomo we would have done so." Mugabe is reported to have said when meeting General Walls later in 1979, "Why are your men trying to kill me?" To which Walls replied, "If they were my men you would be dead."[22]

Technical means were devised for this effort with local ingenuity. A colleague of the Selous Scouts, known as "Q" after a Ian Fleming character in James Bond, handled specialized devices and explosives. He worked on explosive timers, where experience with electronic timers led to a preference for mechanical mechanisms. "The operators like to know: when you push this pin it gets armed and then they've got 15 seconds buggering-off time or whatever. ... In 90 percent of the timers they wanted a delay from zero to up to an hour."[23] Letter bombs were another device, with a 2mm blank cartridge fitted to a modified (flattened to 3mm) "S4" detonator used to set off an ounce of plastic explosive. These letters and cards were mailed from third countries to their final destination. Car bombs were another singular approach for use against targeted leaders.[24]

Specialized demolitions included a South African-developed "cake" landmine which detonated when a mine-detector was used, when exposed to light, when prodded, or when moved. The Council for Scientific and Industrial Research's Dr. Vernon Joynt developed two- and seven-kilogram versions. Terrorist explosives and mines were still used when "plausible deniability" was desired.[25] Other devices developed with CSIR included: the "knock knock" door charge used to blow off door locks, the larger "gate crasher" charge to blow off exterior locks, the "hulk" wall charge to blow man-sized entry holes, the "wreck" or "wrecker" demolitions charge used to demolish buildings, and the "limpet" charge that attached to underwater objects like the hull of a ship using a vacuum rather than magnets. There was also a liquid additive that could freeze up a vehicle power plant and avoid the use of explosives "or anything nasty." Various accessories to attach and apply these special demolitions were also developed such as the binary compound ("wonder glue") used to hang charges on bridges using a 2x4 plank with a hook to hold 100 kilograms of explosives in an ammunition box (usually two devices for 200 kilograms total). It initially took army-trained engineers three hours to demolish a bridge in enemy territory; with specialized demolitions this could be done in five minutes "from touch down to pressing the tit."[26]

In addition to conventional killings and sabotage, chemical and biological means were pursued.[27] Some methods had been used before in Malaya and Kenya by the British colonial police Special Branches who authorized these actions rather than the military. Medical advice came from the University of Rhodesia medical school.[28] Methods included booby-trapping ammunition or weapons left in caches and poisoning tinned goods or clothing. Cyanide, arsenic, thallium, and other agriculture pesticide-type poisons were used to treat clothing with attendant storage and handling problems. Internal distribution was in rural stores that were pillaged by guerrillas or found in stockpiles of guerrilla supplies. External efforts included intercepting and doctoring supplies in transit.[29] Defoliants and poisoning water sources were tried as well. Victims reported becoming dizzy, with blurred vision and vomiting, and shortness of breath. Death followed without immediate medical intervention and hospitalization, not available to guerrillas in the bush.[30] Other extraordinary methods included planting explosives or transponders in portable radios that would indicate locations from the air or would explode when turned off, in a desire to outwit the intuitive course of events.[31]

The goal was as much psychological as it was to inflict casualties as even a general feeling of unease or distrust served a purpose. Control and deconfliction were concerns and not always successfully addressed with the need for clandestine methods. In an anecdotal case, a BSAP Support Unit stick kept terrorists' bush hats after a successful ambush, but suffered headaches, dizziness, and vomiting after wearing them for a short time. In another example, RLI troopers at Chimoio used captured aspirin and canned milk with similar results. The Special Branch representatives present with them were quick to prevent further use.[32]

Outbreaks of natural cholera or anthrax in eastern tribal areas and Mozambique in 1978 and 1979 were attributed to deliberate biological warfare efforts by Rhodesia and South Africa. In reality, these seemed to be postwar fabrications instead of the more logical attribution to the breakdown of internal agricultural and public health controls in proscribed areas.[33] Interviews with CSIR Director J. Wynand de Villiers and senior scientist Vernon Joynt concluded that both chemical and biological weapons were impractical and would have been as much a threat to their own side as the enemy. Killing was hard work and direct methods were the most cost effective rather than getting too clever. The cost of the effort was not justified with the financial restraints that existed although interest continued in a variety of areas: explosives, napalm, teargas, defoliants, and other "special tools" to counter the enemy without direct combat.[34]

South African support for a variety of these methods was evident. In general, the Rhodesians came up with the ideas but lacked the development and industrial base to put the technology into production. This is where the South Africans came in, although the effort was of mutual benefit and certainly cash and carry on the South African side. Mine and anti-mine efforts, night vision technology, communications equipment, and air-delivered weapons resulted from this relationship as well as from sanctions-busting sources. Experience gained in Rhodesia was transmitted through the police presence early on, as except for liaison, training, equipment, and helicopter support, the South African Defense Force did not directly operate in the area until the very end of the conflict in 1979.[35] South African politicians, intelligence, police, and military brought different organizational cultures to the Rhodesian problem and were sometimes at odds with each other. For example, the SADF felt the South African Police picked up a habit of disregarding legality from their border control experience in Rhodesia. In turn, the South African military was unable to adjust to political expediency in the withdrawal of support to what they identified as their fight against African nationalism and worked against their own security and intelligence apparatus. General Constand Viljoen would later recall, although a military task, the police went to Rhodesia where they "became a type of militia using crude methods not within the principles of the Geneva Convention or the principles of a just war."[36] Members of the Rhodesian special forces were also recruited by South African, as well as British and American, intelligence services.[37]

This secret war also had perplexities and disapproval continued from the head of the Central Intelligence Organization and the Rhodesian Army commander even in the face of battlefield success. A source of rancor with the British South Africa Police was that the former guerrillas received amnesty for what had previously been prosecuted as criminal offenses with a death penalty. A more penetrating problem was the fact that the special forces were holding a monopoly on intelligence gathered on the enemy forces that the CIO and MID were resentful of, as well as control of external operations. In this the special forces were allied with Combined Operations.[38] In Lieutenant-Colonel Reid-Daly's favor was a personal relationship with General Walls, Commander, Combined Operations (Reid-Daly and Walls had served together in the SAS in Malaya and the RLI). Regimental paymaster Alexandre Binda felt "that a Selous Scout operator was, for the most part, on his own initiative and allowed to get on with the job as he saw fit and not have his decisions or recommendations turned down out of hand." Reid-Daly knew his men for the most part and would back them to the hilt; as a result "they worked their guts out and did their true best." Binda described "Uncle Ron" as no respecter of persons, "which seemed to earn him quite a few enemies." But, "He certainly did care for his fighting men and their difficult and dangerous work and would move heaven and earth for them."[39] Selous Scout methods were effective and ruthless, making the unit an object of suspicion even to its own side.[40]

This came to a head when the Rhodesian Army Director of Military Intelligence, Colonel John L. Redfern, and the Army Director of Counter Intelligence, Major Trevor G. Des Fountain, engaged in wiretapping Lieutenant-Colonel Reid-Daly's telephone because of concerns over illegal activities in the course of operations. Reid-Daly felt this was an unwarranted compromise of security.[41] Ensuing scandals saw both the pseudo commander Reid-Daly and the army commander Lieutenant-General John S. V. Hickman leave the service at the height of the war.[42] Reid-Daly was replaced under a cloud by Lieutenant-Colonel Patrick W. Armstrong in November 1979. After "red lining" what he would take over, Armstrong remained in command of the Selous Scouts until March 1980. The new army commander, Lieutenant-General Andrew L. C. (Sandy) MacLean, had to go to Walls to find out what his units were doing and afterwards commented, "Shit, I have been in the dark."[43]

Operations *Hectic, Quartz,* and More

After Reid-Daly left his post, more controversial or questionable aspects appeared. In the run-up to the election and independence the SAS and Scouts were required to conduct affairs of dubious value and scruples. One plan called for the elimination of nationalist leadership, particularly ZANU, and the other would attack their followers at designated assembly points throughout the country. *Hectic* and *Quartz* can be considered the last special operations that never really occurred, adding the specter of coup d'etat to the role of special forces.[44] At Combined Operations, Petter-Bowyer recorded General Walls stating, "There is no question of Rhodesians indulging in a military coup." But others in the security forces were told they would prevent a victory by Mugabe over Nkomo and Muzorewa, using force if necessary. Walls used his right to appeal to Prime Minister Margaret Thatcher over the head of the Governor Soames on 1 March 1980, without response. Apparently the intent was deployment of the Rhodesian security forces in case the election results were invalidated because of Patriotic Front coercion. These final internal employments were at odds with the values of a democratic society and perhaps why they were aborted in the end.[45] Robert Mugabe's ZANU-PF won a majority in the February election. Mugabe formed a coalition government with Nkomo's PF-ZAPU and on 18 April 1980 Zimbabwe became an independent republic.[46]

To What End:
Tactical Victory, Strategic Defeat

The impact of the struggle in barest human terms was revealed by some overall statistics that indicated the relative size and scope of the conflict:

- 30,000 were killed during the war, to include 10,000 terrorists inside Rhodesia, 10,000 terrorists outside Rhodesia, 1,120 security force members, 500 European civilians (107 in two airliner attacks), 3,500 African civilians killed by guerrilla actions, and 3,500 African civilians killed by security force actions (violating curfews, caught in crossfire, running with terrorists, etc.).
- 10,000 others were maimed and 275,000 injured.
- 750,000 to 850,000 Africans were displaced in the region, to include:
- 225,000 to 350,000 relocated to government protected or consolidated villages, 330,000 made homeless, and 225,000 to 250,000 made refugees. Not counted were the Europeans and Asians who left the country as a result of the conflict.[1] From the conflict, other consequences were derived in terms of changes made by force to the existing order, which needed to be considered.

A few outside comments are used to conclude. British General Sir Walter C. Walker, a commander in Burma, Malaya, Borneo, and of the North Atlantic Treaty Organization (NATO or OTAN), visited Rhodesia in 1977/8 and felt, "based on more than 20 years' practical experience, from lieutenant to general, of counterinsurgency and guerrilla-type operations, there is no doubt that Rhodesia now [has] the most professional and battle worthy army in the world today for this particular type of warfare. Their army cannot be defeated in the field either by terrorists or even by a much more sophisticated enemy."[2] This was echoed by Royal Military College (RMC) Sandhurst's L. L. Mathews in 1979, who concluded that "Provided with only relatively small forces and equipment sometimes both obsolescent and elderly, General Walls, first as army commander and then as commander combined operations, has waged a campaign of extreme professional competence that will deserve a place in the world's staff college courses for many years to come."[3] Another Sandhurst instructor who was closer to the action, Paul Moorcraft, provided a nonconforming view:

Could soldiers infused with a sense of racial superiority, who rode to battle in helicopters or fought from mine-proofed, ambush-proofed vehicles supported by jet fighter aircraft, hope to defeat guerrillas who slogged everywhere on foot, who could live on a ball of cold maize porridge and tepid water, and who were, except for their ubiquitous AK-47s, often indistinguishable from the rest of the impoverished peasant population?[4]

These were opinions for which conclusions were sought from both sides of the problem. But these are only tentative comments from a work in progress. From this study, the following was found in terms of air–ground general-purpose and special-purpose employment.

Zimbabwe (Department of State, public domain)

Air and Ground Operations

The application of air power in peripheral conflicts has a history and doctrine of its own. In fact, air support has seen more use in marginal areas than it ever has as a strategic force in war. The British were an early proponent of the efficiency of air power in colonial wars with the ability to cover large territory economically. Malaya, Kenya, and Aden provided contemporary examples for the Rhodesians to follow, as well as their own regional experience with Portugal and South Africa.[5] American use of air power in counterinsurgency goes back to the turn of the 20th century as well and paralleled the development of its strategic air force. Air counterinsurgency theory, expressed by John S. Pustay in 1965, outlined the use of aircraft for control of populace, weakening and exposure of the guerrilla forces, engagement and defeat of the guerrillas, and support to civil and military organizations.[6] These "special air warfare tactics" included command and control, airlift, ancillary, forward air control, strike, and reconnaissance duties.[7] While interesting as a point of discussion, actual practice was also available from United States technology and techniques used in Southeast Asia (although the bulk of air operations there were conventional in nature and the antithesis of selectivity demanded for counterinsurgency).

Aerospace doctrine is based on an autonomous air force's place in conventional warfare and obtaining victory through air power. In contrast, air forces configured to provide support to dominate land or naval services have a characteristic focus not viewed by the aerospace community. For example, the U.S. Navy and Marine Corps require a tactical air force equipped, trained, and deployed to ensure the success of tactical operations. This is seen in the doctrinal functions demanded of their air components. These functions provide a basis by which to analyze tactical aviation requirements in a counterinsurgency environment that is more practical than a strategic aerospace view.[8]

Air power proved a key factor for both the Zimbabwean nationalists and Rhodesian government. Rhodesia's enemies knew the value of the air force from the perspective of its impact: "Possession of an air force has enabled the illegal regime to mount devastating bombing raids on targets both inside Zimbabwe and against the front line states. Air superiority is crucial to the regime's survival."[9] It is important to consider this was an asymmetrical application of power: one side had air support while the other did not. It allowed the Rhodesians to overcome a lack of manpower and the demands of space, but did not change the conflict's final outcome. Efficient use was made of finite resources, and because it was felt air power had limited real utility in insurgency situations, air assets were kept within means. Some years after the events, it was acknowledged that air power was an essential element of how the war was fought, but not a factor in the ultimate success or failure of the conflict.

Local analysis augmented first-hand experience, and showed how conventional aircraft could be used for unconventional purposes. There was not always a suitable match of aircraft to tasks: jets were old, fast, and costly; utility aircraft were a not perfect conversion from civil use; helicopters were few in number and performance; and air power lacked the precision to effect "hearts and minds."[10] Also, as Professor Stan Monick wrote for the University of Pretoria in South Africa, the Rhodesian Air Force "was unique in being called upon to function solely within a [counterinsurgency] context; its example would be dangerous for an air force called upon to perform a multi-faceted role."[11]

During the ceasefire period, Group Captain Petter-Bowyer discussed air power's place with ZANLA's Rex Nhongo, and ZPRA's Lookout Masuku, and Dumiso Dabengwa: "They considered themselves to be on an equal footing with the army because they used similar equipment and fought on their feet. The air force was quite different. In their minds it was the complex high-tech force that had been responsible for the devastation visited upon their own forces."[12] Reacting to increased external air attacks in the last year of fighting, ZANLA's Josiah Tongogara noted the Rhodesian's came with, "supersonic jets, bombers, spotter planes and helicopters. Using these aircraft supplied from France, Italy, America and Israel through South Africa he drops bombs and rockets. The aircraft bomb everywhere without any bother to pinpoint targets. ... It is just a way to frighten people."[13] On the other side, Rhodesian morale was boosted as a popular writer observed, when "waves of helicopters loaded with troops, whirled north and west throughout the day, and the elderly Canberra bombers and Hunters followed in their wake, screaming black and lethal against the azure sky, people lifted their heads and watched them go with a strange mixture of pride and awe. The boys were going on a raid across the border."[14]

The multitude of assignments required to fulfill aviation missions in conventional war could be categorized into separate functional areas. Desired capabilities involved reconnaissance, antiair warfare, assault support, offensive support, electronic warfare, and control of aircraft and missiles. Aviation tasks included gaining and maintaining air superiority, seeking out and destroying enemy forces and supporting installations, preventing movement of enemy forces along routes of communications into and within the objective area, and in providing direct air support to surface combat elements in order to assist in the attainment of assigned objectives. The use of an air force configured on conventional lines in unconventional circumstances requires the modification of these functions and tasks based upon a shift of assumptions for aircraft use. The roles remain but the emphasis changes and the question of costs to benefits are dramatic. Observed one Rhodesian air officer, "A pilot trained in conventional operations can easily adapt to [counterinsurgency operations], but not so easily in a vice-versa situation. The Royal Rhodesian Air Force pilot is schooled in all facets of air power, and as such, is rated exceptionally highly by other world air forces."[15]

For the Rhodesian counterinsurgency effort, the air force was needed for transport, reconnaissance, command and control, and lastly offensive air support. This was an approach totally different from its formal role. From study and experience the Rhodesian Air Force determined the types of aircraft required during the different phases of counterinsurgency, weapons suited to these operations, simple and practical modifications to aircraft, the organization and infrastructure required to sustain operations, and the training and tactics necessary to defeat a guerrilla force.

A particular Rhodesian success was the Fire Force concept, "in which troops and aircraft mount combined flexible operations against reported terrorist presence throughout the country. In addition, an efficient air–ground strike capability is available to use if necessary."[16] Found was a balanced use of maneuver, firepower, and communications to win when contact was made. This air–ground task force was the result. Characteristic of the battlefield in the modern era, particularly in insurgency conflicts, is the use of helicopters. Helicopters deliver critical supplies and ensure wounded have a chance for survival that the guerrilla opposition does not usually enjoy. The helicopter adds a dimension of mobility and firepower that gives counterinsurgency units a valuable force multiplier, particularly when insurgent numbers stretch the defenders thin on the ground.

It was easy to take air power for granted, particularly mobility provided on the battlefield by helicopters (for U.S. Marines this began during the Korean War and quickly became an integral part of their amphibious operations). One writer looked at helicopter operations over the past decades from a somewhat different perspective. Journalist Al J. Venter examined the use of vertical envelopment beginning with the French in Algeria who put soldiers with automatic rifles in skid-mounted casualty litters and concluded with American purpose-built gunships in Somalia. His was not a technical or doctrinal study, but a collection of narratives by reporters and players. Surveyed were a host of helicopter operations to include those by British, Portuguese, Rhodesian, South African, and United Nations forces. The lessons presented were recognized by both "air-wingers" and "ground-pounders" who have been introduced to African conflicts. Observations mainly discussed air assault and fire support, although a logical expansion would have been more on air movement of logistic supplies and personnel. The Rhodesians were faced with limited manpower and miles and miles of "bloody" Africa. This obliged them to concentrate infantry and air assets into groupings that allowed response to numerous guerrilla sightings with vertical envelopment and firepower, resembling the Fire Force.

Air force helicopter, transport, and counterinsurgency squadrons provided the air element of helicopters and light aircraft, with fighters and bombers on call. The Air Force Regiment and reserve ran the forward airfields with needed efficiency. The Rhodesian Light Infantry was the backbone of the Fire Force ground elements with the Rhodesian African Rifles being added later to the roster, relieving pressure on the work of the special forces. Afterwards, the South Africans ran their own version of Fire Force during the conflict. By 1979, the most successful combination involved a helicopter gunship carrying air and ground commanders, four helicopter troop transports, and a DC-3 Dakota parachute transport. These were all supported by light fixed-wing aircraft armed with guns, rockets, napalm, and anti-personnel bombs.

The concept required two elements to succeed, other than the air–ground reaction force that receives the most attention. Effective information gathering and reporting by Selous Scout "pseudoterrorists" allowed the callouts of the Rhodesian Light Infantry and African Rifles that accounted for a large number of the enemy killed at the war's end (an 80-to-1 kill ratio) and kept the nationalists from forming "liberated zones" in populated rural areas. It needed a competent patrol and observation element and a large, if not always elite, protection force on the ground for essential infrastructure. These indicated where the terrorists were not, so the specialized units could focus on locating and eliminating terrorists where they were. The border minefield, the cordon sanitaire, also contributed by funneling the arriving guerrillas into desired "killing zones." The Fire Force achievement was enhanced by a late war strategy which designated European population and economic centers as "vital asset ground," defended with "good tactical ground," leaving the African tribal areas as "other ground." With a secure base to operate from, tactical and other ground became in effect free-fire zones to pursue guerrilla concentrations and approach routes.[17]

It proved a purely military solution that neglected effective civic action which was left to the civil administration. In the end this "killing machine" of helicopters, close air support, and aggressive infantry was overwhelmed by the increasing need to engage in cross-border operations to hit base camps and lines of communications to stem a rising tide of guerrilla infiltration. As a tactical measure it bought time and killed "gooks," but could not halt the subversion. This was the classic quandary of modern counterinsurgency, the conflict between combat and civic action to win the war.

Special Operations

Admiral William H. McRaven offered this definition at the U.S. Naval Postgraduate School: special operations were "conducted by forces specially trained, equipped, and supported for a specific target whose destruction, elimination, or rescue (in the case of hostages), is a political or military imperative."[18] McRaven offered six principles for success in these actions: "The theory states that special operations forces are able to achieve relative superiority over the enemy if they prepare a simple plan, which is carefully concealed, repeatedly and realistically rehearsed, and executed with surprise, speed, and purpose."[19] These principles were those followed in planning, preparation, and execution to overcome inherent friction and the enemy's will. Success was based on what he called "relative superiority" that allowed smaller forces to overcome seemingly larger and well-protected adversaries.[20] For this the Rhodesians relied on the straightforward and time-proven "Who Dares Wins." Special Air Service squadron commander MacKenzie felt this meant "after careful calculation of all the risks and the factors involved, then with that extra element of bravery, if you like courage, a calculated decision can produce results totally surprising to everyone, often the operators themselves."[21] Regimental commander Barrett added, "For the special forces soldier the only thing more important than discipline was leadership."[22]

Ken Flower, Director General, Central Intelligence Organization, observed that special operations were "a game that must proceed silently; public applause spells failure. We had proceeded quietly and in a small way in the early years of CIO by probing the weaknesses in the structure of the African nationalist organizations within the country. Later, we went with the nationalist movements into Zambia, Botswana, Mozambique, Tanzania and further still."[23] The full range of *sub rosa* actions were engaged in, from espionage, subversion, and sabotage by individuals for the Central Intelligence Organization; to internal security and surveillance by undercover forces disguised as terrorists for the Special Branch; to the preparation of battlespace and advance force operations by small independent action forces in the Frontline States. In this the Rhodesian Special Air Service and Selous Scouts conducted all the activities that military special forces could be used for: reconnaissance, ambushes, raids, harassment, abductions, targeted leadership eliminations, communications interception, and even guerrilla warfare. Direct action expanded from local camp attacks to full-scale cross-border strikes of a daring nature at multiple locations involving the whole of the security forces. Beyond a certain point, cross-border targets attacked as conventional military objectives required the command and control provided by Combined Operations. All Rhodesian security forces enlarged their participation in unconventional efforts by providing expanded aircraft, firepower, and troop support. In fact, throughout, the air force provided special operations support with the same professionalism as normal operations under more demanding circumstances. With this, special forces had become the supported rather than a supporting unit.

A Rhodesian technique that was part of the total counterinsurgency strategy was the use of pseudoterrorists or guerrillas. Paul Melshen examined this concept at the U.S. Naval War College, and described it as a counterinsurgent force that "completely mirrors" the insurgent in order to infiltrate civilian communities or operational areas to obtain background and combat information upon which to bring force to bear on the insurgent. He concluded that these operations had value because they could 1) gain information; 2) penetrate, isolate, and eliminate insurgent forces; 3) disperse tactical information to government forces; and 4) destroy insurgent political infrastructure.[24]

Further analysis of Rhodesian special operations supported the need for control of these activities at the highest level and indicates the difficulties in maintaining standing special forces when not actively employed. Varying requirements for internal and external operations crossed existing divisions between the civil and military side of counterinsurgency and warfighting. In some areas this was well run but the normal controls and restrictions broke down as the conflict escalated: it appeared terror was being used to match terror. The security and intelligence services were not up to the task of managing either the pseudo or dirty tricks effort. Destabilization and counterterror continued through the end of the war within Rhodesia, at times out of desperation and possibly sanctioned control. Needed was the proposed special forces headquarters to coordinate and plan (a split between force provider and force commander).

Also indicated was the quantity and quality of manpower available (both the SAS and Selous Scouts had to use much younger and older soldiers than normally found in similar organizations with larger national population pools). The Rhodesians had to maintain standing units in wartime from a limited population base and engage creative manpower sources. All units emphasized their "voluntary" nature and incorporated personnel from across the security forces, although consisting of primarily army personnel. Over time, national servicemen, short-term contract, territorial, and reserve personnel were all incorporated. The use of "turned" terrorists in the Selous Scouts was another source of essential manpower. Selection and training produced cohesive units that were desperately short of manpower. While motivation produced initial applicants, special pay and allowances provided additional incentive to remain.[25] McRaven concluded from his study of special operations that in regards to selection and training, "the theory validates the need for a standing special operations force that is trained, equipped, and supported at the best possible levels."[26]

As always, a certain public relations or emotional element existed to ensure the that exploits of "super soldiers" were known or imagined. Lieutenant-General Peter Walls, Commander, Combined Operations concluded, "I really believe that what some of our guys did was as good as anything the Israelis did without anything like the backup or modern equipment. What our guys did was tremendous."[27] Added one commander, Garth Barrett, "Most special forces operations will never be precisely known and some perspectives were created on purpose for deception."[28] By analogy, current U.S. Special Operations Command functions include direct action, reconnaissance, psychological and information operations, counterterrorism, unconventional warfare, civil affairs, and foreign internal defense.[29] This was with comparative resources far and above what the Rhodesian made do with.

Historian and journalist Moorcraft wrote the Selous Scouts were "One of the toughest fighting forces in the world. And certainly one of the most difficult to get into." But, although the Selous Scouts got much of the publicity, "the all-white SAS quietly carry out much of the technical—and deadly—groundwork for the external raids."[30] This aptly depicted the special forces of Rhodesia during the bush war. Some 30 to 35 Selous Scouts were killed, the most during 1978.[31] When it ceased to exist by April 1980, no tribute or ceremony occurred as the losers sought to gratify the victors.[32] During the conflict some 38 SAS men were killed, with 1979 being a costly year.[33] Commanding officer Major Grahame A. ("The Phantom Major") Wilson disbanded the regiment in December 1980. Rhodesian 1SAS stood down with a message from 22SAS that stated: "farewell in part to a much admired sister unit. … Your professionalism and fighting expertise has always been second to none"[34]

Final Words

To conclude, while this analysis started with the opinions of outsiders the participants had their own views, hopefully made evident throughout the narrative. By way of a last word from General Walls, he stated:

> I wouldn't like to upset some of my erstwhile friends in the British Army by making any comparisons. I would merely say that the friends I am talking about would agree with me one hundred percent that practice makes perfect and an army that hasn't fought a war or campaign for a number of years is that much out of date or that much inefficient. This is not casting slurs on people who haven't fought wars. Obviously our whole reason for being soldiers is to avoid wars.[35]

Army commander Lieutenant-General Andrew L. C. MacLean cautioned that:

> A small, thoroughly professional army can defeat a much larger non-professional force, but a small semi-professional army will not defeat a vastly larger non-professional army. It is becoming increasingly evident that in the short term junior officers are not worrying about increasing their military knowledge and are quite happy "slaying gooks." Classical war teaching is erroneously looked upon with disdain. … We cannot afford to degenerate into a semi-professional army with expertise in [counterinsurgency] operations only.[36]

Air Marshal Michael J. McLaren, the air force commander, echoed this view:

> Yet, at this time of attention being focused on our border areas, we are very conscious of the need to avoid putting all our eggs into the anti-terrorist basket. It is imperative that we maintain an ability to defend Rhodesia farther afield than merely from our own backyard. We must have a viable air defense capability and must also retain the vital long-range strike potential which is a powerful deterrent against attack.[37]

McLaren felt this reflected the multiple challenges faced:

> In my view it is vital for us to retain a balanced and viable air force, capable of fulfilling our many and varied roles. In a continent where many countries have [been] rapidly expanding air arms it would be downright foolish for us to concentrate on equipping and provisioning for the anti-terrorist environment alone. The need to continue and improve our conventional war capability is to me so necessary as to be self-evident.[38]

With the higher conduct of the war in the hands of the political leadership, changing outcomes needed for success, and an unfavorable strategic situation, Walls was faced with the choice of using the security forces to simultaneously defend internally and attack externally in order to set the basis for a negotiated settlement, which happened at Lancaster House, rather than victory on the ground. This was done with the establishment of Combined Operations and a National Joint Operations Center.

The internal defense effort was assigned to the police and army commanders using the Joint Operations Center–Brigade model and available part-time and national service units, along with the Special Branch and Selous Scouts internal effort. The offensive effort saw the retention of full-time Fire Forces, special forces, and air forces to fight in the Frontline States. Before March 1977 this was with the intelligence services and special forces who established the model used by general-purpose forces after this date, while expanded special operations continued as well. This also saw special forces establish a lock on "operational" intelligence.

While increased contacts with greater success were a measure of achievement, it also indicated the growing threat from the increased numbers of poorly trained and armed guerrillas, by then quantity having a quality all of its own.[39] What was needed to counter this was a dynamic and aggressive response that pitted limited government resources against increasing nationalist numbers in a classic revolutionary warfare situation. Examination indicates that Fire Force kept the guerrillas moving, dispersed, and fragmented inside Rhodesia. The cordon sanitaire delayed and channelized their entry into Rhodesia. Finally, the cross-border raids pushed the guerrilla sanctuaries away from the border, interdicted their lines of communications and supply, and destroyed their supplies and leadership (to say nothing of those of the Frontline States).

While the Fire Force as a tactical measure was the most efficient application of air and ground forces in the forward area that a joint command had at its disposal, its success masked the failure of security, psychological, population and resource control programs run by the civil authorities (BSAP, IntAf, CMED). The same applied to the cordon sanitaire and the cross-border raids which in some ways were Fire Force writ large. This failure is manifested by the resort the martial law in a majority of African population areas in the country. One controversial element was the Security Force Auxiliaries program which verged on revolutionary, and essential, in securing the tribal areas after the failures of Internal Affairs, the police, and Guard Force.

Some rank and file felt rapid change was deterred by inertia at the top, for example from an aviator:

> The Rhodesian higher command was abysmally slow in adapting to the changing circumstances of the war. Junior officers were constantly devising tactics and taking operational decisions which should have been the responsibility of the Air Staff. Eventually the Air Staff would advocate the right things but they were usually two years too late, as with the cross-border strikes. The limitations and necessity for improving Fire Force operations were apparent to the pilots, but the means for implementing them were not available until too late.[40]

I am not sure Walls and the Combined Operations staff could be faulted for this under the circumstances, although there were plenty of critics of the lack of initiative from the top.

One thing witnessed was the continued presence of personality-driven, bottom-up initiatives rather than policy or strategic efforts from the top. This was found in other areas but was more significant in the special forces and air operations. A byproduct was the factiousness that existed between services and branches whether at the top or at the bottom of the chain. By war's end, the Rhodesian military was trifurcated into special-purpose, general-purpose, and protection forces. Recognized was the need for special forces to carry the fight when national service, reserve, and police units could not or would not. It was seen that the cutting edge was only as good as the support this was based upon.

In the long run, any military success was upset by political failure based in retrospect on the "no-win" goal of continued European minority rule. The military option only bought time for a negotiated settlement in which all parties were forced to the table in 1979 and the subsequent election in 1980. The elusive political solution the nationalists desired and the settlers denied was reached. Judged a success by some and a failure by others, it ended the conflict short of total defeat or victory. Throughout, the Rhodesians searched for a way to defeat external support or basing, infiltration, and insurgency. I am not convinced they ever found a definitive "Rhodesian Way" of countering insurgency, but came up instead with specific responses to definite problems.[41]

Rhodesian
ARMY

TERRORISM STOPS HERE!

Rhodesian Security Forces Troop List[1]

RHODESIAN ARMY (RhA)
Army Headquarters and General Staff
   Chief of Staff, General, Administrative, Quartermaster Branches
   Reserve and Territorial Army
Schools and Depots
District and Brigade Headquarters
Services Headquarters Area
   Ordnance and Supplies Depots
   Base Workshops
   Composite Transport Companies
   Air Supply Platoons
1 Field Regiment Rhodesian Artillery
   Batteries
Psychological Operations Unit
Rhodesian Special Air Service
   Squadrons
Rhodesian Light Infantry
   Commandos
Grey's Scouts
   Squadrons
Rhodesian Defense Regiment
Rhodesia Regiment
   Battalions, Territorial Army
   Independent Companies, National Service
Rhodesian African Rifles
   Battalions
Rhodesian Armoured Car Regiment
   Squadrons
Rhodesian Army Education Corps

Rhodesian Army Medical Corps
   Medical Companies
   Army Health Unit
   Tsanga Lodge
Rhodesian Army Pay Corps
   Pay Companies
   Army Data Processing Unit
Rhodesian Army Services Corps
   Maintenance Companies
Rhodesian Corps of Chaplains
Rhodesian Corps of Engineers
   Engineer Squadrons
   Boat Squadron
Rhodesian Corps of Military Police
   Provost Platoons
   Detention Barracks
Rhodesian Corps of Signals
   Signal Squadrons
Rhodesian Intelligence Corps
Rhodesian Women's Service
Selous Scouts
   Groups

RHODESIAN AIR FORCE (RhAF)
Air Headquarters and Staffs
   Chief of Staff, Director General of Operations, Director General of Supporting
   Services
Main Stations and Forward Airfields
   Thornhill Squadrons 1, 2, 4, 6
   New Sarum Squadrons 3, 5, 7, 8
   Forward Airfields
Volunteer Reserve
Rhodesian Women's Service
Air Force Regiment
   Infantry Squadrons
   Support Squadrons
   Antiaircraft Squadrons
Central Equipment Depot
Technical Training School
Parachute Training School
Flying Training School

1 Squadron (fighter)
2 Squadron (fighter)
3 Squadron (transport)
4 Squadron (utility)
5 Squadron (bomber)
6 Squadron (training)
7 Squadron (helicopter)
8 Squadron (helicopter)

GUARD FORCE (GF)
Commander
Deputy Commander
Training Depot
Headquarters
    SOGD/SOAdmin
    SOLog/SOSpSvcs
Regional Headquarters
Battalions
Group Headquarters (districts)
Guard Headquarters (protected, consolidated villages)

SECURITY FORCE AUXILARIES (SFAs)
Commander
Deputy Commander
    GSO2/Operations and Training
Headquarters SFA
Regional Headquarters
Area Headquarters
Detachments and protection units

INTERNAL AFFAIRS NATIONAL SERVICE UNIT (IntAf)
Secretary (Commander, IntAfNSU)
Deputy Secretary
Training Depot
Headquarters Echelon
Engineering Echelon
A–E Echelons
Provincial and district

BRITISH SOUTH AFRICA POLICE (BSAP)
Police General Headquarters

Commissioner
Deputy Commissioner for Crime and Security
Deputy Commissioner for Personnel and Training
    Uniform Branch
    Police Reserve
    Police Anti-Terrorist Unit
Administrative Branch
Signals Branch
Special Branch (see CIO)
Criminal Investigation Division/Department
Police Support Unit
Provincial and Salisbury headquarters, urban and rural districts, police stations and camps

CENTRAL INTELLIGENCE ORGANIZATION (CIO)
Director General and Deputy Director General
Internal Division (Branch I—Special Branch)
    Sections, Desks—provincial and district
External Division (Branch II)
    Sections, Desks—geographic
Directorate of Military Intelligence
Directorate of Air Intelligence

Glossary of Acronyms, Terms, and Jargon[1]

2IC	second-in-command
AA	antiaircraft
ACR	Armored Car Regiment
AD	accidental discharge
ADF	African Development Fund
African	Black, regardless of extraction
Af	African
Afrikaner	South African of Dutch extraction, native South African
Agric-Alert	agriculture alert, Internal Affairs-run radio network at district level between farmers, police, and security forces
AHQ	Army Headquarters
AK, AKM	Soviet AK-47 or Chinese Type 56 Kalashnikov assault rifle of communist origin used by nationalists and special forces
Alouette III	K-Car (command helicopter from which senior ground and air commander could control operations or contact) with 20mm or quad machine gun and G-Car (troop carriers)
Alpha	first letter of phonetic alphabet used for radio/telephone transmission; others are Bravo, Charlie, Delta, Echo, Foxtrot, Golf, Hotel, India, Juliet, Kilo, Lima, Mike, November, Oscar, Papa, Quebec, Romeo, Sierra, Tango, Uniform, Victor, Whisky, X-ray, Yankee, and Zulu
Alpha bomb	air force one-kilogram anti-personnel bomb that bounced in the air before exploding
Alpha 76, A63, A30	tactical radios

A Luta Continua!	"The struggle continues" (from Portuguese), slogan adopted by nationalists (from FRELIMO and MPLA)
amai	mother (from Shona)
Amandla Ngawethu!	"The power is ours" (from Zulu), slogan adopted by nationalists (from African National Congress)
ammo	ammunition
ANC	African National Congress (South Africa since 1912, Rhodesia since 1934), or African National Council (Rhodesia since 1971)
AP	anti-personnel landmine; assembly point
APAR	Army Pay and Records
apartheid	separateness (from Afrikaans), South African National Party program from 1948; also petty or grand apartheid
APA	African Purchase Area from the Land Apportionment Act
ARNL	Association of Rhodesian Industries
AS	African Staff or Service
Asian	person of Indian extraction, also others of southeast Asian descent
askari	African soldier in the King's African Rifles and Rhodesia Native Regiment; term used by some for the Rhodesian African Rifles
AWOL	absent without leave
baas	sir, mister, boss (from Afrikaans)
baba	father (from Shona)
badza	hoe-style digging implement
baobab	tree with thick trunk and angular branches resembling roots
bazooka	nationalist term for anti-armor rocket launcher
BDESTCOY	Brigade Supply and Transport Company
big means	TR48 high-frequency radio used by tactical headquarters to general headquarters for external operations using manual Morse; B22 used by other units with a weight of 11 kilograms and a range of 3,000 kilometers
biltong	dried meat in thin strips, like jerky
binos	binoculars
bivvy	poncho or bivouac sheet; two troopers used their individual bivvies to form a shelter
blues/blue jobs	army term for air force

Boer	derogatory African term for European (from Afrikaans farmer), *see also Mabunu*
boet	brother (from Afrikaans)
BOSD	Branch of Special Duties, Ministry of Information section devoted to psychological operations projects
BOSS	South African Bureau for State Security
breeker	fighter (from Afrikaans)
Bren gun	British .303 or 7.62mm light machine gun
brew up	popular order in the bush to make tea
Bright Light	police reservist, or others, assigned to guard farms in rural areas
browns/brown jobs	air force term for army
BSAC	British South Africa Company
BSAP	British South Africa Police, established 1890 by BSAC; also known as "The Force" or "The Regiment"
buffalo beans	severe irritant in the bush when clouds of fine hairs come in contact with skin
Bulala zonke!	"Kill them all!" (from Ndebele)
bundu	veld, bush, open space (from Shona)
bunker bomb	one-kilogram bomb with four to six second grenade fuze
bush	the field, as in serving in the bush
call sign	deployed army or police unit, from the alpha-numeric term used to identify units such as "Alpha Four"
callup	orders to active duty for reservists or national servicemen
camarada	comrades (from Portuguese), used by nationalists, synonymous with Shona *vakomana* or "the boys"
cammies/camo/combat kit	camouflaged field uniform
cane	cane liquor
canvas webbing	issue equipment from company stores, also available from commercial sources
casevac	casualty evacuation
CAS	Chief of Air Staff
catch me a glide	give me a lift
CCJPR	Catholic Commission for Justice and Peace in Rhodesia
Central African Federation	merger of Northern Rhodesia, Southern Rhodesia, and Nyasaland from 1953 until 1963; Federation of Rhodesia and Nyasaland

CESC	Civil Executive to the Security Council
CFL	concentrated force level operations
CFMF	Cease Fire Monitoring Force
CGS	Chief of General Staff
chaminuka	spirit medium or *mhnodoro* (from Shona)
chat up	talk to a girl flirtatiously
check you	see you later
chicken run	the migration to South Africa or elsewhere to avoid military service, *see also* take the gap
Chilapalapa	pidgin language used by Europeans with Africans, also South African Fanagolo/kitchen kaffir
chimbambaira	landmine (from Shona)
chibuli	beer
chimbwido	female member of local or underground support to armed nationalists
Chimurenga	rebellion or uprising, from Shona *murenga*; *yekululeko* in Ndebele; used to describe fighting in 1896/7 against Europeans settlement
china	friend, mate
chindunduma	slag dump (from Shona), depending on use it could mean ambush, place to hide a body, or sporadic fighting
chuffed	to be proud
CID	BSAP Criminal Investigation Division
CIIR	Catholic Institute for International Relations
CIO	Central Intelligence Organization, external security service
civil disobedience	campaign to disobey established laws to exert pressure on authorities
civil power	civil administration to include police
clandestine boots	high-ankle boot with flat sole to aid antitracking, made by Bata, had poor ankle support and distinctive (i.e., no) print
classical warfare	general and limited war as opposed to insurgency, also regular army funk
claymore	anti-personnel mine
CO	commanding officer
COIN	counterinsurgency, all civil and military measures taken to prevent or defeat insurgency
COINOps	counterinsurgency operations, actions taken by security forces against armed or suspected armed

	nationalist forces; to consist of antiterrorist operations (ATOPS), psychological operations (PSYOPS), and operations in support of the civil authorities (OSCA)
Colored	person of mixed racial extraction
ComBloc	Union of Soviet Socialist Republics, People's Republic of China, Warsaw Pact, et al.
ComOps	Combined Operations Headquarters
comrade	generic form of address or rank used by communist-trained guerrillas
contact	any encounter with security forces and nationalist forces other than sighting
Cordtex	detonation cord explosives
CorSan	cordon sanitaire, border barrier system
coy	company
CPU	BSAP Crime Prevention Unit
Crippled Eagles	Americans in security forces, from author Robin Moore's organization and residence in Salisbury
CSM	company or commando sergeant-major
CT	Charlie Tango, communist terrorists (from radio/telephone)
cull	kill, from term for reduction of excess stock animals or wildlife herds
CV	consolidated village without fencing, opposed to protected village with fence
Cyclone	radio/telephone term for air force squadrons, such as Cyclone 7 for Squadron
DA	District Assistant of Internal Affairs, African aide to European District Commissioner
Dak	Dakota DC-3C transport aircraft
day-glo	piece of bright orange air-panel sewn inside of combat and bush hats to signal aircraft by ground units
DB	Detention Barracks
DC	District Commissioner of Internal Affairs, European administrator over Africans in rural areas; in 19th century as Native Commissioners they administered hut taxes and forced labor programs
Dep	Depot
desert lily	field urinal or piss-tube
dhobi's itch	jock rot from sweat and dirt (from Indian *dhobi wallah*)
dining in	formal dinner in regimental tradition

dog biscuit	cracker in rations pack
dolly bird	girl, prettier than most, also bird, goose
donga	gully or wash (from Afrikaans)
dop	alcoholic drink (from Afrikaans)
doppie	cartridge case (from Afrikaans)
doro	beer (from Shona)
dress groups	mess, dress, working, denims barracks, drill, and combat uniforms
drifter	cloud
drip	intravenous saline solution in plastic bags
DRR	Depot Rhodesia Regiment (*see* ITD)
DSA	District Security Assistant of Internal Affairs, armed counterpart of District Assistants with the advent of protected villages
DZ	drop zone for parachute landings
dzakutsaku	heavy or clumsy (from Shona)
ek sê	I say (from Afrikaans)
Embodied Volunteer	Territorial Army or Reserve Holding Unit member on a full time active status versus part time call-up
endogamy	marriage within a defined racial or tribal group
ES	European Staff or Service
European	White settler regardless of extraction
Executive Council	cabinet or executive of central government under the 1969 constitution consisting of president, prime minister, and cabinet ministers
extended family	an African kin group of two or more related families, i.e., a man and wife or wives, his married children and their children
FAF	forward airfield
Fire Force	helicopter- and/or parachute-borne reaction force and support constituted at the national or provincial level; radio/telephone term "foxtrot foxtrot"
first field dressing	carried in pocket on denim trousers
flat	angry, as in I got flat
flatdog	crocodile
floppy	dead terrorist
FN-FAL	Fabrique Nationale-Fusil Automatique Leger, standard Rhodesian 7.62mm infantry rifle, equivalent to the British *L1A1* Self-Loading Rifle (SLR)

FNLA	National Front for the Liberation of Angola (from Portuguese Frente Nacional de Libertação de Angola)
42Z	anti-personnel rifle grenade used by security forces
FPLM	Popular Forces for the Liberation of Mozambique (from Portuguese Forças Populares de Libertação de Moçambique)
FR	Field Reservist, BSAP reserve
Frantan	frangible tank, air force fire bomb (nicknamed "fry and tan")
Fred, Freddie	Rhodesian term for FPLM soldier
FRELIMO	Front for the Liberation of Mozambique (from Portuguese Frente de Libertação de Moçambique)
FROLZI, FROLIZI	Front for the Liberation of Zimbabwe, nationalist splinter group in 1970
Frontline States	Tanzania, Zambia, Mozambique, Botswana, Angola
fumba	term for forced march, to get going (from Shona *famba*)
fuzz	police in civil role, also cops, heat
gatecrasher	explosive device used to open gates by destroying the lock
G-Car	Alouette III helicopter troop carrier armed with machine guns
GCU	BSAP ground coverage unit, district informer network
G-gun	*see* MAG
glide	going somewhere
goffle	derogatory Rhodesian term for Colored or mixed-race person
Golf bomb	air force low-drag general-purpose bomb
gomo	hill (from Shona)
gong	medal
gook	derogatory Rhodesian term for terrorist/guerrilla (from American)
graze	food, to eat
GSCTS	Grey's Scouts
GTI	ground of tactical importance
GF	Guard Force, fourth branch of security forces used in tribal areas and for defense of protected villages
gunge	dirt
guti	low-lying mist (from Shona)
HE	high explosive

hondo	war (from Shona)
H-hour	time an attack begins
hot extraction	being pulled from any dangerous situation; in the special forces this was being winched aboard a helicopter while under fire
hot pursuit	cross-border or unit boundary pursuit of nationalists, also known as poaching
hout	wood (from Afrikaans), derogatory for African
houtie slayer	from John Edmond's song "Sling Your Slayer"
HQMASH/HQMAT	Headquarters Mashonaland or Matabeleland, regional headquarters
Hulk	explosive device used to make man-sized holes in walls
I blocked/tuned him	I told him
Icarus	air and ground illumination flare used by security forces
IDA	International Defense and Aid
incident	a criminal or terrorist act committed by nationalists
indaba	meeting or gathering (from Nedebele)
Indep Coy	independent company, national service component of the Rhodesia Regiment, later Rhodesian African Rifles
infiltration	entry into the country by anyone for subversive purposes
IntAf	Rhodesian Ministry of Internal Affairs, formerly Native Affairs branch of central government, appointed to administer Africans in tribal trust areas
intimidator	anyone who tries to impose his will through fear on others
ishe	sir, term used by African servicemen when addressing European seniors (from Shona)
ISOP	Internal Security Operations, support by the army and air force to the police against dissident factions who have not resorted to armed force
ITD	Infantry Training Depot (see DRR)
ja	yes (from Afrikaans)
jacked	smart
jacket webbing	customized combat equipment from commercial sources
jam stealer	noncombatant soldier
jawl	to party (from Afrikaans *jol*)

jesse	thorny brush
jive	leave
JOC	Joint Operations Center, a joint agency established when authorized to control operations for which no single force is responsible; composed of representatives of army, air force, police, and local civil government; with Sub-JOCs as required
JOC	Joint Operations Command, term used after 1977 with the Combined Operations National Joint Operations Center and Brigades Joint Operations Centers in operational areas
joint ops	joint operations, operations with more than one of the security force arms involved
joller	extrovert (from Afrikaans *jol*)
JPS	Joint Planning Staff
JSTC	Joint Staff Targeting Committee
JSPIS	Joint Staff Photographic Interpretation Staff
jumpsuit	flying suit adopted by ground troops on Fire Force duties
just now	shortly, later or in a minute
K-factor	highly derogatory Rhodesian phrase for an explanation of African misadventures or misconduct
kachasu	local moonshine (from Shona)
kaffir	(now highly) derogatory term for African (from Arabic *kafir*, non-believer)
kaffirboetie	derogatory term for anyone who sympathizes with nationalists and/or Blacks (from Afrikaans brother of a kaffir)
kak	shit (Afrikaans)
kamakaze pilot	RL truck driver
kaya	house, used by Europeans for servants quarters (from Ndebele/Shona)
K-Car	Alouette III helicopter gunship armed with 20mm cannon, colloquially "killer car"
keep	IntAf fort in a protected village
KGB	Soviet State Central Security Bureau
kith and kin	relationship of Rhodesian with British security forces by birth, affiliation, and royal commission
knock knock	explosive device used to open door locks
kopje	hill (from Afrikaans), also *koppie*

kraal	African village (from Afrikaans, via Portuguese *curral*)
lekker	great, super, nice (from Afrikaans)
lemon	military operation that fails or produces no results
let's split	let's go
lighty	baby, youngster, kid (from Afrikaans *laaitjie*)
lineage	group who can trace their descent from a common ancestor, either matrilineage or patrilineage
locstat	location statistic, radio/telephone term for grid coordinates
local pops	local population, rural Africans in war zones, also locals
long	excess or extreme, as in long drinks, long culling
long drop	field toilet
LUP	lay-up position
Lynx	Cessna 337 aircraft configured for attack operations
LZ	landing zone for helicopters
Mabunu	derogatory African term for Europeans
mafazi	girl (from Ndebele *umfazi*)
MAG	FN *Mitrailleuse d'Appui Général* 7.62mm general-purpose machine gun (GPMG)
magandanga	thug or terrorist (from Shona), also *gandanga*
magook	derogatory African term for terrorist
MMWC	main man what counts, number one, the boss
maningi	plenty (from Shona)
Mantle	BSAP Police Support Unit call signs
MAP	mine- and ambush-proofed vehicle; also Rhino, Hyena, Leopard, Cougar, Kudu, Hippo, Crocodile, Puma, Zebra
Mashona	largest of the two major tribal groupings in Rhodesia, also Shona
Matabele	smaller, but historically more powerful, tribal grouping in Rhodesia of Zulu extraction, also Ndebele
Mazinzwa?	Do you understand? (from Shona)
MCP	Military Assistance to the Civil Power, use of security forces to maintain essential services
mealie	corn and corn meal used as a staple by rural Africans (from Afrikaans *mielie*)
meloes	music (from melody)
MFC	Military Forces Commendation
MID	Military Intelligence Directorate
mira	halt, wait (from Shona)

M962	fragmentation hand grenade used by security forces
MNR	Mozambique National Resistance, also RENAMO, MRM, and NMR; anti-FRELIMO group supported by the CIO (from Portuguese Resistência Nacional Moçambicana)
mombi	cattle (from Shona *mombe*)
moon buggy	mine- and ambush-proofed vehicle
mopani	tree indigenous to Low Veld areas
morphine	syringe with analgesic carried by stick leaders around their necks
MP	military police, Member of Parliament
MPLA	Popular Movement for the Liberation of Angola (from Portuguese Movimento Popular de Libertação de Angola)
MT	motor transport
mujiba	youth member of local or underground support to nationalists from Shona
mukomana	brother (from Shona), singular of *vakomana*, African term for armed nationalists
mukwichi	clan or tribal name of all male relatives from a specific village or area
munt	derogatory Rhodesian term for African (from Shona *muntu*, a person)
murungu	White man
mushe	great, nice, super (from Shona)
Namibia	South West Africa
nanny	derogatory Rhodesia term for an African female
national defense	steps taken to defend against aggression from other countries
NatJOC	National Joint Operations Center at Combined Operations; present were Commander and Deputy Commander of Combined Operations, Commander of the Army, Commander of the Air Force, Secretary of Internal Affairs, and Director General of the Central Intelligence Organization
NatPAC	National Psychological Action, military staff directed by Psychological Action Secretariat
NCO	noncommissioned officer, enlisted ranks corporal through warrant officer
Ndebele/Sindebele	language of the Matabele
NDP	National Democratic Party

n'ganga	witchdoctor
nine mil/bush hammer	Browning, Walther, or Star 9mm automatic service pistol
NS	national service, the military draft of Europeans, later others
NTR	November Tango Romeo, radio/telephone term for nothing to report; also NFTR nothing further to report
nuclear family	kin group of man, wives, and unmarried children
NUF	National Unifying Force
OAU	Organization of African Unity
OC	officer commanding
OCC	Operations Coordinating Committee, security chiefs' group from 1964
offensive weapon	any object or article capable of causing injury to another
O Group	orders group
old queen	mother
op	operation
OP	observation post
orders	military justice procedure to try offenders of military law
ouen	chap, bloke (from Afrikaans)
PACC	Psychological Action Coordination Committee
PACC sensor team	field research activity in attitudes of target group
paddock	an area enclosed by wooden or wire fence to hold livestock
pamberi	forward (from Shona), as in "*Pamberi ne chimurenga*"
Para-Dak	Dakota DC-3 used in airborne operations
pasi	down with (from Shona), as in "*Pasi ne Ian Smith*"
passive resistance	deliberate acts of a nonviolent nature carried out to defy authority
PATU	Police Anti-Terrorist Unit, BSAP district part-time paramilitary force
PE	plastic explosive
PF	Patriotic Front, nationalist alliance between ZANU and ZAPU, with combined military wings from 1976L ZIPA, Zimbabwe People's Army
piccanin	African child (from Portuguese *pequeño*)
pissed	to be drunk

PJI	air force Parachute Jump Instructor, along with army Assistant Parachute Jump Instructor (APJI); primary and assistant jumpmasters for parachute-delivered forces
place name changes	occurred after 1980
PM	prime minister
PMN	Soviet anti-personnel mine used by nationalists
polygamy	two or more wives
POMZ	Soviet anti-personnel mine used by nationalists
pommy	Englishman
Pookie	mine-detector vehicle used by army and police
Pork	derogatory Rhodesian term for Portuguese, also pork-and-cheese/beans
Porkers	derogatory Rhodesian term for Mozambique
possy	position, see locstat
POU	Psychological Operations Unit
povo	people or masses (from Portuguese)
POW, PW	prisoner of war
PR	public relations
praat	to talk (from Afrikaans)
PRAW	Police Reserve Air Wing
private armies	a product of the Rhodesian regimental system of esprit, terms derogatory or otherwise: browns—army; blues—air force; the Force or the Regiment—British South Africa Police; birds—Rhodesian Women's Service; second-class soldiers—Rhodesia Regiment; garden force—Guard Force; *dagga* (marijuana) regiment—Rhodesian Defense Regiment; dad's army or Mashford's militia—50-plus national service intake or police reserves; Bailey's babes—Police Anti-Terrorist Unit; black boots or chocolate soldiers—Police Support Unit; cherry tops—Internal Affairs national service unit; donkey wallopers—Grey's Scouts; special air safaris/soft as shit—Special Air Service; the incredibles or the saints—Rhodesian Light Infantry; walking armpits—Selous Scouts; the specialists—Police Urban Emergency Units
Pronto	signaler, radio operator
PrtnCoy	Protection Company
ProvOps	Provincial Operations Center
PSA	Public Services Association

pseudo operations	covert police and army units disguised as nationalists
PSYAC	Psychological Action Secretariat
Psyops	psychological operations, planned use of measures to influence others in support of operations and policies
PsyWar Committee	Psychological Warfare Committee
PSU	Police Support Unit, BSAP full time paramilitary unit at province level
PTS	Parachute Training School
PUEU	Police Urban Emergency Unit, BSAP special weapon and tactics teams
pull	to shoot or kill, as in pull him
pull a fade	do not show up or complete a task
pungwe	ZANLA all-night political indoctrination meeting to motivate rural population (from Shona)
PV	protected village, fenced and defended resettlement village in rural tribal areas
Q-car	disguised armed vehicle sent on roads to counter ambushes
QM	quartermaster
rafting up	linking up of kayaks side by side, or other vehicles grouped in tactical situations
RAP	Rhodesian Action Party
RAR	Rhodesian African Rifles
rat pack	ration pack, boxed ration of tinned goods for consumption by troops in the field or on patrol
RBC	Rhodesian Broadcasting Corporation; ZBC after 1980
RCL	recoilless, as in recoilless rifle
RDR	Rhodesian Defense Regiment, formed in 1978 from the RHU and Protection Companies from mixed-race and over-age personnel for static defense and security missions
recce	reconnaissance
revolutionary war	political, diplomatic, psychological, economic, and military means used by dissidents to overthrow existing government
rev/revv	a fusillade
RF	Rhodesian Front, political party of Prime Minister Ian Smith
Rh$	Rhodesian dollar of 10 Rhodesian shillings; used after 1965 instead of Rhodesian pound of 20 shillings; equaled US$1.52 in 1971

RhAF	Rhodesian Air Force
RHU	Reserve Holding Unit
RIC	Rhodesian Intelligence Corps
ring main	use of detonation cord to connect several explosive devices to explode at the same time
RIO	Rhodesian Information Office in the United States of America
RL	Rhodesian lorry, logistics vehicle, motor transport
RLI	Rhodesian Light Infantry
RNFU	Rhodesian National Farmers' Union
RP	regimental police, also rendezvous point
RPD, RPK	general-purpose machine guns of communist origin used by nationalist and special forces
RPG	rocket-propelled grenade of communist origin used by nationalist and special forces
RRAF	Royal Rhodesian Air Force
R&R	rest and recuperation leave
RR	Rhodesia Regiment, also Rhodesian Rifles
RRR	Royal Rhodesia Regiment
RSA	Republic of South Africa
RSF	Rhodesian Security Forces, consisting of army, air force, police, and guard force
RSR	Republic of Southern Rhodesia
RTV	Rhodesian Television
RV	rendezvous
SAANC	South African African National Congress
SABC	South Africa Broadcasting Corporation
Sable	BSAP remote explosive ordnance disposal device
saboteur	anyone who damages property for political goals
SADF	South African Defense Force
SAP	South African Police
savannah	tropical or subtropical grasslands, some trees and shrubs
SAS	Special Air Service special force, both squadron and regiment
SB	BSAP Special Branch, internal security service
scheme	to think, reckon
School of Inf	School of Infantry, also "Hooterville"/"Hooters"
scene	a contact or incident that results in security force intervention
Security Council	prime minister, service and intelligence chiefs

SF	security forces
SFAs	Security Force Auxiliaries, formed in 1978 as paramilitary militia in tribal areas
shebeen	beer drink, place to buy homebrew (from Irish)
sharp	good, number one
sharp end	forward combat area, Zambezi valley through 1972
shell scrape	foxhole
Shona	language of Mashona
Shrike	British detonating control box
Shumba	nickname for Lion Lager beer (from Shona for lion)
sitrep	radio/telephone term for situation report
situpa	identification required to be carried by Africans
sixty mil	60mm mortar
skate	rogue
SKS	Simonov semi-automatic rifle of communist origin used by nationalists
skuz'apo	excuse me, African term for pseudo operations by Selous Scouts, or a Selous Scout
sloot	gully (from Afrikaans *sluit*)
Slope	derogatory Rhodesian term for an Afrikaner
slot	to kill, also zap, cull, take out, waste, off, slay
small means	VHF radio used for short-range communications; A-76 platoon and section
SNEB	*French Societe Nouvelle des Etablissements Edgar Brandt*, air force unguided 68mm air-to-ground rocket
snot squirt	fusillade, volley
sny	to cheat (from Afrikaans *snaai*)
society zoom	prestige car
Sosegan	analgesic syringe carried around neck by troops, morphine alternative
SOP	standard operating procedure
spaced out	killed, drugged
Sparrow	radio/telephone term for tracker
speil	story, account (from Afrikaans)
spoor	track, footprint (from Afrikaans)
SSCTS	Selous Scouts special force
stag	guard duty
start	money, also shekels, bread
stick	basic tactical unit of four to six men, also squad or call sign
stonk	hitting, or being hit by, the enemy
stop	stop group

STPL	Supply and Transport Platoon
Strela	Soviet SA-7 portable surface-to-air missile
stretcher	field cot
SUA	special unit allowance
Sunray	radio/telephone term for commanding officer
Sunray Minor	radio/telephone term for 2IC
SWAPO	South West Africa People's Organization
switched on	alert, motivated
TA/TF	Territorial Army/Territorial Force similar to national guard or organized reserve with regular army cadre consisting of territorial battalions, artillery, and armor units; reinforcement units; intelligence and psychological operations personnel
taal	language (from Afrikaans)
take out	to kill, as in take them out
take the gap	to go absent without leave, also for any European or other migration out of Rhodesia
takkies	track shoes, plimsoles
tank suit	black coverall worn by Armored Car Regiment crews
TCU	Tracker Combat Unit, absorbed by the Selous Scouts
TCV	troop-carrying vehicle
terr/terrorist	any nationalist supporter who is trained or uses armed force or violence for political ends; also surrendered terrorist (STER) and captured terrorist (CTER)
terrorist camp	place inside Rhodesia temporarily occupied by nationalists for training or operations
terrorist hide	place where nationalists temporarily conceal themselves
terrorist base/holding center	place outside Rhodesia occupied by nationalists for indoctrination, training, operations, or support
TM-46	Soviet landmine used by nationalists
toggle rope	line with a loop at one end and a toggle at the other; carried in each infantry squad or section
Tokorev	Soviet automatic pistol
troopie	term for army other ranks or private soldier
trupp	to walk (from Afrikaans *trapp*)
tsumo	the traditional meaning behind a literal meaning (from Shona)
TTL	Tribal Trust Land, from native reserves of the 1930 Land Apportionment Act
tune	to tell

UANC	United African National Council, from ANC, party of Bishop Abel Muzorewa
UDI	Unilateral Declaration of Independence, 11 November 1965
ukwejisa	all-night ZIPRA political indoctrination meetings in tribal areas (from Ndebele)
UNITA	National Movement for the Total Liberation of Angola, anti-MPLA force in Angola (from Portuguese *União Nacional para a Independência Total de Angola*)
UNFP	United National Federal Party, party of Chief Kayisa Ndiweni
UN/UNO	United Nations Organization
UPAM	United People's Association of Matabeleland
Uzi	9mm submachine gun
VAG	vital asset ground
vakomana	the boys (from Shona), name given nationalist "boys in the bush"
VFA	Voice of Free Africa
Viva!	"Long live!" (from Portuguese), as in "*Viva* Mugabe!"
vlei	open marsh plain or marshy area (from Afrikaans)
veldskoen	leather shoe (from Afrikaans), desert boot made by Bata and used by security forces
WCC	World Council of Churches, pro-nationalist religious groups with exception of Catholic Church
webbing	combat equipment
webbing orders	69 Pattern Combat Equipment: drill, patrol, and battle order
What's your buzz?	What's happening?
WO	warrant officer, senior noncommissioned officer
Womble	police reservist
World Bank	International Bank for Reconstruction and Development (IBRD)
WP	white phosphorus
yellow bird	sun
Zamboon	derogatory Rhodesian term for a Zambian
ZANU	Zimbabwe African National Union, political wing of Robert Mugabe's Mashona-oriented party, based initially in Zambia then later in Mozambique; ZANU-PF after 1980

ZANLA	Zimbabwe African National Liberation Army— ZANU's military wing; Chinese supported and Maoist in character
ZAPU	Zimbabwe African People's Union, political wing of Joshua Nkomo's Matabele oriented party based in Zambia
Zhii	nationalist term for civil disobedience and disturbance of early 1960s (from Shona/Ndebele)
Zimbabwe	name used by nationalists for Rhodesia, present name of country
ZIPA	Zimbabwe People's Army
ZIPRA/ZPRA	Zimbabwe People's Revolutionary Army—ZAPU's military wing; Soviet supported and Warsaw Pact in character
ZLC	Zimbabwe Liberation Council, nationalist splinter group
Zulu	radio/telephone term for empty vehicle
ZUPO	Zimbabwe United People's Organization, nationalist splinter group
zut	no

Chronology

c. AD 1000	Emergence of Shona confederacy centered at Great Zimbabwe.
c.1350	Height of Mbire kingdom and Shona confederacy.
c.1450	Decline of confederacy, Munhumutapa state at Mutota in Zambezia region and Changamire in Karanga region.
1513	Portuguese explorers arrive.
1629	Portuguese subdue Munhumutapa state.
c. 1690	Changamire resists and expels Portuguese.
c. 1820	Zulu migration begins in Natal.
1822	Mzilikazi leads Matabele from Natal into Shona territory north of Limpopo.
c. 1840	Matabele establish control of Matabeleland.
1853	Limited European arrival in Matabeleland.
1859	Robert Moffat opens mission at Inyati.
1868	Death of Mzilikazi, Lobengula assumes disputed throne.
1888	Moffat Agreement with Lobengula and Rudd Concession with Cecil Rhodes and British South Africa Company (BSAC) for mineral rights.
1889	British Crown approves BSAC charter.
1890: 12 September	Occupation Day, BSAC Pioneer Column claims Mashonaland for the Crown by occupying Harare hill and establishing Fort Salisbury.
1891	Mashonaland and Matabeleland declared protectorates by order in council in London.
1893–4	Matabele War and death of Lobengula, Matabeleland occupied by BSAC.
1894	First native reserve established.

1895	Protectorate named Rhodesia.
1896–7	Shona revolt, killing 244 settlers; suppressed by British forces; mediums Nehanda and Kagubi hanged.
1897	BSAC establishes separate administrations of Northern and Southern Rhodesia.
1898	Colony named Southern Rhodesia.
1899	Settlers granted participation in legislative council.
1899–1902	Europeans serve in Empire forces during Anglo-Boer War, with Africans used as laborers.
1900	Uprising at Mazoe under Mapondera.
1902	Rhodes dies; Africans over age 14 required to carry passes (*situpas*).
1907	Settlers granted majority role in legislative council.
1914	Variation of native reserve size and quality protested by Nyamanda and Matabele National Home Movement.
1914–18	Europeans and Africans serve in Empire forces during World War I.
1919	Privy council in London assumes control of BSAC land holdings.
1920	Settlers in legislative council press for self-government.
1923: 23 September	BSAC control of colony ends; self-government by settlers as Crown colony through legislative assembly; Rhodesian Bantu Voters' Association formed by Abraham Twala.
1924	First elections under new constitution,
1925–6	Carter Commission advocates separate land development.
1927	African labor movements, The Rhodesian Industrial and Commercial Workers' Union formed.
1930	Land Apportionment Act divides colony into European and African lands.
1934	Europeans adopt separate development policy; African labor movements suppressed; Bantu Congress by Aaron Jacha and African National Congress (ANC) formed.
1939–45	Europeans and Africans serve in Empire and Commonwealth forces in World War II; African labor movement revives.
1945	African railway worker strike under Thompson Samkange.

1946–8	European control of government disputed between liberal United Party and conservative Liberal Party.
1947	British African Voice Association formed.
1948	African workers general strike.
1950	Enforcement of Land Apportionment Act to move Africans to native reserves.
1951	Animal Husbandry Act limits amount and tenure of African grazing practices.
1951	European volunteers to Malaya as part of Special Air Service.
1952	Rhodesian African Rifles to Suez.
1953	Federation of Rhodesia and Nyasaland established combining Southern Rhodesia, Northern Rhodesia, and Nyasaland; Southern Rhodesia controls political and military establishment.
1955: 13 May	City Youth League, later African National Youth League, forms to demand full voting rights for Africans; Public Order Act provides detention and restriction without trial.
1956	Youth League boycotts public transportation in Salisbury, 200 African nationalists detained.
1956	Rhodesian African Rifles to Malaya.
1957: 12 September	Youth League and ANC merge to form Southern Rhodesia African National Congress (SRANC) under Joshua Nkomo.
1958	SRANC meetings in rural areas banned.
1959	ANC throughout Federation engage in civil disorder and intimidation in townships and rural tribal areas; Law and Order (Maintenance) Act, Emergency Powers Act, and Unlawful Organizations Act provide basis to restrict Africans; 29 February, SRANC banned leaders detained and 500 nationalists arrested by BSAP.
1959	Royal Rhodesian Air Force units to Cyprus, Aden, Kuwait.
1960: 1 January	National Democratic Party (NDP) formed with Michael Mawema as president to replace SRANC.
1960	Monckton Commission recommends eventual majority rule for Federation states; "wind of change" speech by British Prime Minister Harold MacMillan in Cape Town, South Africa.

1961	London Constitutional Conference, new constitution enacted, widens franchise to include African representation which NDP rejects.
1961	Congo Border Crisis; Republic of South Africa leaves British Commonwealth.
1961: 9–17 December	NDP banned and replaced by Zimbabwe African People's Union (ZAPU) under Joshua Nkomo, Herbert Chitepo, and Ndabaningi Sithole.
1962	March, anti-Federation Dominion Party reorganized as Rhodesian Front winning December election; Nyasaland secedes from Federation to become Malawi in 1964.
1962	First arrests of nationalists with weapons; ZAPU banned 20 September.
1962–3	Rhodesia Army and Air Force units to Aden.
1963	British establish the "five principles" (no independence before majority rule); Northern Rhodesia secedes from Federation to become Zambia in 1964.
1963	Nationalists split; 8 August, Zimbabwe African National Union (ZANU) formed by Sithole from ZAPU factions; Nkomo forms People's Caretaker Council (PCC) to replace ZAPU on 10 August; first nationalists go to the People's Republic of China for military training (ZANU's Emmerson M'nangagwa).
1963: 31 December	Federation of Rhodesia and Nyasaland dissolved; Southern Rhodesia seeks independence based upon the 1961 Constitution but is rejected by the United Kingdom.
1964: 13 April	Ian Smith becomes prime minister, replacing Winston Field who does not support unilateral independence.
1964	ZANU holds congress at Gwelo, it and PCC banned; Nkomo, Sithole, Mugabe and other nationalists detained.
1964	ZANU first attacks on Europeans since 1897 rebellion (Crocodile Gang incident).
1964: 20–26 October	Domboshawa *indaba* establishes support by chiefs and headmen of Smith and 1961 Constitution.
1964: November	Referendum calls for independence based upon 1961 Constitution on same terms as Zambia and Malawi, Southern Rhodesian to be known as Rhodesia; Law and Order (Maintenance) Act enhanced.

1965: February	Call for referendum for independence based on 1961 Constitution, Europeans and council of chiefs accept; by October after conferring with Nkomo and Sithole, the United Kingdom will not accept this without majority rule.
1965: May	First armed ZAPU guerrillas enter Rhodesia; state of emergency declared.
1965: 25–26 October	British Prime Minister Harold Wilson in Rhodesia.
1965: 5 November	State of emergency declared which will remain in force until 1980.
1965: 11 November	Unilateral declaration of independence declared from United Kingdom based on 1961 Constitution; United Kingdom imposes selective economic sanctions.
1965: 12 November	ZANU forms people's government at Sikombela detention camp.
1965: 19 November	United Nations imposes selective economic sanctions.
1965: 15 December	Ghana breaks relations with United Kingdom over Rhodesia.
1966: January	Lagos Commonwealth Conference held for the first time outside of the United Kingdom to address the illegitimate Smith regime.
1966	Rhodesian security forces conduct operations into Zambia; April 28, seven ZANU nationalists killed near Sinoia by security forces; May, first Europeans killed by nationalists (Viljoen incident).
1966: December	United Nations expands sanctions; Wilson affirms United Kingdom goal of "no independence before majority rule;" Wilson and Smith meet on HMS *Tiger* off Gibraltar.
1967: May	Rhodesian security forces battle nationalists (ZAPU and South African ANC) near Wankie; Republic of South Africa sends police and helicopter support which will remain through 1975.
1967	Operation *Nickel* in Zambezi valley.
1968	Operation *Cauldron* in Zambezi valley.
1968	Captured nationalists hanged for murder despite reprieve by Queen Elizabeth II; United Nations expands sanctions; October, Wilson and Smith meet on HMS *Fearless* off Gibraltar.
1968	"Green and white" flag of Rhodesia adopted.

1969	Referendum approves constitution and establishment of republic on basis of segregation of races similar to South African National Party's apartheid.
1969	Sithole is sentenced to prison for treason and renounces armed struggle during trial leading to his removal as head of ZANU.
1969: 21 February	Forcible expulsion of Chief Tangwena from Gaeresi ranch; Land Tenure Act redefines European and African areas.
1969: September	Nationalist Lusaka Manifesto urges negotiated rather than armed struggle in southern Africa.
1970: 2 March	Republic of Rhodesia declared severing ties with United Kingdom, royal titles and affiliations ended; United Kingdom and United States of America veto United Nations call for expanded sanctions; ZANU moves guerrillas into Mozambique.
1971: 1 October	Nationalist Front for the Liberation of Zimbabwe (FROLIZI) formed.
1971: November	Prime ministers Alec Home and Smith reach agreement on settlement proposals based upon 1969 constitution.
1971: 24 November	Anglo-Rhodesian Settlement Proposal signed in Salisbury.
1971: 4 December	First ZANU guerrillas enter Rhodesia from Tete in Mozambique.
1971: 16 December	African National Council (ANC) formed by Abel Muzorewa to oppose settlement proposals.
1971: 21 December	Up to 60 ZANU nationalists infiltrate into Mashonaland to attack European farms (Altena Farm incident); in reaction Rhodesian security forces begin Operation *Hurricane* in the northeast that will continue through 1980.
1972: 11 January–10 March	Pearce Commission conducts hearings on settlement proposals and concludes they are unacceptable to Africans; United States senate votes against resumptions of embargo on chrome exports from Rhodesia.
1972: March	Security forces conduct cross-border operations into Mozambique; border closed with Zambia, then reopened later; Muzorewa begins negotiations with Smith.

1972: 3 May	Pearce Commission reports rejection of settlement by Africans.
1973: 9 January	Border with Zambia closed.
1973	Nationalist Patriotic Front abducts 295 African staff and pupils from the St. Albert's mission, all but eight are recovered.
1973: 7 December	Lusaka Declaration of Unity signed bringing ANC, FROLIZI, ZAPU, ZANU under an expanded ANC umbrella.
1974: February	Minister of Defense doubles national service intakes and expands call-ups of European males from the 25–38 age group.
1974: 25 April	Coup in Portugal leads to unilateral independence of Angola, Mozambique, and Guinea Bissau; creates 1,100 kilometers of hostile border with Rhodesia, leaving only 200 kilometers open with the Republic of South Africa.
1974: September	Rutenga–Beitbridge rail link with South Africa completed.
1974	ANC rejects negotiations by Smith and Muzorewa; October meetings in Lusaka between representatives of prime ministers John Vorster, Kenneth Kaunda, and Lonrho conglomerate result in detente proposal between South Africa and the Patriotic Front.
1974: November	Ndabaningi Sithole unseated as head of ZANU by Mugabe while both are in Que Que prison, in part due to his denunciation of armed struggle; Rhodesian Front reelected; Smith releases nationalists for ceasefire agreement and Lusaka Conference pressured by South Africa; declaration of unity reached by Muzorewa, Nkomo, Sithole, and Chikerema in Lusaka; Nhari rebellion occurs and ceasefire fails.
1974: November	ZANU meets with Front for the Liberation of Mozambique (FRELIMO) in Lusaka to obtain support access to Rhodesia through Mozambique.
1974	Four South Africa Police ambushed during ceasefire by nationalists.
1975	Mozambican independence.
1975	Mugabe heads ZANU; nationalist joint Zimbabwe People's Army (ZIPA) formed.

1975: March	ZAPU's Herbert Chitepo assassinated in Lusaka; ZANLA leaders arrested and ZANU expelled from Zambia.
1975: July	Dusk to dawn curfew declared for 500 kilometers of border with Mozambique; in August same curfew declared along 640 kilometers of border with Botswana.
1975: 20–23 August	Kaunda and Vorster get nationalists and Smith to meet; South Africa withdraws support from Rhodesia; Victoria Falls Conference with nationalists fails to reach agreement.
1975: October	Smith and Nkomo negotiations commence.
1976: 3 March	Border with Mozambique closed; United Kingdom subsidizes Mozambique.
1976	Terrorist grenade attack in Salisbury.
1976	Fighting resumed by ZANU from Mozambique's Tete, Manica, and Gaza provinces; Operation *Thrasher* begins in February, Operation *Repulse* in May, Operation *Tangent* in August; security forces attack Nyadzonya camp in Mozambique.
1976: 19 March	Smith and Nkomo talks end.
1976: 22 March	United Kingdom and James Callaghan offer settlement proposal.
1976: April	South African civilians killed in ambush on Fort Victoria–Beitbridge road.
1976: 27 April	America's Henry Kissinger starts Africa tour, delivers 10-point proposal in Lusaka.
1976: 23–24 June	Kissinger and Vorster meet in Bodenmais, West Germany.
1976: 9 August	South Africa announces public support of majority rule in Rhodesia and withdraws remaining police and helicopter support.
1976: 4–6 September	Kissinger and Vorster in Zurich push agreement by Smith of principle of majority rule; Zambia releases ZANU leaders; nationalist Patriotic Front (PF) formed.
1976: 19–24 September	Kissinger, Vorster, Smith meet in Pretoria; Smith agrees to majority rule in principle.
1976: 28 October	Geneva Constitutional Conference opens for nine weeks.

1976: 5 December	Catholic Bishop of Bulawayo killed in ambush.
1976: 27 December	27 African workers killed on Honde valley tea estate.
1977	David Owen starts African tour in Dar es Salaam; Rhodesian Front reelected.
1977	Fighting escalates, Rhodesian security forces lose one man a day and kill ratio declines from 10 to 1 to 7 to 1.
1977	Rhodesian defense budget increases 44 percent to almost one million Rhodesian dollars a day; national service extended to 24 months; Europeans in 38–50 age group called up; economic hardship exceptions are eliminated.
1977	400 African students kidnapped by ZAPU to Botswana with less than 100 recovered by security forces.
1977	January, ZAPU's Jason Moyo assassinated in Lusaka.
1977: February	Seven missionaries killed at Musami mission.
1977: March	Combined Operations formed with Lieutenant-General G. P. Walls in command.
1977: July	Rhodesian Action Party (RAP) formed from members of Rhodesian Front (RF).
1977: August	11 killed and 76 wounded by ZANU bombing of Woolworth's in Salisbury.
1977: August	Operation *Grapple* formed; cross-border raids into Zambia; United Kingdom's Owen and United States' Andrew Young arrive in Salisbury for settlement talks; while rejecting these, Smith begins to reach agreement with Muzorewa, Sithole, and Chirau for internal settlement; Land Tenure Act amended.
1977: November	Rhodesians attack Chimoio and Tembué base areas in Mozambique (largest successful security force operation of war).
1978	Dar es Salaam conference by nationalists and Cyrus Vance, Young, Owen; Rhodesian security forces attack base camps in Zambia.
1978: 3 March	Internal agreement reached to form transitional government and constitution; Rhodesia offers safe return for guerrillas; agreement rejected by United Nations.
1978: April	Transition government formed and sworn in; nationalist prisoners released.

1978: June	Nine missionaries and four children killed at Elim mission.
1978: June	Operation *Splinter* formed.
1978: August	Smith and Nkomo talks resume.
1978: September	ZAPU shoots down Air Rhodesia airliner killing 10 survivors on the ground; martial law declared in selected areas; Smith and Nkomo talks end.
1978: October	Africans aged 18–25 subject to national service; railroad traffic reopened with Zambia and South Africa through Rhodesia.
1978: 19 October	Raids on Chikumbi, Mkushi, Mborama camps in Zambia ("Green Leader" incident).
1978: November	Transitional government announces plans for majority rule with government of national unity.
1978: December	Fuel tanks in Salisbury attacked by ZANLA using rockets and gunfire.
1979: January	Martial law extended.
1979: February	ZAPU shoots down second Air Rhodesia plane, killing all 59 on board; four European prisoners released from Mozambique; government schools integrated; raids in Angola, Mozambique, Zambia.
1979: March	ZAPU shoots down two Zambian Air Force planes in Zambia; training of dissidents begins with Mozambique National Resistance; European men in the 50–59 age group called up; raids on Lusaka to kill Nkomo; fighting escalates to conventional phase.
1979: 17 April	Constitution approved by referendum; Land Tenure Act repealed; Muzorewa elected but not recognized; appeals for recognition to United States; fighting continues.
1979: 1 June	Country named Zimbabwe-Rhodesia.
1979: 26 June	Muzorewa government installed, United African National Council (UNAC) holds majority of seats; Europeans control key positions of Defense and Combined Operations.
1979: July	Muzorewa and Smith visit the United States.
1979: 1 August	Commonwealth Conference convenes in Lusaka; United Kingdom petroleum interest in Nigeria nationalized; pressure to obtain United Kingdom intervention and constitutional conference.

1979: 10 September	Lancaster House Conference convenes in London to commence external settlement with United Kingdom and nationalists.
1979: September	Lines of communications in Mozambique destroyed by major raids.
1979: October	Lines of communications in Zambia destroyed by major raids.
1979: 12 December	As a result of Lancaster House conference, direct rule by British governor in Salisbury returns; agreement on new constitution reached.
1979: 21 December	Ceasefire began in accordance with external settlement agreement; sanctions lifted.
1980: 27 February	United Kingdom supervises election won by Mugabe and his ZANU-PF.
1980: March	Coalition government formed with Nkomo and PF-ZAPU.
1980: 18 April	Independence declared for the Republic of Zimbabwe.

Lessons Learned in the Bush

Doctrine and Experience Abstracts, c. 1965–1980

GENERAL (Rhodesian Security Forces, Counter-Insurgency Operational Manual, Part II, Salisbury: GP, 1975, 1-3 to 1-5)

This section emphasizes those factors which have a special application to successful anti-terrorist operations.

1. COOPERATION. The military must never lose sight of the paramount importance of a close understanding and cooperation with their civilian counterparts. This principle must be followed at all levels of cooperation, e.g. army/air force, military/police, etc.
2. HEARTS AND MINDS. Unless the trust, confidence and respect of the people are won by the government and the military forces, the chance of success is greatly reduced. If the people support the government and the military forces, the enemy becomes isolated and cut off from its supplies, shelter and intelligence …
3. INTELLIGENCE. Successful [anti-terrorist operations] depend upon an efficient integrated intelligence organization, planned and controlled on a national or theater of operations basis. Good intelligence is the key to successful operations. Very little value will be achieved without timely and accurate intelligence, and commanders will often have to plan special operations and take considerable risks to obtain valuable intelligence. Before undertaking military operations against terrorists the district in which they are operating should be thoroughly studied and a dossier prepared by the security police, working in conjunction with the local civil authorities, where necessary.
4. SECURITY OF BASES. It is fundamental to the success of [anti-terrorist operations] that all bases are secure, whether it be a major base, mobilization center, installation, airfield, police post or patrol base. All members of the military forces, whatever their tasks, must be trained to take an effective and active part in the defense and protection of installations.

5. PLANNED PATTERN OF OPERATIONS. Operations must be planned on the basis of systematically gaining and maintaining control of the country or area concerned, by the establishment and constant expansion of controlled areas. By establishing controlled or safe areas, enemy freedom of movement is curtailed and it provides a safe place for the local indigenous people away from the influence and intimidation of the enemy.

6. SEIZING AND HOLDING INITIATIVE. A clear cut political policy, and offensive action by the military forces, is essential for seizing and holding the initiative. Every effort must be made to dominate any area in which the military forces are operating.

7. SPEED, MOBILITY AND FLEXIBILITY. Military forces must be equipped, trained and accustomed to operating for long periods under the same conditions as the enemy, while full use must be made of air support to provide additional mobility, reconnaissance, airstrike capability and a flexible administrative system.

8. SURPRISE AND SECURITY. The strictest security in planning is essential if surprise is to be achieved. Loss of surprise probably means an unsuccessful operation and a least a temporary loss of initiative.

9. GROUND FORCES. If success is to be achieved it is essential that sufficient infantry, together with armor and other supporting arms, are deployed on the ground. The infantry must be highly trained, acclimatized and masters of modern techniques. Air mobility, modern weapons, good communications and fire support, as well as first class foot mobility is also essential.

10. TRAINING. Success in [anti-terrorist operations] is only possible if troops are highly trained, supremely fit and sufficiently tough, cunning and skillful to outfight the enemy on his own ground. While full use must be made of the technical superiority in firepower, mobility and equipment, all troops must nevertheless be trained to such a pitch that they are fully confident that man for man they are better fighters than the enemy. The two most important training requirements are supreme physical fitness and the ability to shoot accurately at fleeting targets at short and medium ranges.

11. AIR SUPPORT. Although air power in itself does not guarantee success in [anti-terrorist operations], the tactical concept relies primarily on it for strategic and tactical movement, fire support and logistic support, with particular emphasis on the use of helicopters and light aircraft in reconnaissance, armed and support roles....

12. OFFENSIVE ACTION. The tactical concept is essentially offensive from the beginning. The commander must, however, bear in mind the protracted nature of operations, the great boost to morale of success and the corresponding danger of failure. He must avoid acting on too great a scale prematurely and he must ensure that his initial offensive operations are within the capabilities of the forces he has available.

13. CONCLUSION. The outstanding lesson from recent revolutionary wars is that no single program—political, social, psychological, economic or military—will in itself succeed. It is a combination of all these elements together with a joint government/police/military approach to the problem, which will counter the efforts of the enemy, and restore lawful authority.

GENERAL (Army Headquarters, Operations Aide Memoire, Salisbury: GP, 1979, 8)

1. As in all matters, military commanders must realize that troops will only act efficiently if they are commanded efficiently. Remember the adage "There are no bad troops only bad leaders."
2. War is basically common sense, therefore:
   a. Expect enemy action.
   b. Think, think, and keep on thinking (anticipate).
   c. Never present the enemy with a good target.
   d. Always have a reserve (one foot on the ground).
   e. Teach your men to respect and have confidence in their weapons. Teach them to use the weapons correctly, accurately, and economically.
   f. Keep people involved and active.
   g. Never stop training.
   h. Never take short cuts.
   i. Let people know what is going on—information must not only be demanded from below, it must be passed down from above.
3. Efficiency in [counterinsurgency] relies on:
   a. Understanding of tactical doctrine.
   b. An aggressive attitude.
   c. Alertness.
   d. Common sense and logic.

TRAINING (Army Headquarters, Operations, 1)

1. Commanders at all levels must motivate the men under their command and instill an aggressive attitude.
2. An aggressive attitude must not be confused with offensive operations. It is just as important, if not more so, to instill and maintain an aggressive attitude during defensive operations.
3. Being aggressive involves:
   a. Maintaining a constant state of alertness.
   b. Being determined to kill the enemy while at the same time taking all reasonable measures to preserve security force lives, i.e.: not being idle and

careless. The attitude should be that the terrorist is always close at hand and that he could strike within seconds.

c. Commanders and men should always be trying to improve their military knowledge.

d. Basic tactical procedures must be obeyed. Short cuts must be avoided.

4. There is never enough time for training. It is the responsibility of all officers and [noncommissioned officers] to acquaint themselves with Rhodesian army manuals and training directives and to ensure that the information therein is imparted to the rank and file.

5. Training must be continuous and constant. The attitude that training only takes place on courses and the short predeployment period must be eradicated. Training can and must be carried out during quiet periods on operations.

6. Aspects which require special attention are:
   a. Basic tactics.
   b. Weapons handling.
   c. Safety.
   d. Shooting.

SECTION LEADER'S CHECKLIST (Rhodesia Regiment Pocket Book, Salisbury: City Printers, July 1978, G3)

1. Physical condition of men in section—that no one is suffering from any ailment which is likely to hinder the patrol activities.
2. Physical check of all boots—that they are in good condition.
3. Physical check on items of equipment, rucksack straps, belt fittings, identity disks, rations.
4. Physical check of all firearms, magazines, ammunition and cleaning material.
5. First aid kits and that each man in his section has taken anti-malaria tablets.
6. Each man has his field dressing.
7. Each man is properly camouflaged.
8. That all water containers are full, plus water tablets.
9. Compasses, protractors, maps, and heliograph.
10. Wireless sets, on correct channel. Receiver and transmitter are working, spare batteries, call signs and distress signals, codes.
11. Transport check.

MOVEMENT, MILITARY (Army Headquarters, Operations, 2-3)

Movement to, from, and within the operations area. Troops are at their most vulnerable when confined to a small space, especially a vehicle. Two factors are therefore of vital importance:

1. Troops must be doubly alert. This means:
   a. Sentries must be posted on all four corners of the vehicle.
   b. All persons in the vehicle must hold their weapons so that they are pointing outward.
   c. Troops must be ready for ambush and look as though they are ready. The mere fact that troops look efficient provides a strong deterrent to surprise attack.
2. The state of confinement or concentration of troops under unfavorable conditions must not be allowed to exist for longer than is absolutely necessary. Therefore:
   a. Whenever a vehicle halts, for whatever reason, troops must debus and disperse.
   b. Sentries must immediately be posted to a position where they can be effective.
   c. When a vehicle halts it should do so in an area which makes effective terrorist action difficult, i.e. high and open ground on straight stretches of road.
   d. When in vehicles troops must wear all items of equipment.

MOVEMENT, CIVIL (General Convoy Instructions, GP&S 79951, n.d.)

GENERAL
1. These instructions are issued for the benefit of all persons who travel in convoy. Please make sure all your passengers are aware of these instructions and comply with them.
2. Before the convoy departs ensure that you have sufficient fuel, that your vehicle tires are correctly inflated and you have a spare wheel in case of punctures.
3. Attendance in the convoy is voluntary. However, once you join the convoy you come under the command and control of the convoy commander.

ROAD RULES
4. Whilst on the road the normal rules of the road will apply and they must be observed.

SPACING
5. The spacing between vehicles should be 100 meters behind any escort vehicles and 50 meters between other vehicles. Large gaps are to be avoided.

ESCORT VEHICLES
6. There will be three escort vehicles; one at the head of the convoy, one approximately in the center and the third at the rear. All these vehicles are in radio contact with each other as well as with other patrol vehicles on the road.

BREAKDOWNS

7. Should any vehicle break down, it must pull off to the left of the road and assistance will be given by one of the escort vehicles, or by one of the other patrol vehicles on the road.

AIR COVER

8. If aeroplanes are heard or seen overhead, do not worry as from time to time we provide air cover for convoys as well.

ANIMALS

9. You are likely to meet game and also cattle on the road, so be prepared for them.

NATURE'S CALLS

10. […] please make sure that all calls of nature are attended to before the convoy sets on.

OVERTAKING

11. Whilst driving, please do not overtake or attempt to jump the queue. We have enough to deal with without having to investigate road accidents on the way.

MEDICAL

12. In the event of an accident or attack which necessitates medical attention, casevac will be arranged by the quickest means available.

BRIEFING

13. Fifteen minutes before the convoy sets off, a briefing will be held at the center escort vehicle. The signal to attend will be the hooter of the center escort vehicle. At this briefing you will be instructed as to what action to take in the event of an attack.

PERSONAL WEAPONS

14. If you have personal weapons remember that they are for your personal protection. Please handle them carefully with due regards for the other members of the convoy. Personal weapons must be "made safe" just before you arrive at your convoy destination.

AT DESTINATION

15. Once you have completed your journey with the convoy, please hand in these instructions to the Police in charge of your convoy. If you forget to do this please destroy this document as the detail in contains may be of some interest to our enemies.

Thank you. We hope you have a pleasant journey.

BASES (Rhodesia Regiment, Pocket Book, G5)

1. General:
   All stops, however temporary. Security: site base tactically. Good communications. Tasks: base to be sited so that patrol tasks can be adequately carried out from there. Avoid game trails.
2. For longer term add:
   Water availability. Hard standing. Resupply, ease, landing zones.
3. Set up:
   Patrol commander locates. Recce group forward, dogleg in. Sentries out. Two riflemen guide in patrol via dogleg. Patrol commander indicates 12/4/8 o'clock positions for section arc of fire. Sections move in. Stand to, clearance patrol out, commander checks all-around defense, sites GPMGs [general-purpose machine guns]. Clearance patrol returns. Patrol commander's orders group (see orders). Stand down, sentry on duty.
4. Orders:
   To include base security, alarm scheme and action. Stand to and stand down, passwords and sentries—who and where. Clearance patrols, digging-in, defence measures (Claymores). Routine tomorrow, maintenance of weapons—who and when. Tasks, cooking, restrictions, smoking, water, rubbish, latrines.

OBSERVATION POSTS (Rhodesia Regiment Pocket Book, G8)

1. Move at night, debus 6 kilometers plus from [observation post] on move, singly, over side of vehicle (tracks).
2. In daylight observe your [observation post] and rear from halfway point.
3. Next night move into [observation post], dogleg in.
4. Two men at first light look for terrorists, routes, paths, fields, dogs. Remainder watch for signs of compromise.
5. No movement during day.
6. Make a track plan, avoid accidents.
7. Keep a log, establish routine of locals.
8. Concealment and camouflage of the highest order, avoid glint, obvious places, crest lines.
9. Cook with gas low; avoid smell, rear feeds all at rear after dark.
10. Re-water at night, same place as locals use, go barefoot, and avoid rifle or water bottle spoor. Change around, one man only each day.
11. Minimize on radio.
12. Remove all rubbish from [observation post], use plastic liner.
13. Pull out if compromised.
14. Review Fire Force deployment.

OBSERVATION POST AIDE MEMOIRE/FIRE FORCE CALL OUT (Rhodesia Regiment Pocket Book, W2.)

1. Information to be passed to [Control] includes:
   a. Grid reference, channel and call sign of the observation post.
   b. Method of identifying observation post to Fire Force.
   c. Number of terrorists if known and their dress/weapons.
   d. Terrorist position/activity and direction of last move (magnetic).
   e. Possible escape routes.
   f. Dress and size of feeding parties (if applicable).
   g. Areas of population.
   h. Nature of surrounding country (possible helicopter landings zones and paratroop drop zones).
   i. Suggested direction of approach.
   j. How Fire Force will be directed to target.
   k. Location of neighboring observations posts and/or troops (if applicable).
2. Minimize conversation.
3. Observation post must remain clandestine throughout and after contact.
4. Triple check before calling Fire Force.
5. Avoid crest lines.
6. Don't move about.
7. Don't alter the observation post (cut trees/move rocks).
8. Don't smoke or cook.
9. Avoid talking.
10. Always keep fully camouflaged.
11. Keep all equipment hidden/camouflaged.
12. Keep an observation post log.
13. No soap, toothpaste or deodorant to be taken.

ON ARRIVAL: Ask Control for channel and call sign of Fire Force—especially K-Car. Standby to talk in Fire Force. Pass on any changes in the situation to Control as they occur.
   a. Establish communication with K-Car at earliest opportunity.
   b. Latest situation.
   c. Talk K-Car over communist terrorist's position. K-Car will invariably pull up before flying over target area. It will therefore be the aircraft flying highest. If not sure request identification.
   d. Indicate target by using marker of ground features.

FIRE FORCE STICK BRIEFING AIDE (School of Infantry, Gwelo, n.d.)

1. EQUIPMENT

a. Check on amount of magazines and belts carried and condition.

b. Detail number and types of grenades to be carried and by whom.

c. Detail who should carry spare radio batteries.

d. Detail who will carry pangas and toggle ropes.

e. Check medic pack and detail who will carry it.

f. Make sure each man has a field dressing.

g. Show your stick where you carry your morphine.

h. Check that each man has rations for at least 36 hours.

i. Check that each man has enough water.

j. Check that sleeping kit is secure and protected.

k. Make sure that you have camouflage cream and it is used.

l. Make sure that your controlled stores are secure.

m. Make sure that your codes are secure and waterproof.

n. Make sure that you have a white map.

2. USE OF HELICOPTERS

a. Detail positions in aircraft.

b. Detail regrouping drills after deplaning.

c. Remember to put your headset on in the aircraft.

3. PARA STICK BRIEFING

a. Detail stick order.

b. Tell stick to watch where the rest of the stick lands.

c. Brief stick on regrouping, channel, and senior stick.

4. MOVEMENT

a. Detail pairs, formations, and individual positions.

b. Remind stick of system of clearing kraals.

c. Detail system of cave clearing.

d. Detail how and when suspect areas will be cleared both before and after contact is made.

e. Detail how you want fire and movement conducted over open ground and other obstacles.

f. Detail arcs of responsibility on sweeps and halts.

g. Show your stick all the hand signals you will use.

h. Remember to detail the directing flank on sweeps and action on loss of contact with other sticks.

5. ACTIONS

a. Detail action on halts and use of map.

b. Detail action on radio going unserviceable.

c. Detail action on contact and use of smoke.

    d.   Detail action on indicating targets to stick and aircraft.

    e.   Detail action on grenade thrown at stick and own use.

    f.   Detail how you will use fire and movement in contact.

    g.   Detail who will search bodies and kit and when.

    h.   Warn stick on looting.

    i.   Detail action on casualties both on our side and the terrorists.

    j.   Detail action on being separated from stick.

6.   COMMAND AND SIGNALS

    a.   Detail the chain of command.

    b.   Inform stick on call sign and channel used, include aircraft.

7.   REMINDER TO STICK COMMANDER

    a.   Remember to answer your radio the first time.

    b.   Put your map out whenever static.

    c.   Remember that you are responsible for the success of your stick, if: i. You have wankers in your stick report them to the troop commander; ii. Debriefs are done and faults will be corrected; iii. You don't brief your stick properly you will have your arse kicked.

BATTLE APPRECIATION (Rhodesia Regiment, Pocket Book, G4)

Divide ground into left/center/right, and consider each in turn as under:
1. Enemy dispositions, fields of fire, dead ground.
2. Cover for movement.
3. Assault positions, distance from.
4. Positions for supporting fire, best angle in relation to assault.
5. Obstacles and distances, their effect on speed.
6. Select best alternative and implement.

LESSONS LEARNED (Army Headquarters, Military Support to the Civil Power [MCP], Salisbury: GP, 1967, as amended 1975, 8-11—8-12; Rhodesian Security Forces, Counter-Insurgency Operational Manual, Part II, Salisbury: GP, 1975, 10-15 to 10-16)

Wisdom in retrospect—The following are some reasons for failure which have been reported by ambush commanders in Malaya and Kenya. These may help in the training for, and mounting of, ambushes in Rhodesia:

1. Disclosure of the ambush by the noise made by cocking weapons and moving safety catches or change levers. Check weapons, practice men in their silent handling and ensure that all weapons are ready to fire.
2. There was a tendency to shoot high at the light face of the terrorist. This must be corrected on the jungle range.
3. Disclosure of the ambush position by footprints made by the ambush party moving into position and by movement of individuals at the crucial time when the terrorists were approaching.
4. There was a lack of fire-control and commanders were unable to stop the firing and start the immediate follow-up.
5. Commanders were badly sited with consequent lack of control.
6. There was a lack of all-around observation, resulting in terrorists arriving at the area of the ambush unannounced.
7. There were misfires and stoppages through failure to clean, inspect and test weapons and magazines.
8. There was a lack of clearly defined drill for opening fire and orders were contradictory.
9. There was a tendency for all to fire at the same target.
10. Fire was opened prematurely.
11. It has been found that, provided you achieve surprise, the disadvantage of being outnumbered can be overcome.

LESSONS LEARNED (Rhodesian Light Infantry, operational procedure notes, Cranborne Barracks, n.d.)

1. Assign every trooper an area to be covered: front, back, left or right. Make sure you have assigned flank security.
2. Assign one other trooper besides the stick leader to check the compass bearings.
3. Brief every trooper on an operation the details of the operation and the initial plan of action.
4. Double check your communications before departure and double-check again.
5. Keep control of the stick and make sure covering distance does not take priority over security.
6. Make sure every trooper knows the route of the mission.
7. Always have a rendezvous point.
8. Make sure standard operating procedures are adhered to.
9. Make sure the stick has a password known only to its own troops.
10. Be prepared once the patrol or bush trip has started to stay alert at all times.
11. Be aware of the area around you whether in the bush or rural village.

12. Be sure weapons are loaded and safety off. Check, double-check minutes later and check again hours later.
13. Be aware of broken trees or bushes which are being used to camouflage the terrorists.
14. Remember intelligence reports on what the terrorist group favors in the way of ambushes.
15. If the terrorist group has superior numbers, make every effort to prevent a flanking maneuver.
16. Open fire at the terrorist immediately when you can identify them. Don't wait, unless it endangers the stick.
17. Always deny the terrorist group the tactical advantage. Put yourself in his position and guard against his actions.
18. Rehearse your actions and stick actions in various combat contingencies and make sure each trooper will deploy in the action practiced.
19. Contacts are lost because of the lack of proper liaison between troopers of the stick. Make sure you assist one another and vice versa. Practice it.
20. During a firefight expose only as much of your body as is absolutely necessary to effect a kill.
21. When a terrorist group's presence is known or suspected, avoid moving in the open in a straight line or parallel to them.
22. Remember fire and movement.
23. Do not move until supporting fire is supplied.
24. Fire your weapon in short bursts during a firefight (double-tap at center mass). Long bursts tend to decrease accuracy, may overheat your weapon, and give your body more exposure time to terrorist fire.
25. Be prepared for night contacts, never let down.
26. Never do the same routine twice. Change, double back, halt, advance slow, force march, or move to a flank for a couple of clicks from the objective.
27. Surprise is important. Make sure of your security, keep the stick tight both in the bush and on R&R. Keep it close to the unit.
28. When you base-up overnight, or even for a few hours, dig shell scrapes, don't relax.
29. Proceed, [pause,] and peer. Proceed.
30. Keep formations and maintain loose control.

LESSONS LEARNED (Police Headquarters, n.d.)

Don't be an easy target, don't get killed for comfort, don't get caught, regularity is a casualty!

1. If alone, be extra alert. Use a back-up where possible. Avoid suspicious areas and always look for cover. Change your firing position. Remember shape, shine, shadow, silhouette, smell and movement. Casualties help the enemy.
2. Avoid a hasty and careless return to base at dusk—stay the night in the sticks. Eliminate all unnecessary movement at dusk—contacts at this time hinder backup Fire Force, casevacs, etc. Don't trade your life for one extra night of comfort. At night, avoid sound and light—don't smoke—it's deadly.
3. Don't regulate routes and times. Change routines often. Don't give the enemy a chance to plan. Let's not lose the game by default.
4. Always post sentries. Avoid movement at dusk. Keep your firearm in constant readiness. Know your arcs of responsibility. Avoid typical ambush or suspicious situations. Be sure of your anti-ambush drills and tactics. Be sure your mates know them. Be sure, be safe—surprise means a successful ambush.

The FN Rifle in Rhodesia

Modern military small arms fall into two categories, those that were successful and those that were not. The success stories are repeated while the failures slide into ridicule or obscurity. An example of achievement is the Fabrique Nationale-Fusil Automatique Leger (FN-FAL) light automatic rifle, which was used during the 1965 to 1980 Rhodesian Bush War. Revered as the troopie's "slayer," it is possible to conclude that in this example of success for almost two decades the FN-FAL and its R1 variation proved to be a classic infantry rifle in every sense of the word.

Southern Rhodesia first received the FN in 1961 to equip new units of the Rhodesia and Nyasaland Federal Army: the Rhodesian Light Infantry, the Special Air Service, and the Selous Scout armored car unit. The 7.62mm FN rifle was soon adapted as the standard rifle by the rest of the army, Rhodesian Air Force, and British South Africa Police. The weapons were British-made inch-pattern L1A1s, already in service with British, Canadian, and Australian forces.

Sources of Commonwealth supply were cut off by 1965 sanctions after Rhodesian independence and replacement weapons were needed by 1970. The Republic of South Africa's Lyttelton Engineering Works (LEW) at Verwoerdburg made a metric-pattern version of the Belgium FN used as the South African Defense Force's infantry rifle, the R1 (later models included the R2 and R3). Alternatives were the German Heckler & Koch G3 7.62mm rifle used by the Portuguese in Guinea, Angola, and Mozambique. While illicit trade existed with Belgium, Germany, and Portugal, South Africa appeared the most reliable source for arms and they also made the MAG 58 machine gun, and 7.62mm NATO ammunition used by the Rhodesians.

Hardware

The FN rifle was a gas-operated automatic weapon with a breech block which mechanically locked before firing could take place. The R1 version was defined in technical terms as gas operated, full or semi-automatic; caliber 7.62x51mm, 150g bullet weight, with 2,750 feet-per-second muzzle velocity; four grooves, right-hand-twist rifling, with one turn in 20 inches; 43 inches in length with a 21-inch barrel; effective range 600 meters; protected post front sight, aperture graduated to 600 meters rear sight; weighing 9 pounds unloaded, 10.4 pounds loaded; with a standard magazine capacity of 20 rounds; with a cartridge weight (per 100 rounds) of 5.4 pounds. For the average rifleman the complete rifle, 200 rounds, and four magazines weighed in at 23 pounds (10.4kg).

Accessories included a bayonet, sling, and cleaning kit. Telescopic and night vision devices were available as well. Both wood and synthetic stock, grip, and forearms were used. During the war, the tubular bayonet was eventually withdrawn from service and kept in the armory for parades. The carrying handle was removed to discourage sloppy handling and some units went as far as to remove the sling swivels for the same reason and to prevent rattling. The distinct black outline of the weapon was broken up with olive drab PVC paint applied as needed.

The Rhodesians found there were more stoppages with the R1 than the L1A1. At first it was believed this was due to poor quality control during manufacture. In fact the opposite was proven in that the Lyttleton weapons were made with narrower tolerances than other versions. This required a break-in period to function smoothly and allowed for more interference from rust or grit that would occur particularly around the gas port. Eventually the bore and chamber were chromed to prevent this and gas regulation remained the key to proper functioning. Another critical factor was that a unique combination tool was required for required field stripping past a certain point.

Software Theory

Instructors described the FN as a rifle, machine gun, and mortar all in one. This was because of its ability to fire aimed single shots, semi, and automatic fire, and used an FN rifle grenade. Rhodesian training was incremental, without unnecessary repetition. Skills and facts were learned in basic lessons followed by practice to speed up application of what was taught.

Basic training was in some nine lessons over six periods that covered disassembly, cleaning, loading and unloading, stoppages, sight adjustment, aiming and holding, grouping, sight offsets for elevation and windage, deliberate, snap, and rapid fire, positions, cover, and close quarters firing, shooting at night, bayonet fighting, and the assault course. Each of these subjects had a measured training test to demonstrate skill.

Firing practice was at either a 44½x17-inch silhouette (with a 8x16-inch center) or a 15-inch bull's eye. This started with 25-meter grouping, then progressed 100- to 200-meter preclassification and classification firing. Training was then expanded to close quarter firing, night shooting, and "jungle lane" shoots used to maintain skill at arms.

Software Practice

It should be kept in mind that the basic tactical unit for the war was a four-man team or "stick" that was built around the MAG 58 machine gun and three FN-armed riflemen working in mutual support. Contacts were often sudden at close range with victory going to the side that established a high volume of effective fire. Individual use of the rifle was anything from vehicle anti-ambush drills to the defense of isolated farm homes. As a mark of respect for the weapon's reliability and effectiveness, it was preferred for border control and counterinsurgency operations, with only the special forces using communist bloc firearms for cross-border operations. This was due as much to security and logistical reasons as employment, and for special forces combat was often the last resort.

The desired field use was firing the so-called "Mozambique tap" of one or two center-of-mass body shots followed by a head shot. This could be at a visible target or in the form of the "Drake" shoot that saw "double tap" shot placement across an assigned zone of fire into likely enemy hiding places. The 7.62mm round was more than capable of penetrating natural concealment and most cover. Its impact on the terrorists was dramatic and there was no debate about stopping or killing power.

Riflemen were told that firing more than two magazines (40 rounds) on full automatic would overheat that barrel and they should only fire single rounds. A more logical reasons was recorded: "It is generally accepted that it is impossible to fire the FN rifle at full auto from the shoulder due to the tremendous recoil." From my own experience in shooting the FN and American M14 and M16 rifles, the FN had superior pointing and recoil handling qualities in semiautomatic fire that allowed it to acquire and return to the target efficiently.[1]

Rhodesian ARMY

TERRORISM STOPS HERE!

Endnotes

Abbreviations Used with Endnotes & Bibliography

AHQ	Army Headquarters
AirHQ	Air Force Headquarters
BSAP	British South Africa Police
c.	circa
CCJP	Catholic Commission for Justice and Peace
CIIR	Catholic Institute for International Relations
CIO	Central Intelligence Organization
C&S	Combat and Survival
DirCIO	Director General CIO
DirAI	Director Air Intelligence
DMI	Director Military Intelligence
ed., eds.	editor, editors
EngD	Engineer Directorate
et al.	and others
GP	Government Printer
HMSO	Her Majesty's Stationary Office
ISSUP	Institute for Strategic Studies, University of South Africa (Pretoria)
misc.	miscellaneous
JPS	Joint Planning Staff
MID	Military Intelligence Directorate
n.d.	no publication date given
n.p.	no place, no publisher, or no page given
OCC	Operations Coordinating Committee
PTS	Parachute Training School
RA	Rhodesia Army vice RhA
RhAF	Rhodesian Air Force
RIC	Rhodesian Intelligence Corps
RSA	Republic of South Africa
RSF	Rhodesian Security Forces
RUSI	Royal United Services Institute
SADF	South Africa Defense Forces
SBHQ	Special Branch Headquarters
SFA	Security Forces Auxiliary
SFHQ	Special Forces Headquarters
SInf	School of Infantry

SOF	Soldier of Fortune
UNESCO	United Nations Educational, Scientific, and Cultural Organization
UNISA	University of South Africa (Pretoria)
USGPO	United States Government Printing Office
ZMS	Zimbabwe Medal Society
( )	source or collection
[ ]	added information

Preface

1. Quoted in Richard Hamley, *The Regiment* (Weltevreden Park: Covos Day Books, 2000), vii.
2. Quoted in A. J. Arniel, *Badges and Insignia of the Rhodesian Security Forces* (Germiston: Alec Kaplan & Son, 1987), 5.
3. For example, Cold War-Era Military Lesson Learned: South Africa and Rhodesia Symposium, UNSW, Canberra, ADFA, 1 October 2013.
4. Laurence Binyon, "For the Fallen;" Rhodesian use of these verses was for Empire and Commonwealth service with the Southeast Asia Command of Lord Louis Mountbatten in World War II.
5. See Charles D. Melson, Lessons Learned in the Bush: Southern Rhodesia, 1965–1980 (HQMC, 1986); Killing Machine (HQMC, 2003); and "Top Secret War: Rhodesian Special Operations," *Small Wars and Insurgencies*, vol. 16 no. 1, March 2005, 57–82.

Introduction

1. From a Shona expression for resistance or rebellion.
2. Robert Blake, *A History of Rhodesia* (London: Eyre Methuen, 1977); Martin Meredith, *The Past is Another Country* (London: André Deutsch, 1979); and Paul Moorcraft, *A Short Thousand Years: The End of Rhodesia's Rebellion* (Salisbury: Galaxie, 1979), 227.
3. Charles M. Lohman and Robert I. MacPherson, *Rhodesia: Tactical Victory, Strategic Defeat* (USMC C&SC, 1983).
4. David W. Lovell and Deane-Peter Baker, eds., *The Strategic Corporal Revisited: Challenges Facing Combatants in 21st Century Warfare* (Cape Town: UCT Press, 2017).
5. Colin McInnes, *Hot War, Cold War: The British Army's Way in Warfare 1945–1995* (London: Brassey's, 1996); Michael Dewar, *Brush Fire Wars: Campaigns of the British Army since 1945* (London: Robert Hale, 1987).
6. Charles D. Melson, 14th Naval History Symposium, USNA, Annapolis, MD., 1999.
7. Put forward in *Assegai*, 1973, *Military Review*, 1979, *Naval Institute Proceedings*, 1981, *Naval Institute Proceedings*, 1982, *Marine Corps Gazette*, 1989, *Marine Corps Gazette*, 1995, and *Marine Corps Gazette*, 2000.
8. Wood was an invited guest of the Marine Corps University, wrote for the *Marine Corps Gazette*, and gave papers to the Society for Military History, the Army–Air Force Center for Low Intensity Conflict, the U.S. Air Force Special Operations School, and at the U.S. Naval Academy.
9. Center for the Study of Intelligence and Society for Military History conference, Rosslyn, VA, 18–21 April 1996, panel on "The Use and Abuse of Intelligence in Low-Level Conflict: the British Commonwealth Approaches and Experience." Chair Michael F. Noone, commentor Charles D. Melson, panelists J. R. T. Wood, Raffi Gregorian, and John R. Cronin.

Chapter 1

1. W. V. Brelsford, ed., *Handbook of the Federation of Rhodesia and Nyasaland* (London: Cassell, 1960), 1–2; Harold D. Nelson, ed., *Zimbabwe: A Country Study* (Washington, DC: American University, 1983).

2. Kees Maxey, *The Fight for Zimbabwe* (London: Rex Collings, 1975), 191–3.

3. J. R. T. Wood, *The Welensky Papers: A History of the Federation of Rhodesia and Nyasaland* (Durban: Graham Publishing, 1983), passim.

4. Compiled by Ian J. Johnstone (NAZ).

5. Rhodesian Army, Military Support to the Civil Power, RhCodeNo 0104, 1 May 1967; selected chapters were reprinted in an abbreviated edition, 1 June 1975, xiv (PMML).

6. RA, MCP, xiv.

7. Rhodesian Security Forces, Counter-Insurgency Operations Manual, RSF/101, June–July 1975; Parts I through IV, v (PMML).

8. RSF, COIN, II, v.

9. RA, MCP, xiv.

10. RA, MCP, xv.

11. RA, MCP, v.

12. RA, MCP, v.

13. RSF, COIN, II, v.

14. RA, MCP, xv–xvi.

15. Walls was born in 1926 in Salisbury, Southern Rhodesia, and graduated from Sandhurst and was commissioned into the Black Watch Regiment in 1946. He returned to Rhodesia in 1948 and became an officer with the Rhodesian African Rifles the following year. In 1950, he went to Somalia with the King's African Rifles and from 1951–3 was in Malaya as a Special Air Service squadron commander. Assigned to the School of Infantry in 1956, he then served with the Northern Rhodesia Regiment as a company commander and battalion executive officer. After staff courses in the Great Britain, Walls returned to the Northern Rhodesia Regiment before being named adjutant general of the Rhodesian army in 1962. He commanded the Rhodesian Light Infantry from 1964–7 and then 2 Brigade. He was the army chief of staff from 1968 and army commander from 1972. In 1977, then a lieutenant-general, Walls was named Commander, Combined Operations. Though this position never achieved the military and civilian powers associated with "supremos" in Malaya, Cyprus, or Kenya, it was still the most powerful security position in Rhodesia by 1980. Walls ended the war at odds with both sides, being accused by the nationalists of plotting a coup and by the settlers for not carrying one out. With this situation Walls has kept his own counsel since, other than dealing with the Rhodesian Army and SAS associations, and anonymous interviews.

16. Extended interview from late 1976, published in Al J. Venter, *Vorster's Africa* (Johannesburg: Ernest Stanton Publishers, 1977), 347–62; and "War in Rhodesia," *SOF*, Fall 1976, 20–9; and was edited for continuity and circumstance.

17. Venter & Walls, *Vorster*, 352–3.

18. Venter & Walls, *Vorster*, 362.

19. Venter & Walls, *Vorster*, 350.

20. Venter & Walls, *Vorster*, 356.

21. Venter & Walls, *Venter*, 354–5.

22. Venter & Walls, *Vorster*, 351.

23. Paul Moorcraft and Peter McLaughlin, *Chimurenga: War in Rhodesia* (Johannesburg: Sygma & Collins, 1982), 66; also published as *The Rhodesian War* (Barnsley: Pen & Sword Books, 2008).

24. Moorcraft was a university lecturer, editor, and wartime journalist in Salisbury, while McLaughlin was a historian of the Rhodesian security forces.

25. Rajesh Rajagopalan, "Restoring Normalcy: The Evolution of the Indian Army's Counterinsurgency Doctrine." *Small Wars and Insurgencies*, vol. 11, no. 1, Spring 2000, 45.

26. See Appendix: Lessons Learned in the Bush.

27. RSF, COIN, II, iv.

28. RSF, COIN, II, ii.

29. RSF, COIN, II, iv.

30. Venter & Walls, *Vorster*, 349.

31. Venter & Walls, *Vorster*, 348–9.

32. Venter & Walls, *Vorster*, 355.

33. Venter & Walls, *Vorster*, 349.

34. Venter & Walls, *Vorster*, 349.

35. Venter & Walls, *Vorster*, 352.

36. Venter & Walls, *Vorster*, 351–2.

37. Venter & Walls, *Vorster*, 349–50.

38. RSF, COIN, II, ii.

39. RSF, COIN, II, ii.

40. RSF, COIN, II, vi.

41. RSF, COIN, II, ii.

42. RSF, COIN, II, v.

43. RSF, COIN, II, vi.

44. RSF, COIN, II, vi.

45. Some confusion existed on dates and locations of JOCs and sub-JOCs as they evolved.

46. ComOps, A Brief Operational History of the Campaign in Rhodesia Covering the Period 1964–1978, 31 May 1978 (PMML); Michael Evans, *Fighting Against Chimurenga* (Salisbury: Historical Association of Zimbabwe, 1981); John R. Cronin and Robert C. MacKenzie, *Counter-Insurgency in Southern Africa* (Washington, DC: Center for Stategic and International Studies, 1986).

47. AHQ, *A Brief History of the Rhodesia Army* (Salisbury: City Printers, 1968); Beverley Whyte, *A Pride of Men: The Story of Rhodesia's Army* (Salisbury: Graham Publishing, 1975).

48. Lewis H. Gann, *The Development of Southern Rhodesia's Military System* (Salisbury: National Archives of Rhodesia, 1965) and "From Ox Wagon to Armored Car in Rhodesia," *Military Review*, April 1968, 63–72.

49. Peter McLaughlin, *Ragtime Soldiers: The Rhodesian Experience in the First World War* (Bulawayo: Books of Zimbabwe, 1980); "The Thin White Line: Rhodesia's Armed Forces Since the Second World War," *Zambezia*, vol.6, no.2, 1978, 175–85.

50. Eugene Pomeroy, The Origins and Development of the Defense Forces of Northern and Southern Rhodesia from 1890 to 1945, thesis, Portland State University, 1994.

51. Richard Miers, *Shoot to Kill* (London: Faber & Faber, 1959), passim. It was believed that Africans held up better in the bush and that the Europeans were more subject to disease and wastage. Observed as far back as Burma in World War II and then in Malaya, was the use of rural African troops to conduct extended ground operations while the generally urban Europeans were retained as reaction forces.

52. Unit histories include: Peter Baxter, Hugh Bomford, and Gerry van Tonder, *Rhodesia Regiment, 1899–1981* (Tauranga: Rhodesian Services Association, 2014); Alexandre Binda, *Masodja* (Johannesburg: 30 Degrees South Publishers, 2009); Alexandre Binda, *The Saints* (Johannesburg: 30 Degrees South Publishers, 2007); and Mark Adams and Chris Cocks, *Africa's Commandos: The Rhodesian Light Infantry* (Solihull: Helion & Co., 2013).

53. Timothy Stapleton, *African Police and Soldiers in Colonial Zimbabwe, 1923–1980* (Rochester: University of Rochester Press, 2011), passim.

54. Sections on the police and armed forces in Brelsford, ed., *Handbook*, 657–9, 666–7.

55. Terrorist Incursions from Zambia, A statement by the Prime Minster, the Hon I.D. Smith, and other proceedings of the Rhodesian parliament, 30 August 1967 (PMML).

56. AHQ, *History*, 15–16.

57. Dudley Cowderoy and Roy C. Nesbit, *War in the Air* (Alberton: Galago Publishing, 1987), 35.

58. AHQ, *History*, 16; John Lovett, *Contact* (Salisbury: Galaxie Press, 1977) provides an overview of the armed response.

59. SInf, Organization and Roles of the Rhodesian Army, n.d., 4 (PMML).

60. David Scott-Donelan, *Tactical Tracking Operations* (Boulder: Paladin Press, 1998), 77–8.

61. The increasing manpower demands of the conflict were met in small part by overseas recruiting; this reached a peak of 2,000 that fell off to 500 by 1979. The relative ease in which United Kingdom subjects could move about created a cosmopolitan complexion to the security forces with British, South Africans, Portuguese, and even American nationals. John Coleman estimated some 200–300 Americans served overall, while Robert MacKenzie felt that no more than 50 were ever fully attested security force members (Coleman, MacKenzie, personal communications, n.d.).

62. With the Queen Mother as its Honorary Commissioner, BSAP records were kept by the British Army Museum that normally excluded Empire and Commonwealth units.

63. Richard Hamley, *The Regiment* (Weltrevreden Park: Covos Day Books, 2000), 71–2; British South Africa Police, *COIN and I.S. Training Manual* (Salisbury: Police Headquarters, 1969); Arnold, personal communication, n.d.

64. Hamley's narrative was based on lectures about the history of the BSAP to recruits, using as a theme the depiction of uniforms and personal equipment. It was previously published in 1971 and 1980; David W. Arnold, Counterinsurgency, SOF Convention, Las Vegas, NV, 1986.

65. Peter Gibbs and Hugh Phillips, *The History of the British South Africa Police* (North Ringwood: Something of Value, 2000). The revised volumes were the product of the police regimental association. While authoritative in sources and sponsorship, the accounts are anecdotal and nostalgic in narrative. With more recent events not on par with past glories, being published at the start of the major fighting that saw the respect of the police decline as the need for military solutions increased.

66. There was no single document as specific provisions crossed government lines. BSAP Inspector Jon L. Milner recalled a classified, black-covered publication at the station level titled the *B.S.A. Police Instruction Book* (Salisbury: Police Headquarters, 1965) which summarized the main features of the acts and regulations. (PMML)

67. BSAP Superintendent Arnold gave an overview of emergency regulations; specific legislation included the Federation of Rhodesia and Nyasaland Emergency Powers Act (1960), as amended 1964, 1976; Law and Order (Maintenance) Act (1961), as amended 1964, 1976; and the Southern Rhodesia Emergency Powers (Maintenance of Law and Order) Regulations, 1974; Indemnity and Compensation Act, 1975 as amended; Official Secrets Act; Exchange Control Regulations.

68. Hoffman, Arnold & Taw, *Rhodesian Experience*, 47–51; Michael Noone, "Legal Issues in Low Intensity Warfare: the British and Israeli Experience," Inter University Seminar, Catholic University Columbus School of Law, 3 May 1990.

Chapter 2

1. For example in 1978, there were an estimated total of 19,765 security force members opposed by 15,375 communist terrorists; RIC Research Report No. 30, 31 December 1978, 4 (RAA). Unless otherwise cited, used were JPS, Analysis of Past Operations, 28 January 1971; DirCIO,

An Assessment of the Threat to Rhodesia from Terrorism over the Three Year Period, 8 September 1971 (RAA).

2. Vital Ground and Key Areas, 1980 Election, n.d. (RAA).

3. SAS narratives were by Barbara Cole, *The Elite* (Amanzimtoti: Three Knights, 1984) followed by *The Elite Pictorial* (Amanzimtoti: Three Knights, 1986). These were written by a journalist whose access to the SAS was through husband Peter Cole and mates Colin Willis and Robert MacKenzie. Both provide a wealth of detail on the SAS but organization, chronology, and analysis are lacking. One major fault is the use of pseudonyms. These narratives have been charitably described as the view of the war from the sergeants' mess and the regiment deserved better; for example the unit history by Johnathan Pittaway and Craig Fourie, *SAS Rhodesia* (Durban: Dandy Agencies, 2003).

4. Reid-Daly's memoir first saw the light of day told to Peter Stiff as *Selous Scouts: Top Secret War* (Alberton: Galago Publishing, 1982). This was followed by Peter Stiff, *Selous Scouts: A Pictorial Account* (Alberton: Galago Publishing, 1984). *Pamwe Chete* (Weltevreden Park: Covos Day Books, 1999) was an edition which revised the previous editing style which read like an interview transcript. New information concerned South Africa's involvement in Rhodesia and identified individuals who had previously kept out of sight. No information was provided for more controversial or dubious aspects, for example, the period through the 1980 election. Included were rosters of personnel and award citations that give a face to some exceptional soldiering. A unit history was published by Johnathan Pittaway, *Selous Scouts Rhodesia* (Durban: Dandy Agencies, 2015); and Ron F. Reid-Daly, Counterinsurgency, seminar, Soldier of Fortune Convention, Las Vegas, NV, 1985.

5. The Special Air Service, Selous Scouts, Grey's Scouts, and Psychological Operations Unit were administratively part of the Rhodesian Corps of Infantry. The Grey's Scouts was associated with the border minefield and cordon sanitaire effort. The 1 Psychological Operations Unit was not considered a special force, although by current American criteria it would be; Formation Order Number 5: Rhodesian Corps of Infantry, 28 August 1978, 8–12 (RAA).

6. Reid-Daly, was known as "Uncle Ron" to his men. Rhodesian-born, he was a founding member of the Special Air Service that served in Malaya in 1951–3. Remaining in the army, he helped establish the Rhodesian Light Infantry and was its first sergeant-major. He retired from the service as a captain commanding the RLI Support Commando. In 1973, he was asked to form the Selous Scouts as a major and commanded it through 1979 as a lieutenant-colonel through 1979. He lived in South Africa. Reid-Daly, personal communications, 13 October 1993.

7. Quoted in Hilton Hamann, *Days of the Generals* (Cape Town: Zebra Press, 2001), 130. The South Africans formed special forces in 1971 based on the Rhodesian example and their own needs in South West Africa. See Kevin A. O'Brien, "Special Forces for Counter-Revolutionary Warfare: The South African Case," *Small Wars and Insurgencies*, vol. 12, no. 2, Summer 2001, 79–109.

8. Security and intelligence accounts were found in Ken Flower, *Serving Secretly* (Alberton: Galago Publishing, 1987), Henrik Ellert, *The Rhodesian Front War* (Gweru: Mambo Press, 1989), and William Crabtree, *Came the Fourth Flag* (Lancaster: Scotforth Books, 2002); Henrick Ellert, "The Rhodesian Security and Intelligence Community," in Ngwabi Bhebe and Terence Ranger, eds., *Soldiers in Zimbabwe's Liberation War* (Harare: University of Zimbabwe Publications, 1995), 87–103, 183; Glenn Cross, Rhodesian Intelligence in a Counter-insurgent/Counter-terrorist Conflict paper, Georgetown University, 2007. Flower and Crabtree were director general and deputy director of the Central Intelligence Organization. As to be expected, these provide circumscribed insight into the secret war undertaken before and after independence. BSAP Special Branch member Henrik Ellert observed that some actions were taken "because it's there!" rather than for any planned aim. From Denmark, he worked the Branch One European Desk monitoring threats inside and outside the country. He lives in Zimbabwe.

9. Working definitions of these terms: overt actions are those in which the act and actor are known; covert actions are those where the act is known but not the actor; clandestine actions are those where both the act and the actor are not obvious or deflected elsewhere.

10. The basis for listing these general- and special-purpose operations, as for the rest of the narrative, were the RAA archive operations index of 13 July 1994 and Wood's named operations list of 11 July 2003 (PMML); J. R. T. Wood, *Zambezi Valley Insurgency: Early Rhodesian Bush War Operations* (Pinetown: 30 Degrees South Publishers, 2012) provided a detailed narrative of the early border actions.

11. Known as such by the Organization of African Unity (OAU) from December 1974.

12. Kenneth "Ken" G. Harvey, a World War II Distinguished Service Order recipient, was the Rhodesian SAS's honorary colonel; Ken Harvey, "SAS Operational Wings," *ZMS Journal*, April 2001, 16–18. Spencer Chapman's memoir *The Jungle is Neutral* (London: Chatto & Windus, 1949) was mentioned by Reid-Daly as motivation.

13. Calvert advocated the postwar need for Commonwealth special forces in 1945 and employed them at first opportunity in 1950 in Malaya; J. M. Calvert, The Future of SAS Troops, HQSAS, 12 October 1945 (PMML).

14. Keith Meadows, *Sand in the Wind* (Bulawayo: Thorntree Press, 1997), 14–16.

15. Reid-Daly, personal communications, 13 October 1993.

16. Scott-Donelan, *Tactical Tracking*, 10–11.

17. Cole, *Pictorial*, 6; SAS unit ephemera including nominal roll and newsletters (NAZ).

18. Reid-Daly, *Pamwe Chete*, 40.

19. When the Rhodesian SAS formed, the British 22SAS was still evolving and the Rhodesians made their own way. The SAS scheme was replicated in France, Belgium, Rhodesia, Australia, New Zealand, and even with the U.S. Army's Special Forces Operations Detachment Delta (a figure of Col David Stirling stands in its Fort Bragg conference room). While Brig Michael Calvert was credited with founding the postwar Special Air Service, Lt-Col John Woodhouse and Maj Dare Newell were recognized for the modern SAS selection process and organization. "Mister SAS" Woodhouse had a surreptitious visit to wartime Rhodesia.

20. John Evans, "C Squadron Trooper," *Lion & Tusk*, March 1997, 19–24; David Scott-Donelan, letter, *Lion & Tusk*, March 1997, 13–14.

21. Wood, *Welensky*, 783, 801, 1214; Eugene Pomeroy, "The Origins of the Rhodesian SAS Title," *Lion & Tusk*, February 1994, n.p.; Army Career Office, *You're Someone Special in the S.A.S.*, "History of the SAS," n.d. (PMML).

22. "The Squadron's First Big Para Drop Near Salisbury," *Lion & Tusk*, August 1996, n.p; Rhodesia Herald, "Action Stations and Air Devils Plunge into Big Dawn Drop" in *Lion & Tusk*, March 1997, 24–6. The next squadron mass-jump would be to celebrate its establishment; "10th Anniversary," *Assegai*, August 1971, 18–21.

23. Beverley Whyte, "Tough Guys," *Illustrated Life Rhodesia*, 7 August 1975, 113; W. D. Gale, "Men Who Dare," *Fighting Forces of Rhodesia*, (3) 1976, 41; Wood, *Welensky*, 1087.

24. Gale, "Men Who Dare," *Fighting Forces of Rhodesia*, 41.

25. Coventry went to the office of the prime minister after leaving command of the SAS as a lieutenant-colonel. From 1970, he directed "undercover" operations including the training and support of MNR/RENAMO. He remained in this capacity in Zimbabwe after independence. Obituary by Barbara Cole, *Lion & Tusk*, Autumn 1993, n.p.

26. SD Instruction 2: Order of Seniority, 26 February 1979; SD Instruction 9: Formation and Location Statements, 28 August 1978; 1 (Rhodesian) Special Air Service Regiment, 5 (RAA); Cole, *Elite*, 14–24; Cole, *Pictorial*, 9–12.

27. A patrol had command, navigation, and stores vehicles with two to three men in each. At the time, this was based on the short-wheelbase Land Rover modified to SAS needs by removing doors and windscreen. Added were front- and rear-firing GPMG machine guns, grenade launchers, space for a 3.5-inch rocket launcher and Bren light machine gun, additional fuel and ammunition storage, radios, and navigation gear; David Mills, "The Pink Panther," *SOF*, July 1984, 54–5.

28. Army Careers Office, *You're Someone Special in the S.A.S.*, n.d. (PMML).

29. Ian Henderson and Philip Goodhart, *Manhunt in Kenya* (New York: Bantam Books, 1988).

30. Barrett, personal communications, 2 June 2003.

31. David Martin and Phyllis Johnson, *The Chitepo Assassination* (Harare: Zimbabwe Publishing House, 1985).

32. Established in 1963, the CIO was headed throughout the war by Director General Ken Flower, appointed from the BSAP. From Great Britain and a policeman by experience, he and his organization were distrusted because of continued contacts with Great Britain and other countries opposed to Rhodesian independence. He remained in this post in Mugabe's Zimbabwe after independence. Wood, Never Enough Intelligence, SMH, 4.

33. Crabtree, *Fourth Flag*, 211–65.

34. Ellert, "Rhodesian Security and Intelligence," *Zimbabwe's Liberation War*, 87–103, 183, provides the best overview of the subject; Ellert, *Rhodesian Front War*, addresses the same topic in broader terms from 1962–80. See also Ron Reid-Daly, "War in Rhodesia," in *Challenge: Southern Africa within the African Revolutionary Context* (Gibraltar: Ashanti Publishing, 1989), 163–4; Jakkie K. Cilliers, *Counterinsurgency in Rhodesia* (Dover: Croom Helm, 1985), 218–37.

35. Cole, *Pictorial*, 64–9. Insight into these activities is found in Roy Christie, *For the President's Eyes Only* (Johannesburg: Hugh Keartland Publishers, 1971); Peter Stiff, *See You in November* (Alberton: Galago Publishing, 1984); and Martin & Johnson, *Chitepo Assassination*.

36. Army Careers Office, *You're Someone Special in the S.A.S.*, "History of the SAS," n.d. (PMML).

37. Peter Godwin, *Mukiwa* (London: Picador, 1996), 13–14.

38. Robinson passed SAS selection in 1964 and was attached to 22SAS. He subsequently served as the troop commander, adjutant, and squadron second-in-command. During this time he was instrumental in external and internal operations, including the tracking effort. He commanded the SAS from 1972 through 1978 and finished the war as special operations action officer at ComOps headquarters. He lives in South Africa.

39. Crabtree, *Fourth Flag*, 242–3.

40. *The Conduct of Anti-Terrorist Operations in Malaya* (Kuala Lumpur: GPO, 1958), Chapter 21; *A Handbook on Anti-Mau Mau Operations* (Nairobi: GPO, 1954), Chapter 6.

41. RA, *MCP*, Chapter 7, Sections 3, 4, and Annex E; RSF, *COIN*, Chapters 7, 8.

42. Scott-Donelan, *Tactical Tracking*, 9; Cole, *Pictorial*, 30–3; Cole, *Elite*, 89; Reid-Daly, "War in Rhodesia" in *Challenge*, 156–7; Reid-Daly, *Pamwe Chete*, 67, 75, 77; Flower, *Secretly*, 113; Tracking Wing, operational procedure notes, Kariba: n.d. (HQMC).

43. Allan Savory letter to AHQ, G(Ops) dated 5 July 1966 (RAA).

44. Tracking: COIN, correspondence with AHQ, G(Ops)1/37 (RAA).

45. JPS, Analysis, Part II, Chapter 2, Section 5, 1 (RAA).

46. Wood, *Zambezi Valley*; "Infiltration of African Nationalists," Maxey, *Fight for Zimbabwe*, 107, 161.

47. Barrett, personal communications, 21 August 2003.

48. MacKenzie, an American, served in the SAS from 1970 rising from trooper to captain and squadron commander.

49. Robert C. MacKenzie, Rhodesian SAS, seminar, Soldier of Fortune Convention, Las Vegas, NV, 1986.

50. Wood, personal communications, 7 November 2003.

51. Flower, *Secretly*, 115; The Sinoia incident was one example.

52. Flower, *Secretly*, 107; Peter P. H. Petter-Bowyer, Winds of Destruction manuscript, 137 (PMML).

53. Stiff, *Selous Scouts*, 48–55.

54. Paul Melshen, Pseudo Operations, U.S. Naval War College, 1986, 26–7.

55. Reid-Daly, *Staying Alive*, 5.

56. Donald H. Grainger, *Don't Die in the Bundu* (Cape Town: Howard Timmins, 1967), 93.
57. "The talk of lack of trackers and the need for army trackers which came out at the Operation Nickel debrief appalled me after all we have tried to do since last year;" Allan Savory memo, 17 October 1967 (RAA).
58. Grainger, *Bundu*, 73; Scott-Donelan, *Tactical Tracking*, 29.
59. Reid-Daly, "War in Rhodesia" in *Challenge*, 158–9; Ellert, *Rhodesian Front War*, 80–92.
60. Binda, personal communications, 20 June 2003.
61. Cole, *Pictorial*, 30–3; Reid-Daly, "War in Rhodesia" in *Challenge*, 164–5. For useful details see Ron Reid-Daly, *Staying Alive* (Gibraltar: Ashanti Publishing, 1990); Scott-Donelan, *Tactical Tracking*, and Grainger, *Bundu*.
62. Venter & Walls, *Vorster*, 354–5.
63. AHQ, G(Ops) 1/37, minute sheet, 22 December 1967 (RAA).
64. Tony Geraghty, *Inside the SAS* (Nashville: Battery Press, 1980), 223.
65. Reid-Daly, "War in Rhodesia" in *Challenge*, 157, 162–3, 165.
66. Preller M. Geldenhuys, Nickel Cross manuscript, 126; Cole, *Elite*, 30.
67. Reid-Daly, "War in Rhodesia" in *Challenge*, 162–3.
68. Scott-Donelan, *Tactical Tracking*, 62.
69. A civilian African tracker unit (CATU) was formed in 1977 using Shangaan tribesman in the Low Veld to support the Rhodesia Regiment in that area. They used a six-man combat tracker team adding a European stick leader and second-in-command. They operated on a rotating three days on patrol, three days off, and split operations could be conducted with two separate four man sections; Jack Lott, "CATU Tracks Terrorists," *SOF*, July 1979, 46–51.
70. AHQ, GSO I, Guerrilla Anti-Terrorist Units, 17 October 1967; JPS, Analysis, Part II, Chapter 2, Section 5, 1–3 (RAA).
71. Tracker combat teams were formed by the Rhodesia Regiment along with existing reconnaissance troops that served better than might be reasonably expected from these part-time soldiers.
72. JPS, Analysis, Part II, Chapter 2, Section 5, 1 (RAA).
73. Joe Skehel, District Commissioner Kariba, letter, *Lion & Tusk*, November 1991, n.p.
74. After the tennis or gym shoes favored by the rapidly moving trackers.
75. Reid-Daly, "War in Rhodesia" in *Challenge*, 156–7.
76. JPS, Analysis, Part II, Chapter 2, Section 6, 2 (RAA).
77. JPS, Analysis, Part II, Chapter 2, Section 5, 1–3 (RAA).
78. Tracking Wing, operational procedure notes, Kariba, n.d. (HQMC); Scott-Donelan, personal communications, 16 March 1990.
79. Counter- or anti-tracking was studied both to deal with its use by the guerrillas and as an aid to "friendly" efforts to avoid being tracked by the enemy; JPS, Analysis, Part II, Chapter 2, Section 5, 1 (RAA).
80. From Great Britain, Scott-Donelan was as an original member of C Squadron, Special Air Service and the Tracker Combat Unit. He went on to the Rhodesian Light Infantry and Selous Scouts, two successful counterinsurgency units based in large part on essential bushcraft. He lives in the United States.
81. "Combat Tracking (Mantracking)," *Selous Scouts*, www.members.tripod.com, accessed 3 January 2002.
82. Reid-Daly, *Staying Alive*, 6.
83. Reid-Daly, "War in Rhodesia" in *Challenge*, 156–7.
84. JPS, Analysis, Part II, Chapter 2, Section 6, 3 (RAA).
85. Reid-Daly, Counterinsurgency Warfare, SOF, 1985.
86. Jack Thompson, "Tracking Techniques," *SOF*, September 1989, 16–19, 78.

87. When this was disclosed through the news media, the terrorists changed their shoes!

88. John Early, "Combat Tracking," *SOF*, July 1979, 52–5, 78–9; Thompson, "Tracking," *SOF*, 16–19, 78; "Bush Tracking and Countertracking," *C&S*, (19) 1991, 1097–101.

89. Early, "Tracking," *SOF*, 52–5, 78–9.

90. Scott-Donelan, *Tactical Tracking*, 2–3.

91. Early, "Tracking," *SOF*, 53.

92. Reid-Daly, "War in Rhodesia," in *Challenge*, 157–8; Early, "Tracking," *SOF*, 52.

93. P. Coetzee, "Pamwe Chete," *Paratus*, December 1979, 18.

94. Reid-Daly examined in detail the development of tactical doctrine and techniques and the clash within the army and the police over the right way to deal with terrorism; Reid-Daly, "War in Rhodesia" in *Challenge*, 152–5, 159–63.

95. Nick Downie, "Rhodesia," *Defence*, May 1979, 343.

96. Venter & Walls, *Vorster*, 354–5.

97. "C Squadron SAS," *Assegai*, May 1969, 16–17.

98. "C Squadron SAS Notes," *Assegai*, June 1969, 31.

99. Rhodesian Information Service, *They Who Dare* film, n.d. (Rhodesian Forces Two)

100. Cole, *Elite*, 6

101. Reid-Daly, "War in Rhodesia" in *Challenge*, 164; Ellert, *Rhodesian Front War*, 21–2, 60.

Chapter 3

1. With exceptions, most artillery and armor was used for counterbattery fire and defense of fixed points along the border areas. Armored cars patrolled road and rail networks with escort duties.

2. Ian Douglas Smith flew for the Royal Air Force in World War II as a fighter pilot in North Africa, the Middle East, and Italy.

3. Rhodesian Air Force, Add up the offers, Then give us a call, n.d. (PMML).

4. Beverley Whyte, *Pride of Eagles* (Salisbury: Graham Publishing, 1976), passim.

5. This did not mean neglected, rather they were late blooming: "They were always well equipped and manned and greatly valued by the forces and the nation." Paintin, personal communications, 7 June 2002.

6. Defense Working Party Paper No. 111B (Revised), Royal Rhodesian Air Force, 30 June 1963 (RAA); Dudley Cowderoy, Roy C. Nesbit, and Andrew Thomas, *Britain's Rebel Air Force* (London: Grub Street, 1998), 21–2, 112, 134–5; Beryl Salt, *Pride of Eagles* (Weltevreden Park: Covos Day Books, 2001), 456; Geldenhuys, Nickel Cross, 381–4; Petter-Bowyer, personal communications, 21 June 2002.

7. Geldenhuys, Nickel Cross, viii.

8. Armored car security specialist WO Ken R. Salter noted that the senior officers were of Rhodesian or South African background and this limited the advancement of those not of this set. In addition, "Very few of the 'birdmen' had come through the ranks whilst the 'penguins,' particularly the warrant officers, had. There were often two totally different schools of thought and I had difficulty attributing some of the comments made in your study to those who, supposedly, made them." Salter, personal communications, 24 June 2002.

9. *Bateleur*, December 1976, 1.

10. AM Norman Walsh stressed the humanitarian support to civil sector aspects needed by an emerging nation, where the air force is often called upon "to participate in casualty evacuation, flood relief support, search and rescue operations, anti-poaching and game culling exercises and photographic survey on a national scale;" Air Force of Zimbabwe, *Air Force 81* (n.p.: Irwin, 1981), 1.

11. *Financial Gazette*, 17 November 1978, n.d.; Whyte, *Eagles*, 18–21; "I always understood deterrence to be the primary role," Petter-Bowyer, personal communications, 21 June 2002.

12. AFZ, *AF81*, 1.

13. The pre-Federal air force contributed to Empire and Commonwealth defense with fighters and bombers under the control of the Royal Air Force, a system that saw personnel used interchangeably throughout rather than as separate formations and was similar to the Royal Navy scheme. This model continued through the Federal period with the development of a more balanced force by the time of UDI. One training document stated the roles of the air force were "a. Defense against external attack in any form, b. Close support of the Rhodesian armed forces in the field, c. Support of the civil power in the maintenance of internal security and law and order;" Roles of the RRAF, Its Aircraft and Weapons, n.d., 1 (PMML).

14. Salt, *Pride*, viii.

15. Nesbit, Cowderoy & Thomas, *Rebel Air Force*, passim.

16. Petter-Bowyer noted that "This may have been so before 1973 but thereafter the air force was in direct support." Petter-Bowyer, personal communications, 21 June 2002.

17. Peter I. Wilkins, *Chopper Pilot* (Nelspruit: Freeworld Publications, 2000), 59; Abdul S. Minty, *Fire Force Exposed* (London: Anti-Apartheid Movement, 1979), 27; For example, one pilot did some 24 tours in the bush ranging from one week to three months (on the average of three to six weeks in length) flying 1,000 hours on Alouettes and another 300 on Pumas. South Africa's security arrangements found him employed almost continuously in operational flying starting in 1966, first deploying on "bush trips" to Portuguese Angola and then Rhodesia with the mainstay of the counterinsurgency effort, the Alouette III. This was an effortless move to support other countries, the police, and navy that might teach "jointness" to more rigid institutions.

18. Service staff included: Air branch—meteorology, public relations, photography, research, physical fitness; technical branch—aeronautical inspection; administrative branch—public works, motor transport, fire services, statistics, legal, provost, chaplain, accounting, catering, medical, educational, postal, dental, and movement.

19. Geldenhuys, Nickel Cross, 56.

20. Marine Corps Schools, Present Organization of a Typical RAF Command Headquarters, 1957; Whyte, *Eagles*, 95–104; Career Opportunities in the Rhodesian Air Force, n.d.; Air Force Careers, n.d. (PMML).

21. Whyte, *Eagles*, 91–3.

22. Newnham, personal communication 2 September 2002.

23. Whyte, *Eagles*, 31–2, 49–51.

24. Whyte, *Eagles*, 61–7; AFZ, *AF81* 27; Beverley Whyte, "Strike From Above," *Fighting Forces of Rhodesia*, (3) 1976, 59–65; *Bataleur*, April 1977, 2.

25. Peter R. Briscoe, Third World Air Power in Relation to COIN Operations, RAF Staff College, 19; Salt, *Pride*, 422

26. Petter-Bowyer, personal communications, 21 June 2002.

27. Peter Petter-Bowyer commented, "Like all our forces, we did not really know our enemy. What should have been known at every level was withheld by our intelligence agencies. The 'need to know' syndrome was, in my opinion, often counter-productive." Petter-Bowyer, personal communications, 21 June 2002.

28. Whyte, *Eagles*, 32.

29. Briscoe, COIN, 17–18.

30. Brand, personal communications, 24 August 2002.

31. Francis Tusa, "Out of Isolation," *Armed Forces Journal*, April 1994, 42–3.

32. *Bataleur*, December 1976, 2.

33. AFZ, *AF81*, 4–5, 18–19.
34. Briscoe, COIN, 18.
35. Minty, *Fire Force*, 30–1.
36. Briscoe, COIN, 18.
37. Sally Brown, "Successful Anti-Insurgency Operations [Fire Force Bravo]," *Fighting Forces of Rhodesia*, (5) 1978, 4–5; The air force could move to any location in Rhodesia with a suitable runway and have a fully operational airfield and support base established within 24 hours, "everything in fact, from portable toilets to knives and forks." Whyte, *Eagles*, 19.
38. Briscoe, COIN, 18.
39. Petter-Bowyer, personal communications, 21 June 2002.
40. Grand Reef was attacked in force on 17 December 1977. Salt, *Pride*, 601–3.
41. Whyte, *Eagles*, 73–81.
42. Paintin, personal communications, 7 June 2002.
43. Minty, *Fire Force*, 46–9.
44. Geldenhuys, Nickel Cross, 179ff for Operation *Hottentot*; see also Operations *Polo* and *Sand*, 193, 266–7.
45. Briscoe, COIN, 12.
46. Briscoe, COIN, 1.
47. Briscoe, COIN, 7.
48. Briscoe, COIN, 7.
49. Mienie, personal communications, 20 August 2002.
50. Salt, *Pride*, 405.
51. Briscoe, COIN, 12.
52. Minty, *Fire Force*, 46–9; AMNorman Walsh quoted by Wood, personal communication, 3 April 2002.
53. Nesbit, Cowderoy & Thomas, *Rebel Air Force*, 56ff.
54. Squadron mottos were used in the sections on aircraft types.
55. For example, UH-1, AH-1, OV-10, Pucara, A-10, DHC-5 Buffalo, C-160, C-130, CASA C-202 were all mentioned as preferred substitutes for existing aircraft used.
56. On 1 July 1975, the air force's strength was given as 11 Hunters, 21 Vampires (13 trainers), 11 Dakotas (4 VIP passenger), 7 Provosts, 7 Trojans, 8 Canberras (2 photo reconnaissance), 20 helicopters (2 gunships) for 85 aircraft of all types and 92 pilots including volunteer reserve; JP/205 dated 5 August 1975, Annex A, Aircraft and Aircrew Availability, 1–6 (RAA).
57. "Radius of action is calculated on fuel load plus weapons load and is the distance the aircraft can fly to a target and return to base. Normally 10 minutes is allowed in or over the target area unless otherwise stated;" JPS, Memorandum to OCC: Security Forces Offensive Capabilities in the event of a Hostile Mocambique, 5 August 1975, Annex A–C (RAA); AFZ, *AF81*; and Roles of the RRAF (PMML).
58. Canberras planned on reaching a target at 5 miles per minute, accelerating to 6.7 miles per minute for low-level delivery of bouncing bombs for "air bursts." This was limited, because of the stress placed on frame 21 and the wing roots, "which bore the high loads in turbulent flight situations." Petter-Bowyer, personal communications, 21 June 2002.
59. Robert Jackson, *Canberra: The Operational Log* (Washington, DC: Smithsonian Institution, 1989), 102–6; AFZ, *AF81*, 12–13; Winston A. Brent, *Rhodesian Air Force: The Sanctions Busters* (Nelspruit: Freeworld Publications, 2002), 13–23.
60. Robert Jackson, *Hawker Hunter: The Operational Record* (Washington, DC: Smithsonian Institution, 1989), 140–3; AFZ, *AF81*, 20–1; Brent, *RhAF*, 13–23.
61. AFZ, *AF81*, 22–3; Brent, *RhAF*, 13–23.

62. AFZ, *AF81*, 14–15; Brent, *RhAF*, 13–23, 145–6, 151–2; Geldenhuys, Nickel Cross, 266; Wilkins, *Chopper Pilot*, Annexure, 144–52, lists some nine Alouette IIIs and one Puma as being shot down or written off in operations in Rhodesia by the South African Air Force.

63. AFZ, *AF81*, 16–17; Brent, *RhAF*, 13–23.

64. Paintin, personal communications, 7 June 2002.

65. Fairey, personal communications, 2 July 2002.

66. "Cessna 337 Lynx, Rhodesian Operations," War Zone: Africa, *Air Warfare*, n.d., 1681–5; AFZ, *AF81*, 10–11; Brent, *RhAF*, 13–23.

67. Fairey, personal communications, 2 July 2002.

68. Different models of this aircraft were apparently used by both 2 and 6 Squadrons; AFZ, *AF81*, 24–5; Brent, *RhAF*, 13–23.

69. AFZ, *AF81*, 8–9; *Rhodesia Regiment Pocket Book*, B1–B17; Brent, *RhAF*, 13–23.

70. Tasks included low-level flying, message dropping, aerial reconnaissance, search and rescue, liaison with ground personnel, courier duties, conversion courses, and training personnel for the above. By 1976, this included some 85 aircraft flown by 92 PRAW pilots. JPS, Air Support, annex 2 (RAA).

71. JPS, Non Offensive Air Support for Rhodesian Army, 16 December 1976, 1 (RAA); Graffiti at FAF 8 observed by Wood, personal communications, 13 August 2001.

72. JPS, Non Offensive Air Support for Rhodesian Army, 16 December 1976, passim (RAA); Briscoe, COIN, 11.

73. Both Rhodesians and South Africans used British airborne procedures. Specific techniques were from the Royal Air Force's *Parachute Training Manual* and South African Army's *Manual for Parachute Jumping Instructors*.

74. PTS, operational procedures, New Sarum, 4 (HQMC).

75. Salt, *Pride*, 434, 586–587, 614, 923, 925; Paul Moorcraft, *Contact II* (Johannesburg: Sygma Books, 1981), 181; Helen Treloar, "The Parachute Training School, *Fighting Forces of Zimbabwe-Rhodesia*, (6) 1979, 48–50; Archer B. Campling, "A Brief History of Parachuting in the Rhodesian Army," *Lion & Tusk*, October 1999, 16–25.

76. Salt, *Pride*, 586–7. Also "They're 'Chuting High," *Illustrated Life Rhodesia*, 22 July 1976, 86–9; "Para School," *Focus on Rhodesia*, vol. 2, no. 9, 3.

77. These were thought to provide an aiming point for ground fire; but according to Flt Lt John Fairey, "Roundels and fins flashes were not removed because they could be used as an aiming point, it was never a problem in World War II." Fairey, personal communications, 2 July 2002.

78. Bruce Robertson, et al., *Aircraft Markings of the World, 1912–1967* (Letchworth: Harleyford, 1967), 74–5, 128.

79. Wilkins, *Chopper Pilot*, 59.

80. Fairey, personal communications, 2 July 2002.

81. Paintin, personal communications, 19 June 2002.

82. Mark E. Dawson, interview by Ian J. Johnstone, 1 November 1983, Oral 232, 12 (NAZ).

83. Fairey, personal communications, 2 July 2002.

84. RSF, COIN (ii), 15-3–15-4.

85. Briscoe, 9–10.

86. Petter-Bowyer, personal communications, 21 June 2002.

87. Martin S. Hatfield, interview by Ian J. Johnstone, n.d. (NAZ).

88. Cronin, personal communications, 14 April 2000.

89. Armor added to the Alouette reduced its ability to carry five troops to four. Armor for the already overloaded Lynx did not progress beyond a trial installation.

90. Fairey, personal communications, 2 July 2002.

91. Geldenhuys, Nickel Cross, 249, 325; Salt, *Pride*, 493–4; RhAF, The Tactical Avoidance of Strela, April 1975 (RAA); Cronin, personal communications, 14 April 2000.
92. Briscoe, COIN, 10.
93. Petter-Bowyer, personal communications, 21 June 2001.
94. Salt, *Pride*, 611.
95. Fairey, personal communications, 2 July 2002.
96. Geldenhuys, Nickel Cross, 372; see Operation *Tepid*.
97. Briscoe, COIN, 9.
98. Salt, *Pride*, 658.
99. Fairey, personal communications, 2 July 2002.
100. Brand, personal communications, 24 August 2002.
101. Rhodesian expression used to explain why the guerrillas did something that did not seem to make sense or was counterproductive, like jumping up and down on a landmine while laying it.
102. Moorcraft & McLaughlin, *Chimurenga*, 121; Salt, *Pride*, 658.
103. Briscoe, COIN, 3.
104. Whyte, *Eagles*, 21.
105. JPS, An Analysis of Past Counter Insurgency Operations in Rhodesia: Terrorist Tactics, 28 January 1971, Chapter 8 (RAA).
106. MID, Terrorist Tactics, 29 March 1977, 6 (RAA); RIC, 1Bde, Operation Repulse: Captured ZANLA Ters, 22 March 1977, 5–6 (RAA); MID, CT Tactics, 21 June 1978, 3 (RAA); BSAP, Basic Terrorist Tactics: Op Hurricane, 5–6 (PMML).
107. Firing vertically in front of an approaching aircraft was a standard communist tactic used in Korea, Malaya, and elsewhere, "It was not frightening or distracting unless the aircraft was hit. Otherwise one did not know what was happening." Fairey, personal communications, 2 July 2002.
108. RIC, 1Bde, Operation Repulse: Captured ZANLA Ters, 22 March 1977, 5–6 (RAA).
109. Les Payne, "Report from Zimbabwe-Rhodesia: U.S. Built Planes Leading Attack," *Newsday*, 13 July 1979, n.p.
110. JPS, An Analysis of Past Counter Insurgency Operations in Rhodesian: Terrorist Tactics, 28 January 1971, Chapter 8 (RAA).
111. W. N. B. Jackson, "Some Problems of Being a Freedom Fighter," *British Army Review*, April 1987, 38.
112. ZANU, Headquarters of Security and Intelligence Department, ZANLA Headquarters Chimoio, Security and Intelligence Opinion on How Best We Can Organize Our Forces and Build Our Defense Works so as to Encounter Stereoscopic Warfare, 29 August 1978, manuscript 536/7/3 (NAZ).
113. Martin Gutu, manuscript 591/4. (NAZ)
114. Gutu (NAZ).
115. Minty, *Fire Force*, 26.
116. Stan Monick, "The Rhodesian Air Force 1935–1980," *ISSUP Contemporary Air Strategy Studies*, April 1986, 53–90.

Chapter 4

1. Whyte, *Eagles*, 5.
2. Briscoe, COIN, 3.
3. Briscoe, COIN, 21.
4. Briscoe, COIN, 3.
5. Geldenhuys, Nickel Cross, 106.

6. Briscoe, COIN, 2–12.
7. By mid-war, the air force addressed "land/air operations" in terms of capabilities rather than missions: the need for combat, reconnaissance, transport, and utility efforts. This indicated a more flexible approach and sophistication to support based on experience; RSF, *COIN* (ii), 15-1–15-36.
8. Colin Black, "Wings Guard Our Country," *Fighting Forces of Rhodesia*, (1) 1974, 29.
9. Geldenhuys, Nickel Cross, 106.
10. Briscoe, COIN, 3.
11. Wood felt that the air force preferred the tactical headquarters in lieu of the joint operations center as it gave a degree of autonomy from the army and police. Wood, personal communications, n.d.
12. JPS, Past Operations, II, Chp 3, Sec 1, 1 (RAA).
13. AirHQ, Policy Directive on the Employment of the New FFU Organization, 18 December 1975 (RAA).
14. RA, MCP, 12-1–12-16; as early as 1967, some 159 pages of material were devoted to standardized procedures for the use air support; this doctrine continued in RSF, COIN (ii), 15-1ff which paraphrased the RhAF's *Air Support Procedures Manual.*
15. AHQ, Air Parts: ISOPS (SR Code 0104), 4 March 1965, passim (RAA).
16. AHQ, Air Parts: ISOPS (SR Code 0104), 4 March 1965, Chp XII, passim (RAA).
17. RSF, COIN (ii), 15-1ff.
18. RSF, COIN (ii), 4–12.
19. Rhodesian Information Service, *Pride of Eagles* film, n.d. (Rhodesian Forces Two).
20. JPS, Analysis, Chp 3, Sec 2, 1 (RAA).
21. RSF, COIN (ii), 1–5.
22. Minty, *Fire Force*, 27.
23. Whyte, *Eagles*, 5.
24. *Assegai*, December 1976, 39.
25. Briscoe, COIN, i.
26. RA, MCP, 12–12-2.
27. RSF, COIN (ii), 15–19.
28. A local brewing company canned water for delivery in the field.
29. JPS, Analysis, Chp 3, Sec 5, 1 (RAA).
30. Salt, *Pride*, 486.
31. Whyte, *Eagles*, 37.
32. Briscoe, COIN, 9.
33. Wilkins, *Chopper Pilot*, 56.
34. Salt, *Pride*, 556–7.
35. Salt, Pride, 530.
36. Whyte, *Eagles*, 55; Beverley Whyte, "Casualty Evacuation," *Fighting Forces of Rhodesia*, (3) 1976, 77–9; Between 1963 and 1973, some 500 medical evacuations were conducted by both rotary- and fixed-wing aircraft. Salt, *Pride*, 484.
37. *Assegai*, December 1976, 39; enemy casualties were moved before friendly wounded and dead, but guerrilla dead were recovered only if convenient or necessary for identification. JPS, Analysis, Chp 3, Sec 6, 1 (RAA).
38. Salt, *Pride*, 400.
39. In fact, fuel staged throughout the country was used to extend the helicopter range and later the Dakotas carried pre-rigged fuel drums on pallets for emergencies. At first a hand pump was needed to manually refuel from 44-gallon drums, but modification to the Alouette provided a self-contained pressure refueling system. Instead of 15 minutes a drum, this system could refuel in three and a half minutes. Salt, *Pride*, 404.

40. Mienie, personal communications, 20 August 2002.
41. Dawson interview, 8–9 (NAZ).
42. Whyte, *Eagles*, 83.
43. See also Cowderoy, Nesbit & Thomas, *Rebel Air Force*, 43.
44. *Bateleur*, April 1977, 2.
45. This involved the air force and police in an action that precipitated the evolution of the joint operations system and the recognition that policemen alone were not adequate for combat roles; and was distributed by then Major John S. V. Hickman with G(Ops); AHQ, Incident at Sinoia, 29 April 1966, 17 May 1966 (RAA).
46. AHQ, Incident at Sinoia, 29 April 1966, 17 May 1966, passim (RAA).
47. The terms evolved for ease in radio communications and were based in part on television and popular usage of "Zed" car and "Bee" car for police vehicles. Other references used "T" for troop ship, "G" for gun ship, and "C" for command ship. Petter-Bowyer, personal communications, 21 June 2002.
48. The numbers of aircraft and crews from Portuguese and South African sources is hard to determine, but were never enough for increasing needs.
49. Wilkins, *Chopper Pilot*, 100.
50. Tusa, "Isolation," *Armed Forces Journal*, 42–3.
51. Operation Parker dealt with helicopter support to special forces. Geldenhuys, Nickel Cross, 287–8.
52. Briscoe, COIN, 6.
53. "Cessna 337," *Air Warfare*, 1681–865.
54. Fairey, personal communications, 2 July 2002.
55. Petter-Bowyer, Winds of Destruction, 313, 333, 371–2.
56. Salt, *Pride*, 421.
57. On a single sortie, aircrews could find themselves tasked in combination to conduct radio relay, top cover, armed reconnaissance, casualty evacuation, resupply, flare, courier, and airborne "stop-line" flights.
58. Whyte, *Eagles*, 43.
59. Wilkins, *Chopper Pilot*, 56.
60. Whyte, *Eagles*, 43.
61. RA, MCP, 12-2.
62. "This small unit was commanded by an air force officer, Flight Lieutenant Bill Buckle, with an army lieutenant as his assistant. Most interpreters on the staff were females in service with [the] air force or army. I cannot recall the entire staff running to more than eight people, six of whom were females;" Petter-Bowyer, personal communications, 15 July 2002.
63. "By the time JPS gave way to ComOps, all our internal and external mapping was already of a high order," according to Petter-Bowyer. For example, a JPS effort to secure mapping of Mozambique from the Portuguese, which in turn was updated by the Rhodesian Government Surveyor General with fresh aerial photography; Petter-Bowyer, personal communications, 15 July 2002.
64. Jackson, *Canberra*, 102–6; Jackson, *Hawker Hunter*, 140–3; AFZ, *AF81*, 12–13, 20–1; Brent, *RhAF*, 13–23.
65. Petter-Bowyer, personal communications, 15 July 2002.
66. Salt, *Pride*, 407.
67. Geldenhuys, Nickel Cross, 259–260; note the aerial reconnaissance missions by this one pilot over a two-and-one-half–year period.
68. Briscoe, COIN, 6.
69. Petter-Bowyer, Winds of Destruction, 226–7.
70. Mienie, personal communications, 20 August 2002.

71. Petter-Bowyer, personal communications, 21 June 2002.

72. Paintin, personal communications, 7 June 2002.

73. Wilkins, *Chopper Pilot*, 91.

74. Petter-Bowyer, personal communications, 21 June 2002.

75. Briscoe, COIN, 8.

76. Geldenhuys, Nickel Cross, 362; Cowderoy, Nesbit & Thomas, *Rebel Air Force*, 78ff.

77. Fairey, "Op Uric," *Lion & Tusk*, July 1991, n.p.

78. Cowderoy, Nesbit & Thomas, *Rebel Air Force*, 79ff.

79. Fairey, "Op Uric," *Lion & Tusk*, July 1991, n.p.

80. RA, MCP, 12-2.

81. Briscoe, COIN, 6–7.

82. Briscoe, COIN, 5.

83. Briscoe, COIN, 5–6.

84. Wilkins, *Chopper Pilot*, 104.

85. Briscoe, COIN, 12–13; quoting Frank Kitson, *Bunch of Fives* (London: Faber & Faber, 1967), 147.

86. "Cessna 337," *Air Warfare*, 1681–5.

87. For an account of a PRAW search and rescue mission, see "Valley of the Shadow," *Outpost* (Cape Town: Books of Africa, 1970), 265–70.

88. Gibbs & Phillips, *BSAP*, 318.

89. Gibbs & Phillips, *BSAP*, 318–21.

90. RA, MCP, 12-2.

91. Briscoe, COIN, 8–9; JPS, Analysis, Chp 3, Sec 2, 1 (RAA).

92. Flower, *Secretly*, 107; Salt, *Pride*, 400–3.

93. Petter-Bowyer, personal communications, 21 June 2002.

94. The fighter-trained pilots subscribed to Wing Cdr A. G. "Sailor" Malan's 10 rules from World War II; Geldenhuys, Nickel Cross, 100–1.

95. Whyte, "From Above," *Fighting Forces of Rhodesia*, 59–65.

96. AHQ, Air Parts: ISOPS (SR Code 0104), 4 March 1965, Chp XII, Sec 2 (RAA).

97. Whyte, *Eagles*, 25, 47.

98. Petter-Bowyer, personal communications, 21 June 2002.

99. For example, references cited the Hunter with some 26 variations of ordnance, listing four 30mm guns and 12 to 16 rockets as "normal" with fuel drop tanks in place.

100. Whyte, *Eagles*, 47.

101. Salt, *Pride*, 561–2.

102. JPS, Analysis, Chp 3, Sec 2, 1–3 (RAA). Procedures remained under review and occasional reminders were needed, such as that subsequent corrections for airstrikes were based on the direction the aircraft was flying rather than the observer, but that the strike aircraft should try to overfly the ground observer en route to the target to make the effort easy for all concerned; AirHQ message, 21 June 1978 (RAA).

103. RSF, COIN (ii), 15-6.

104. Salt, *Pride*, 628.

105. RSF, COIN (ii), 15-7.

106. Salt, *Pride*, 621.

107. Briscoe, COIN, 10.

108. The Lynx was preferred in this role rather than the later arriving SF260 Genet. Perhaps because dual-seating the trainer would degrade its focus and training was still a vital part of the total effort; Briscoe, COIN, 11.

109. Petter-Bowyer, personal communications, 21 June 2002.

110. RSF, COIN (ii), 15-7–15-8.

111. JPS, Past Operations, Pt II, Chp 3, Sec 2, 2 (RAA).

112. Briscoe, 11; "Cessna 337," *Air Warfare*, 1681–865.

113. A useful summary of aircraft ordnance configuration is given in JP/205, 5 August 1975, The Offensive Capability of the Rhodesian Air Force to Strike at Targets in Mocambique [Mozambique], Annex A (RAA).

114. Petter-Bowyer, personal communications, 21 June 2002.

115. Aeronautical and Chemical Divisions, CSIR.

116. Petter-Bowyer, Winds of Destruction, 300–8, 326–31, 340–2, 364–6, 369–71, 371–5, 483–5.

117. The Rhodesians considered the use of fixed-wing gunships to counter infiltration by guerrillas, similar to the Americans in Vietnam; Cronin, personal communications, 14 April 2000. But the air force did not have the aircraft available and one 3 Squadron pilot commented "I do not think the idea of using a Dakota as gunships was ever seriously considered" as transports were in short supply; Fairey, personal communications, 2 July 2002.

118. Wood, personal communications, 14 November 2000; Cronin, personal communications, 31 March 1996.

119. "Cessna 337," *Air Warfare*, 1681–865.

120. Geldenhuys, Nickel Cross, 249–50; Salt, *Pride*, 492–3.

121. Petter-Bowyer, personal communications, 21 June 2002.

122. Salt, *Pride*, 541–3.

123. Petter-Bowyer, personal communications, 21 June 2002; Jackson, *Hawker Hunter*, 143; Salt, *Pride*, 653.

124. Petter-Bowyer, personal communications, 21 June 2002.

125. "Cessna 337," *Air Warfare*, 1681–865; Salt, *Pride*, 606–7, 624–6.

126. Brand, personal communications, 24 August 2002.

127. RhAF airstrike report forms (AF 1621) were filled out for missions similar to the police and army's contact reports and actions could be covered by all three. This eight-page document was forwarded to the AirHQ via the chain of command (RAA).

128. Extracts of comments by air staff on strike reports, c. 1974 (RAA); Preller Geldenhuys, *Rhodesian Air Force Operations Strike Log* (Durban: Just Done Publishing, 2007).

129. "The air force was strongly opposed to arming PRAW aircraft because no police pilot had … been subjected to the demands and disciplines considered essential to avoid errors and misuse of air power. In spite of objections, some PRAW pilots illegally acquired weapons." Petter-Bowyer, personal communications, 21 June 2002.

130. Arnold Woolley quoted by Wood, personal communications, 2 April 2001.

131. Dawson interview, 12 (NAZ).

132. Dawson interview, 12 (NAZ).

133. Paintin, personal communications, 7 June 2002.

Chapter 5

1. JOC Hurricane, SitRep No. 1, 21–22 December 1972 (RAA); Reid-Daly, "War in Rhodesia" in *Challenge*, 164–5.

2. Sabre Land Rovers continued to be used by the SAS until the mine threat caused them to be replaced by specialized mine- and ambush-proofed vehicles.

3. Formation Order Number 5: Rhodesian Corps of Infantry, 28 August 1978, 8–10 (RAA).

4. Rhodesian-born Hickman served in Malaya where he earned a Military Cross. He was an original thinker who played a part in the development of counterinsurgency tactics, techniques, and

procedures from the beginning. He remained in Zimbabwe after independence. A son, Richard J. S. Hickman, died serving in the SAS.

5. Reid-Daly, "War in Rhodesia" in *Challenge*, 165.
6. Reid-Daly, "War in Rhodesia" in *Challenge*, 164–5; Cole, *Pictorial*, 48–9.
7. Cole, *Pictorial*, 50–56.
8. Robinson, personal communications, 2 April 2003.
9. Barrett, personal communications, 21 August 2003.
10. Barrett, personal communications, 2 June 2003.
11. John A. Coey, "Counter Insurgency Patrol," *Assegai*, June 1974, 9–11; John A. Coey, *A Martyr Speaks* (Fletcher: New Puritan Library, 1988), 135–46.
12. Coey, "Patrol," *Assegai*, 10.
13. Coey, "Patrol," *Assegai*, 9.
14. Coey, "Patrol," *Assegai*, 10.
15. Cole, *Pictorial*, vi–vii, 15, 20, 30–3, 42–7, 50–6. SAS, operational procedure notes, Kabrit, n.d. (HQMC).
16. Barrett, personal communications, 21 August 2003.
17. Coey, "Patrol," *Assegai*, 11.
18. Whyte, "Tough Guys," *Illustrated Life Rhodesia*, 11.
19. Army Career Office, *You're Someone Special in the S.A.S.*, "Recruits Life," n.d. (PMML).
20. Army Careers Office, *You're Someone Special in the S.A.S.*, "Recruits Life," n.d. (PMML).
21. Gale, "Those Who Dare," *Fighting Forces of Rhodesia*, 41.
22. MacKenzie, Rhodesian SAS, SOF, 17.
23. Cole, *Pictorial*, 19.
24. Barrett, personal communications, 21 August 2003.
25. The SAS disagreed, "because in the dark even a white man is black;" Barrett, personal communications, 21 August 2003.
26. Savory memorandum to AHQ, (GSO I) dated 17 October 1967; AHQ, GSO (Ops) 1/37 and responses dated 22 December 1967, 15 January 1968 (RAA).
27. DirCIO, memorandum dated April 1974 in Flower, *Secretly*, 300–2; John P. Cann, *Counterinsurgency in Africa* (Westport: Greenwood Press, 1997), 101–2; "Mozambique: The White Devil of Niassa," *Newsweek*, 14 January 1974, 15–16; S. S. Nielsen, "The White Devil of Mozambique," *SOF*, October 1979, 78–83, 87.
28. Flower, *Secretly*, 115, 123–5; Stiff, *Selous Scouts*, 48–56.
29. Reid-Daly, "War in Rhodesia" in *Challenge*, 164–6.
30. Geraghty, *SAS*, 228.
31. Stiff, *Selous Scouts*, 60–1; Flower, *Secretly*, 124–5. See also Ellert, *Rhodesian Front War*, 93–123; Cilliers, *Counterinsurgency in Rhodesia*, 118–34.
32. Named formally in October 1974, though a Federal army armored car unit had the same title. African soldiers had difficulty pronouncing "Selous Scouts" and reduced this to "Selousie."
33. Stiff, *Selous Scouts*, 60–1.
34. SD Instruction 2: Order of Seniority, 26 February 1979; SD Instruction 9: Formation and Location Statements, 28 August 1978; Selous Scouts, 2 (RAA).
35. Rhodesian Information Service, *Pamwe Chete* film, n.d. (Rhodesian Forces One).
36. Scott-Donelan, personal communications, 16 March 1990.
37. "The Men Who Hunt Down Terrorists," *Focus on Rhodesia*, vol. 2, no. 3, 2.
38. A commander, political cadre, security cadre, logistics cadre, medical cadre, and five others armed with seven rifles, a light machine gun, mortar, and grenade launcher.
39. Eventually officer ranks were expanded to include to Africans. Despite this, and national service, there was not an influx of personnel.

40. The distribution of Selous Scouts "02" situation reports was tightly controlled by their Special Branch representatives.

41. Cronin felt 200 was more realistic, with two operational groups always being deployed. The 420 deployed strength cited by Cilliers and RAND was the most accurate total figure seen according to him, although up to 700 had been cited; John R. Cronin, Counterinsurgency in Rhodesia, Society for Military History, paper, Roslyn, VA, 1996, 14; Cronin, personal communications, 1 June 1992.

42. Stiff, *Selous Scouts*, 116; Reid-Daly, *Pamwe Chete*, 52–4, 490–500, 502–80.

43. Ellert, *Rhodesian Front War*, 101–2.

44. Ellert, *Rhodesian Front War*, 100.

45. Selous Scouts, operational procedure notes, Inkomo, n.d. (HQMC).

46. An American serving in Rhodesia stated in a four-year period some 1,200 terrorists were eliminated for the loss of 10 Selous Scouts. Vietnam veteran Travis Tucker went on to quip, "these guys are the best when it comes to the bush … If you sent 10 Marines into the Zambezi Valley against 10 Selous Scouts, you'd end up with 10 dead Marines;" *The Washington Post*, 19 April 1977, A17.

47. Cilliers, *Counterinsurgency in Rhodesia*, 124.

48. Robert K. Brown and Jay Mallin, "Capt John Early," *SOF*, December 1979, 86–7.

49. Brown & Mallin, "John Early," *SOF*, 86–7. Events of February 1978 in the Wankie area. This technique was used by the Selous Scouts and Special Branch with some success, but this meant the technique became known and incidents decreased. Variations are described in Poos and Gaudet.

50. Cronin, a graduate of the Citadel and former U.S. Marine, served with the RLI and Selous Scouts up to the rank of captain. At the time he arrived in Rhodesia, he was not aware of the SAS or its activities. He is currently a college professor living in the United States.

51. SD Instruction 2: Order of Seniority, 26 February 1979; SD Instruction 9: Formation and Location Statements, 28 August 1978 (RAA); Grey's Scouts manuscript, 6 (PMML). See Alexandre Binda, *The Equus Men* (Solihull: Helion & Co., 2016).

52. Formation Order Number 5: Rhodesian Corps of Infantry, 28 August 1978, 8–10 (RAA).

53. Cronin, personal communications, 17 June, 1992.

54. J. R. T. Wood, There Was Never Enough Intelligence, paper, Society for Military History, Roslyn, VA, 1996, 12.

55. Wood, Never Enough Intelligence, SMH, 12.

56. Peter Stiff, *Taming the Landmine* (Alberton: Galago Publishing, 1986); EngD, An Analysis of Mine Incidents Encountered in Zimbabwe-Rhodesia During 1979, March 1980; Terrorist Mines and Explosives Encountered in Rhodesia, n.d.; Mine Position Indicators and Terrorist Tactics Associated with Mine Warfare, n.d.; Col I. R. Stansfield, A Paper on Mine Protection of Military Vehicles, n.d. (PMML).

57. "The Army's Fighting Vehicles," *Assegai*, February 1980, 5–13. Hoffman, Arnold & Taw, *Rhodesian Experience*, Appendix B, "Mine Countermeasures," 62–76; Don Blevin, Strange Beasts: The Evolution and Use of Rhodesian Mine and Ambush Protected Vehicles manuscript (PMML).

58. SADF, Rhodesian Minefield Devices, n.d. (PMML).

59. Briscoe, COIN, 13.

60. Reid-Daly, *Pamwe Chete*, 158ff.

61. Venter & Walls, *SOF*, 22–3.

62. Roger Marston, "Resettlement as a Counter-Revolutionary Technique," *RUSI Journal*, December 1979, 46–50.

63. Venter & Walls, *SOF*, 23.

64. AHQ, The Guard Force: A Study, 1975; SFAHQ, Security Force Auxiliaries, September 1979 (PMML).

65. Parliamentary Debates, 2 July 1976.
66. Unless otherwise cited, used were AHQ, Psychological Warfare, August 1966; RSF, *COIN Manual: Psychological Action*, July 1975; JPS/OCC Memorandum on a National Surrender Policy, 4 October 1976; SBHQ, Psychological Action, 30 June 1977; SBHQ, Reward Policy, 23 September 1977; GP, Rewards, November 1974; SFHQ, Amnesty Directorate, Amnesty Policy, Safe Return Policy, Amnesty, 1979 (PMML); Herbert A. Friedman, "Rhodesia Psyop, 1965–1980," www.psywar.org, accessed 3 October 2008.
67. Venter & Walls, *SOF*, 27.
68. Unless otherwise cited, used were Catholic Commission for Justice and Peace in Rhodesia (London: CIIR); *The Man in the Middle* (1975); *Civil War in Rhodesia* (1976); *Rhodesia the Propaganda War* (1977); *Rhodesia at War* (1979) (PMML).
69. Venter & Walls, *SOF*, 27.
70. Unless otherwise cited, used were JPS, Command and Control of Rhodesian Security Forces at National Level, 30 November 1976; JPS, Command and Control of Rhodesian Security Forces at National Level, 1 December 1976; JPS/OCC, Report on Current Security Force Counter-Insurgency Operations, 28 December 1976; JPS, Consolidated Replies by Air Force, Army, and Police Headquarters to JPS Paper, 21 January 1977; JPS/OCC, Report on Current Security Forces Counter-Insurgency Operations, 21 January 1977 (RAA).
71. Form RA/G/25 contact report; RIC Research Report No. 30, Contact Report Index and Basic Data, 31 December 1978 (RAA).
72. RIC No. 30, 3–4; In 1978; total security force strength was listed as 19,765 in comparison to a ZIPRA/ZANLA guerrilla strength of 15,375 (RAA).
73. RIC No. 16/2, 11 August 1978, 6, 15–19; database of 272 actions, figures rounded up to whole numbers (RAA).
74. Robinson, personal communications, 12 September 2002.
75. Innovations included the use of pseudo and, motorcycle, and mounted forces; JPS, Memorandum to Commanders, 29 July 1975 (RAA).
76. Briscoe, COIN, 13.
77. Reid-Daly, *Pamwe Chete*, 85.
78. Salt, *Pride*, 484; Petter-Bowyer, Winds of War, 314.
79. RSF, COIN (ii), 15-13–15-16.
80. Ron Reid-Daly, "Fire Forces, General Observations," in J. R. T. Wood, ed., *The War Diaries of André Dennison* (Gibraltar: Ashanti Publishing, 1989), 373.
81. Robinson, personal communications, 5 June 2002.
82. "Cessna 337," *Air Warfare*, 1681–1685.
83. Wood, a senior history lecturer at the University of Durban-Westville, was a Rhodesia Regiment territorial and Rhodesian Intelligence Corps reservist. One project was to analyze the impact of helicopter reactions forces on the course of the war.
84. In 1976, twin .303 Browning Mk 2s replaced the flexible 7.62mm MAG on the Alouette troopships and in 1978 a quad-gun fit was used as a gunship supplement; Wood, personal communications, 14 November 2000.
85. See J. R. T. Wood, *Counter-Strike from the Sky* (Johannesburg: 30 Degree South Publishers, 2009); also the video *Counter-Strike from the Sky* (30 Degrees South Production, 2009).
86. RSF, COIN (ii), 15-13.
87. Reid-Daly, *Pamwe Chete*, 279ff.
88. RSF, COIN (ii), 15-13.
89. Brown, "Succesful Anti-Insurgency," *Fighting Forces of Rhodesia*, 4–13.
90. RSF, COIN (ii), 4-12–4-13.

91. The RLI pushed for independent parachute deployments after integration with Fire Force, to include the possibility of using paratroopers to relieve farms under attack at night. AHQ, PTS comment on Para Fire Force Deployment, 23 June 1977 (RAA).

92. The SADF provided parachute training from 1974 to augment the more limited Rhodesian parachute facilities and eventually fielded their own Fire Force in the Beitbridge–Messina area beginning in 1978. The SADF used Aloutte gunships, Puma troopships, and Dakota parachute transports with Parachute Brigade personnel ("Parabats") manning reaction forces and Reconnaissance Commandos ("Recces") serving with the Rhodesian special forces, primarily the SAS.

93. J. R. T. Wood, "Fire Force," *Military Illustrated*, MI/72, 21–4; A Fire Force Action manuscript, n.d.; and Fire Force manuscript, n.d.

94. ComOps, Rationalization of Fire Forces/Strike Force, 5 January 1978; ComOps, Command and Control: Fire Forces, 3 February 1978; 13 March 1978; 28 April 1978 (RAA).

95. ComOps, Record of a Meeting on Fire Force Tactics, 18 May 1978. Also see RIC, Research Report 16, 9 May 1978; Research Report 16/2, 11 August 1978; Research Report 30, 31 March 1979. The Detailed Index–Contact Reports, and Additional Coding of Fire Force both indicated the statistics used by the Automatic Data Processing Unit and the Rhodesian Intelligence Corps to reach a variety of conclusions at the request of Army Headquarters (RAA).

96. So-called Fire Force Zulu, operating from Buffalo Range as part of Operation *Bowler*, 1979–80. See Mathew Paul, *Parabat* (Weltevreden Park: Covos Day Books, 2001); Paul Els, *We Fear Naught but God* (Weltevreden Park: Covos Day Books, 2000); Wilkins, *Chopper Pilot*, 104.

97. Briscoe, COIN, 15.

98. Reid-Daly, *Pamwe Chete*, 366ff.

99. Reid-Daly, "Fire Forces" in Wood, *War Diaries*, 376–7.

100. Wood, "Fire Force," *Military Illustrated*, 21–4; Fire Force Action; Fire Force.

101. LaDuke, personal communications, 30 September 2002, 21 October 2001.

Chapter 6

1. "Best Genre on Rhodesia Bush War," *The Citizen*, 17 March 1997; members.tripod.com, accessed 8 May 2001.

2. See video *Frontline Rhodesia* (30 Degrees South Productions, n.d.); for the evocative 1979 BBC/Channel 4 documentary by Nick Downie and Richard Cecil.

3. Cronin, personal communications, 14 April 2000.

4. Downie, "Rhodesia," 343.

5. Pat Lawless, "Fire Force Operations in Rhodesia," *Army Air Corps Journal*, (11) 1985, 8–11; events of 1977–80.

6. RSF, COIN (ii), 15-13–15-19.

7. RSF, COIN (ii), 15-13; RIC, Research Report 16, 9 May 1978; Research Report 16/2, 11 August 1978; Research Report 30, 31 March 1979 (RAA).

8. "Cessna 337," *Air Warfare*, 1681–5.

9. RIC, Research Report 30, 31 March 1979, 12, 14–15 (RAA).

10. Thomas Arbuckle, "Rhodesian Bush War," *RUSI Journal*, December 1979, 27–31.

11. Lt Pat Lawless' Fire Force Operation, June 1990, interview by Donald Blevin, n.p.; events of November 1979 (PMML).

12. John W. Coleman, "Five AK Rounds," *SOF*, February 1983, 38; events of October 1977.

13. Frank Terrell, "Fireforce Ops with the Rhodesian Light Infantry," *C&S*, June 1989, 36–44; events of 1978–9.

14. The Rhodesian Intelligence Corps noted that paratroops and Dakotas were present in 64 percent of the Fire Force incidents; RIC, Research Report 3, 31 March 1979, 12 (RAA); Reid-Daly, *Pamwe Chete*, 172.
15. Robinson, personal communications, 24 May 2002.
16. AHQ, PTS Comments on Para Fire Force Deployment, 23 June 1977, 2–3 (RAA).
17. RSF, COIN (ii), 15-15–15-16.
18. 3Cdo RLI, Para Fire Force Deployments, 25 May 1977, appendix B (RAA).
19. AHQ, PTS comments on Para Fire Force Deployment, 23 June 1977, 2–3 (RAA).
20. Coleman, "Five AK Rounds," *SOF*, February 1983, 38; events of October 1977.
21. John W. Coleman, "LALO Jump," *SOF*, January 1984, 39; events of August 1978.
22. LaDuke, personal communications, 21 October 2001.
23. "Guerrilla Contact in the Bush War," *C&S*, (22) 1991, 1270, 1276.
24. "Counter-Terrorist Airborne Attack," *C&S*, (8) 1991, 436.
25. "The Encounter or the Day in the Life of an RAR Soldier," *Lion & Tusk*, March 1990, n.p.; events of 1976.
26. Lawless's Fire Force Operation, n.p.; events of November 1979.
27. Briscoe, COIN, 13.
28. Briscoe, COIN, 14.
29. RSF, COIN (ii), 15-13.
30. Lawless, "Fire Force," *AAC Journal*, 10; events of 1977–9.
31. Lawless, "Fire Force," *AAC Journal*, 10; events of 1977–9.
32. Scouts also collected the cash reward for terrorist kills or captures while the regular security forces did not.
33. Briscoe, 13.
34. Coleman, "Five AK Rounds," *SOF*, February 1983, 39; events of October 1977.
35. Coleman, "LALO Jump," *SOF*, January 1984, 39; events of August 1978.
36. Naturalists from the Parks Service serving with the Rhodesian Intelligence Corps considered the guerrillas to be "riparian creatures" following the water drainage system; Wood, personal communications, 29 October–7 November 2000.
37. Experience from the 1976–8 period when Lt Cronin served as a Fire Force commander in absence of his commanding officer, Maj Jeremy T. Strong (Strong had gone to parachute training in South Africa and was injured, Cronin was the unit's second-in-command); Cronin, personal communications, 14 April 2000.
38. ComOps, Record of a Meeting on Fire Force Tactics, 18 May 1978, 2–3 (RAA); for a pilot's viewpoint see Wilkins, *Chopper Pilot*, 82–3.
39. Briscoe, COIN, 16; et al.
40. Referencing RIC Research Report Number 30, 17 March 1979 (RAA).
41. ComOps, Rationalization of Fire Forces/Strike Force, 5 January 1978, passim; ComOps, Command and Control: Fire Forces, 3 February 1978, 13 March 1978 (RAA).
42. RSF, COIN (ii), 15-13.
43. Peter Younghusband, Kim Willenson, and Francois Darquennes, "Tea and Terrorists," *Newsweek*, 8 May 1978, 52–3; events of May 1978.
44. Frank Terrell, "RLI Fire Force," *The Elite*, (113) 1985, 160–6; events of June 1979.
45. ComOps, Record of a Meeting on Fire Force Tactics, 18 May 1978, 3 (RAA).
46. OP Aide Memoire; see also *COIN* manual or *Rhodesia Regiment Pocket Book* (PMML).
47. A noisy light aircraft could be used to fly over and mask the sound of approaching helicopters; top cover could also be flown if a prolonged search was involved and could facilitate communications as a relay. RSF, COIN (ii), 15-15.

48. RSF, COIN (ii), 15-13–15-14.
49. Lawless, "Fire Force," *AAC Journal*, 11; events of 1977–9.
50. Dick Pitman, *You Must be New Around Here* (Bulawayo: Books of Rhodesia, 1979), 180; events of October 1978.
51. Hornet One [Peter R. Briscoe], "Day of the Hornet," *SOF*, September 1989, 63; events of August 1979.
52. Terrell, "Fire Force," *The Elite*, 160–6; events of June 1979.
53. Robinson, personal communications, 24 May 2002.
54. "Before boarding, the 'gypsies warning' would be given that the green light constitutes an order to jump. Anyone failing to do so would be subject to court martial. In the event of a light failure you are to take your orders from the parachute jumping instructor. Any questions?;" Robinson, personal communications, 24 May 2002.
55. Robinson, personal communications, 24 May 2002.
56. Coleman, "LALO Jump," *SOF*, events of August 1978.
57. During 1978–9 three combat jumps a day were logged by 1Cdo, RLI; PTS, operational procedures, New Sarum, 3–5 (HQMC).
58. Pitman, *You Must be New Around Here*, 180–1.
59. "The Encounter," *Lion & Tusk*, n.p.; events of 1976.
60. Robinson, personal communications, 4 June 2002.
61. Quoted in Nesbit, Cowderoy & Thomas, *Rebel Air Force*, 43; events of March 1976.
62. "Cessna 337," *Air Warfare*, 1681–5.
63. Wood, personal communications, 6 June 2002.
64. Wilkins, *Chopper Pilot*, 82–3.
65. Mienie, personal communications, 20 August 2002.
66. Wood, personal communications, n.d.
67. "Airborne Attack," *C&S*, 436.
68. Robinson, personal communications, 24 May 2002.
69. Lawless's Fire Force Operation, n.p.; events of November 1979.
70. Briscoe, COIN, 14–15.
71. Briscoe, COIN, 15.
72. "Helicopter Engagement with Terrorists," *C&S*, (21) 1991, 1210; events of April 1976.
73. Cronin, personal communications, 14 April 2000; LaDuke, personal communications, 21 October 2001; Coleman, "LALO Jump," *SOF*, 38–9.
74. William Norris, "Fireforce Commandos," *SOF*, November 1987, 65–6; events of 1978–9.
75. Terrell, "Fire Force," *The Elite*, 160–6; events of June 1979.
76. Cronin, personal communications, 14 April 2000.
77. Robinson, personal communications, 24 May 2002.
78. Cronin, personal communications, 14 April 2000.
79. Robinson, personal communications, 24 May 2002.
80. Caffin, personal communications, 6 June 2002.
81. Briscoe, COIN, 15.
82. Cronin, personal communications, 14 April 2000.
83. LaDuke, personal communications, 30 September 2001.
84. Norris, "Fireforce Commandos," *SOF*, 66, events of 1978–9.
85. Caffin, personal communications, 6 June 2002.
86. Cronin, personal communications, 14 April 2000.
87. Terrell, "Fireforce Ops," *C&S* 38; events of 1978–1979.

88. Robinson, personal communications, 24 May 2002.
89. Norris, "Fireforce Commandos," *SOF*, November 1987, 64–5; events of 1978–1979.
90. Briscoe, personal communications, 30 May 1990.
91. "Guerrilla Contact," *C&S*, 1270, 1276.
92. "Airborne Attack," *C&S*, 436.
93. "Cessna 337," *Air Warfare*, 1681–5.
94. Wilkins, *Chopper Pilot*, 81–2; events of September 1975.
95. Anthony Rogers, *Someone Else's War* (London: Harper Collins, 1998), 46; events of 1978–9.
96. Norris, "Fireforce Commandos," SOF, 66; events of 1978–9.
97. "Hunting the Terrorist," *C&S*, (6) 1991, 357; events of 1979.
98. Downie, "Rhodesia," 343; events in 1978.
99. Robert Young Pelton, *The Hunter, the Hammer, and Heaven* (Guilford: Lyons Press, 2002), 92–3.
100. LaDuke, personal communications, 21 October 2001.
101. Quoted in Rogers, *Someone Else's War*, 62–3; events of December 1978.
102. Quoted in Rogers, *Someone Else's War*, 62; events of December 1978.
103. Support Cdo, RLI, under command of Maj Nigel Henson, killed or captured 165 insurgents in April and May 1979, for a cost of four killed and several wounded or injured. By December 1979 this was a record total of 470 insurgents of the RLI's 1,680 tally; Al J. Venter, ed., *The Chopper Boys: Helicopter Warfare in Africa* (London: Greenhill Books, 1994), 110–22.
104. Rogers, *Someone Else's War*, 63–5; events of April 1979.
105. "Fire Force Mission," *C&S*, (4) 1991, 190; events of March 1979.
106. Rogers, *Someone Else's War*, 65; events of April 1979.
107. Eventually the SAS was asked to come in, as they had night vision devices that the RLI lacked, and near midnight SAS Lt Robert C. MacKenzie confirmed the guerrillas were gone.
108. Coey, *A Martyr Speaks*, 227–30; events of July 1975.
109. Robinson, personal communications, 12 September 2002.
110. Rogers, *Someone Else's War*, 60–3; events of December 1978.
111. Rogers, *Someone Else's War*, 60–3; events of December 1978.
112. Rogers, *Someone Else's War*, 64–5; events of April 1979.
113. Although basic military training had included house and street fighting, cave clearing was not anticipated or covered; J. R. T. Wood, "Cave Clearing in the Rhodesian Bush War," *Lion & Tusk*, March 2003, 16–27.
114. Rogers, *Someone Else's War*, 60; events of December 1977.
115. Lawless's Fire Force Operation, n.p.; events of November 1979.
116. Venter, *Chopper Boys*, 110–22.
117. Cronin, personal communications, 14 April 2000.
118. Robinson, personal communications, 4 June 2002.
119. Norris, "Fireforce Commandos," *SOF*, November 1987, 64–5; events of 1978–9.
120. Coleman, "LALO Jump," *SOF*, 38; events of August 1978.
121. Coleman, "Five AK Rounds," *SOF*, February 1983, 39; events of October 1977.
122. LaDuke, personal communications, 21 October 2001.
123. Reid-Daly, "Fire Forces" in Wood, *War Diaries*, 376; Reid-Daly, *Pamwe Chete*, 366ff.
124. Briscoe, COIN, 15.
125. "Cessna 337," *Air Warfare*, 1681–5.
126. Lawless, "Fire Force," *AAC Journal*, 11; events of 1977–9.
127. RSF, COIN (ii), 15-15.
128. Rogers, *Someone Else's War*, 60; events of December 1978.

129. ComOps, Record of Meeting on Fire Force Tactics, 18 May 1978, 2 (RAA).

130. Lt Cronin was called over to 2 Group (the group he later served with) fort and was counseled on patience, being known as "Lieutenant Lighting" for not remaining around long enough for results. Cronin, personal communications, 14 April, 2000; LaDuke felt, "The RAR were good fighters, but they probably got their kills because they could interface with the locals better and the locals did not like most of the terrs. But they were not comfortable with the white soldier either." LaDuke, personal communications, 21 October 2001.

131. Both moved ahead between 1977 to 1979, with A Coy, 2RAR achieving 403 kills between September 1977 and July 1979 and Support Cdo, RLI obtaining 470 kills alone in 1979 in somewhat different circumstances; Wood, personal communication, n.d.

132. Annotation on RIC Research Report Number 16, 9 May 1978 (RAA).

133. Robinson, personal communications, 12 September 2002.

134. RSF, COIN (ii), 15-15.

135. David W. Arnold interview, RAND Corporation Rhodesia manuscript, 1989, 236 (PMML).

136. According to an RLI trooper, "Sometimes we would do our own observation post–listening post work because the police and reserves were so inept at it. When we did, we got massive kills because we were good at it;" LaDuke, personal communications, 21 October 2001.

137. "The SAS killed 108 terrorists in a nine-year period in Malaya. ... We of Fire Force killed 1,690 terrorists in nine months, 187 times the British SAS monthly kill rate! ... For the 1,690 terrorists killed in nine months mentioned at the beginning, all 1 RLI commandos lost 24 men total. That is a 70-to-1 kill ratio;" LaDuke, personal communications, 30 September 2001.

138. LaDuke, personal communications, 21 October 2001.

139. Terrell, "Fire Force," The Elite, 160–6; events of June 1979.

140. Salt, Pride, 604–5; events of January 1978.

141. "The Encounter," Lion & Tusk, n.p.; events of 1976.

142. "Airborne Attack," C&S, 436.

143. "Helicopter Engagement," C&S, 1210; events of April 1976.

144. Younghusband, Willenson & Darquennes, "Tea and Terrorists," 53; events of May 1978.

145. Norris, "Fireforce Commandos," SOF, 67; events of 1978–9.

146. Results attributed in part to the use of ill-trained Mashona auxiliaries in a Matabele area; LaDuke, personal communications, 24 October 2001.

147. Coey, Martyr Speaks, 224; events of July 1975.

148. Norris, "Fireforce Commandos," SOF, 67; events of 1978–9.

149. Reid-Daly comments in ComOps, Record of Meeting on Fire Force Tactics, 18 May 1978, 2 (RAA); RSF, COIN (ii), 15-14–15-15.

150. Jackson, "Freedom Fighter," 38.

151. As oddly reported, including with acronyms: "During a recent FF [Fire Force] callout an SF [security force] group engaged in a sweep found a naked AFA [African female adult] sitting in a tree. The AFA stated she was engaged in conversation with a CT [communist terrorist] when the Fire Force arrived on scene. CT then instructed her to remove her clothes which the CT then donned. The transvestite CT then made good his escape." Combined Operations warned, "All JOCs are advised to be on the alert for possible transvestite CTs [communist terrorists];" Message G/4/6 G13, dated 22 June 1978 (RAA).

152. Maj Jeremy T. Strong and Flt Lt Michael Borlace watched a guerrilla launch a rocket-propelled grenade that passed through the Alouette propeller arc, with the comment of "Oh shit!" coming over the tactical net; Cronin, personal communications, 14 April 2000.

153. RSF, COIN (ii), 15-15.

154. Reid-Daly, "Fire Forces" in War Diaries, 375.

155. Petter-Bowyer, Winds of Destruction, 366–7.
156. LaDuke, personal communications, 30 September 2001.

Chapter 7

1. RIC, Rpt No 30, 31 December 1978, Appendix I, CT Sectors (RAA); guerrilla infiltration routes in Cilliers, 38, and Moorcraft & McLaughlin, 74–5.

Unless otherwise cited, used were JPS, Memorandum to the OCC: Security Force Offensive Capability in the Event of a Hostile Mocombique [sic], 5 August 1975; JPS, National Operational Plan Memo, 26 November 1975; JPS, Termination of Operation Hurricane, 1 December 1975 [declare war and go home memo]; JPS, National Operational Plan Redraft, 4 December 1975; JPS, Changes to JPS Establishment, 8 December 1975; JOC Hurricane, Standing Down Operation Hurricane, 18 December 1975; JPS, Notes of Action: Visit by JPS to JOC Hurricane, 24 December 1975; OCC, Notes on Civil Activities During Widespread Operations, 24 December 1975; OCC, Urban Terrorism, 29 December 1975 (RAA).

2. RAND subject matter expert Arnold was the cousin of historian Wood. Hoffman, Arnold & Taw, *Rhodesian Experience*, 77–92, Appendix C, "Cross Border Raids," 77–92 with maps; also Arnold, RAND Rhodesia draft manuscript as expanded by RAA/BECM index and Wood's named operations listing (PMML).

3. Some of these were listed by codenames, others used a physical location. The RAND study grouped operations geographically by Rhodesian unit involved, while examined here in their chronological sequence.

4. Hoffman, Arnold & Taw, *Rhodesian Experience*, 77–92; Reid-Daly, *Pamwe Chete*, 99–102; Stiff & Reid-Daly, *Top Secret War*, 98–101.

5. A Sandhurst graduate, Barrett joined the SAS in 1970 as a captain, serving as a section, troop, and squadron second-in-command and acting commander before going to staff college and other postings in 1974, including brigade major. He returned as SAS regimental commander in 1978 through the war's end. He lives in the United States.

6. Barrett, personal communications, 21 August 2003.

7. Hoffman, et al, *Rhodesian Experience*, 77–92; Cole, *Elite*, 66–77; Cole, *Pictorial*, 70–1.

8. Hoffman, Arnold & Taw, *Rhodesian Experience*, 77–92; Reid-Daly, *Pamwe Chete*, 123–125; Stiff & Reid-Daly, *Top Secret War*, 117–19.

9. Hoffman, Arnold & Taw, *Rhodesian Experience*, 77–92; Reid-Daly, *Pamwe Chete*, 144–6; Stiff & Reid-Daly, *Top Secret War*, 133–4.

10. Reid-Daly, "War in Rhodesia" in *Challenge*, 169.

11. JP/205, 5 August 1975, Annex B and C (RAA).

12. "It is not possible for SAS troops to 'live off the land' in the strictest sense. Under normal circumstances the acquisition of food from the local population presents unwarranted risk of compromise … planning consideration must therefore be given to fairly regular resupply;" JP/205, 5 August 1975, Annex B, B3 (RAA).

13. "Parachutes are normally considered expendable during operations. Aircraft can best effect quick extraction e.g.: light aircraft or helicopter although the availability of suitable landing strips and the operating range of applicable aircraft are limiting factors. Troops can of course march out to safe areas;" JP/205, 5 August 1975, Annex B, B3 (RAA).

14. Considered "unsophisticated specialist operations;" JP/205, 5 August 1975, Annex C, C1 (RAA).

15. JP/205, 5 August 1975, Annex C, C1–C2 (RAA).

16. Barrett, personal communications, 21 August 2003.

17. Hoffman, Arnold & Taw, *Rhodesian Experience*, 77–92; Reid-Daly, *Pamwe Chete*, 176–7; Stiff & Reid-Daly, *Top Secret War*, 157; Stiff, *Selous Scouts*, 85.

18. Hoffman, Arnold & Taw, *Rhodesian Experience*, 77–92; Reid-Daly, *Pamwe Chete*, 183–5; Stiff & Reid-Daly, *Top Secret War*, 162–4.

19. Hoffman, Arnold & Taw, *Rhodesian Experience*, 77–92; Reid-Daly, *Pamwe Chete*, 187–8; Stiff & Reid-Daly, *Top Secret War*, 165–6.

20. Cronin, personal communications, 4 September 1993.

21. Hoffman, Arnold & Taw, *Rhodesian Experience*, 77–92; Reid-Daly, *Pamwe Chete*, 191–202; Stiff & Reid-Daly, *Top Secret War*, 169, 178; Stiff, *Selous Scouts*, 88.

22. Reid-Daly, "War in Rhodesia" in *Challenge*, 169–70.

23. Hoffman, Arnold & Taw, *Rhodesian Experience*, 77–92; Reid-Daly, *Pamwe Chete*, 202–47; Stiff & Reid-Daly, *Top Secret War*, 178–222; Stiff, *Selous Scouts*, 92; Salt, *Eagles*, 543–5.

24. David Martin and Phyllis Johnson, *The Struggle for Zimbabwe* (New York: Monthly Review Press, 1981), 246–7.

25. Reid-Daly, "War in Rhodesia" in *Challenge*, 170.

26. Wood, personal communications, 17 November 2003.

27. Hoffman, Arnold & Taw, *Rhodesian Experience*, 77–92; Cole, *Elite*, 111; Reid-Daly, *Pamwe Chete*, 258–68; Stiff & Reid-Daly, *Top Secret War*, 231–9; Stiff, *Selous Scouts*, 100; Salt, *Eagle*, 544–6.

28. Hoffman, et al, *Rhodesian Experience*, 77–92; Reid-Daly, *Pamwe Chete*, 268–72; Stiff & Reid-Daly, *Top Secret War*, 239–44; Stiff, *Selous Scouts*, 102.

29. Venter & Walls, *Vorster*, 362.

30. Venter & Walls, *SOF*, 20–9; Venter & Walls, *Vorster*, 348–62.

31. Venter & Walls, *Vorster*, 361.

32. Venter & Walls, *SOF*, 20–9.

33. Venter & Walls, *Vorster*, 360.

34. Venter & Walls, *Vorster*, 353–4.

35. Hoffman, Arnold & Taw, *Rhodesian Experience*, 77–92; Cole, *Elite*, 116–29; Cole, *Pictorial*, 75–82; Barbara Cole, "Cockleshell Heroes," *SOF*, March 1986, 74–7, 107.

36. Unless otherwise cited, used were AHQ, Miltary Strategy Within the Rhodesian Context, 18 July 1977; MI/106, External Operations in Mozambique, August 1977; ComOps, Internal Strategy, 13 March 1979; ComOps, National Strategy Guidelines for Zimbabwe-Rhodesia for the Period of the First Government or Five Years, 22 March 1979; ComOps, Higher Defence Operation, 10 April 1979; ComOps, Short Term Strategy Directive, 12 April 1979; ComOps, Internal Strategy, 19 April 1979; R & A Team, Draft Aide Memoire for Prime Minister of Zimbabwe-Rhodesia (ZR): Total National Strategy, July 1979; Vital Ground and Key Areas, 1980 Election, n.d. (RAA).

37. Barrett, personal communications, 21 August 2003.

38. Reid-Daly, "War in Rhodesia" in *Challenge*, 172.

39. Robinson, personal communications, 2 April 2003.

40. Robinson, personal communications, 2 April 2003; Barrett, personal communications, 2 June 2003.

41. Barrett, personal communications, 2 June 2003.

42. Geraghty, *SAS*, 226–7.

43. While the SAS used a unique communications code system, reports were sent to CIO, ComOps, DMI, and DAI. This was stopped in 1978 and replaced by a daily briefing at Combined Operations headquarters to restrict information. Barrett, personal communications, 2 June 2003.

44. Chris Vermaak, "Rhodesia's Selous Scouts," *Armed Forces*, May 1977, n.p.

45. Vermaak, "Selous Scouts," *Armed Forces*, n.p.

46. "The Men Who Hunt Down Terrorists," *Focus on Rhodesia*, vol. 2, no. 3, n.d., 2–3; "Selous Scouts," *Assegai*, April 1977, 21–4; Vermaak, "Selous Scouts," *Armed Forces*, n.p.

47. Vermaak, "Selous Scouts," *Armed Forces*, n.p.; "Men Who Hunt Down Terrorists," *Focus on Rhodesia*, 3.
48. Hoffman, Arnold & Taw, *Rhodesian Experience*, 77–92; Salt, *Eagles*, 568.
49. Hoffman, Arnold & Taw, *Rhodesian Experience*, 77–92; Reid-Daly, *Pamwe Chete*, 302–12; Stiff & Reid-Daly, *Top Secret War*, 274–80; Stiff, *Selous Scouts*, 108; Salt, *Eagles*, 578–81.
50. Hoffman, Arnold & Taw, *Rhodesian Experience*, 77–92.
51. Cole, *Pictorial*, 13; as well recruiting literature and training film.
52. Cole, *Pictorial*, vi.
53. Barrett, personal communications, 21 August 2003.
54. Hoffman, Arnold & Taw, *Rhodesian Experience*, 77–92.
55. Operation Dingo Order for Security Forces Assault on ZANLA Forces Base Camp at Chimoio, Mocambique in Chris Cocks, *Fireforce* (Weltevreden: Covos Day Books, 1997), 265–88.
56. Geraghty, *SAS*, 227.
57. No African troops were deployed to avoid any "friendly fire" mistakes.
58. Hoffman, Arnold & Taw, *Rhodesian Experience*, 77–92; Cole, *Elite*, 169–89; Robert MacKenzie, "Fast Strike on Chimoio," *SOF*, January 1994, 40–8, 83–4; February 1994, 44–7, 71–82; Salt, *Eagles*, 593–8.
59. Reid-Daly, "War in Rhodesia" in *Challenge*, 171–2; J. R. T. Wood, *Counter-Strike*, 123ff; J. R. T. Wood, Operation Dingo, Airborne Assault in Mozambique, 23–27 November 1977 manuscript (PMML).
60. Wood, personal communications, 16 October 2000.
61. Robinson, personal communications, 5 June 2002.
62. Robinson, personal communications, 2 April 2003.
63. Robinson, personal communications, 14 April 2003.
64. Barrett, personal communications, 21 August 2003.
65. Geraghty, *SAS*, 226.
66. Pomeroy, personal communications, 29 December 1997.
67. This was subject to debate, as postwar accounts indicate the South Africans continued Operation *Polo* after August 1976 with Rhodesian uniforms and markings.
68. Brown & Mallin, "John Early: Rhodesian Adventures," *Merc*, 173–5.
69. Brown & Mallin, "John Early: Rhodesian Adventures," *Merc*, 173–5.
70. De Kock, OCPTS, comments memorandum, 20 June 1977, 2 (RAA).
71. Notes on Basic Pathfinder Technique, Appendix C to letter dated 25 May 1977 (RAA).
72. "In the past the SAS have had extreme difficulty in carrying out RV [rendezvous] procedures at night." De Kock, OCPTS, comments memorandum, 20 June 1977, 2 (RAA); Parachute Training School, operational procedure notes, New Sarum, n.d. (HQMC).
73. Hoffman, Arnold & Taw , *Rhodesian Experience*, 77–92; Cole, *Elite*, 205–217.
74. Hoffman, Arnold & Taw , *Rhodesian Experience*, 77–92.
75. The extent of guerrilla infiltration is reflected in the extended mining of roads throughout the country; EngD, An Analysis of Mine Incidents in Zimbabwe-Rhodesia During 1979, Total Mine Incidents, 8 (PMML).
76. Hoffman, Arnold & Taw, *Rhodesian Experience*, 77–92.
77. Those who had previously served with the SAS remained on the rolls and continued to receive special pay if qualified. They were recalled for operations as reinforcements. The "old and the bold" also provided security for administrative bases in enemy territory as "they were trusted." Barrett, personal communications, 21 August 2003.
78. Barrett, personal communications, 21 August 2003.
79. Robert MacKenzie, "Lengthening the Reach," *SOF*, February 1994, 82.
80. Pomeroy, personal communications, 6 April 1993.
81. Barrett, personal communications, 21 August 2003, 2 May 2003.

82. Cole, *Pictorial*, 54.
83. Barrett, personal communications, 21 August 2003.
84. MacKenzie, "Lengthening the Reach," *SOF*, 82.
85. Barrett, personal communications, 21 August 2003.
86. Barrett, personal communications, 2 June 2003.
87. Cronin, Rhodesian Counterinsurgency, SMH, 6–8.
88. Reid-Daly, "War in Rhodesia" in *Challenge*, 172.
89. Heppenstall, personal communications, 14 October 2000; Barrett, personal communications, 21 August 2003.
90. Formation Order Number 4: Headquarters Special Forces, 28 August 1978 (RAA).
91. Cilliers, *Counterinsurgency in Rhodesia*, 196.
92. Operations other than those considered by RAND were indicated by asterisks (*); Salt, *Eagles*, 621.
93. Hoffman, Arnold & Taw, *Rhodesian Experience*, 77–92; Cole, *Elite*, 224–32; Salt, *Eagles*, 626–63.
94. Salt, *Eagles*, 643.
95. Hoffman, Arnold & Taw, *Rhodesian Experience*, 77–92; Reid-Daly, *Pamwe Chete*, 367–72; Stiff & Reid-Daly, *Top Secret War*, 331–6; Stiff, *Selous Scouts*, 136–9; Salt, *Eagles*, 643.
96. Hoffman, Arnold & Taw, *Rhodesian Experience*, 77–92; Cole, *Elite*, 239–41.
97. Hoffman, Arnold & Taw, *Rhodesian Experience*, 77–92; Cole, *Elite*, 232–7.
98. Hoffman, Arnold & Taw, *Rhodesian Experience*, 77–92.
99. Hoffman, Arnold & Taw, *Rhodesian Experience*, 77–92; Reid-Daly, *Pamwe Chete*, 412–23; Stiff & Reid-Daly, *Top Secret War*, 369–85; Stiff, *Selous Scouts*, 150.
100. Hoffman, Arnold & Taw, *Rhodesian Experience*, 77–92 with map. Petter-Bowyer, Winds of Destruction, 472; Salt, *Pride*, 646–8; Cowderoy & Nesbit, *War in the Air*, 646–8; Cowderoy, Nesbit & Thomas, *Rebel Air Force*, 85–8; Salt, *Eagles*, 247–8.
101. Hoffman, Arnold & Taw, *Rhodesian Experience*, 77–92 with maps; Cole, *Elite*, 254–60; Salt, *Eagles*, 650–1.
102. Scott-Donelan, personal communications, 16 March 1990.
103. Reid-Daly, *Pamwe Chete*, 54, 466–7, 490–500; Julie Frederikse, *None But Ourselves* (Johannesburg: Raven Press, 1982), 368.
104. Binda, personal communications, 20 June 2003.
105. Cronin, Rhodesian Counterinsurgency, SMH, 14–15.
106. Petter-Bowyer, Winds of War, 472.
107. Hoffman, Arnold & Taw, *Rhodesian Experience*, 77–92; Robert MacKenzie, "The Big Bang," *SOF*, November 1994, 38–43, 71–94.
108. Salt, *Eagles*, 652–3.
109. Hoffman, Arnold & Taw, *Rhodesian Experience*, 77–92; Cole, *Elite*, 270–96; Cole, *Pictorial*, 107–14; Barbara Cole, "Storming the Bastille," *The Elite*, (49) 1986, 961–6; Reid-Daly, *Pamwe Chete*, 405; George Gordon, "Rhodesian SAS Tried to Kill Joshua Nkomo," *Daily Mail*, 27 May 1980, 20–1; Craig Roberts, "Killers," *Modern Warfare*, November 1989, 8, 56–62; Stiff, *See You in November*, passim.
110. Hoffman, Arnold & Taw, *Rhodesian Experience*, 77–92; Cole, *Elite*, 296–304; Cole, *Pictorial*, 115–17.
111. Hoffman, Arnold & Taw, *Rhodesian Experience*, 77–92; Cole, *Elite*, 305–23; Salt, *Eagles*, 655–7.
112. Hoffman, Arnold & Taw, *Rhodesian Experience*, 77–92; Cole, *Elite*, 323–6.
113. Stephen J. Stedman, The Lancaster House Conference on Rhodesia, Pew Case Studies in International Affairs, 1993.
114. Hoffman, Arnold & Taw, *Rhodesian Experience*, 77–92; Salt, *Eagles*, 258–61; Cole, *Elite*, 327–39, 357; Alex Binda, "Operation Uric, Gaza, Mocambique, 1–7 September 1979," *Lion & Tusk*,

February 1994, n.p.; "Operation Uric," letters, *Lion & Tusk*, September 1994, n.p.; J. R. T. Wood, Operation Uric manuscript, n.d. (PMML).

115. See Chapter Eight.
116. Hoffman, Arnold & Taw, *Rhodesian Experience*, 77–92; Cole, *Elite*, 339–46; Salt, *Eagles*, 661–2.
117. Hoffman, Arnold & Taw, *Rhodesian Experience*, 77–92.
118. Hoffman, Arnold & Taw, *Rhodesian Experience*, 77–92; Reid-Daly, *Pamwe Chete*, 434–47; Stiff & Reid-Daly, *Top Secret War*, 392–404; Stiff, *Selous Scouts*, 154; Salt, *Eagles*, 663–4).
119. Hoffman, Arnold & Taw, *Rhodesian Experience*, 77–92.
120. Hoffman, Arnold & Taw, *Rhodesian Experience*, 77–92; Cole, *Elite*, 358–73; Salt, *Eagles*, 265–6.
121. Hoffman, Arnold & Taw, *Rhodesian Experience*, 77–92; Cole, *Elite*, 378–93; Salt, *Eagles*, 667–8.
122. Salt, *Eagles*, 670.
123. Part of an extended area operation from 12 September to 26 December 1979; Hoffman, Arnold & Taw, *Rhodesian Experience*, 77–92; Cole, *Elite*, 393–412; Cole, *Pictorial*, 145–51; Stiff & Reid-Daly, *Top Secret War*, 404–20; Stiff, *Selous Scouts*, 162; Salt, *Eagles*, 670–1.
124. For example JOC Tangent consisted of the provinces of North and South Matabeleland.

Chapter 8

1. Cilliers, *Counterinsurgency in Rhodesia*, 205.
2. Reid-Daly, "War in Rhodesia" in *Challenge*, 174; SFAHQ, An Abridged History: Security Force Auxiliaries, n.p., n.d. (PMML); Ellert, *Rhodesian Front War*, 140–51; Cilliers, *Counterinsurgency in Rhodesia*, 202–17.
3. SFAHQ, Security Force Auxiliaries, 7 September 1979; SFAHQ, Administrative Instruction 3/79, 29 November 1979 (PMML).
4. Ken Flower, 1987 interview in "Mozambique," *Public Broadcasting System/WHUT Channel 32*, accessed 17 May 1989.
5. Flower, interview in "Mozambique."
6. Ellert, *Rhodesian Front War*, 69.
7. Jack Wheeler, "RENAMO," *SOF*, February 1986, 64; Paul L. Moorcraft, "The Savage Silent Civil War," *Army*, April 1987, 42–52; William Finnegan, *A Complicated War* (Berkeley: University of California Press, 1992); C. J. Jacobs, The Conflict Between South Africa and Mozambique, 1975–1989, paper, International Commission on Military History, Cape Town, RSA, 2007.
8. Hamann, *Generals*, 105.
9. Petter-Bowyer, Winds of Destruction, 466.
10. Pomeroy, personal communications, 6 April 1993.
11. Petter-Bowyer, Winds of Destruction, 466–7.
12. Other estimates put this at some 500 fighters with 2,000–3,000 camp followers. Reid-Daly, "War in Rhodesia" in *Challenge*, 175; Petter-Bowyer, Winds of Destruction ms, 465–7; Ellert, *Rhodesian Front War*, 54–79; Cilliers, *Counterinsurgency in Rhodesia*, 172–201; Hamann, *Generals*, 105–14.
13. Flower, interview in "Mozambique."
14. Again, as defined by the more doctrinaire South Africans. Substances, primarily toxic or narcotic, played a role in the "elimination" effort. Hamann, *Generals*, 141; Cole, *Pictorial*, 64–9.
15. Barrett, personal communications, 21 August 2003.
16. Cronin, personal communications, 17 September 1992.
17. An indicator was the small number of nationalist bodies relocated after the war for burial at national and local "Heroes Acres." During the conflict the BSAP recovered dead terrorists for identification with photographs, fingerprints, and weapons profiles. These were retained, then later buried, in mass graves near the joint headquarters often at the end of the airfields. Others were

reported as killed by the Selous Scouts to claim the reward bounty. Those that were not reported could have ended dumped in mine shafts. Ellert, *Rhodesian Front War*, 197–8; Scott-Donelan, personal communications, 16 March 1990.

18. Kenneth B. Brown, "Counter Guerrilla Operations: Does the Law of War Proscribe Success," *Naval Law Review*, (44) 1997, 123–73.

19. Elsewhere RAND has examined the problems in leadership targeting and assessing the consequences of these efforts to ensure unintended results are avoided.

20. Ellert, "Rhodesian Security and Intelligence," *Zimbabwe's Liberation War*, 103; Barrett, personal communications, 21 August 2003.

21. Of interest is that Rhodesian interviews with RAND did not mention leadership elimination, either because it fell outside of the military effort or because of continued sensitivity of the topic.

22. *The Washington Post*, 15 April 1979, n.p.

23. Hamann, *Generals*, 144–5.

24. Hamann, *Generals*, 144–6.

25. Robinson, personal communications, 19 May 2003; Barrett, personal communications, 21 August 2003.

26. Barrett, personal communications, 21 August 2003.

27. A discussion of more conventional means reflecting South African involvement is in Hamann, *Generals*, 139–59.

28. Innocent Chofamba-Sithole and Norman Mlambo, "Ex-Rhodesian under probe for US anthrax attacks," *The Sunday Mirror*, www.africaonline.co.zw, accessed 9 July 2002; Scott-Donelan, personal communications, 16 March 2004.

29. Scott-Donelan, personal communications, 16 March 1990; Crabtree, *Fourth Flag*, 252.

30. "Reconciliation or Chaos?," *Mother Jones*, June 1999, 52–7, 82–3.

31. Scott-Donelan, personal communications, 16 March 1990.

32. Milner, Rhodesian police, personal communications, 15 February 1990; Cronin, personal communications, 21 April 1998.

33. Some 10,738 human anthrax cases were reported in 1979/80 in Zimbabwe resulting in 182 deaths; Tom Mangold and Jeff Goldberg, *Plague Wars* (New York: St. Martin's Press, 1999), 214–24; Glenn A. Cross, *Dirty War: The Rhodesian Chemical and Biological Warfare Effort, 1975 to 1979*, dissertation, George Mason University, 2006; again as reflected through South African sources.

34. One result was that up until 1980, the South Africans maintained a chemical and biological capability. See Stephen Burgess and Helen Purkitt, *The Rollback of South Africa's Chemical and Biological Warfare Program* (Maxwell Air Force Base: USAF Counterproliferation Center, 2001), 4–16, 81, 85–7, 99–103.

35. Ellert, *Rhodesian Front War*, 80–92; Reid-Daly, "War in Rhodesia" in *Challenge*, 158–9; Hamann, *Generals*, 139–59, passim; Wood, Never Enough Intelligence, SMH, passim.

36. Hamann, *Generals*, 9.

37. Ellert, *Rhodesian Front War*, 90.

38. Cronin, Rhodesian Counterinsurgency, SMH, 6–8.

39. Binda, personal communications, 20 June 2003.

40. Melshen, Pseudo Operations, 38–9, in which he describes the Selous Scouts as a law unto themselves. This was a part of the US Naval War College Advanced Research Program. Melshen was in Rhodesia in 1979 with the auxiliaries.

41. Some questioned CIO's Flower and Branch One's Robinson's judgment and loyalty with the compromise of operations seemingly at the highest level. Communications security may have had problems in access and routing rather than interception. The counterargument was the intelligence services did not want to disrupt the known quantity of the nationalist leadership. In later years, Reid-Daly speculated this was an effort by Flower to get him and Walls out of the way before

a negotiated settlement could be reached; Reid-Daly, "War in Rhodesia" in *Challenge*, 173–4; Barrett, personal communications, 21 August 2003.

42. Ironically, Hickman was considered to be an innovative and "in touch" leader compared to others in the Rhodesian high command. Ron Reid-Daly, Selous Scouts regimental association newsletter 3/2006, Appendices A through M. (PMML)

43. Barrett, personal communications, 21 August 2003.

44. Petter-Bowyer, Winds of Destruction, 528–9. Edward Luttwak, *Coup d'Etat: A Practical Handbook* (Cambridge: Harvard University Press, 1979) provides broader insights. Another reference to the role of special forces in society is Eliot A. Cohen, *Elite Military Units in Modern Democracies* (Cambridge: Harvard CFIA, 1978).

45. SADF took personnel and records that allowed special operations to continue with former SAS and Selous Scout operators, but never truly accepted their service.

46. Walls to Thatcher, 1 March 1980; Carrington to Salisbury, 3 March 1980 (PMML); Richard Allport, "Operation Quartz: Rhodesia 1980," www.ourworld.compuserve.com, accessed 9 July 1997; MacKenzie, Rhodesian SAS, SOF, passim; Reid-Daly, "War in Rhodesia" in *Challenge*, 175–6; Ellert, *Rhodesian Front War*, 122–3, 153–4; Ellert, "Rhodesian Security and Intelligence," *Zimbabwe's Liberation War*, 101–3.

Conclusion

1. Harold D. Nelson, ed., *Zimbabwe: A Country Study* (Washington, DC: American University, 1983), 58; Cilliers, *Counterinsurgency in Rhodesia*, 241; Frederikse, *Ourselves Alone*, 345; Cronin and MacKenzie cited BSAP Special Branch sources for 40,000 killed (PMML).

2. Walter Walker, *The Bear at the Back Door* (Sandton: Valiant Publishers, 1978), 5.

3. John Keegan, ed., *World Armies* (New York: Facts on File, 1979), 588.

4. Moorcraft & McLaughlin, xii–xiii.

5. Bruce Hoffman, *British Air Power in Peripheral Conflicts, 1919–1976* (Santa Monica: RAND Corporation, 1989); James S. Corum, "The Myth of Air Control: Reassessing the RAFs Role in Imperial Policing in the Interwar Period" presents a differing view (Society for Military History, April 2000); James D. Corum and Wray R. Johnson, *Airpower in Small Wars* (Lawrence: University Press of Kansas, 2003).

6. John S. Pustay, *Counter-Insurgency Warfare* (New York: The Free Press, 1965), 116–35.

7. Special Air Warfare Tactics, USAF Manual 3–5, 1965.

8. Marine Aviation, US Marine Corps Command and Staff College, 1988.

9. Minty, *Fire Force*, 26.

10. RSF, COIN (ii), 15-5–15-6.

11. Monick, "Rhodesian Air Force," *ISSUP Contemporary Air Strategy Studies*, 53–90.

12. Petter-Bowyer, Winds of War, 520.

13. *Zimbabwe News*, vol. 11, no. 1, January–June 1979, n.p.

14. Sylvia Bond Smith, *Ginette* (Bulawayo: Black Eagle Press, 1980), 241.

15. Geldenhuys, Nickel Cross, 110.

16. *Financial Gazette*, 17 November 1978, n.p.

17. Alan Lindner quoted in Reid-Daly, *Pamwe Chete*, 365–7; Cilliers, *Counterinsurgency*, 207, 249–52.

18. Adm McRaven was a career naval special warfare officer, who later led both the U.S. Joint and Special Operations Commands. This was his thesis at the Naval Postgraduate School, Monterey, California. William H. McRaven, *Spec Ops* (Novato: Presidio Press, 1995), 2–3.

19. McRaven, *SpecOps*, 381–2.

20. McRaven, *SpecOps*, 1–27, 381–92.

21. MacKenzie, Rhodesian SAS, SOF, 4.
22. Barrett, personal communications, 21 August 2003.
23. Flower, *Secretly*, 114–15.
24. Melshen, Pseudo Operations, ii–iii.
25. Special unit allowance was paid to the RLI, SAS, and Selous Scouts at the rate of $51.93 a month in 1975 U.S. dollars. The SAS and Selous Scouts received an additional allowance of $1.38 a day. A bounty was also collected on kills and captures by the Scouts.
26. McRaven, *SpecOps*, 387.
27. Cole, *Pictorial*, vii.
28. Barrett, personal communications, 2 May 2003.
29. It also has a more esoteric counterproliferation role; See Special Operations in War and Peace, US Special Operations Command Publication 1, 25 January 1996.
30. Moorcraft, *Contact II*, 92, 104.
31. Stiff, *Selous Scouts*, 7; also Reid-Daly, *Pamwe Chete*, 489; a number that did not include "turned-terrorists."
32. Scott-Donelan, personal communications, 12 April 1990; The regimental standard migrated with a number of its members to South Africa but now resides with the Imperial War Museum in London. The uniform on exhibit wears rank insignia donated by the author to the Rhodesian Army Association.
33. Cole, *Pictorial*, vi.
34. 22SAS message dated 191005Z December 1980 (006) in Cole, *Pictorial*, 159.
35. Venter & Walls, *Vorster*, 352.
36. Glen St. J. Barclay, "Rhodesia's Hand-Picked Professionals," *SOF*, April 1984, 30–3.
37. Salt, *Pride*, 5.
38. *Bateleur*, April 1977, 2.
39. The development of successful Fire Force tactics raised the kill ratio up to 80 to 1; Wood, personal communications, n.d.
40. Quoted in Cowderoy, Nesbit & Thomas, *Rebel Air Force*, 44.
41. Greg Mills and Grahame Wilson, "Who Dares Loses? Assessing Rhodesia's Counter-Insurgency Experience," *RUSI Journal*, December 2007, 22–31.

Appendix 1

1. Order of Seniority and Re-naming of Army Units, 22 September 1980, Appendix Z to G (SD) 113 (RAA); Order of Seniority of Units for Correspondence, Signals and Distribution Lists, 19 October 1976, Appendix to SD Instruction 6 (RAA); AFZ, *AF81*; AHQ, The Guard Force, 1975 (PMML); SFAHQ, AdminInst 3/79, 29 November 1979 (PMML).

Appendix 2

1. RA, Military Symbols and Abbreviations, RhCodeNo 12, n.d.; SInf, Alphabetical Glossary of Abbreviations, n.d.; "A Story for the 'Ohns," *Assegai*, January 1970, 32; Keith Simpson, "Just Gonk this Lekker Lingo as Tuned by the 'Saintly' Owens," *Rhodesia Herald*, n.d., n.p.; these were just a start on the topic of jargon and acronyms.

Appendix 5

1. "The 7.62mm FN Light Automatic Rifle," BSAP, *Handbook of Information for the Guidance of the BSA Police Field Reserve* (Salisbury: GP,1974); D. A. Scott-Donelan, "The Armalite in Africa," *Assegai*, June 1973, 20–2; RA, *Skill at Arms, Training Record Book and Recruit Aide Memoire*; RA, *The 7.62mm FN Rifle and Bayonet* (Salisbury: GP, 1972); Fabrique Nationale, *FAL User's Manual*, n.d.; *This is Armscor*, n.d.; *Armscor*, n.d.; Arnold, Cronin, Scott-Donelan, and Wood, personal communicatons, various dates.

Bibliography

Archives & Collections

British Empire and Commonwealth Museum (BECM)
Flame Lily Association of South Africa (FLASA)
Headquarters, United States Marine Corps (HQUSMC)
Hoover Institution for War, Peace, and Revolution (HIWPR)
Library of Congress (LOC)
National Archives of Zimbabwe (NAZ)
Pritzker Military Museum and Library (PMML)
Rhodesian Army Association & Archive (RAA)
RAR Regimental Association (RAR Regt Assoc)
RLI Regimental Association (RLI Regt Assoc)

Personal Communications

Mark Adams. Rhodesian Army. Durban, RSA.
David W. Arnold. Rhodesian Police. Santa Monica, CA.
Mark Axworthy. Guard Force. UK.
Deane-Peter Baker. University of New South Wales/Australian Defense College. Canberra, AU.
Garth J. M. Barrett. Rhodesian Army. Charleston, SC.
Alexandre Binda. Rhodesian Army. London, UK.
Richard J. Brand. Rhodesian Air Force. UK.
Peter R. Briscoe. Rhodesian Air Force. Cypress, CA.
Kenneth B. Brown. Joint Special Operations Command. Fayetteville, NC.
James K. Bruton. U.S. Army. Tulsa, OK.
Harry F. Byrd. U.S. Senator. Washington, DC.
Jean-Michel Caffin. Rhodesian Army. Washington, DC.
John P. Cann. Marine Corps University. Quantico, VA.
M. J. Chinyanganya. Zimbabwean Army. ZW.
Jakkie Cilliers. South African Defense Force. RSA.
Chris M. Cocks. Rhodesian Army. Stroud, UK.
John W. Coleman. Rhodesian Army. Boulder, CO.
John R. Cronin. Rhodesian Army. Alexandria, VA.
Glenn A. Cross. George Mason University. Quantico, VA.
Peter Duignan. Hoover Institution. Stanford, CA.
Michael Evans. Deakin University, Australian Defense College. Canberra, AU.
John S. Fairey. Rhodesian Air Force. Bristol, UK.
Deon F. S. Fourie. University of South Africa (Pretoria). Cape Town, RSA.

Lewis H. Gann. Hoover Institution. Stanford, CA.
Donald R. Gardner. Marine Corps University. Quantico, VA.
Douglas Garret. Businessman. Washington, DC.
Preller M. Geldenhuys. Rhodesian Air Force. Durban, RSA.
Patrick Gericke. Rhodesian Army. Alexandria, VA.
Raffi Gregorian. Johns Hopkins University. Washington, DC.
F. G. D. Heppenstall. Rhodesian Army. London, UK.
Bruce Hoffman, RAND Corporation. Alexandria, VA.
Keith Holshausen. Zimbabwe Medal Society. Cary, NC.
John W. Hopkins. Rhodesian Army. Bristol, UK.
Hebert M. Howe. Georgetown University. Washington, DC.
Wray R. Johnson. Marine Corps University. Quantico, VA.
Ian J. Johnstone. Researcher. Harare, ZW.
Rob J. Johnstone. Rhodesian Army. Chimanimani, ZW.
Norma J. Kriger. Johns Hopkins University. Baltimore, MD.
John J. LaDuke. Rhodesian Army. Las Vegas, NV.
Patrick Lawless. Rhodesian Army. Bristol, UK.
Robert C. MacKenzie. Rhodesian Army. Seattle, WA.
Christopher A. Marquardt. St. Antony's College. Washington, DC.
Matthew C. Mason. U.S. Embassy. Harare, ZW.
Paul Melshen. Armed Forces Staff College. Norfolk, VA.
Jan W. Mienie. Rhodesian Air Force. Washington, DC.
Jon L. Milner. Rhodesian Police. Washington, DC.
Paul L. Moorcraft. University of South Africa (Pretoria). Cardiff, UK.
David P. Newnham. Rhodesian Air Force. UK.
Michael F. Noone. Catholic University. Washington, DC.
Morgan Norval. Selous Foundation. Washington, DC.
Sue Onslow. London School of Economics. London, UK.
Edward H. Paintin. Rhodesian Air Force. UK.
Chris Pearson [Ted Bishop, et al.]. Rhodesian Army, Air Force. Marathon, TX.
Peter J. H. Petter-Bowyer. Rhodesian Air Force. London, UK.
Eugene P. J. Pomeroy. Rhodesian Army. Chatham, NY.
Terrence O. Ranger. St. Antony's College. Oxford, UK.
Ron F. Reid-Daly. Rhodesian Army. Simon's Town, RSA.
Brian G. Robinson. Rhodesian Army. Durban, RSA.
Ken R. Salter. Rhodesian Air Force. UK.
Barry M. Schutz. Defense Intelligence Agency. Washington, DC.
David A. Scott-Donelan. Rhodesian Army. Moscow, PA.
Chris Smith. Businessman. Columbus, GA.
Peter Stiff. Rhodesian Police. Alberton, RSA.
Al J. Venter. Journalist. Chinook, WA.
John Vollaire. Rhodesian Police. Nerja, Malaga, ESP.
Edward J. Wages. U.S. Marine. Alexandria, VA.
Peter S. Walton. British Military Advisory Training Team. Alexandria, VA.
Carl P. Watts. London School of Economics. London, UK.
Luise White. Woodrow Wilson Center. Washington, DC.
J. R. T. Wood. Rhodesian Army, University of Durban-Westville. Durban, RSA.

Unpublished Sources

Arnold, David W. Counterinsurgency. Seminar. Las Vegas, NV: SOF Convention, 1986.

Arnold, David W. RAND Rhodesia draft. Manuscript. US: 1989.

Blevin, Don. Strange Beasts: The Evolution and Use of Rhodesian Mine and Ambush Protected Vehicles. Manuscript. UK: 1990.

Briscoe, Peter R. Third World Air Power in Relation to COIN Operations. Thesis. Bracknell, UK: Royal Air Force Staff College, 1981.

Chronology: Rhodesia UDI, Road to Settlement. London, UK: London School of Economics and Political Science, 2006.

Corum, James R. The Myth of Air Control: Reassessing the RAFs Role in Imperial Policing in the Interwar Period. Paper. Quantico, VA: Society for Military History, 27–30 April 2000.

Cronin, John R. Counterinsurgency in Rhodesia from the Viewpoint of a Participant. Paper. Roslyn, VA: Society for Military History, 18–21 April 1996.

Cronin, John R. & Robert C. MacKenzie. Counter-Insurgency in Southern Africa. Study. Washington, DC: Center for Strategic and International Studies, 1986.

Cross, Glenn A. Dirty War: The Rhodesian Chemical and Biological Warfare Effort, 1975–1979. Dissertation. Arlington, VA: George Mason University, 2006.

Cross, Glenn A. Rhodesian Intelligence in a Counter-Insurgent, Counter-Terrorist Conflict. Paper. Washington, DC: Georgetown University, 2007.

Fourie, D. F. S. Advanced Study of the Theory and Practice of Internal War. ATHPIW-4. Study Guide. Pretoria: University of South Africa, 1996.

Geldenhuys, Preller. Nickel Cross. Manuscript. RSA: 2001.

Howe, Herbert M. Dancing on Cobwebs: American Diplomatic Participation in the 1976 Rhodesian Peace Process. Study. Washington, DC: Pew Charitable Trusts, 1988.

Jacobs, C. J. The Conflict Between South Africa and Mozambique, 1975–1989. Paper. International Commission on Military History. Cape Town, RSA: 2007.

Joint Low-Intensity Conflict Study, Final Report. Ft Monroe: U.S. Army Training and Doctrine Command, 1986.

Lawless, Patrick & Peter J. H. Petter-Bowyer. The Relevance of the Rhodesian Bush War to Current COIN Operations in Afghanistan. Study. UK: 2009.

Lohman, Charles M. & Robert I. MacPherson. Tactical Victory, Strategic Defeat. Thesis. Quantico, VA: U.S. Marine Corps Command and Staff College, 1983.

MacKenzie, Robert C. Rhodesian SAS. Seminar. Las Vegas, NV: SOF Convention, 1986.

Melshen, Paul. Pseudo Operations. Thesis. Newport, RI: U.S. Naval War College, 1986.

Melson, Charles D. Killing Machine. Manuscript. Washington, DC: 2003.

Melson, Charles D. Lessons Learned in the Bush. Staff Study. Washington, DC: Headquarters, U.S. Marine Corps, 1986.

Melson, Charles D. Separate and Equal Status: The Response of the Johnson Administration to the Rhodesian Crisis of 1965. Paper. London, UK: London School of Economics and Political Science, 5–6 January 2006.

Melson, Charles D. Top Secret War: Rhodesian Special Forces Operations. Paper. Bethesda, MD: Society for Military History, 20–23 May 2004.

Noone, Michael. Legal Issues in Low Intensity Warfare: The British and Israeli Experience. Seminar. Washington, DC: Catholic University Columbus School of Law, 3 May 1990.

Petter-Bowyer, Peter J. H. Winds of Destruction. Manuscript. UK: n.d.

Plans of Rhodesian Mine Protected Vehicles. Alberton: South African Book Society, n.d.

Pomeroy, Eugene. The Origins and Development of the Defense Forces of Northern and Southern Rhodesia from 1890–1945. Thesis. Portland: Portland State University, 1994.

Reid-Daly, Ron F. Counterinsurgency Warfare. Seminar. Las Vegas, NV: SOF Convention, 1985.

Scott-Donelan, David. Tactical Tracking Operations for Police, Military, and Corrections Special Response Teams. Lesson plan. Mooreton: Tactical Tracking School, 1993.

Special Air Warfare Tactics. AF Manual 3-5. Washington, DC: Department of the Air Force, 1965.

Special Operations in War and Peace. SoCom Pub 1. Tampa, FL: U.S. Special Operations Command, 25 January 1996.

Stedman, Stephen John. The Lancaster House Constitutional Conference on Rhodesia. Study. Washington, DC: Pew Charitable Trusts, 1993.

Sunderland, Riley. Antiguerrilla Intelligence in Malaya, 1948–1960. Study. Santa Monica: RAND Corporation, 1964.

Wood, J. R. T. The Double Edged Sword: The South African Rhodesian Alliance. Paper. Kingston, ONT: Society for Military History, 20–24 May 1993.

Wood, J. R. T. A Fire Force Action. Manuscript. RSA: n.d.

Wood, J. R. T. Fire Force. Manuscript. RSA: n.d.

Wood, J. R. T. Operation Uric. Manuscript. RSA: n.d.

Wood, J. R. T. There Was Never Enough Intelligence: The Role of Intelligence in the Rhodesian Counter-Insurgency Campaign, 1962–1980. Paper. Roslyn, VA: Society for Military History, 18–21 April 1996.

Published Sources

Abbot, Peter & Philip Botham. Modern African Wars: Rhodesia, 1965–1980. London: Osprey Publishing, 1986.

Abbot, Peter & Manuel Ribeiro Rodrigues. Modern African Wars: Angola and Mozambique, 1961–74. London: Osprey Publishing, 1988.

Abrahams, Beverley & Lesley Humphrey. Study Guide to Harvest of Thorns. Harare: Academic Books, 1993.

Adams, Mark & Chris Cocks. Africa's Commandos: The Rhodesian Light Infantry. Solihull: Helion & Co., 2012.

Air Force of Zimbabwe. Air Force 81. Salisbury: Irwin, 1981.

Alexander, Jocelyn, JoAnn McGregor & Terence Ranger. Violence and Memory: One Hundred Years in the Dark Forest of Matabeleland. Oxford: James Currey, 2000.

Alexander, McGill. "The Liberation Struggle in Africa: Airborne Tactics in an Insurgency War." In An Art in Itself: The Theory and Conduct of Small Wars and Insurgencies, edited by Peter Dennis & Jeffrey Grey. AU: Australian History Military Publications, 2006.

Aellen, Richard. "Rhodesia's Secret Army." Soldier of Fortune, July 1978, 36–8.

Allen, Don & George Gamble. "Bounce-Bombs for Breakfast." Eagle, April 1977, n.p.

"An Ingenious Bomb Disposal Device: The Sable." Fighting Forces of Zimbabwe-Rhodesia, (6) 1979, 27.

Arbuckle, Thomas. "Rhodesian Bush War Strategies and Tactics." RUSI Journal, December 1979, 27–31.

Army Careers Office. You're Someone Special in the S.A.S. Salisbury: n.p., n.d.

Arniel, A. J. Badges and Insignia of the Rhodesian Security Forces. Germiston: Alex Kaplan & Son, 1987.

"The Army's Fighting Vehicles." Assegai, February 1980, 5–13.

Arnold, Dave. "How to use Cover and Concealment." Handguns for Sport & Defense, February 1992, 23–7, 72.

Arnold, Dave. "Shooting Hints: Handgun." Guns & Ammo Annual, 1992, 117–21.

"A Story for the 'Ohns.'" Assegai, January 1970, 32.

Astrow, André. *Zimbabwe: A Revolution that Lost its Way?* London: Zed Press, 1983.

Auret, Diana. *Reaching for Justice: The Catholic Commission for Justice and Peace, 1972–1992.* Gweru: Mambo Press, 1992.

Ayittey, George B. *Africa Betrayed.* New York St. Martin's Press, 1992.

Baker, Jill. "Co-ord-a-nation." *Assegai,* July 1976, 11.

Balaam, Andrew. *Bush War Operator: Memoirs of the Rhodesian Light Infantry, Selous Scouts, and Beyond.* Solihull: Helion & Co., 2014.

Ballinger, Anthony J. *A Walk Against the Stream: A True Story of Love Set Against a Background of War in Rhodesia.* Victoria: Trafford Publishing, 2007.

Banana, Canaan. *The Gospel According to the Ghetto.* Harare: Mambo Press, 1981.

Barclay, Glen St. J. "Rhodesia's Hand-Picked Professionals: Making Do with the Chosen Few." *Soldier of Fortune,* April 1984, 30–3.

Bax, Tim. *Three Sips of Gin: Dominating the Battlespace with Rhodesia's Elite Selous Scouts.* Solihull: Helion & Co., 2013.

Baxter, Peter. *Selous Scouts: Rhodesian Counter-Insurgency Specialists.* Pinetown: 30 Degrees South Publishers, 2011.

Baxter, Peter, Hugh Bomford, & Gerry van Tonder, et al. *Rhodesia Regiment, 1899–1981.* Tauranga: Rhodesian Services Association, 2014.

Baynham, Simon. *Africa from 1945.* New York: Franklin Watts, 1987.

Beckett, Ian F. W., ed. *Encyclopedia of Guerrilla Warfare.* Santa Barbara: ABC-Clio, 1999.

Beckett, Ian F. W. *Modern Insurgencies and Counter-Insurgencies.* London & New York: Routledge, 2001.

Beckett, Ian F. W. "Portuguese Africa: Angola, Guinea, Mozambique, 1961–1976." In *War in Peace,* edited by Robert Thompson, et al. New York: Harmony Books, 1981, 152–7.

Beckett, Ian F. W. "The Portuguese Army: The Campaign in Mozambique." In *Armed Forces and Modern Counter-insurgency,* edited by Ian F. W. Beckett & John Pimlott. New York: St. Martin's Press, 1985, 136–62.

Beckett, Ian, F. W. "The Rhodesian Army: Counter-insurgency." In *Armed Forces and Modern Counter-insurgency,* edited by Ian F. W. Beckett & John Pimlott. New York: St. Martin's Press, 1985, 163–89.

Bennett, D. C. "Mugabe's Bloody Christmas Gift." *Soldier of Fortune,* November 1986, 12.

Bell, J. Bowyer. "The Frustration of Insurgency: The Rhodesian Example in the Sixties." *Military Affairs,* vol. 35, no. 4, 1971.

Bhebe, Ngwabi & Terence Ranger, eds. *Society in Zimbabwe's Liberation War.* Harare: University of Zimbabwe Publications, 1995.

Bhebe, Ngwabi & Terence Ranger, eds. *Soldiers in Zimbabwe's Liberation War.* Harare: University of Zimbabwe Publications, 1995.

Binda, Alexandre. *The Equus Men: Rhodesia's Mounted Infantry, The Grey's Scouts, 1896–1980.* Solihull: Helion & Co., 2015.

Binda, Alexandre, et al. *Masodja: The History of the Rhodesian African Rifles and its Forerunner The Rhodesia Native Regiment.* Johannesburg: 30 Degrees South Publishers, 2009.

Binda, Alexandre. *The Rhodesia Regiment.* Alberton: Galago Publishing, 2012.

Binda, Alexandre, et al. *The Saints: The Rhodesian Light Infantry.* Johannesburg: 30 Degrees South Publishers, 2007.

Black, Colin. "The RAF Volunteer Reserve." *Fighting Forces of Rhodesia,* (1) 1974, 53–71.

Black, Colin. "Wings Guard Our Country." *Fighting Forces of Rhodesia,* (1) 1974, 21–31.

Blake, Robert. *A History of Rhodesia.* London: Eyre Methuen, 1977.

Blaufarb, Douglas S. *The Counterinsurgency Era.* New York: Fress Press, 1977.

Blevin, Don. "Here are Signs for the Wise: Lessons of the Rhodesian War." *British Army Review,* December 1991, 45–56.

Blue and Old Gold: A Selections of Stories from the Outpost, the Regimental Magazine of the British South Africa Police. Cape Town: Howard B. Timmins, 1953.

de Boer, Marno. "Rhodesia's Approach to Counterinsurgency: A Preference for Killing." *Military Review*, November–December 2011, 35–45.

Bond, Geoffrey. *The Incredibles: The Story of the 1st Battalion, The Rhodesian Light Infantry.* Salisbury: Sarum Imprint, 1977.

Boorman, Scott A. *The Protracted Game: A Wei-chi Interpretation of Maoist Revolutionary Strategy.* New York: Oxford University Press, 1969.

Bopela, Thula & Daluxolo Luthuli. *Umkhonto we Sizwe: Fighting for a Divided People.* Alberton: Galago Publishing, 2005.

de Braganca, Aquino & Immanuel Wallerstein, eds. *The African Liberation Reader: The Strategy of Liberation.* London: Zed Press, 1982.

Brelsford, W. V. *Handbook of the Federation of Rhodesia and Nyasaland.* London: Cassell, 1960.

Brent, Winston A. *Rhodesian Air Force: A Brief History, 1947–1980.* Kwambonambi: Freeworld Publications, 1987.

Brent, Winston A. *Rhodesian Air Force: A Brief History, 1947–1980* (Revised Edition). Kwambonambi: Freeworld Publications, 1988.

Brent, Winston A. *Rhodesian Air Force: The Sanctions Busters.* Nelspruit: Freeworld Publications, 2001.

Briscoe, Peter [Hornet One]. "Day of the Hornet: Fire Force Deadly Swarm Draws Last Blood." *Soldier of Fortune*, September 1989, 60–7, 78–80.

Brown, Kenneth B. "Counter Guerrilla Operations: Does the Law of War Proscribe Success." *Naval Law Review*, no. 44, 1997, 123–73.

Brown, Robert K. "The Black Devils." *Soldier of Fortune*, January 1979, 38–43.

Brown, Robert K. & Jay Mallin. "Capt John Early." *Soldier of Fortune*, December 1979, 86–7.

Brown, Sally. "Successful Anti-Insurgency Operations," *Fighting Forces of Rhodesia*, (5) 1978, 4–13.

Burgess, Stephen E. & Helen E. Burkitt. *The Rollback of South Africa's Chemical and Biological Warfare Program.* Maxwell AFB: USAF Counterproliferation Center, 2001.

Cabot, John. *Strike Back at Terror.* Pretoria: Thelaw, 1987.

Callwell, Charles E. *Small Wars: Their Principles and Practices.* London: HMSO, 1906 [University of Nebraska Press reprint, 1996].

Campling, Archer B. "A Brief History of Parachuting in the Rhodesian Army." *Lion & Tusk*, October 1999, 16–25.

Cann, John P. *Counterinsurgency in Africa: The Portuguese Way of War, 1961–1974.* Westport: Greenwood Press, 1997.

Cann, John P., ed. *Memories of Portugal's African Wars, 1961–1974.* Quantico: MCUF, 1998.

Cann, John P. "The Portuguese Colonial Experience in Southern Africa, 1961–74." In *An Art in Itself: The Theory and Conduct of Small Wars and Insurgencies*, edited by Peter Dennis & Jeffrey Grey. AU: Australian History Military Publications, 2006.

Cary, Robert & Diana Mitchell. *African Nationalist Leaders in Rhodesia: Who's Who.* Bulawayo: Books of Rhodesia, 1977.

Caute, David. *Under the Skin: The Death of White Rhodesia.* Evanston: Northwestern University Press, 1983.

Celso, Anthony C. & Robert Nalbandov, eds. *The Crisis of the African State: Globalization, Tribalism, and Jihadism in the Twenty-First Century.* Quantico: Marine Corps University Press, 2016.

"Cessna 337 Lynx, Rhodesian Operations," *War Zone: Africa. Air Warfare*, n.d., 1681–5.

Chan, Stephen. *The Commonwealth Observer Group in Zimbabwe: A Personal Memoir.* Gweru: Mambo Press, 1985.

Chan, Stephen. *Robert Mugabe: A Life of Power and Violence*. Ann Arbor: University of Michigan Press, 2003.

Charlton, Michael, ed. *The Last Colony in Africa: Diplomacy and the Independence of Rhodesia*. Oxford: Basil Blackwell, 1990.

Chinodya, Shimmer. *Harvest of Thorns*. Harare: Baobab Books, 1989.

Christie, Roy. *For the President's Eyes Only*. Johannesburg: Hugh Keartland Publishers, 1971.

Cilliers, J. K. *Counter-Insurgency in Rhodesia*. Dover: Croom Helm, 1985.

Civil War in Rhodesia: A Report from the Rhodesian Catholic Commission for Justice and Peace. London: Catholic Institute for International Relations, 1976.

Clark, K. D. "I Was There: RLI Meets the Wild Bunch." *Soldier of Fortune*, December 1985, 10, 108–9.

Clayton, Anthony. *Frontiersmen: Warfare in Africa since 1950*. London: UCL Press, 1999.

Clayton, Anthony & David Killingray, eds. *Khaki and Blue: Military and Police in Colonial Africa*. Athens: Ohio State University, 1989.

Cline, Sibyl. "Forgotten Freedom Fighters: Mozambique's RENAMO Lost in Maelstrom of Misinformation." *Soldier of Fortune*, January 1990, 30–9, 88–9.

Cobb, Charles E., et al. "After Rhodesia, A Nation Named Zimbabwe." *National Geographic*, November 1981, 616–51.

Cocks, Chris. *Fireforce: One Man's War in the Rhodesian Light Infantry*. Weltevreden Park: Covos Day Books, 1997.

Cocks, Chris. *Survival Course*. Weltevreden Park: Covos Day Books, 1999.

Cocks, Kerrin. *Rhodesian Fire Force, 1966–80*. Pinetown: 30 Degrees South Publishers, 2015.

Coetzee, P. "Grey's Scouts: An Invaluable Friend on the Borders." *Paratus*, January 1980, 16–17.

Coetzee, P. "Pamwe Chete: Selous Scouts, Carve Their Name With Pride." *Paratus*, December, 1979, 18–19.

Coey, John A. *A Martyr Speaks: The Journal of the Late John Alan Coey*. Fletcher: New Puritan Press, 1988.

Coey, John A. "Counter Insurgency Patrol." *Assegai*, June 1974, 9–11.

Cohen, Barry. "The War in Rhodesia: A Dissenter's View." *African Affairs*, n.d., 483–4.

Cohen, Eliot A. *Commandos and Politicians: Elite Military Units in Modern Democracies*. Cambridge: Harvard University CFIA, 1978.

Cole, Barbara, et al. *Sabotage and Torture*. Amanzimtoti: Three Knights, 1988.

Cole, Barbara. *The Elite: Rhodesian Special Air Service Pictorial*. Amanzimtoti: Three Knights, 1986.

Cole, Barbara. *The Elite: The Story of the Rhodesian Special Air Service*. Amanzimtoti: Three Knights, 1984.

Cole, Barbara. "Cockleshell Heroes: SAS Hit and Float in Mozambique." *Soldier of Fortune*, March 1986, 74–7, 101.

Cole, Barbara. "SAS: Storming the Bastille." *The Elite*, (49) April 1986, 961–6.

Coleman, John W. "Combat Weaponcraft: Ambush!" *Soldier of Fortune*, December 1986, 24, 105–6.

Coleman, John W. "Combat Weaponcraft: Ops Order, Don't Leave Home Without It." *Soldier of Fortune*, September 1987, 28–9, 89–90.

Coleman, John W. "Five AK Rounds: American Survives Rhodesian Ambush." *Soldier of Fortune*, February 1983, 38–41.

Coleman, John W. "Flak from the Terrs—Mission: Mozambique Ambush." *New Breed*, n.d., 32–9, 59–60.

Coleman, John W. "LALO Jump: RLI Almost Inherits the Earth." *Soldier of Fortune*, January 1984, 38–41.

Coleman, John W. with Dick DeLany. "I Was There: Where Did I Go Wrong?" *Soldier of Fortune*, June 1985, 18.

"Combat Report Rhodesia: Alouette Raid, Part 1." *Combat & Survival*, (11) 1991, 610.

"Combat Report Rhodesia: Alouette Raid, Part 2." *Combat & Survival*, (11) 1991, 616.

"Combat Report Rhodesia: Fire Force Mission." *Combat & Survival*, (4) 1991, 190.

"Combat Report Rhodesia: Anti-Guerrilla Patrol." *Combat & Survival*, (7) 1991, 417.

"Combat Report Rhodesia: Counter-Terrorist Airborne Attack." *Combat & Survival*, (8) 1991, 436.

"Combat Report Rhodesia: Guerrilla Ambush near Mkumbura." *Combat & Survival*, (18) 1991, 1077.

"Combat Report Rhodesia: Guerrilla Contact in the Bush War, Part 1." *Combat & Survival*, (22) 1991, 1270.

"Combat Report Rhodesia: Guerrilla Contact in the Bush War, Part 2." *Combat & Survival*, (22) 1991, 1276.

"Combat Report Rhodesia: Helicopter Assault Tactics." *Combat & Survival*, (19) 1991, 1085–9.

"Combat Report Rhodesia: Helicopter Engagement with Terrorists." *Combat & Survival*, (21) 1991, 1210.

"Combat Report Rhodesia: Hunting the Terrorists." *Combat & Survival*, (6) 1991, 357

"Combat Report Rhodesia: I let loose round after round." *Combat & Survival*, (85) 1988, n.p.

"Combat Report Rhodesia: Those monkeys are headed right towards one of our OPs." *Combat & Survival*, (85) 1988, n.p.

"Combat Report Rhodesia: Zambian Border Action." *Combat & Survival*, (12) 1991, 721.

"Combat Skills: Ambushing the Terrorists." *Combat & Survival*, (19) 1991, 1091–5.

"Combat Skills: Anti-Terrorist Operations." *Combat & Survival*, (22) 1991, 1265–9.

"Combat Skills: Bush Patrolling." *Combat & Survival*, (22) 1991, 1277–81.

"Combat Skills: Bush Tracking and Countertracking." *Combat & Survival*, (19) 1991, 1097–101.

"Combat Skills: Helicopter Assault Tactics." *Combat & Survival*, (19) 1991, 1085–9.

"Combat Skills: Intelligence Operations in the Bush." *Combat & Survival*, (22) 1991, 1271–5.

"Commanders: Walls." *The Elite*, (#) 1986, 164–5.

Cope, Terence Peter. "Rhodesian Goatman: $15,000 for 480 Goats and Lots of Terrs." *Soldier of Fortune*, January 1979, 54–5, 88–90.

Cornwall, Barbara. *The Bush Rebels: A Personal Account of Black Revolt in Africa*. New York: Holt, Rinehart & Winston, 1972.

Corum, James D. & Wray R. Johnson. *Airpower in Small Wars*. Lawrence: University Press of Kansas, 2003.

"Counter-Terrorist Airborne Attack." *Combat & Survival*, (8) 1991, 436.

"C Sqdn 22 SAS (Rhodesia): The Squadron's First Big Para Drop Near Salisbury." *Lion & Tusk*, August 1996, n.p.

"C Squadron SAS," *Assegai*, May 1969, 16–17.

"C Squadron SAS Notes," *Assegai*, June 1969, 31

Coventry, Dudley. Obituary by Barbara Cole, *Lion & Tusk*, Autumn 1993, n.p.

Cowderoy, Dudley & Roy C. Nesbit. *War in the Air: Rhodesian Air Force, 1935–1980*. Alberton: Galago Publishing, 1987.

Cowderoy, Dudley, Roy C. Nesbit, & Andrew Thomas. *Britain's Rebel Air Force: The War from the Air in Rhodesia, 1965–1980*. London: Grub Street, 1998.

Coyle, R. G. & C. J. Millar. "A Methodology for Understanding Military Complexity: The Case of the Rhodesian Counter-Insurgency Campaign." *Small Wars and Insurgencies*, vol. 7, no. 3, Winter 1996, 360–378.

Crabtree, William. *Came the Fourth Flag*. Lancaster: Scotforth Books, 2002.

Crocker, Chester A. *High Noon in Southern Africa: Making Peace in a Rough Neighborhood*. New York: W. W. Norton & Co., 1992.

Cronin, John R. "South African Mine-Resistant Personnel Carrier One of a Kind." *Armed Forces Journal*, March 1992, 35.

Cross, Glenn. *Dirty War: Rhodesia and Chemical Biological Warfare, 1975–1980*. Solihull: Helion & Co., 2017.

Croukamp, Dennis. *Only My Friends Call Me Crouks: Rhodesian Reconnaissance Specialist*. Cape Town: Pseudo Publishing, 2006.

Custis, Jon A. "Fire Force: Vertical Envelopment During the Rhodesian War." *Marine Corps Gazette*, March 2000, 48–51.

Davidow, Jeffrey. *A Peace in Southern Africa: The Lancaster House Conference on Rhodesia, 1979*. Boulder: Westview Press, 1984.

Davidson, Basil. *Africa in History*. New York: Collier Books, 1991.

Des Fountain, T. G. "Military History and the Professional Soldier." *Assegai*, December 1978, 13–21.

Dodgen, Bill. *Reflections of a God Botherer*. Springs: Rhodesia Association of South Africa, 1991.

Dornan, Jr., James E., ed. *Rhodesia Alone*. Washington, DC: Council on American Affairs, n.d.

Downie, Nick. "Rhodesia: A Study in Military Incompetence." *Defence*, May 1979, 342–5.

Doyle, Mick. "Bush Bobbies: Rhodesia's British South Africa Police." *Soldier of Fortune*, July 1985, 32–7, 80–3.

Doyle, Mick. "The Black Boots: British South Africa Police Makes War on Terrorists." *Fighting Elite*, n.d., 46–9, 75–6.

Dzimba, John. *South Africa's Destabilization of Zimbabwe, 1980–89*. London: Macmillan Press, 1998.

Early, John. "Combat Tracking Techniques: How to Track Your Enemy." *Soldier of Fortune*, July 1979, 52–5, 78–9.

Early, John. "Big John Murphy, 1943–1980." *Soldier of Fortune*, July 1981, 46–7.

Early, John. "John Early: Rhodesian Adventures." In *Merc: American Soldiers of Fortune*, edited by Robert K. Brown & Jay Mallin. New York: Macmillan, 1979, 169–87.

Edmond, John. *Bushcat: Minstrel of the Wild*. Leeuport: Roan Antelope Books, 1997.

Edwards, Clare Kelly, ed. *Cartoons of Rhodesia, 1965–1979*. Salisbury: Hansel Books, 1979.

Ellert, Henrik. *The Rhodesian Front War: Counterinsurgency and Guerrilla Warfare, 1962–1980*. Gweru: Mambo Press, 1989.

Ellert, Henrik. "The Rhodesian Security and Intelligence Community." In *Soldiers in Zimbabwe's Liberation War*, edited by Ngwabi Bhebe & Terence Ranger. Harare: University of Zimbabwe Publications, 1995, 87–103.

Elliot-Bateman, Michael. *Defeat in the East*. New York: Oxford University Press, 1969.

Els, Paul. *We Fear Naught but God: The Story of the South African Special Forces*. Johannesburg: Covos Day Books, 2000.

"The Encounter or the Day in the Life of an RAR Soldier." *Lion & Tusk*, March 1990, n.p.

Evans, John. "C Squadron Trooper." *Lion & Tusk*, March 1997, 19–24.

Evans, Michael. *Fighting Against Chimurenga*. Salisbury: Historical Association of Zimbabwe, 1981.

Evans, Michael. "The Wretched of the Empire: Politics, Ideology, and Counter-Insurgency in Rhodesia, 1965–80." In *An Art in Itself: The Theory and Conduct of Small Wars and Insurgencies*, edited by Peter Dennis & Jeffrey Grey. AU: Australian History Military Publications, 2006.

Fanon, Frantz. *The Wretched of the Earth*. New York: Grove Weidenfeld, 1968.

Finnegan, William. *A Complicated War*. Berkeley: University of California Press, 1992.

Flower, Ken. *Serving Secretly: Rhodesia's CIO Chief on Record*. Alberton: Galago Publishing, 1987.

Ford, Jeremy. *Hello, Soldier!* Salisbury: Graham Publishing, 1975.

Foster, Don, Dennis Davis, & Diane Sandler. *Detention and Torture in South Africa: Psychological, Legal, and Historical Studies*. New York: St. Martin's Press, 1997.

Fredrickson, George M. *White Supremacy: A Comparative Study in American and South African History*. New York: Oxford University Press, 1981.

Frederikse, Julie. *None But Ourselves: Masses vs. Media in the Making of Zimbabwe*. Johannesburg: Ravan Press, 1982.

French, David. *The British Way in Counter-Insurgency*. New York: Oxford University Press, 2012.

French, Paul. *Shadows of a Forgotten Past: To the Edge with the Rhodesian SAS and Selous Scouts*. Solihull: Helion & Co., 2012.

Fuller, Alexandra. "Letter from Zimbabwe: The Soldier." *The New Yorker*, 1 March 2004, 54–67.

Gale, W. D. "Men Who Dare," *Fighting Forces of Rhodesia*, (3) 1976, 41.

Gann, Lewis H. *The Development of Southern Rhodesia's Military System*. Salisbury: National Archives of Rhodesia, 1965.

Gann, Lewis H. "From Ox Wagon to Armored Car in Rhodesia." *Military Review*, April 1968, 63–72.

Gann, Lewis H. & Peter Duignan. *Burden of Empire: An Appraisal of Western Colonialism in Africa South of the Sahara*. Stanford: Stanford University Press, 1971.

Gann, Lewis H. & Peter Duignan. *The Rulers of British Africa, 1870–1914*. Stanford: Stanford University Press, 1978.

Gann, Lewis H. & Thomas H. Henriksen. *The Struggle for Zimbabwe: Battle in the Bush*. New York; Praeger Publishers, 1981.

Gaudet, Kenneth J. "Big Magic: AKM Bayonet Prize Trophy." *Soldier of Fortune*, November 1982, 60–1.

Gaudet, Kenneth J. "Deadly Deception." *Soldier of Fortune*, May 1988, 62–3, 73–4.

Geldenhuys, Preller. *Rhodesian Air Force Operations with Strike Log*. Durban: Just Done Publishing, 2007.

Gericke, Patrick, et al. *Terrorist Weapons and Explosive Devices: Posters, Aides-Memoire, and Supplementary Technical Data*. Amersham: Security Awareness & Promotions, 1988.

Gibbs, Peter & Hugh Phillips. *The History of the British South Africa Police*. North Ringwood: Something of Value, 2000.

Gjerstad, Ole, ed. *The Organizer: The Story of Temba Moyo*. Richmond: LSM Press, 1974.

Gledhill, Dick. *One Commando: Rhodesia's Last Years and the Guerrilla War it Never Lost*. Castletown: RLI Publishing, 1997.

Godfrey, F. A. "War in the Bush: Rhodesia, 1957–1980." In *War in Peace*, edited by Robert Thompson, et al. New York: Harmony Books, 1981, 241–7.

Godwin, Peter. *Mukiwa: A White Boy in Africa*. London: Picador, 1996.

Godwin, Peter & Ian Hancock. *Rhodesians Never Die: The Impact of War and Political Change on White Rhodesia, c. 1970–1980*. Oxford: Oxford University Press, 1993.

Good, Robert C. *UDI: The International Politics of the Rhodesian Rebellion*. Princeton: Princeton University Press, 1973.

Gordon, George. "The Day the Rhodesian SAS Tried to Kill Joshua Nkomo." *Daily Mail*, 27 May 1980, 20–1.

Gordon, John [sic]. "Operation Assassination." *Soldier of Fortune*, October 1980, 30–2.

Grainger, D. H. *Don't Die in the Bundu*. Cape Town: Howard B. Timmins, 1967.

Grant, Neil. *Rhodesian Light Infantryman, 1961–80*. Oxford: Osprey Publishing, 2015.

Greeff, Jack. *A Greater Share of Honour*. Ellisras: Ntomeni Publishers, 2001.

Grensoorlog 1966–1989 Border War. Journal for Contemporary History, vol. 31, no. 3, December 2006.

"Grey's Scouts Ride Again." *Focus on Rhodesia*, vol. 2, no. 1, 8–9.

Gumbo, Mafuranhunzi. *Guerrilla Snuff*. Harare: Baobab Books, 1995.

Hallencrutz, Carl & Ambrose Moyo, eds. *Church and State in Zimbabwe*. Gweru: Mambo Press, 1988.

Hamilton, Alex W. "The Spirit of Augsburg Lives On." *Fighting Forces of Rhodesia*, (4) 1977, 41–53.

Hamley, Richard. *The Regiment: A History and the Uniforms of the British South Africa Police*. Weltevreden Park: Covos Day Books, 2000.

Hammann, Hilton. *Days of the Generals: The Untold Story of South Africa's Apartheid-era Military Generals*. Cape Town: Zebra Press, 2001.

Hanlon, Joseph. *Beggar Your Neighbors: Apartheid Power in Southern Africa*. London: Catholic Institute for International Relations, 1986.

Harvey, Ken G. "SAS Operational Wings." *ZMS Journal*, April 2001, 16–18.

Hatchard, John. *Individual Freedoms and State Security in the African Context: The Case of Zimbabwe*. London: James Currey, 1993.

Heaton, Bob. "Camouflaged Cleric's Vital Role." *Focus on Rhodesia*, vol. 2, no. 10.

Heitman, Helmoed-Römer. *Modern African Wars: Southwest Africa*. London: Osprey Publishing, 1991.

Heitman, Helmoed-Römer. *South African War Machine*. Novato: Presidio Press, 1985.

Henderson, Ian & Philip Goodhart. *Manhunt in Kenya*. New York: Bantam Books, 1988.

Hoffman, Bruce. *British Air Power in Peripheral Conflicts, 1919–1976*. Santa Monica: RAND Corporation, 1989.

Hoffman, Bruce, Jennifer M. Taw, & David W. Arnold. *Lessons for Contemporary Counterinsurgencies: The Rhodesian Experience*. Santa Monica: RAND Corporation, 1991.

Hopkins, John W. "Rhodesian Mine and Ambush Protected Vehicles." *Army and Navy Modelworld*, January 1988, 14–18.

Howe, Herbert M. "The Rhodesia Conflict, 1966–1979." In *Prolonged Wars: The Post-Nuclear Challenge*, Karl P. Magyar & Constantine P. Danopouls, eds. Maxwell AFB: Air University Press, 1994.

Hubbard, Jr., Douglas H. *Bound for Africa: Cold War Fight Along the Zambezi*. Annapolis: Naval Institute Press, 2008.

Hudson, Miles. *Triumph or Tragedy: Rhodesia to Zimbabwe*. London: Hamish Hamilton, 1981.

Jackson, Neill & Rick van Malsen. *The Search for Puma 164: Operation Uric and the Assault on Mapai*. Johannesburg: 30 Degrees South Publishers, 2011.

Jackson, Robert. *Canberra: The Operational Log*. Washington, DC: Smithsonian Institution, 1989.

Jackson, Robert. *Hawker Hunter: The Operational Record*. Washington, DC: Smithsonian Institution, 1989.

Jackson, W. N. B. "Some Problems of Being a Freedom Fighter." *British Army Review*, no. 85, April 1987, 36–9.

Jatras, Jake. "Mushonga: Magic Charms No Substitute for Flak Jackets." *Soldier of Fortune*, June 1980, 63.

Johnson, Chalmers. *Autopsy of People's War*. Berkeley: University of California, 1973.

Jokonya, T. J. B. "The Effects of the War on the Rural Population of Zimbabwe." *Journal of Southern African Affairs*, 1981, 135–47.

Jones, M. L. "I Was There." *Soldier of Fortune*, November 1980, 2021.

Jordon, Frank. "Le Rat Pack Rhodesien." *Raids*, no. 17, October 1987, 36–7.

Kadhani, Muderei & Musaemura Zimunya, eds. *And Now the Poets Speak: Poems Inspired by the Struggle for Zimbabwe*. Gweru: Mambo Press, 1981.

Kaplan, Robert D. *The Coming Anarchy*. New York: Random House, 2000.

Kazembe, Musosa. "Why Should I Die?: A Chinese-trained Guerrilla of Africa, His Personal Story." *Atlas*, June 1968, 19–21.

Keegan, John, ed. *World Armies*. New York: Facts on File, 1979, 588.

Kriger, Norma J. *Zimbabwe's Guerrilla War: Peasant Voices*. New York: Cambridge University Press, 1992.

Lake, Anthony. *The Tar Baby Option: American Policy Toward Southern Rhodesia*. New York: Columbia University Press, 1976.

Lan, David. *Guns and Rain: Guerrillas and Spirit Mediums in Zimbabwe*. London: James Currey, 1985.

Lapping, Brian. *End of Empire*. New York: St. Martin's Press, 1985.

Latham, Jim. "Shona Belief in the Supernatural." *Assegai*, November 1973, 8–11.

Lawless, Patrick. "Fire Force Operations in Rhodesia, 1977 to 1980." *Army Air Corp Journal*, (11) 1985, 8–11.

Lee, Jerry. "A Night at Vila Salazar: Keeping Freddie Fired Up." *Soldier of Fortune*, April 1981, 32–3.

Lemon, David. *Never Quite a Soldier: A Rhodesian Policeman's War, 1971–1982*. Alberton: Galago Publishing, 2006.

Lessing, Doris. *African Laughter: Four Visits to Zimbabwe*. New York: Harper Collins, 1992.

Locke Peter G. & Peter D. F. Cooke. *Fighting Vehicles and Weapons of Rhodesia, 1965–1980*. Wellington: P&P Publishing, 1995.

Lott, Jack P. "CATU Tracks Terrorists: Rhodesia's Civilian Tracking Unit." *Soldier of Fortune*, July 1979, 46–51.

Lott, Jack P. "Bounty Hunting in Rhodesia." *Combat Illustrated*, n.d., 43–62.

Lott, Jack P. "Forensic Ballistics: When Sherlock Homes Isn't Enough!" *Handgun Annual*, n.d., 92–7.

Lotter, Charles. *Echoes of an African War*. Weltevreden Park: Covos Day Books, 1999.

Lovett, John. *Contact: A Tribute to Those Who Served Rhodesia*. Salisbury: Galaxie Press, 1977.

Lunt, James. *Imperial Sunset: Frontier Soldiering in the 20th Century*. London: McDonald, 1981.

Luttwak, Edward. *Coup d'Etat: A Practical Handbook*. Cambridge: Harvard University Press, 1979.

MacBruce, James. *When the Going Was Rough: A Rhodesian Story*. Pretoria: Fremina Publishing, 1983.

MacDonald, Peter. "Rhodesia: Lessons Learned." *Military Operations*, vol. 1, no. 4, Spring 2013, 11–14.

MacGregor, Thomas. "Grey's Scouts Ride Again." *Soldier of Fortune*, n.d., n.p.

MacGregor, Thomas. "In Rhodesia: Civilian Ambush Protection." *Soldier of Fortune*, n.d., 60.

MacIntyre, Alexander N. O. *Rough Diamonds and Other Gems*. Lexington: Xlibris, 2013.

MacKenzie, Robert C. "I Was There: Last Bayonet Charge." *Soldier of Fortune*, January 1991, 20, 88–92.

MacKenzie, Robert C. "Fast Strike at Chimoio: Rhodesian SAS Blitz Terrorist Nerve Center." *Soldier of Fortune*, January 1994, 40–3, 83–4; February 1994, 43–7, 71, 82.

MacKenzie, Robert C. Obituary, *Lion & Tusk*, June 1995, n.p.

MacKenzie, Robert C. Obituary by Sibyl W. MacKenzie, *Soldier of Fortune*, July 1995, 36–41.

MacKenzie, Sibyl. "Death of a Warrior: Robert MacKenzie, 1948–1995." *Soldier of Fortune*, July 1995, 36–41, 82–5.

MacLean, Joy. *The Guardians: A Story of Rhodesia's Outposts and the Men and Women Who Served in Them*. Bulawayo: Books of Rhodesia, 1974.

Mangold, Tom & Jeff Goldberg. *Plague Wars*. New York: St. Martin's Press, 1999.

Marks, Tom. "Remembering RENAMO: The Counterinsurgency that Almost Won." *Soldier of Fortune*, January 2000, 40–3, 68; February 2000, 56–9.

Marston, Roger. "Not Ordinary White People: The Origins of Rhodesian COIN Theory and Practice." *RUSI Journal*, December 1986, 25–31.

Martin, David & Phyllis Johnson. *The Chitepo Assassination*. Harare: Zimbabwe Publishing House, 1985.

Martin, David & Phyllis Johnson. *The Struggle for Zimbabwe*. London: Faber & Faber, 1981.

Martin, Faan. *James and the Duck: Tales of the Rhodesian Bush War, 1964–1980*. Central Milton Keynes: Author House, 2007.

Maxey, Kees. *The Fight for Zimbabwe*. London: Rex Collins, 1975.

Mazorodze, I. V. *Silent Journey from the East*. Harare: Zimbabwe Publishing House, 1989.

McAleese, Peter. *No Mean Soldier*. London: Cassell, 2000.

McCallion, Harry. *Killing Zone: A Life in the Paras, the Recces, the SAS and the RUC*. London: Bloomsbury Publishing, 1995.

McKenna, Bob [Robert C. MacKenzie]. "The Big Bang: Beira Oil Depot Annihilated in SAS Revenge Raid." *Soldier of Fortune*, n.d., 38–43, 71, 82.

McKenna, Bob. "Combat Weaponcraft: At my command." *Soldier of Fortune*, May 1987, 18, 92–4.

McKenna, Bob. "Combat Weaponcraft: SAS Knock-Knocks and Bunker Bombs. *Soldier of Fortune*, November 1986, 14–17, 84.

McLaughlin, Janice. *On the Frontline: Catholic Missions in Zimbabwe's Liberation War*. Harare: Baobab Books, 1996.

McLaughlin, Peter. *Ragtime Soldiers: The Rhodesian Experience in the First World War.* Bulawayo: Books of Zimbabwe, 1980.

McLaughlin, Peter. "The Thin White Line: Rhodesia's Armed Forces Since the Second World War." *Zambezia*, no. 6, vol. 2, 1978, 175–85.

McLaughlin, Peter. "Victims as Defenders: African Troops in the Rhodesian Defence System, 1890–1980." *Small Wars and Insurgencies*, vol. 2, no. 2, August 1991, 240–75.

McLoughlin, T. O. *The Sound of Snapping Wires: A Selection of Zimbabwean Short Stories.* Harare: College Press, 1990.

McRaven, William H. *Spec Ops: Case Studies in Special Operations Warfare.* Novato: Presidio Press, 1995.

Meadows, Keith. *Sand in the Wind.* Bulawayo: Thorntree Press, 1997.

Melshen, Paul. "Pseudo Ops: Defeating Terrorists from Within." *U.S. Naval Institute Proceedings*, November 1988, 98–101.

Melshen, Paul. "ZANLA's War in Zimbabwe-Rhodesia: A Lesson in Strategy and Tactics." *U.S. Naval Institute Proceedings*, August 1982, 118–19.

Melson, Charles D. "SAS Operational Wings." *ZMS Journal*, August 2001, 26–7.

Melson, Charles D. "Top Secret War: Rhodesian Special Operations." *Small Wars and Insurgencies*, vol. 16, no. 1, March 2005, 57–82.

"The Men Who Dare." *Fighting Forces of Rhodesia*, (3) 1976, 41.

"The Men Who Hunt Down Terrorists." *Focus on Rhodesia*, vol. 2, no. 3, n.d., 2–3

Meredith, Martin. *Our Votes, Our Guns: Robert Mugabe and the Tragedy of Zimbabwe.* New York: Public Affairs, 2002.

Meredith, Martin. *The Past is Another Country: Rhodesia, 1890–1979.* London: André Deutsch, 1979.

M'Gabe, Davis. "Guerrilla Activity in Zimbabwe." *Monthly Review*, March 1969, n.p.

Miers, Richard. *Shoot to Kill.* London: Faber & Faber, 1959.

Mills, David. "The Pink Panther," *Soldier of Fortune*, July 1984, 54–5.

Mills, Greg & Grahame Wilson. "Who Dares Loses? Assessing Rhodesia's Counter-Insurgency Experience." *RUSI Journal*, December 2007, 22–31.

Minty, Abdul S. *Fireforce Exposed.* London: The Anti-Apartheid Movement, 1979.

"The Mobile Resuscitation Unit." *Assegai*, September 1979, 21–5.

"Mobile Surgical Unit." *Assegai*, July 1977, 11–14.

Mockaitis, Thomas R. *British Counterinsurgency, 1919–1960.* New York: St. Martin's, 1990.

Mockaitis, Thomas R. *British Counterinsurgency in the Post-Imperial Era.* Manchester & New York: Manchester University Press, 1995.

Monick, Stan. "The Rhodesian Air Force, 1935–1980." *ISSUP Contemporary Air Strategy Studies*, no. 23, 1986, 53–90.

Monick, Stan. "The War of the Zambezi Salient: The Portuguese and Rhodesian Responses to Insurgencies." *Armed Forces*, February 1981, 20–7; March 1981, 18–26; April 1981, 27–31; May 1981, 13–17.

Montfort, Robert. "La Septieme Compagne Independante." *Raids*, September 1987, 16–20; October 1987, 28–31.

Moorcraft, Paul L. *Africa's Super Power.* Johannesburg: Sygma Books & Collins Vaal, 1981.

Moorcraft, Paul L. *African Nemesis: War and Revolution in Southern Africa, 1945–2010.* London: Brassey's, 1994.

Moorcraft, Paul L. *Contact II: Struggle for Peace.* Johannesburg: Sygma Books, 1981.

Moorcraft, Paul L. "Rhodesia's War of Independence." *History Today*, September 1990, 11–17.

Moorcraft, Paul L. "The Savage Silent Civil War." *Army*, April 1987, 42–52.

Moorcraft, Paul L. *A Short Thousand Years: The End of Rhodesia's Rebellion.* Salisbury: Galaxie Press, 1979.

Moorcraft, Paul L. *What the Hell am I Doing Here: Travels with an Occasional War Correspondent.* London: Brassey's, 1995.

Moorcraft, Paul L. & Peter McLaughlin. *Chimurenga: War in Rhodesia.* Johannesburg: Sygma & Collins, 1982.

Moorcraft, Paul L. & Peter McLaughlin. *The Rhodesian War: A Military History.* London: Pen & Sword Books, 2008.

Moore, Robin. *Rhodesia.* New York: Condor Publishing, 1977.

Moore-King, Bruce. *White Man Black War.* Johannesburg: Penguin Books, 1988.

Morris, Michael. *Armed Conflict in Southern Africa.* Cape Town: Jeremy Spence, 1974.

Morris-Jones, W. H., ed. *From Rhodesia to Zimbabwe: Behind and Beyond Lancaster House.* London: Frank Cass & Co., 1980.

"Mozambique: The White Devil of Niassa." *Newsweek,* 14 January 1974, 15–16.

Mumford, Andrew. *The Counterinsurgency Myth: The British Experience of Irregular Warfare.* Abingdon: Routledge, 2011.

Mumford, Andrew. *Counterinsurgency Wars and the Anglo-American Alliance.* Washington, DC: Georgetown University Press, 2017.

Mungazi, Dickson A. *Education and Government Control in Zimbabwe: A Study of the Commissons of Inquiry, 1908–1974.* New York: Praeger Publishers, 1990.

Mungazi, Dickson A. *The Last Defenders of the Laager: Ian D. Smith and F. W. de Klerk.* Westport: Praeger Publishers, 1998.

Munro, Gordon & Henton Jaaback. *Bush Telegraph: The Rhodesian Corps of Signals.* Randpark Ridge: Print Factory, 2002.

Murphy, John K. Obituary by John Early, *Soldier of Fortune,* July 1981, 46–7.

Murphy, Philip. "Creating a Commonwealth Intelligence Culture: The View from Central Africa, 1945–1965." *Intelligence and National Security,* vol. 17, no. 3, Autumn 2002, 131–63.

Muzorewa, Abel. *Rise Up and Walk.* London: Sphere Books, 1978.

Neate, Tim. "Counter Insurgency Vehicles." *Military Modeling,* December 1985, 892–4.

Nelson, Harold D., ed. *Zimbabwe: A Country Study.* Washington, DC: American University, 1982.

Nelson, Keith A. *Shadow Tracker.* Johannesburg: 30 Degrees South Publisher, 2007.

Nielsen, S. "The White Devil of Mozambique." *Soldier of Fortune,* October 1979, 78–83, 87.

Nkomo, Joshua. *The Story of My Life.* London: Methuen, 1984.

Nkrumah, Kwame. *Handbook of Revolutionary Warfare: A Guide to the Armed Phase of the African Revolution.* New York: International Publishers, 1969.

Norman, Charles. "A Hide and Seek War, Played in the Dark." *Scope,* 22 August 1975, 6–10.

Norris, William. "Rhodesia's Fireforce Commandos: Sweep Lines, Stop Groups, and Flying K-Cars." *Soldier of Fortune,* November 1987, 64–7.

Norval, Morgan. *Red Star Over Southern Africa.* Washington, DC: SFP, 1988.

Nyamubaya, Freedom T. V. *On the Road Again.* Harare: Zimbabwe Publishing House, 1986.

Nyangoni, Christopher & Gideon Nyandoro, eds. *Zimbabwe Independence Movements: Selected Documents.* New York: Barnes & Noble Books, 1979.

O'Brien, Kevin A. "Special Forces for Counter-Revolutionary Warfare: The South African Case." *Small Wars and Insurgencies,* vol. 12, no. 2, Summer 2001, 79–109.

Oldham, Scott. "Tactical Tracking Operations School." *Tactical Response,* Spring 2004, 82–5.

Oliver, Roland. *The African Experience.* New York: Harper Collins, 1992.

Onslow, Sue. "A Question of Timing: South Africa and Rhodesia's Unilateral Declaration of Independence, 1964–65." *Cold War History,* vol. 5, no. 2, May 2005, 129–59

Onslow, Sue. "South Africa and the Owen–Vance Plan of 1977." *South African Historical Journal,* (51) 2004, 130–58.

Onslow, Sue, ed. "White Power, Black Nationalism and the Cold War," in *Cold War History,* vol 7, no. 2, May 2007.

Osborn, Jr., John W. "Operation Dingo: Rhodesia 1977." *Modern Warfare*, September–October 2015, 28–38.

Outpost: Stories of the Police of Rhodesia. Cape Town: Books of Africa, 1970.

Owen, Christopher. *The Rhodesian African Rifles*. London: Leo Cooper, 1970.

Pandya, Paresh. "Foreign Support to ZANU and ZANLA During the Rhodesian War." *ISSU Strategic Review*, November 1987, 1–31.

Pandya, Paresh. *Mao Tse-tung and Chimurenga*. Braamfontein: Skotaville Publishers, 1988.

"Para School." *Focus on Rhodesia*, vol.2, no.9, n.d., 3.

Parker, Jim. *Assignment Selous Scouts: Inside Story of a Rhodesian Special Branch Officer*. Alberton: Galago Publishing, 2006.

Paul, Mathew. *Parabat*. Johannesburg: Covos Day Books, 2001.

Payne, Les. "Report from Zimbabwe-Rhodesia: U.S. Built Planes Leading Attack." *Newsday*, 13 July 1979, n.p.

Peirce, Michael. "Rebel in Rhodesia." *Soldier of Fortune*, November 1981, 42–7, 81–5; December 1981, 37–43, 83–9; January 1982, 27–32, 66–77.

"A Penthouse Interview with Mtabuko Joshua Nkomo." *Penthouse*, 1979, 58–61, 142–4.

[Pessarra, Chris, ed.] *African Combat: Rhodesian Security Forces*. Hinton: Rhodesia was Super, 2010.

Petter-Bowyer, P. J. H. *Winds of Destruction: The Autobiography of a Rhodesian Born Pilot Covering the Rhodesian Bush War of 1967–1980*. Victoria: Trafford Publishing, 2003.

Pitman, Dick. *You Must be New Around Here*. Bulawayo: Books of Rhodesia, 1979.

Pittaway, Jonathan, ed. *Selous Scouts Rhodesia: The Men Speak*. Durban: Dandy Agencies Publishing, 2015.

Pittaway, Jonathan & Craig Fourie, eds. *SAS Rhodesia: The Men Speak*. Avondale: Dandy Agencies Publishing, 2003.

Pongweni, Alex J. C., ed. *Songs that Won the Liberation War*. Harare: College Press, 1982.

Pomeroy, Eugene. Letter, *Lion & Tusk*, November 1992, n.p.

Pomeroy, Eugene. "The Origins of the Rhodesian SAS Title." *Lion & Tusk*, February 1994, n.p.

"The Pony Pilots." *Fighting Forces of Zimbabwe Rhodesia*, (6) 1979, 13, 19.

Poos, Robert. "Night Ambush in Southern Africa." *Soldier of Fortune*, August 1980, 70–1.

Powell, Heather. *Tsanga: Place of Reeds, Place of Healing*. AU: Bayprint, 2005.

Preston, Mathew. "Stalemate and Termination of Civil War: Rhodesia Reassessed." *Journal of Peace Research*, vol. 41, no. 1, 2004, 65–83.

Proctor, André & Hannie Koch. *The School We Made*. Harare: Baobab Books, 1998.

Pullin, W. J. "The Kill: A Firefight in Rhodesia." *Soldier of Fortune*, November 1977, 31, 69.

Pullin, W. J. "Afternoon Firefight: Rhodesians Refine the Counter-Ambush." *Soldier of Fortune*, May 1979, 52–3.

Pustay, John S. *Counter-Insurgency Warfare*. New York: The Free Press, 1965.

Raeburn, Michael. *We Are Everywhere: Narratives from Rhodesian Guerrillas*. New York: Random House, 1979.

Rajagopalan, Rajeh. "Restoring Normalcy: The Evolution of the Indian Army's Counterinsurgency Doctrine." *Small Wars and Insurgency*, vol. 11, no. 1, Spring 2000, 44–68.

Ranger, Terence. "The Death of Chaminuka: Spirit Mediums, Nationalism, and the Guerrilla War in Zimbabwe." *African Affairs*, 1982, 349–69.

Ranger, Terence. *Peasant Consciousness and Guerrilla War in Zimbabwe*. London: James Currey, 1985.

Ranger, Terence. *Voices from the Rocks: Nature, Culture and History in the Matopos Hills of Zimbabwe*. Oxford: James Currey, 1999.

Rea, Fred B., ed. *Southern Rhodesia: The Price of Freedom*. Bulawayo: Stuart Manning, 1964.

Reed, Jonathan. "War in the Bush." *The Elite*, (52) 1986, 1036–40.

Reid-Daly, Ron F. *Pamwe Chete: The Legend of the Selous Scouts*. Weltevreden Park: Covos Day Books, 1999.

Reid-Daly, Ron F. *Staying Alive: A Southern Africa Survival Handbook*. Gibraltar: Ashanti Publishing, 1990.

Reid-Daly, Ron F. "War in Rhodesia: Cross-Border Operations." In *Challenge: Southern Africa in the African Revolutionary Context*, edited by A. J. Venter. Gibraltar: Ashanti Publishing, 1989, 8, 56–62.

Reid-Daly, Ron F. & Peter Stiff. *Selous Scouts: Top Secret War*. Alberton: Galago Publishing, 1982.

Renwick, Robin. *Unconventional Diplomacy in Southern Africa*. New York: St. Martin's Press, 1997.

Rhodesia Herald. "Action Stations and Air Devils Plunge into Big Dawn Drop." In *Lion & Tusk*, March 1997, 24–26.

"Rhodesian Dustoff." *Soldier of Fortune*, November 1987, 76.

Rhodesian Leader's Guide. Boulder: Paladin Press, 1980.

"Rhodesian Raiders: Helicopters at War." *Lion & Tusk*, February 1998, 21–3.

Roberts, Craig. "Killers in Sand-colored Berets: The Exclusive Ranks of the Rhodesian SAS Always Dared and Usually Won." *Modern Warfare*, April 1979, 8, 56–62.

Roberts, Craig. "War Against Impossible Odds: Among Other Handicaps, There was a Mole in Rhodesia's Headquarters." *Modern Warfare*, September 1989, 50–2.

Robertson, Bruce, et al. *Aircraft Markings of the World, 1912–1967*. Letchworth: Harleyford, 1967.

Rogers, Anthony. *Someone Else's War: Mercenaries from 1960 to Present*. London: Harper Collins Publishers, 1998.

Rubert, Steven C. & R. Kent Rasmussen. *Historical Dictionary of Zimbabwe*. Lanham: Scarecrow Press, 2001.

Saffery, David, ed. *Rhodesian Medal Roll*. London: Jeppestown Press, 2006.

Salt, Beryl, et al. *A Pride of Eagles: The Definitive History of the Rhodesian Air Force, 1920–1980*. Johannesburg: Covos Day Books, 2001.

Schorr, Douglas. *The Myth of Smith: Rhodesia Revealed*. US: CreateSpace, 2015.

Scott-Donelan, David. "The Armalite in Africa." *Assegai*, June 1973, 20–2.

Scott-Donelan, David. Letter, *Lion & Tusk*, March 1997, n.p.

Scott-Donelan, David. *Tactical Tracking Operations*. Carey: First Impressions, 1997.

Scott-Donelan, David. *Tactical Tracking Operations*. Boulder: Paladin Press, 1998.

Scott-Donelan, David. "Zambezi Valley Manhunt: Tracker Combat Unit Trails Terrs." *Soldier of Fortune*, March 1985, 70–3.

"Selous Scouts." *Assegai*, April 1977, 21–4.

"Selous Scouts: The Men the Terrorists Dread." *Focus on Rhodesia*, vol.2, no.3, n.d., 2–3.

Shay, Reg & Chris Vermaak. *The Silent War*. Salisbury: Galaxie Press, 1971.

Simpson, Keith. "Just Gonk the Lekker Lingo as Tuned by the 'Saintly' Owens." *Rhodesia Herald*, n.p., n.d.

Sinclair, Wayne A. "Answering the Landmine." *Marine Corps Gazette*, July 1996, 37–40.

Sinclair, Wayne A. *The Last Defense: Vehicle Survivability and Guerrilla Mine Warfare*. Quantico: MCUF, 2004.

Slipchenko, Sergei. *In Southern Africa*. Moscow: Progress Publishers, 1987.

Smith, David, Colin Simpson, & Ian Davies. *Mugabe*. London: Sphere Books, 1981.

Smith, Ian. *The Great Betrayal: The Memoirs of Africa's Most Controversial Leader*. London: Blake Publishing, 1997.

Smith, Sylvia Bond. *Ginette*. Bulawayo: Black Eagle Press, 1980.

"The Squadron's First Big Para Drop Near Salisbury." In *Lion & Tusk*, August 1996, n.p.

Stapleton, Timothy J. *African Police and Soldiers in Colonial Zimbabwe, 1923–80*. Rochester: University of Rochester Press, 2011.

Stapleton, Timothy J. *Warfare and Tracking in Africa, 1952–1990*. London: Taylor & Francis, 2015.

Stedman, Stephen John. *Peacemaking in Civil War: International Mediation in Zimbabwe, 1974–1980*. Boulder: Lynne Rienner Publishers, 1991.

Steyn, Douw & Arne Soederlund. *Iron Fist from the Sea: South Africa's Seaborne Raiders, 1978–1988*. Solihull: Helion & Co., 2014.

Stiff, Peter. "Scouting for Danger: Selous Scouts, Rhodesia, 1973–80." *The Elite*, no. 1, 1985, 16–20.

Stiff, Peter. *See You in November: Rhodesia's No-holds-barred Intelligence War*. Alberton: Galago Publishing, 1985.

Stiff, Peter. *Selous Scouts: A Pictorial Account*. Alberton: Galago Publishing, 1984.

Stiff, Peter. *The Silent War: South African Recce Operations, 1969–1994*. Alberton: Galago Publishing, 1999.

Stiff, Peter. *Taming the Landmine*. Alberton: Galago Publishing, 1986.

Stoneham, Lewis. "Rhodesian Terrorist Hit Man Confesses." *Soldier of Fortune*, June 1979, 32–3.

Summers, Harry G. *On Strategy*. Novato: Presidio, 1982.

Sutton-Pryce, Ted. Zimbabwe: *A Model for Namibia?: A Comparison of Events in Zimbabwe-Rhodesia 1979–80 with the Situation in SWA in 1989*. Pretoria: Academica, 1989.

Tamarkin, M. *The Making of Zimbabwe: Decolonization in Regional and International Politics*. London: Frank Cass, 1991.

Tekere, Edgar. *A Lifetime of Struggle*. Harare: Sapes Books, 2007.

Telfer, Andy & Russell Fulton, eds. *Chibaya Moyo: The Rhodesian African Rifles, An Anthology, 1939–1981*. Pinetown: 30 Degrees South Publishers, 2015.

"10th Anniversary, C Squadron SAS." *Assegai*, August 1971, 18–21.

Terrell, Frank [Anthony Rogers]. "Combat Report Mozambique: Rhodesian Raid on ZANLA Base." *Combat & Survival*, (2) 1990, 117.

Terrell, Frank. "Combat Report Rhodesia: Fire Force Mission." *Combat & Survival*, (4) 1991, 190.

Terrell, Frank. "Combat Report Rhodesia: Hunting the Terrorists." *Combat & Survival*, (6) 1991, 357.

Terrell, Frank. "Fireforce Ops with the Rhodesian Light Infantry." *Combat & Survival*, (#) June 1989, 36–44.

Terrell, Frank. "Galloping Greys: Greys Scouts, Rhodesia, 1975–80." *The Elite*, (80) 1986, 1588–93.

Terrell, Frank. "RLI Fire Force." *The Elite*, (25) [113] 1985, 488–94 [160–6].

Terrell, Frank. "RLI Support Commando." *The Elite*, (113) 1987, 2241–7.

"They're 'Chuting High." *Illustrated Life Rhodesia*, 22 July 1976, 86–9.

Thompson, Jack [Andy V. Langley]. "Combat Weaponcraft: Before the Medic Comes." *Soldier of Fortune*, January 1988, 28, 101.

Thompson, Jack. "Combat Weaponcraft: Checking Up on the Checkout." *Soldier of Fortune*, May 1988, 18, 83–4.

Thompson, Jack. "Combat Weaponcraft: Combat Fire Control." *Soldier of Fortune*, November 1989, 14–15, 77.

Thompson, Jack. "Combat Weaponcraft: Core Skills for Combat." *Soldier of Fortune*, April 1988, 18, 82–3.

Thompson, Jack. "Combat Weaponcraft: Effective Fire, Noise or Bodycount?" *Soldier of Fortune*, October 1985, 22–3.

Thompson, Jack. "Combat Weaponcraft: Fire Control Orders." *Soldier of Fortune*, February 1990, 16.

Thompson, Jack. "Combat Weaponcraft: Firefights and Battle Sights. *Soldier of Fortune*, February 1986, 22.

Thompson, Jack. "Combat Weaponcraft: Getting on Target." *Soldier of Fortune*, January 1990, 12–13.

Thompson, Jack. "Combat Weaponcraft: Hidden Enemies." *Soldier of Fortune*, June 1988, 21, 83–4.

Thompson, Jack. "Combat Weaponcraft: In Time-On Target." *Soldier of Fortune*, April 1987, 22.

Thompson, Jack. "Combat Weaponcraft: Magazine, Military Rifle's MREs." *Soldier of Fortune*, March 1986, 12.

Thompson, Jack. "Combat Weaponcraft: Password by the Numbers." *Soldier of Fortune*, February 1987, 28.

Thompson, Jack. "Combat Weaponcraft: Quick and the Dead. *Soldier of Fortune*, March 1987, 22, 81–2.

Thompson, Jack. "Combat Weaponcraft: Tracers, The Good, the Bad, and the Deadly. *Soldier of Fortune*, November 1985, 14, 96–7.

Thompson, Jack. "Combat Weaponcraft: Tracking Techniques for Predator and Prey." *Soldier of Fortune*, September 1989, 16–19, 76.

Thompson, Leroy. "Rhodesian Guerrilla Fighters: The Legend of the Selous Scouts." *Fighting Elite*, n.d., 50–3.

Thompson, Robert. *Defeating Communist Insurgency*. New York: Praeger Publishers, 1966.

Thow, Iain. "Combat Report Rhodesia: Caught in an Ambush." *Combat & Survival*, (16) 1991, 916.

Thrush, Alan. *Of Land and Spirits*. Guernsey: Transition Publishing, 1997.

Toase, Francis. "Out of Isolation: South Africa's Helicopter Fleet Plays Key Role in its Military Doctrine." *Armed Force Journal*, April 1994, 42–3.

Toase, Francis. "The South African Army: The Campaign in South West Africa/Nambia since 1966." In *Armed Forces and Modern Counter-insurgency*, edited by Ian F. W. Beckett & John Pimlott. New York: St. Martin's Press, 1985, 190–221.

Todd, Judith. *The Right to Say No*. London: Sedgwick & Jackson, 1972.

Treloar, Helen. "The Parachute Training School." *Fighting Forces of Zimbabwe-Rhodesia*, (6) 1979, 48–50.

Trethowan, Anthony. *Delta Scout: Ground Coverage Operator*. Johannesburg: 30 Degrees South Publishers, 2008.

Tucker, Daryl. "Danger in the Night: SOF Staffer on Rhodesian Ranch Patrols." *Soldier of Fortune*, August 1979, 54–9, 65, 86.

Turner, John W. *Continent Ablaze: The Insurgency Wars in Africa, 1960 to Present*. London: Arms & Armour Press, 1998.

The U.S. Army–Marine Corps Counterinsurgency Field Manual. Chicago: University of Chicago Press, 2007.

Vambe, Lawrence. *An Ill-Fated People: Zimbabwe Before and After Rhodes*. London: William Heinemann, 1972.

van der Waals, W. S. *Portugal's War in Angola, 1961–1974*. Rivonia: Ashanti Publishing, 1993.

Veit-Wild, Flora. *Teachers, Preachers, Non-Believers: A Social History of Zimbabwean Literature*. Harare: Baobab Books, 1993.

Venter, Al J. *Barrel of a Gun: A War Correspondent's Misspent Moments in Combat*. Philadelphia: Casemate Publishers, 2010.

Venter, Al J., ed. *Challenge: Southern Africa within the Revolutionary Context*. Gibraltar: Ashanti Publishing, 1989.

Venter, Al J., ed., *The Chopper Boys: Helicopter Warfare in Africa*. London: Greenhill Books, 1994.

Venter, Al J. "Old Soldiers Never Die, They Join Dad's Army." *Scope*, 22 August 1975, 22–3.

Venter, Al J. *Vorster's Africa: Friendship and Frustration*. Johannesburg: Ernest Stanton Publishers, 1977.

Venter, Al J. "War in Rhodesia: An Exclusive Interview With Lt Gen G. P. Walls." *Soldier of Fortune*, Fall 1976, 20–9.

Venter, Al J. *The Zambesi Salient: Conflict in Southern Africa*. Old Greenwich: Devin-Adair Co., 1974.

Venter, Paul. "Ballad of Two Soldiers." *Scope*, 22 August 1975, 11.

Vermaak, Chris. "Rhodesia's Selous Scouts." *Armed Forces*, May 1977, n.p.

Verrier, Anthony. *The Road to Zimbabwe, 1890–1980*. London: Jonathan Cape, 1986.

Vines, Alex. *RENAMO: Terrorism in Mozambique*. Bloomington: Indiana University Press, 1991.

Walker, Walter C. *The Bear at the Back Door*. Sandton: Valiant Publishers, 1978.

Walton, Peter S. "Detect and Protect." *Military Modeling*, November 1987, 790–1.

"The War: General Controls all Forces." *Focus on Rhodesia*, vol. 2, no. 4, 2–3.

Ward, Alexander John. *The Call of Distant Drums*. Edinburgh: Pentland Press, 1992.

Warren, Charlie. *Stick Leader: RLI*. Durban: Just Done Publishing, 2007.

"War Zone Africa: Cessna 337 Lynx Rhodesian Operations." *Air Warfare*, n.d., 1681–5.

Watts, Carl P. "Dilemmas of Intra-Commonwealth Representations during the Rhodesian Problem, 1964–65." *Commonwealth & Comparative Politics*, vol. 45, no. 3, 2007, 323–44.

Watts, Carl P. *Rhodesia's Unilateral Declaration of Independence: An International History*. New York: Palgrave Macmillan, 2012.

Wessels, Hannes. *A Handful of Hard Men: The SAS and the Battle for Rhodesia*. Philadelphia: Casemate Publishers, 2015.

Wheeler, Jack. "RENAMO." *Soldier of Fortune*, February 1986, 64.

White, Luise. *The Assassination of Herbert Chitepo: Text and Politics in Zimbabwe*. Bloomington: Indiana University Press, 2003.

White, Luise. "Precarious Conditions: A Note on Counter-Insurgency in Africa after 1945." *Gender & History*, vol. 16, no. 3, November 2004, 603–25.

Whyte, Beverley, ed. *A Pride of Men: The Story of Rhodesia's Army*. Salisbury: Graham Publishing, 1975.

Whyte, Beverley, ed. *A Pride of Eagles: The Story of Rhodesia's Air Force*. Salisbury: Graham Publishing, 1976.

Whyte, Beverley. "Casualty Evacuation." *Fighting Forces of Rhodesia*, (3) 1976, 77–9.

Whyte, Beverley. "No. 7 Squadron." *Fighting Forces of Rhodesia*, (3) 1976, 76–9.

Whyte, Beverley. "Strike from Above." *Fighting Forces of Rhodesia*, (3) 1976, 59–76.

Whyte, Beverley. "They're Chuting High." *Illustrated Life of Rhodesia*, 22 July 1976, 86–9.

Whyte, Beverley. "The Tough Guys: C Squadron, Rhodesian Special Air Service Regiment." *Illustrated Life Rhodesia*, 7 August 1975, 112–17.

Wigglesworth, Tom. *Perhaps Tomorrow*. Salisbury: Galaxie Press, 1980.

Wilkins, Peter I. *Chopper Pilot: The Adventures and Experience of Monster Wilkins*. Nelspruit: Freeworld Publications, 2000.

Williams, L. H. "The Cavalry Rides Again: Riding and Fighting with Grey's Scouts." *Soldier of Fortune*, November 1978, 40–4; December 1978, 58–63, 70–1; January 1979, 68–78.

Williams, L. H. "Do Not, Repeat, Do Not Fire!: Rhodesia Prepares to Become Zimbabwe." *Soldier of Fortune*, August 1980, 33–5, 86–7; September 1980, 22–5.

Williams, L. H. "The Ice-Cube Lunch." *Eagle*, n.d., 58–61, 78–80.

Williams, L. H. "L. H. 'Mike' Williams: Kraals and Galloping Goffles." In *Merc: American Soldiers of Fortune*, edited by Robert K. Brown & Jay Mallin. New York: Macmillan, 1979, 109–21.

Williams, L. H. "Rhodesia's No Win War." *Soldier of Fortune*, September 1980, 22–5.

Williams, L. H. & Robin Moore. *Major Mike*. New York: Ace Charter, 1979.

Willis, G. "Low-level Parachutes." *International Defense Review*, no. 4, 1989, 419.

Windrich, Elaine. *The Mass Media in the Struggle for Zimbabwe*. Gweru: Mambo Press, 1981.

Wood, J. R. T. *A Matter of Weeks Rather than Months: The Impasse between Harold Wilson and Ian Smith, 1965–1969*. Victoria: Trafford Publishing, 2008.

Wood, J. R. T. "Cave Clearing in the Rhodesian Bush War." *Lion & Tusk*, March 2003, 16–27.

Wood, J. R. T. *Counter-Strike from the Sky: The Rhodesian All-Arms Fireforce in the War in the Bush, 1974–1980*. Johannesburg: 30 Degrees South Publishers, 2009.

Wood, J. R. T. "Countering the Chimurenga: The Rhodesian Counterinsurgency Campaign, 1962–1980." In *Counterinsurgency in Modern Warfare*, edited by Daniel Marston & Carter Malkasian. Oxford: Osprey Publishing, 2008.

Wood, J. R. T. *Kwete—No!: The Veto of Four Per Cent of the Governed, The Ill-Fated Anglo-Rhodesian Settlement Agreement, 1969–1972*. Pinetown: 30 Degrees South Publishers, 2015.

Wood, J. R. T. *Operation Dingo: Rhodesian Raid on Chimoio and Tembué, 1977*. Pinetown: 30 Degrees South Publishers, 2011.

Wood, J. R. T. "The Pookie Mine Detector." *Marine Corps Gazette*, January 1997, 25.

Wood, J. R. T. *So Far and No Further: Rhodesia's Bid for Independence during the Retreat from Empire, 1959–1965*. Victoria: Trafford Publishing, 2005.

Wood, J. R. T., ed. *The War Diaries of André Dennison*. Gibraltar: Ashanti Publishing, 1989.

Wood, J. R. T. "Weaponry: Developed During a Guerrilla War in Rhodesia, the Pookie is One of the World's most effective Mine-clearing Vehicles." *Military History*, December 1998, 18–22.

Wood, J. R. T., ed. *The Welensky Papers: A History of the Federation of Rhodesia and Nyasaland*. Durban: Graham Publishing, 1983.

Wood, J. R. T. *Zambezi Valley Insurgency: Early Rhodesian Bush War Operations*. Pinetown: 30 Degrees South Publishers, 2012.

Wood, Richard. "Counter-Punching on the Mudzi: D Company, 1st Battalion Rhodesian African Rifles on Operation Mardon, 1 November 1976." *Small Wars and Insurgencies*, vol. 9, no. 2, Autumn 1998, 64–82.

Wood, Richard. "Fire Force: Helicopter Operations, 1962–1980." *Military Illustrated*, (72) 1994, 21–4.

Wylie, Dan. *Dead Leaves: Two Years in the Rhodesian War*. Pietermaritzburg: University of Natal Press, 2002.

Younghusband, Peter, Kim Willenson, & Francois Darquennes. "Tea and Terrorists." *Newsweek*, 8 May 1979, 52–3.

Zimfep. *Children of History*. Harare: Academic Books, 1992.

Internet & Audiovisual Sources

Allport, Richard. "Operation Quartz: Rhodesia 1980," *Rhodesia and South Africa: Military History*. www.ourworld.compuserve.com, accessed 9 July 1997.

Atkinson, Dave & Michael G. Quintana. "The Fire Force Concept," *African Defense Journal*. ADJ@ mango.zw, accessed 5 June 2001.

C Squadron Rhodesian SAS. www.csqn.co.za, accessed 9 August 2001.

Chofamba-Sithole, Innocent & Norman Mlambo. "Ex-Rhodesian under probe for US anthrax attacks," *The Sunday Mirror*. www.africaonline.co.zw, accessed 9 July 2002.

Counter-Strike from the Sky. Video. 30 Degree South Productions, 2009.

Flower, Ken. "Mozambique." Public Broadcasting System, *WHUT Channel 32*, accessed 17 May 1989.

Friedman, Herbert A. *Rhodesia Psyop, 1965–1980*. www.psywar.org, accessed 3 October 2008.

Frontline Rhodesia. Video. 30 Degree South Productions, n.d.

Ken Flower: Rhodesian CIO. Video. Wilmington: Memories of Rhodesia, 2004.

Pamwe Chete. By the Rhodesian Information Service. Video. Benoni: Msasa Enterprises, 1997.

"Pamwe Chete: Selous Scouts, Carve Their Name With Pride." *Paratus*, December 1979. members. aol.com, accessed 19 October 1998.

Pettis, Stuart. "The Role of Airpower in the Rhodesian Bush War, 1965–1980." *Air & Space Power Journal*. www.airpower.maxwell.af.mil/airchronicles, accessed 25 January 2010.

Pride of Eagles, The Rhodesian Air Force Today. By the Rhodesian Information Service. Video. Benoni: Msasa Enterprises, 1997.

Rhodesia Remembered. Video. Westminster King Productions, 2009.

The Saints: The Rhodesian Light Infantry. Video. 30 Degrees South Productions, 2008.

Selous Scouts. www.members.tripod.com, accessed 9 August 2001, 3 January 2002.

They Who Dare. By the Rhodesian Information Service. Video. Benoni: Msasa Enterprises, 1997.

Tactical Tracking Operations School. www.mantrack.aol.com, accessed 5 January 1998.

Vermaak, Chris. Rhodesia's Selous Scouts," *Armed Forces,* May 1977. ourworld.compuserve.com, accessed 9 July 1997.

Watts, Carl P. "Killing Kith and Kin: The Viability of British Military Intervention in Rhodesia, 1964-5." *Twentieth Century British History,* 2005, accessed on-line 19 October 2005.

Wood, J. R. T. Roll of Honour. www.jrtwood.com, accessed 17 July 2018.

Index